Feminism, Children, and the New Families

PERSPECTIVES ON MARRIAGE AND THE FAMILY
Bert N. Adams and David M. Klein, Editors

FEMINISM, CHILDREN, AND THE NEW FAMILIES
Sanford M. Dornbusch and Myra H. Strober, Editors

HELPING THE ELDERLY
The Complementary Roles of Informal Networks and Formal Systems
Eugene Litwak

COMMUTER MARRIAGE
A Study of Work and Family
Naomi Gerstel and Harriet Gross

WIFE BATTERING
A Systems Theory Approach
Jean Giles-Sims

Feminism, Children, and the New Families

Edited by

SANFORD M. DORNBUSCH
Reed–Hodgson Professor of Human Biology,
Sociology, and Education, Stanford University;
Director, Stanford Center for the Study of
Families, Children, and Youth

MYRA H. STROBER
Associate Professor of Education,
Stanford University;
Former Director, Stanford Center for
Research on Women

THE GUILFORD PRESS
New York   London

© 1988 The Guilford Press
A Division of Guilford Publications, Inc.
72 Spring Street, New York, NY 10012

Printed in the United States of America

Last digit is print number: 9 8 7 6 5 4 3 2

Library of Congress Cataloging-in-Publication Data

Feminism, children, and the new families / edited by Sanford M.
   Dornbusch and Myra H. Strober.
      p.   cm. — (Perspectives on marriage and the family)
   Bibliography: p.
   Includes index.
   ISBN 0-89862-078-3 (cloth)   ISBN 0-89862-514-9 (paper)
   1. Family—United States. 2. Feminism—United States. 3. Child
care—United States. 4. Divorce—United States. I. Dornbusch,
Sanford M. II. Strober, Myra H. III. Series
HQ536.F45 1988
306.8′5—dc 19   88-21350
                                           CIP

To the late Michelle Zimbalist Rosaldo, Associate Professor of Anthropology at Stanford, who cared and thought deeply about feminism, children, and families.

Contributors

JANE BECKER-HAVEN, Ph.D. Palo Alto, California.

SUSAN COHEN, Ph.D. candidate. Government Department, Cornell University, Ithaca, New York.

MARGARET CROSBIE-BURNETT, Ph.D. Department of Counseling Psychology and Counselor Education, University of Wisconsin, Madison, Wisconsin.

KINGSLEY DAVIS, Ph.D. Department of Sociology, University of Southern California, Los Angeles, California; Hoover Institution, Stanford University, Stanford, California.

SANFORD M. DORNBUSCH, Ph.D. Department of Sociology, Stanford University, Stanford, California; Stanford Center for the Study of Families, Children, and Youth, Stanford, California.

JEANNE J. FLEMING, Ph.D. Public Response Associates, San Francisco, California.

ROBERT FUHR, Ph.D. Adult and Child Guidance Center, San Jose, California, Bramer Medical Center, Palo Alto, California.

KATHRYN D. GRAY, M.A. Department of Sociology, Drew University, Madison, New Jersey.

MARY FAINSOD KATZENSTEIN, Ph.D. Government Department, Cornell University, Ithaca, New York.

SUSAN KRANTZ, Ph.D. Bay Area Center for Cognitive Therapy, Palo Alto, California.

NANCY LANGTON, Ph.D. School of Business, University of Toronto, Toronto, Ontario.

JOHN W. MEYER, Ph.D. Department of Sociology, Stanford University, Stanford, California.

HARRIET NERLOVE MISCHEL, Ph.D. Department of Psychology, Columbia University, New York, New York; New York State Psychiatric Institute, New York, New York.

SORCA M. O'CONNOR, Ph.D. Department of Education, Washington University, St. Louis, Missouri.

FRANCISCO O. RAMIREZ, Ph.D. School of Education, Stanford University, Stanford, California.

KAREN SKOLD, Ph.D. Institute for Research on Women and Gender, Stanford University, Stanford, California.

ADA SKYLES, Ph.D. Wisconsin Department of Health and Social Services, Madison, Wisconsin.

MYRA H. STROBER, Ph.D. Stanford School of Education, Stanford University, Stanford, California.

HENRY A. WALKER, Ph.D. Department of Sociology, Stanford University, Stanford, California.

LENORE J. WEITZMAN, Ph.D. Department of Sociology, Harvard University, Cambridge, Massachusetts.

Preface

This book is an outgrowth of a project entitled "Public Policy Implications of Perceived Conflicts Between Children's Interests and Feminists' Interests," supported by the Ford Foundation. The Ford grant enabled us to assemble a group of interested scholars drawn from the faculty of Stanford University and visitors to that campus. A series of group meetings helped to set general guidelines for areas of interest and for the style of the enterprise. Three persons provided leadership for the group: sociologist Lenore Weitzman, formerly of the Department of Sociology at Stanford and now on the faculty of the Department of Sociology at Harvard; economist Myra H. Strober, on the faculty at the Stanford School of Education, and formerly the Director of the Stanford Center for Research on Women; and sociologist Sanford M. Dornbusch, Director of the Stanford Center for the Study of Families, Children, and Youth and a faculty member of the Stanford Department of Sociology and the Program in Human Biology.

In addition to the authors of the chapters, the participants in our discussions came from a broad cross-section of Stanford University. Persons who assisted include: P. Herbert Leiderman, a psychiatrist; LaDoris Cordell, Catherine MacKinnon, Robert Mnookin, and Michael Wald from the Law School; the late Michelle Rosaldo and Sylvia Yanagisako, anthropologists; Estelle Freedman and Carl Degler, historians; Diane Middlebrook from the English Department; Eleanor Maccoby, psychologist; William J. Goode, Alex Inkeles, and Seymour Martin Lipset, sociologists; and Victor Fuchs, economist. We thank them for their suggestions and criticisms.

This enterprise grew out of discussions between two groups of scholars at Stanford: those at the Center for Research on Women (CROW), (now the Institute for Research on Women and Gender), who have been studying feminist ideology and changing gender roles, and those at the Stanford Center for the Study of Families, Children, and Youth, who have been investigating processes of development in childhood and adolescence. Each group had been broadening its research focus and each wished to learn about the other's theories, research findings, and policy prescriptions. The Ford Foundation felt it important that we explore the public policy implications of putting together these perspectives.

Feminist writers have placed women at the center of their analyses and have not usually examined the interests of others. This emphasis on women's interests has served to redress past imbalances, where often the interests of women were not considered at all. By 1981, however, feminist scholars at the Center for Research on Women wished to begin to analyze explicitly the effects of feminist principles on the welfare of all family members.

In the same fashion, some of those doing research on children were, by 1981, widening their sphere of concern. The unidirectional image of the parent socializing the child began to give way to an interactive image, in which the child's characteristics and responses affect the parents and their behavior. Moreover, researchers at the Stanford Center for the Study of Familes, Children, and Youth felt the need to be more informed about trends and possibilities with respect to mothers, taking into account the varied roles that women now play.

The arena of greatest interest for examining public policies related to feminist and children's concerns is that of the "new families." These new families we consider to be two-earner families, single-parent families, and stepfamilies. Our decision to exclude from our discussion gay and lesbian families and heterosexual couples who are cohabitating was made reluctantly and reflected only the virtual absence of social science research on them when we began our project, rather than any judgement that these new families are unimportant. On the contrary, we encourage social science research on these latter types of new families. Such research will contribute to framing and shaping more informed policy debates on their needs and interests.

Social science research, as well as political ideology, has often assumed that there is a major conflict between the needs of "the family" and women's independent interests. For example, Carl Degler's thesis is that, as women's power and independence has increased historically both inside and outside the home, the family has been weakened. In the policy domain, traditional images of the family and women's changing roles conflict when decisions are made that purportedly defend the family or children, but in fact are not responsive to the realities of the current situation. For example, President Nixon in 1971 vetoed a bill that would have provided funds for child care, stating that the bill would have harmed "the family." We argue that analyses of families are far more enlightening when scholars and policymakers can be induced to drop the notion of "the family" and instead examine the variety of family types now on the American scene.

Our view is that there is not a necessary conflict between the interests of women and children. Indeed, we find that women's interests and children's interests are more often consonant than dissonant. Similarly, we suggest that the survival of the family does not entail a reduction in the concern for women's development and well-being. Rather, if families are to survive, they must be beneficial to all their members.

Why this book at this time by these scholars? The authors are all behavioral scientists. It is their professional task to analyze social and psychological processes, trying to understand the basic elements of a swiftly changing society. Each of these authors is a specialist, and that lends strength to this broad summary volume. No single person could be equally well-informed. Yet there is a limit to the ability of any expert to understand the ramifications of their policy recommendations outside of a narrow band of expertise; such breadth and depth of understanding is at best rare. This group of specialists, brought together for occasional meetings and the exchange of commentary on the written drafts of their fellow contributors, has been exposed to a diversity of skill and expertise that afforded an opportunity to create a richer and more unified approach.

The audience for this book will be varied. Feminists, educators, and scholars interested in the family and in children are all likely to be readers, as is the educated public that influences policymakers. We also hope to gain the attention of policymakers themselves—those responsible for public policy decisions not only in government but also in corporations, unions, educational institutions, and philanthropic organizations. A central purpose of this book is to bring to policymakers the research they need for enlightened decision making. Too often policies regarding families are based on outmoded stereotypes. This volume seeks to substitute social science analyses for such stereotypes.

Contents

xiii

Feminism, Children, and the New Families

PART I

FEMINISM AND FAMILIES

1

Our Perspective

SANFORD M. DORNBUSCH AND MYRA H. STROBER

In an era of increasing advocacy for children's interests and feminists' interests, we believe that a thoughtful and scholarly approach to the intersection of these interests will be helpful to all those who seek to understand current trends and respond appropriately to them. We want to complicate the public policy questions both by making feminists think about children's needs and by making those concerned with children think about feminist issues.

Feminist writings have justifiably put women at the center of research and analysis on the family and society. Yet this leads to an imbalance; the interests of other actors in the family drama are not usually taken into account. We believe that feminist scholarship is ready for a new stage of development in which women are perceived as part of organic working wholes, such as families. This does not mean that we should discuss families as homogeneous units without regard to the individuals who compose them; we seek to relate feminist principles to their impact on other persons and groups. Fathers and children are usually also part of families, and feminist ideology and practices can affect all members of the household, often in positive ways. There is not, in our view, a direct conflict between the interests of children and the feminist perspective.

There also needs to be an increased complexity of thought and research about children. In the policy arena, advocates for children are urging mothers and fathers to change behaviors in order to improve the lives of children. Such advocates need to be better informed about the trends and possibilities in family life produced by feminist thinking. The varied roles played by women have major effects on their children. One brief example may help to illustrate the need for this approach. Kenneth Keniston's report to the Carnegie Commission (1977), a major review of issues related to children and the family, devoted little attention to women's changing roles in the family. We believe this gap made some of his recommendations less practical.

Sanford M. Dornbusch, Ph.D. Department of Sociology, Stanford University, Stanford, California; Stanford Center for the Study of Families, Children, and Youth, Stanford, California.

Myra H. Strober, Ph.D. Stanford School of Education, Stanford University, Stanford, California.

A central feature of our approach is recognizing the diversity of family forms in the current environment. Our continual concern with "families" instead of "the family" is a major part of the reconciliation between feminism and family rights and responsibilities. While the male/breadwinner-female/homemaker model is still present in millions of American homes and should not be omitted from our examination, it is the presence of numerous other forms of family life that has transformed the issues involved in the fulfillment of both genders and in the successful raising of the next generation. Feminists emphasize that the traditional model of family relations does not apply to the bulk of contemporary families. Thinking about the relationships between men, women, and children must take into account the variety of families in which they are embedded.

Our approach is relational rather than individual, social rather than personal, focused on the societal structure rather than on individual families. Such emphases constitute both a weakness and a strength. Each person, each family, and each community faces specific challenges and must meet them with a specific set of resources in a specific set of circumstances. Thus, no general statement in a volume like this one can be directly applied to any immediate problem faced by interacting human beings. The best that can be hoped for is that the consideration of general issues can provide some guidance for dealing with particular problems.

There are, however, numerous gains to be obtained from taking a broader ecological perspective, from examining the interaction of general social trends, specific ideologies, social and economic circumstances, and the welfare of various family members. At its best, the attempt to view the interaction of feminism and family functions from a more global perspective can enrich the vision of the actors in the drama. Too often in American life, problems that are institutional in nature are treated as problems of the individual. Rhetoric for individual action and for change in individual morality is often, under such circumstances, a barrier to effective thinking and social action, and the attempt to generalize from the experiences of millions of individuals can go beyond ideology to provide guidance for policymakers.

Among proponents of feminism, there are some who are suspicious of the motives of those who have introduced familial language into the national agenda. Is concern for the family only a ruse, a device for transmuting the terms of national debate in ways that result in a vote for stability in the relations between men and women? We think not. Advocates of social change and social reformers have found it useful for their goals to bring debate about families into the policy arena (Diamond, 1983). Families do matter. Concern about families can lead to changes in major social policies, just as it can lead to a vote for a return to a mythical past. Devising appropriate strategies for dealing with family issues can advance the interests of women and their children.

What about men? Gender equality must, by definition, lead to a decline in the relative power of men over women. But life is not a zero-sum game: The current lives of American men are not so full of success, love, and joy that we must assume that changes in current arrangements between the sexes will lead to a diminution of male happiness. In fact, we believe that a more equal society will bring more happiness to the majority of men as well as women.

As W. I. Thomas put it, things that people believe, even if false, are real in their consequences. Accordingly, judgments about the probability of humans being happy in any specific situation must consider not only the actual circumstances but also the values and standards that people use in judging their condition. As more men become feminists, more men will be uncomfortable with family arrangements that are based on an unthinking assumption of male dominance. In addition, most modern American marriages seek some level of happiness for both partners; increased happiness for one partner is likely to affect the quality of the relationship in ways that increase the happiness of the other partner.

The concern with the interests of men has a pragmatic political goal as well. As Betty Friedan says,

> It also seems clear to me that we will never solve the new problems and bring about the changes in the workplace and childcare options so necessary for the well-being of families if their only supporters and beneficiaries are women. . . . The solutions will come about only because more and more men demand them, too—not to "help" the women, but because of their own new problems and needs and choices, as fathers and for themselves as men. (1981, p. 121)

In contrast to this pragmatic concern, a few feminist ideologists espouse views that are so critical of current arrangements between the sexes as to endorse women never marrying or, if married, voluntarily remaining childless. Nevertheless, voluntary childlessness is still a relatively uncommon choice, though it may be increasing in frequency (Veevers, 1979). Most feminists support marriage and having children.

Family households, that is, related individuals living together, now compose about three fourths of all households. Despite the great growth in persons living alone, nonfamily households, made up of unrelated or single people, still represent only about a quarter of all households. Nine out of ten young adults will marry, although perhaps a little later in the life cycle. That 10% of young adults will never marry represents a doubling of the rate for 1970, but it still is a minority option. About 3% of the nation's households consists of persons of the opposite sex sharing living quarters, a quadrupling since 1970 ("Death of the Family," 1983).

From our perspective, the task is not to denounce those women who find either marriage or parenthood unappealing. Most studies conclude that childless marriages that survive are happier, on the average, than marriages that produce offspring. Paradoxically, comparing the reported happiness of husbands and wives in families with children and families without children, it is the husbands in childless marriages who show the highest level of marital satisfaction (Bernard, 1982). Such findings indicate that our society faces a novel and important task: finding ways in which the institutions of marriage and parenthood can be assisted so as to reduce the pain and increase the joy.

Part I of this book addresses the relation between feminist ideology and the functioning of families. The emphasis is on family functions as they affect individual family members, rather than on the overall welfare of "the family," since there is no single entity that forms the family as an institution, but rather a variety of family types. The institution of the family is resilient precisely because its variety permits adjustment to changing social and economic conditions.

Although the feminist perspective would be worthy of scholarly attention even if only women shared this perspective, happily for the future of both sexes, feminist attitudes are a product of experiences that are not limited to women. Feminist views are shared increasingly by both men and women, and, even for those who disagree, understanding them will become a necessary part of learning to live with others in the modern world.

Chapter 2, by Susan Cohen and Mary Fainsod Katzenstein, directly addresses the diversity that is found within feminism and within the right-wing advocates of traditional roles within the family. Cohen and Katzenstein explore that diversity, and their summary makes clear that there is little argument about the importance of the family, about the fundamental requirement that children be nurtured and encouraged to develop their talents, and even about the importance of marriage to the functioning of society. The issues that truly divide feminists from the traditional right, they hold, are about adult roles rather than children's needs. Writings about the family exemplify different images of the roles to be played by adult men and adult women. Both positions use the family as part of their arguments; both claim that children, the family as an institution, and the society will be harmed if the views of opponents prevail.

Concern with the needs of children has only recently become a central topic of the ongoing debate. Children's needs tend to be derived from assumptions about desirable gender arrangements. The preferred roles for men and women in the society determine, both for feminists and for the traditional right, the appropriate image of children and their potential. Cohen and Katzenstein show that gender roles have important implications for images of the relation between women and the family. Without portraying either the position of the traditional right or the feminist position as monolithic, they make clear that female autonomy is the key issue. Feminists and the traditional right agree on the importance of autonomy and community, but their differing visions of men and women affect their ideal image of the family. Accordingly, the two groups—with the exception of some radical feminists—accept the importance of the nuclear family, but differ on the ease with which autonomy and community can be found within the family. Feminists are far more likely to see autonomy and community as in constant tension within even a restructured family institution. The traditional right emphasizes community within the family, and individualism outside the family, which emphases, feminists claim, produce an individualism that embraces mostly men, leaving women out. Thus, Chapter 2 concludes, the battle over the family is really a struggle about the roles and values of men and women.

While Chapter 2 explores the ideological positions of feminism and the traditional right by examination of the writings of their leading exponents, Chapter 3 by Jeanne J. Fleming examines the views of the American public concerning the acceptance of various parts of each ideological position. Fleming analyzes changes in the American public's support for feminism and its goals. Paradoxically, her analysis of public attitudes aids in the determination of what is central in the vision of feminism. The very act of recording which beliefs tend to be found together helps to determine those aspects of the debate that are part of cohesive belief systems and those that are not. A central finding is that the attitudes of the general public increasingly support the goals of the women's movement. In a variety of arenas, there is no evidence of a recent counterrevoltuion: The feminist position is increasingly the majority position, although a substantial proportion of the public takes a more traditional view of women's rights and roles. The recent victories of the antifeminist movement do not come from a growth in the number of their supporters.

Chapter 3 also explores who is likely to take a more feminist or less feminist position among members of the general public. Fleming shows that women are not a unitary class with a single set of interests. Women whose primary focus is in the family, that is, homemakers, are more concerned about legislating the male's contribution to the family. Key items on the agenda for this group include the male's legal responsibility for financial support of the family. Those women who are relatively well-paid participants in the labor force are concerned with their chances for success in the labor market, while women who do work outside the home, but only at low-paying jobs, have mixed interests. Thus, an important factor in determining the attitudes of women is whether they perceive their life chances to be located primarily in the market for paid labor or primarily in the institution of the family.

Fleming indicates ways in which these different interests shape the opinions of women who differ in education or employment status; who are single, married, or divorced; who have few or many children. She also demonstrates the link between feminism and particular political and religious perspectives. One arena is striking in its distinctiveness: Opinions on abortion appear to have an ideological basis different from other feminist issues. Thus, her analysis shows the extent to which the conceptualization of women's issues as a coherent whole can be misleading.

Fleming also looks at activists among feminists and among the traditional right. The opinions of activists help us better to understand the motivations of those who carry the burden of battle, as well as the symbolic goals of the two movements. Combining an analysis of the responses of the general public with an analysis of the responses of activists provides rich data for understanding of the political battles between the active converts to the two main positions. Such understanding is necessary for those interested in the policy implications of the feminist movement and the reaction to it. One noteworthy finding is that, though men and women in the general public are about equally likely to express pro-feminist attitudes, men are much less likely to join movements that act on these beliefs. Accordingly, feminist organizations are primarily female, while organizations with an antifeminist program have numerous male members.

Chapter 4 by Kingsley Davis and Chapter 7 by Meyer, Ramirez, Walker, Langton, and O'Connor both find it useful to put American data on feminist and family issues within an international context and to examine historical data to try to understand the bases for major changes in contemporary American society. Davis portrays in Chapter 4 a revolution that is still in process. Throughout the world, female participation in the labor force is growing as societies industrialize. He links this social trend to the Industrial Revolution, which, by separating the workplace from the home, changed the nature of the division of labor between husband and wife. The "traditional" male/breadwinner family, in Davis's broad-ranging treatment, is actually an unusual and short-lived arrangement. It is only in the early stages of industrialization that men leave home to work and women remain outside of the labor force. Davis not only depicts the increase in female labor-force participation in various countries, but he also predicts the future for countries at various stages of industrialization.

The male/breadwinner–female/homemaker sytem was triumphant largely because of the number of children to be cared for in each household. That system became deeply embedded in social thought and in governmental policy. Davis argues that this system seemed natural to people because it continued the dominance of the husband and assumed the devotion of women to child care.

The dichotomies between the workplace and the home, and between the breadwinner and the homemaker, created a system that could not continue without strong normative controls. Gradually those controls broke down, at least in part because postponement of marriage was onerous for the young. This led to both partners entering the labor force among young couples who lived together, whether or not they were married. Low fertility also provided a basis for attacking the male/breadwinner system. It was not just having fewer children that released wives for employment. Instead of spreading out the childbearing period, women simply stopped having babies at an earlier age. Combined with the increase in life expectancy, this led to women living more than half their married lives without a child in the household. The loss of face-to-face sharing when husbands' work moved out of the home and the later breakdown of the division of labor within the household when wives entered the workforce, Davis believes, led to a decline of the bonds between husband and wife. The anomalies in the new system slowly increased the likelihood of divorce. And, once the risk of divorce reached a threshold, the system unraveled further as wives used work outside the home as a hedge against divorce. (Strober in Chapter 8 and Weitzman in Chapter 10 return to this theme.)

Davis is pessimistic about the chances for success of the current movement towards egalitarianism. The lack of normative expectations, the lack of agreement on what the husband and the wife should expect from each other, produces a situation in which each couple must try to create its own standard for assigning household tasks and childrearing. Since economic opportunity for both women and men currently lies primarily outside of the home, childrearing and housework will have to be shared, but on what basis? The diversity in current arrangements makes it difficult for couples to work out norms for themselves, yet external normative controls are hard to imagine. Still, because people care so deeply about marriage and the family as goals in themselves, some resolution of the dilemmas of home and workplace may yet come out of the diverse efforts to accomplish a meaningful movement toward egalitarianism.

Chapter 5 by Henry Walker examines the special circumstances of black families, and illustrates the importance of examining family structures and processes within a specific ethnic context. As indicated by Dornbusch and Gray in Chapter 12, black families in America are currently unique in the extent to which children are not living in two-parent households. Walker attempts to understand the development of this pattern. Compared to whites, blacks are less likely to marry, less likely to remain married, more likely to have children out of wedlock, and more likely to raise children in households headed by women. Why might this be so?

One explanation proposed for these black–white differences is a difference in culture, related to the African experience, to slavery, or to migration. According to this explanation, blacks are culturally deviant or have a different, though equivalent, culture. Walker shows that a cultural explanation is incapable of explaining the data, which show similarity in marital patterns and family structure for the two racial groups from 1890 to 1940. It is only in recent years that we observe the remarkable differences in family structures, and the recent data give no support for these cultural explanations.

What then is likely to be the explanation? The divergence in family patterns since World War II is likely to be based on some change in the social context within which marriage patterns are observed. Walker argues that, as compared with white women, black women are less likely to marry and more likely to divorce because the latter group participates in a marriage market that is increasingly disadvantageous for them. The sex ratio among blacks—the number of males per 100 females—has fallen precipitously in the prime marriageable ages. Moreover, black men, compared with white men, have evidenced lower rates of labor-force participation and higher rates of unemployment than were found in the pre-World War II period. Given the increased labor-force participation of young women, women need not accept less than satisfactory relations with male partners. At the same time, black women have continued to have higher labor-force participation rates than white women, although the difference in participation rates has decreased.

Further, changes in the wage structure of the society also affect the marriage market for black females. The relative improvement in wages for black women over the past 20 years has been greater than the increase for black men. Walker contends that this reduction in the male–female wage ratio among blacks has lessened the dependence of black women on men. The combination of all these factors provides bases for both a lower incidence of marriage among blacks and less tolerance for the continuance of a relationship that is unsatisfying for the black female. In conjunction with this, Walker notes the differential costs incurred by black women and white women who leave a relationship. Because the combined earnings of a black couple are likely to be low, black women have less of a decline in their standard of living if a relationship is terminated. In addition, black women who head families may have more social and economic support from the black community. Thus, the breakup of a household is less costly for black females despite their lower economic resources.

Walker closes with a provocative point. He believes that white family patterns are following trends similar to those of blacks, with a lag in time. His emphasis on the marriage market suggests that strengthening the economic position of all women might reduce the economic dependence of women and increase the proportion of single-parent households. The proportion of couple-headed families will, he believes, increase only after a renegotiation of family roles that leads to greater egalitarianism. The increasing independence of women, based on improvements in their material condition compared with men, has given them options that include living more independently of men. For all groups, two-parent families will increase only after changes occur in the internal organization of families that enable men and women to live together in a more stable and egalitarian mode.

Karen Skold in Chapter 6 addresses the problem of child care, an issue that is central to the discussion of feminism, children, and the new families. Skold locates the source of the conflict between child care and female labor-force participation in the inflexibility of work organization and the inequity of family organization. The implication is that conflict is not inevitable. Changes in the structure of work and family, some of which have already begun to appear, could reduce current strains. We need not view children as barriers to women's equality nor see women's departure from full-time motherhood as harmful to children.

Skold summarizes the current problems in child care. They include issues of cost, the availability of care for certain age groups, care for sick children, and the definition of child care as the responsibility of women. Skold sees the necessary social changes as far-reaching, but the societal payoffs make the effort worthwhile. The problem of child care is usually resolved by job discontinuity for women. If men were more involved in child care, women would be less often faced with the choice between sacrifice of their career goals and the needs of their children. Were men to share the child-care burden more equitably, society as a whole would be more likely to invest in child care. Such an investment would not only assist children but would also reduce the enormous burden now carried by working mothers, especially single parents. Feminists, Skold urges, should seek the adoption of children's needs as congruent with their own, thereby increasing the probability of a transformation towards equality in the public sphere.

In Chapter 7, John Meyer and his colleagues examine trends in the role of the state in institutionalizing the relations between women and children. Their central point is a simple one: The extent to which the relations of women and their children are on the public agenda is a function of the nature and development of state control. As the state has increased its power and authority on a worldwide basis, there has grown a perception of increased conflict between women and children. Meyer *et al.* assert that there is good reason to believe that the level of conflicts between women and children within the family has *decreased* as the state has taken over some responsibilities and duties formerly assigned to parents. But how then account for the perception of a *rising* tide of conflict?

Meyer *et al.* hypothesize that expansion of the citizenship rights of women and children put intrafamilial conflicts on the public agenda. As the state grants rights to individuals, thereby giving them more "freedom," the state is drawn into disputes over the operation and coordination of those rights. The result is that private issues become defined as public issues. There can be a general and shared perception of increasing conflict within the family without an increase in the true frequency of such conflict. The testing of this perspective on some cross-national data is at least suggestive of support for its validity. The national agenda of major issues seems to be more a result of incorporation of areas of life under state control than a reflection of increases in problematic situations. When women and children are incorporated into the polity as individuals, as in liberal democratic societies, family conflicts are more likely to reach the public arena than in situations where there is a more corporate form of incorporation (such as using the family as the unit). The expansion of state power to the relations of individuals within the family is part of the reason that books like this one are written: Issues formerly perceived as private have come to be viewed as social problems.

Part II of this book is concerned with the "New Families." Let us briefly describe here what we do and do not mean by that term. The term "new" is not meant to imply discontinuity with the past; current families are not all different in kind from those found in earlier generations. But there is a major shift in the proportion of families of various types, a shift of a magnitude sufficient to indicate the necessity of a thoughtful examination of the implications of the new composition of the American family system.

"Traditional" families are a smaller proportion of American families today than in the recent past. When families with a male breadwinner and female homemaker are a minority of American families, we must examine the roots and implications of the variant forms of family life. The American family is changing, but then it always seems to be changing. It is stable in its flexibility, its adaptation to changing social conditions. Instead of viewing with alarm the rapidity of change in family structures, we should step back a bit and be aware of the continuity of familial change. Those who emphasize the continuity of the family are quick to note its persistence in various forms. Those who emphasize the threat to the family are eager to point to the breakdown of traditional values and behaviors. The feminist literature on the family notes the extent to which the structures and processes within the traditional family fail to take into account female capabilities and aspirations. Many of the changes that have occurred in family structure within the United States can be viewed as adaptations to changing images of women, their desires, and their resources.

We will be discussing several variant forms of the American family, each of which is increasing in frequency. These alternative family forms have effects on mothers, fathers, and children, and they also have implications for policy designed to improve family functioning. These family forms do not exist in a vacuum. In discussing them, we will examine ethnic and racial differences in family structures and their effects, as well as the impact of differences in family income or parental education. We title this section "The New Families" because, although the nontraditional family structures we will describe and analyze are not new, their relative contribution to the mix of families is now so massive that the perception of American families must itself change to incorporate the increased importance of diversity.

In Chapter 8 Myra Strober examines an increasingly prevalent family form, the two-earner family. Much of the book up to this chapter has presaged the importance of female participation in the labor force—for example, Fleming's description in Chapter 3 of how differences in work patterns, at home or away from home, influence the attitudes or ideology of women, and Davis's description of female labor-force participation as a key element in the decline of the traditional male-dominated household and of the development of satisfying egalitarian relationships between husband and wife as both threatened and assisted by both spouses working outside the home.

Although the proportion of married women working outside the home has recently evidenced spectacular increases, the continuity of the process is shown by a four-fold increase from 1900 to 1940 in the percentage of married women in the labor force. Strober is not dealing with a temporary phenomenon, subject to change without notice, but with a profound shift in the life experience of most American women. Exhortations to return to the home will not be heeded. Therefore, Strober's attempt to understand the meaning of this shift for women and their families is designed to provide a solid framework for policy. Too often our policymakers continue to view the traditional male/breadwinner–female/homemaker roles as typical in American families. Strober shows that the occupational role of the female is fundamental to understanding contemporary families and their problems.

When the husband is present and there is no child under 18, it was not considered inappropriate earlier in this century for the wife to work prior to the arrival of the first child. A young child was supposed to tie the mother, as childrearer as well as childbearer, to the home. As recently as 1950 the proportion of mothers with children under 6 and a husband present who were working outside the home was 11.9%. By 1985, the percentage of mothers with children under 6 and a husband present who were in the labor force had zoomed to 53.7% (Hayghe, 1986).

Women are currently handicapped in their attempt to gain equality on the job. In 1985, women who worked full-time, year-round had median earnings equal to 64% of those of men who worked full-time, year-round (Council of Economic Advisors, 1987). Although this earnings discrepancy results in part from the fact that in today's labor force men have slightly more formal education, more on-the-job training, and more continuous work experience than do women, about half of the earnings differential does result from employment discrimination. Strober shows how occupational segregation discriminates against women and points out that both the male–female earnings differential and occupational segregation have persisted despite the remarkable rise in women's labor force participation.

Strober discusses the importance of wives' income to their families and reports on the similarity in spending patterns among two-earner and single-earner married couple families. In examining the literature on the complex relations between wives' employment and marriage, childbearing, divorce, and marital satisfaction. Strober finds that, although women's employment leads to a delay in marriage, it does not result in a decline in the marriage rate. With respect to fertility, women who are employed have fewer children than women who are not, but disentangling causal directionality is an ongoing exercise. Similarly, it is difficult to analyze the possible causal relation behind the positive correlation over time between the increasing divorce rate and the increasing female labor force participation rate. Research on the effects of wives' employment on marital satisfaction gives some cause for optimism to those participating in this new family form. Both husbands and wives in a recent national study scored higher on measures of marital solidarity when the wife was employed.

Today there is enough of a discrepancy between work and rewards for husbands and wives that traditional roles in the household are not yet fully challenged by economic forces. But as women gradually gain more equal responsibilities and pay in the workplace, it is likely that they will expect from men more equal participation in the home. Housework and child care cannot remain largely feminine responsibilities. Employed married women spend 2½ to 3 times as many hours on housework as do their husbands. And husbands of employed wives spend virtually the same number of hours on housework as husbands of full-time homemakers. We think that as wives' earnings play a greater role than they do today in the economic well-being of the family, husbands' participation in housework and childrearing will increase commensurately.

Strober's assessment of the strains and changes as women move toward occupational equality suggests an agenda for policymakers oriented toward dealing with the evolving family forms. She argues in favor of changes in the workplace, including more effective enforcement of antidiscrimination legislation. She points to the central importance of child care as an arena in which private and public initiatives can make a difference for millions of women. Her discussion of suggested changes in income taxation and the social security system for two-earner families reflects the transition to a new era in which women will rely more on their own earnings for material well-being.

In Chapter 9, Mischel and Fuhr continue to explore the impact of maternal employment, focusing on its psychological effects on children and on family life. Their summary of research findings may reduce the concerns of those who think that maternal employment harms the cognitive and social development of children. Indeed, the attitudes of the parents toward the mother's working and the involvement of the father in childrearing are found to have more of an impact than does maternal employment. Studies suggest that helping all families to make the choices that fit their values would lead to the best results for children.

There is now a large body of research that indicates that most children of working mothers are not disadvantaged by maternal employment. The children, on the average, do no worse than children in comparable settings whose mothers do not take jobs outside the home with respect to physical development, intellectual development, school performance, and interpersonal and societal adjustment. Mothers' interests in employment appear not to be in conflict with their children's well-being. This message is getting through to the general public. One response to the increasing labor-force participation of mothers and the lack of clear negative results of their entry into paid employment, is a gradually increasing tolerance towards working mothers. For example, when asked during 1978 and 1979 whether working mothers take as good care of their children's health as do mothers not in the labor force, most members of American families saw no jeopardy to the health of children when mothers work outside the home. Only among persons 65 years and older was there a majority who felt that employed mothers harmed the health of their children. Every other group, including nonemployed mothers, thought that working mothers took good care of their children's health.

The importance of a more egalitarian ideology is evident in Mischel and Fuhr's analyses of the impact of maternal employment upon female and male children. The results for sons are more often inconclusive or negative than are those for daughters. Both sexes show increased sex role flexibility when mothers work, but mothers are obviously operating as role models more often for their female children. Mischel and Fuhr suggest that greater parental, and especially paternal, attention and involvement with sons can probably prevent some of the possible negative effects on cognitive development. They find no consistent demonstration of negative effects of maternal employment for the husband, and find that work outside the home provides numerous benefits for the wife. Labor-force participation increases social integration, protects against depression, and increases satisfaction and self-esteem. Instead of providing evidence that maternal employment is deleterious to the women themselves, the data suggest that women who work only at home are more at risk.

Like Strober, Mischel and Fuhr note that studies of the effects of married women's employment have been cross-sectional and correlational, and that it is difficult to analyze causality. They call for longitudinal studies and for more precision in research regarding the occupations of married women. They also suggest the need for additional studies within specific racial and ethnic groups.

Chapter 10 by Weitzman examines divorce as a fundamental aspect of the American family system. The high divorce rate in the United States is part of a long-term historical trend—in fact, every study of divorce since 1860 shows an increase in the rate of divorce compared to the previous period (Stannard, 1979). Weitzman (1981) has suggested that, paradoxically, a high divorce rate will remain a stable feature of American society, and may reflect a belief in the possibility of a more perfect union.

Weitzman points out that one aspect of this increase in divorce is the increased economic capability of women and the reduction in dependence on the male breadwinner. Yet the income of men in our society remains so much greater than the income of women that the impact of divorce very often leads to the impoverishment of the mother and her children. When divorce occurs among families with children, the husband typically becomes single while the wife becomes a single parent. The spouse who assumes or is assigned the burden of supporting the family is usually less capable of fulfilling the financial obligations associated with childrearing. Weitzman notes that the level of child support ordered by the courts after divorce is inadequate to relieve the economic burden on the mother, so that failures of enforcement merely exacerbate an already difficult situation. No-fault divorce, Weitzman shows, has harmed women and children because legal institutions have optimistically presumed gender equality in the marketplace. The assumption has been that wives and mothers who are entering the labor force after years of duty in the home are fully capable of competing for jobs and income. The result has been court-ordered settlements that shortchange the wives and children, ignore new forms of assets (such as professional training), and lead to further disruptions of the children's patterns of living.

Chapter 11 by Susan Krantz examines the evidence concerning this disruption of family functioning by divorce. She finds the psychological stress associated with divorce to be well documented—children, for example, often exhibiting emotional difficulties that persist for long periods. Such children often have problems with respect to deviance as well as to intellectual performance, but Krantz's survey of findings reveals considerable variation in the results for groups differing in age, social class, employment of mother, and other variables. Her summary indicates that, despite the paucity of well-controlled studies, the pattern of results seems to support the view that divorce and its stresses have long-term psychological consequences for mother and children.

Some policymakers have recently talked of the consequences of divorce as only temporary problems. Krantz has demonstrated that such a view is overly optimistic. People have a great capacity for overcoming difficulties given the appropriate amount of time and resources, but there is little in the aftermath of divorce to indicate that the psychological problems it brings are trivial or short-lived. Family members need both emotional and economic support in order to overcome the psychological difficulties of divorce.

Another group at risk is single-parent families. Chapter 12 by Dornbusch and Gray goes beyond the usual description of single-parent families as a major focus of problems and concern. They examine the *processes* that produce the problems faced by single-parent families. The growth in this family form has been dramatic and is continuing. Most single-parent families are in transition between two-parent households and a remarriage. About half of all divorced women remarry within 3 or 4 years, yet at any single moment more than one fifth of all American children today are in single-parent families. This is a sharp increase from 9% in 1959, more than a doubling. The rise in the proportion of single-parent families has produced a situation in which half of all American children can be expected to live in a single-parent household before the age of 18. The vast majority of single-parent families are headed by women, almost 90% in 1984 (U.S. Bureau of the Census, 1985), so that when we discuss single-parent families, we are talking predominantly about women and their children.

The incidence of single-parent families varies dramatically by ethnic and racial background. The modal form of family life among blacks is now the single-parent family, a fact increasingly recognized by policymakers. As we have noted, Henry Walker in Chapter 5 discusses some probable causes of this ethnic variation in family forms.

The rise in single-parent families has contributed greatly to the feminization of poverty. If we look at female-headed families, the proportion who are living in poverty ranges from 54% for non-Hispanic whites to 70% among blacks. The proportion of single-parent families who are poor is so high that they constitute half of all the families in poverty. We cannot develop policies to deal with American families without taking account of this family form. Social welfare policies must deal with the feminization of poverty. The program of Aid to Families with Dependent Children (AFDC) has been characterized as aid to *children* with dependent children, so large is the number of teenagers who are having children in and out of wedlock and require welfare as single parents. Between 1970 and 1982, the number of one-parent families headed by never-married women rose by 367%. This increase has been most apparent among teenage mothers. Dornbusch and Gray's chapter includes a discussion of the special problems of this group of single parents.

The processes given particular attention in Dornbusch and Gray's discussion of single-parent families include the forms of family decision making, the styles of parenting, and family participation in schooling. Their main point is that poverty is not the only problem that weighs heavily on single-parent families; the tasks of single parenthood produce additional problems as overburdened mothers try to cope with their diverse responsibilities.

Chapter 13 on stepparents by Crosbie-Burnett, Skyles, and Becker-Haven discusses the processes that lead that family form to have difficulties in parenting. As in the previous chapter, the emphasis is on the processes within the family that produce negative outcomes for children. The rise in the number of stepfamilies indicates that Americans are not rejecting marriage. Their marriage rate has continued to be among the very highest in the world. Of course, that is partly explained by a high divorce rate that gives millions of Americans the opportunity to marry more than once. But since the rate of remarriage continues to be very high, divorce does not represent a rejection of the institution of marriage. Divorced persons are more likely to get married than single persons who have never been married (Laslett, 1979). Dr. Johnson would call this the triumph of hope over experience.

Stepfamilies are an increasingly frequent form of American family. Since about five out of six divorced men remarry, and three out of four divorced women remarry, a high proportion of all marriages in the United States, about 41%, have a ghost at the wedding—that is, they involve at least one person who was previously married. The result is the continual creation of new stepparent households: About 13% of all children under 18 are now living in stepfamilies. Given the magnitude of that number, one might expect that our society would have developed clear and shared understandings of how stepparents should behave. But, as will be clear in Chapter 13, Crosbie-Burnett *et al.* note that norms for behavior within stepfamilies are not well formulated or agreed upon, leaving each stepfamily the difficult task of working out its own mode of operation.

Since physical custody of the child after divorce continues to be granted to the mother about 90% of the time, remarriages produce stepfathers far more often than they produce stepmothers. Thus, it is the male parental role that is most often at issue in stepfamilies. The low participation of most fathers in childrearing thus takes on additional dimension in stepfamilies. The stepfather is often unsure of his rights or responsibilities, and the children, particularly older children, often object to intrusions by the interloper. Under these conditions, it appears that stepfathers are even less active than fathers in families containing both natural parents. Since stepmothers also are less active in childrearing than are mothers in families with both natural parents, stepfamilies on average provide somewhat lower levels of child care. The result is a lack of clear definition of the role of the stepparent that produces difficulties for the child and for the relations between husband and wife.

In addition, remarriage separates the remarrying parent from children for whom custody has been granted to the other parent. The remarriage of the noncustodial father often breaks the frail links between the father and his own children. The work of building a new family interferes with the continuity of fathering, and remarriage often creates a final rupture between the father and his offspring by a previous marriage. Since continued contact between father and children after divorce has been shown to be associated with the mental health of the child, this deterioration of relations has profound significance.

In Chapter 14 we (Strober and Dornbusch) discuss the numerous policy suggestions incorporated in the various chapters. Their analysis of these suggestions indicates that most of them are helpful to children, to women, and, more surprisingly, to men. Policies that have positive short-term and long-term consequences are numerous and worthy of consideration. The chapter begins by noting that the new family forms are here to stay. Public policy must assist all citizens, regardless of the type of family to which they belong. Policies thus need to address the problems of all families and not focus on male/breadwinner–female/homemaker families, recognizing the diversity of family types and thus becoming more flexible in application.

The actors in the policy arena are also diverse. The federal government has a major role, but numerous initiatives concerning families are reserved to state action. In addition, many policies are not the product of legislative enactments or administrative edicts; often important policy actions stem from the activities of decentralized actors operating in local communities. Schools, churches, local courts, businesses, unions, and foundations are among the groups influencing the situation of families in each community. Therefore, a comprehensive national policy for families is neither likely nor desirable. Policy recommendations are grouped in this chapter into three general categories: (1) enabling young people and adults to perform nontraditional tasks more effectively at home and at work; (2) developing new arrangements for childcare; and (3) assisting in the difficult transitions after divorce. Although numerous recommendations for assisting the new families are included, some have had to be eliminated because of lack of space. With respect to changing roles of men and women in the new families, we begin with suggestions for educational changes. Textbooks and teachers are beginning to emphasize the labor-force participation of women, but they have been slow to introduce curricular changes that stress nurturance by boys and men. A "curriculum for caring" is needed.

In addition, both boys and girls need to learn basic domestic skills, including training in childrearing. The special problems of single parents and stepparents should be discussed in the classroom. The prevention of teenage pregnancy through sex education does not seem to have worked, but schools can provide special assistance for teenage parents. Not only should schools stress the importance of prenatal care, but they should encourage teenage mothers to stay in school, helping to form support groups that will increase opportunities for the young parents and reduce the frequency of neglect and abuse of the children of teenage parents.

Parent–school communication is now much more difficult, for mothers are no longer so available to meet with teachers or act as classroom aides. Care for children during school holidays, vacations, or periods of illness has become problematic. Among desirable measures are increased flexibility in scheduling of parent–teacher conferences, development of communication with stepparents and noncustodial parents, and weekend field trips accompanied by parents.

With respect to employment, affirmative action has had only a modest effect so far in reducing occupational segregation or the gender gap in wages. Better enforcement mechanisms are needed, including the possibility of less harsh penalties that will be more likely to be applied. But gender segregation in occupations is tenacious and likely to persist for a long time, which leads to concerns about pay equity. In our decentralized system, immediate changes in pay equity through the introduction of "comparable worth" are unlikely. Yet current initiatives could include the assessment of relative wages for key occupations on the basis of comparable worth principles. That would assist unions and employers in moving towards more equitable pay for men and women.

Most parents would not reduce their hours of work because they cannot afford the loss of income. Part-time employment does not appear to be a popular way of adjusting the demands of work and family. Still, the offer of part-time employment would assist some parents of young children without producing an exodus away from full-time employment. New career paths, emphasizing more flexibility in career mobility, should be tested. Intergenerational transfers, guaranteed loans to be paid back after the childrearing years, and a reduction in the current stress on long work weeks for young professionals should also be examined.

The program of Aid to Families with Dependent Children requires substantial revision. It currently increases the probability of long-term dependency. It is unacceptable that AFDC, in practice, calls for full-time motherhood. Training programs, subsidized child care for mothers of preschool children, ameliorating the punitive taxation of AFDC recipients who work, providing health benefits for working mothers during a period of transition, and improving mechanisms for collecting child support payments would all be steps towards a more rational system.

With respect to housing, we need spatial designs that increase sharing across family units. The current regulatory system hampers the development of innovative forms of housing. There is a market for new types of housing; what is needed is a broader vision within the construction industry and its regulators.

The increasing number of stepfamilies require the states to recognize that stepparents have both rights and responsibilities. Stepparents need to be educated about their role in child care, and the state has to encourage their concern and active parenting.

We next turn our attention in Chapter 14 to the second general category of policy recommendations: the provision of new arrangements for child care. The male/breadwinner–female/homemaker household is not ordinarily seen as problematic, so that even those traditional households that are experiencing problems in childrearing are not viewed as requiring interventions by the community. But with respect to single-parent and two-earner families, public policy is increasingly designed to improve the quality of child care.

Public policy must be concerned with child care because we now perceive children as a public good, requiring investments by the society and later providing a return on that public investment. Whatever the legal and economic situation, some people are having children who do not have the resources to care for them. Who will care for those children? Single-parent families and two-earner families must often have the parent or parents of young children enter the labor force in order to get enough income for the family. Who is to provide for the physical and psychological care of the child when no parent can be home? Finally, among high-earning two-career couples, the demands of childrearing often are perceived as so onerous that prospective parents frequently decide not to have children. There is now little debate; our society needs to develop a system for child care.

The provision of child care is an organizational problem, not just a matter of money. A child-care system would differ from our current ad hoc arrangements primarily in its degree of coordination. We need conscious decisions about the types of services to provide, and their ownership and control. The current nonsystem has too many gaps and flaws. Infant care is very difficult to obtain; sick children are expected to return home even though there are no adults there to care for them; there are long waiting lists for available places in child-care facilities; there is high turnover among the low-paid caregivers; and parents do not have enough information as they try to find a safe and high-quality setting for their child. The nonsystem is both inefficient and expensive. We must search for innovative solutions to the daycare crisis.

Research on child-care systems is needed and likely to be fruitful. The numerous state and local initiatives require careful evaluation, along with studies in other countries of the cost-effectiveness of alternative forms of child care. But research should be more than evaluations of existing child care arrangements. We need to create and evaluate demonstration projects. Building on our awareness of the ubiquity of the new families, we should look at the costs and benefits of alternative forms of child care at different age levels for different types of families. For example, we need to study, for varied types of households, the effectiveness and efficiency of infant care, preschool care for toddlers, before- and after-school care, care during school vacations, and care for sick children. There is much to be learned, and active research will stimulate more imaginative thinking about the parts of the system and their integration.

The development of a child-care system need not lead to an inflexible, centralized bureaucracy. There is ample room for decentralization at the community level, with numerous groups jointly participating in the creation of an integrated system. Schools should play an active role in the child-care system. School holidays, extended vacations, and the hours before and after the usual school day all require alternative forms of care if no parent is at home. We do not believe it necessary that schools themselves provide alternative forms of care; they can, however, act as advocates for children in urging that local agencies take on the responsibility for school-age children who need care and monitoring.

Alternatives for the care of sick school-age children need to be developed. These may include a community infirmary, a set of persons trained to provide home care for sick children, or vouchers to permit parents to be paid while staying home with a sick child. School districts should take the lead in collaborating with nurses, physicians, and employers to reduce the additional strain that the illness of a child brings to the family in which there is no parent at home full-time.

A vital part of any child-care system is the availability of a parent to care for a newborn infant. The United States is the only industrial society that does not mandate maternity leave. We urge that paid leave for pregnancy, childbirth, and early care be viewed as a care benefit for infants rather than as a sick benefit for women. It should be paid for by a combination of employee insurance, employer benefits, and the public. Despite the large public benefit of parental leaves, the public contribution should be limited to those employees unable to pay for needed insurance or to receive employer benefits.

It is important that parental leave for infant care not be limited to women. Although the experience of Sweden indicates that most fathers will choose not to take paternal leave, the existence of the option for both parents reduces the likelihood of discrimination against women in employment and wages. Finally, research indicates that early bonding between fathers and infants is desirable for the children and both parents. National policies should encourage new norms for fathering.

Children also require economic support as part of the child-care system. Children in the new families rely either on both parents or solely on the single mother. Improvement of employment prospets for women contributes directly to the economic well-being of children. Another element of economic care for children is support from the noncustodial parent. Moral pressure and legislative remedies should make it more difficult for absent fathers to fail to live up to their responsibilities. We favor support payments based on a percentage of the noncustodial parent's income. Payments from AFDC should supplement the mother's earnings and child support payments so that the child's economic level will not fall below minimum standards.

The other side of the child support bargain is to assist the noncustodial parent, usually the father, in preserving ties to the child. As we turn our attention to the dislocations of divorce, our third category of policy recommendations, we note that most noncustodial fathers soon become estranged from their children. Except in rare cases, we believe it would be good public policy to guarantee the visitation rights of the father and to encourage the mutually beneficial contacts between divorced fathers and their children.

Since about half of all children will experience the divorce of their parents, public policies related to divorce are important. We are pleased by the growing movement for revision of child support laws and better enforcement of support agreements across state lines. Much remains to be done with respect to the division of "career assets" and real property. Children are often disadvantaged by custodial mothers being given too small a share of the career assets, and by their home being sold in order to provide each parent with a share of its value. Divorce settlements that demand immediate sale of the family home are robbing the children, tearing them away from neighborhood and friends during a particularly difficult period.

Since the acrimony of divorce proceedings often harms the children, we urge continuing experimentation with mediation and with training of lawyers in conflict resolution. Schools could also assist children of divorce during difficult periods of transition; workshops for teachers, and support groups among children whose parents are involved in separation and divorce are two activities to consider.

How do our policy recommendations affect men, women, and children? All the recommendations appear to be beneficial to women and to children. There are some policies that would usually assist women and children at the financial expense of men. Fathers who do not now pay child support would be injured financially by better enforcement of support agreements. The calculation of the level of child support on the basis of the noncustodial parent's income would negatively affect fathers with relatively high incomes. Postponing the sale of a home keeps the father from getting half of the proceeds. Finally, if the husband's career assets are larger than the wife's, he loses if career assets are divided at the time of divorce. Yet we do not believe this list of financial losses for some men shows that men would necessarily lose if these policies were introduced. Improved relationships with children are a likely consequence, and those interpersonal gains would help balance the financial losses.

Even a cold-blooded financial analysis does not lead to clear losses for men as a group. Most mothers remarry, and the increased costs to natural fathers may be exactly matched by the financial gains for the stepfathers. Similarly, improving employment opportunities for women does not lead to a commensurate economic loss for men in the aggregate. If one man fails to get a job because a woman gets it, another man is likely to be economically better off because his wife or mother or daughter got that very job.

We have found few conflicting interests among men, women, and children as we have examined the new families. Men, women, and children live together in families. Policies to assist the new families generally serve all of the family members.

REFERENCES

Bernard, J. (1982). *The future of marriage*. New Haven, CT: Yale University Press.
Council of Economic Advisors. (1987). *Economic report of the President*. Washington, DC: U.S. Government Printing Office.
Death of the family. (1983, January 17). *Newsweek Magazine*, pp. 26–27.
Diamond, I. (Ed.). (1983). *Families, politics and public policy: A feminist dialogue on women and the state*. New York: Longman.
Friedan, B. (1981). *The second stage*. New York: Summit Books.

Hayghe, H. (1986). Rise in mothers' labor force activity includes those with infants. *Monthly Labor Review*, *109*(2), 43–45.

Keniston, K. (1977). *All our children: The American family under pressure*. New York: Harcourt, Brace, Jovanovich.

Laslett, B. (1979). The significance of family membership. In V. Tufte & B. Myerhoff (Eds.), *Changing images of the family*. New Haven, CT: Yale University Press.

Stannard, D. E. (1979). *Changes in the American family: Fiction and reality*. New Haven, CT: Yale University Press.

U.S. Bureau of the Census. (1985, March). *Marital status and living arrangements* (Current Population Reports, Series P-20, No. 399). Washington, DC: U.S. Government Printing Office.

Veevers, J. E. (1979). Voluntary childlessness: A review of issues and evidence. *Marriage and Family Review*, *2*(2).

Weitzman, L. J. (1981). *The marriage contract: Spouses, lovers and the law*. New York: The Free Press.

2

The War over the Family
Is Not over the Family

SUSAN COHEN AND MARY FAINSOD KATZENSTEIN

The War over the Family (Berger & Berger, 1983), *In Defense of the Family* (Kramer, 1983), and *Rethinking the Family* (Thorne & Yalom, 1982) are but a few of the books produced over the last decade in the political encounters between feminists and traditionalists. Curiously, the battle is not fundamentally about the family, but rather a conflict over the roles and relationships of men and women. Moreover, the differences of opinion over the needs and interests of children constitute a skirmish more than a war. This essay advances an argument: Feminists and traditionalists disagree deeply about issues fundamental to the nature of society and the role of men and women within it. Finding a middle ground is neither easy nor perhaps even possible. But to say that the controversy is over who is pro- or antifamily obscures rather than illuminates the issue. The debate is fundamentally about the places in society of men and women. The discourse about what is good for children is simply not so polarized; to see it as such would be to misspecify the nature of the feminist–traditional division.

We recognize, of course, that there is a close connection between children's interests and the interests of adults. Suppositions about the roles and relationships of men and women have implications for the upbringing of children. How we raise our children depends on our conceptions of the adults we want them to become. At the same time, people who otherwise have widely varying world views may hold similar ideas about the kind of care children should receive and the persons from whom they should receive it.

In this chapter, we will analyze the arguments about the family that have preoccupied the American public over the last decade or so. Our intention is threefold:

> 1. To convey an understanding of the multiplicity of views among both traditionalists and feminists that, while they do not deny the differences between the two ideological camps, do complicate the easy stereotypes to which popular debate so readily resorts;

Susan Cohen, Ph.D. candidate, and Mary Fainsod Katzenstein, Ph.D. Government Department, Cornell University, Ithaca, New York.

2. To explore the idea that the rift between feminists and traditionalists revolves largely around issues of adult roles rather than children's needs;

3. To explicate the tensions that exist among both feminists and traditionalists in their attempts to reconcile the sometimes conflicting values embodied within their writings on the family.

Feminism and the traditionalist Right are terms that require definition if our discussion is to proceed. When we speak of feminism and the Right, we will be distinguishing between two theoretical perspectives that are themselves extraordinarily heterogeneous. By feminist views, we refer to arguments that start from the premise that society now and in the past has been arranged hierarchically by gender and that such arrangements must be challenged. Within this feminist perspective, however, we discuss a range of views: revisionist theories, such as those of Jean Elshtain (1982) that exhort feminists to return to "female-created and -sustained values" of mothering and nurturance, as well as the more radical views of such theorists as Adrienne Rich (1976), that insist on a basic restructuring of family life.

By rightist, traditional, or conservative views (we use the terms interchangeably), we refer to writings of wide-ranging perspectives on the economic, social, and moral responsibility of the state to its citizens. What these writings share is a belief either in the different natures of men and women, or in the desirability of a continued division of labor by gender whatever might be the similarity or difference in men and women's nature (Christensen, 1977). Thus the writings of the New Right speak of the religious and biologically mandated differences in the life callings of men and women. Neoconservatives, by contrast, emphasize the desirability of gender-neutral, nonintrusive laws that afford equal educational and job opportunities for men and women even as they "prefer" that women elect different life priorities from those men choose (see Berger & Berger, 1983). Absolutely central to both views is the assumption that the government has now done all it can do, that virtually all antidiscrimination laws that might provide guarantees of equal opportunity are now in place.[1]

THE REAL WAR OVER THE FAMILY: GENDER ROLES AND THE VIEW FROM THE RIGHT

Diverse as different components of the Right are, they are united around an idealization of the traditional nuclear family. Contained in this idealization is a particular view of men's and women's roles that is absolutely crucial to an understanding of the ideological divide between feminism and the Right.

The Right's view of gender roles is remarkably invariant across neoconservative and New Right positions. A man's responsibility to his family is best met by his success in the market, his ability as a wage earner to support his wife and children; a woman's worth is measured by her dedication to her role as wife and mother. This case is made with evangelical conviction by Phyllis Schlafly in *The Power of the Positive Woman* (1978) and *The Power of the Christian Woman* (1981). Motherhood is a woman's calling. If a woman wants love, emotional, social, or financial security, or the satisfaction of achievement, no career in the world can compete with motherhood. That is not to say that women can never find fulfillment outside the home. The rare woman (Mother Theresa is one example that Schlafly offers) may find fulfillment in life's other options, and some may successfully pursue both marriage and career. But this pursuit of dual responsibilities is possible only if two conditions are met: (1) if a woman relies on her own resourcefulness rather than expecting others, the government in particular, to come to her assistance; and (2) if she does not allow her primary role as wife and mother to be superseded by other interests or responsibilities. Here Schlafly offers the example of "Mrs." Thatcher, who managed both to become Prime Minister of Great Britain and to cook breakfast every morning for her husband (in contrast to Mrs. Betty Ford "who stayed in bed while her husband cooked his own breakfast during the many years he was Congressman" (1978, p. 44).

Brigitte Berger and Peter Berger, who have written in defense of the bourgeois family from a neoconservative perspective, are less proselytizing but no less convinced:

> Individual women will have to decide on their priorities. Our own hope is that many will come to understand that life is more than a career and that this "more" is above all to be found in the family. But however individual women decide, they should not expect public policy to underwrite and subsidize their life plans. (1983, p. 205)

The emphasis on the primacy of motherhood and the secondary concession to women's other sources of identity and fulfillment (as long as women don't expect any special help) are common to New Right and neoconservative perspectives alike.

Greater differences do exist within the Right over the question of why this arrangement of gender roles is socially desirable. Schlafly and the evangelical Right accept a traditional sexual division of labor as natural—biologically destined and God-given. Schlafly (1978, pp. 17, 33, 49–50) and Falwell (1980, p. 150) both speak of an "innate maternal instinct," of a "natural maternal need," and of God-given roles. The Bergers are less sure. Whether or not there is a maternal instinct in the human species, it should still be evident, the Bergers argue, that the division of labor embodied in the bourgeois family is preferable to any other arrangement (Berger & Berger, 1983, p. 152). The bourgeois family produced individuals whose traits made possible both capitalism and a democratic order (1983, p. 157).[2] The more secular, supply-side exponents of the New Right, as evidenced in the writing of George Gilder (1981, pp. 69–71), makes a similar argument, proposing that the heterosexual nuclear family is essential to an efficient and productive society. Married men form stable work patterns and contribute more productively to the economic well-being of the nation than do bachelors who have no family responsibilities and dissipate their energies in nonproductive sexual and economic concerns.

Gender Roles and Public Policy

According to the Right, the traditional bourgeois family as it is now constituted offers women and men nearly all the options they should want. In contrast to the feminist position, the Right seeks a roll-back of state initiatives, maintaining that there is little the state should do beyond what it has already done to lend support to women or men who might seek to alter the traditional gender arrangements both within and outside the family. The list of public policy measures that most feminists would see as essential to the enlargement of life options for men and women (legalized abortion [but see Chapter 3], expanded day-care services, programs to assist victims of domestic violence, insurance provisions for maternity/paternity leaves, protection of homosexual rights) are either actively opposed or simply ignored by virtually all sections of the Right. The New Right's position on these issues is well known: opposition to federal legislation on domestic violence, opposition to the legalization of abortion, and support for the Family Protection Act (barring governmental recognition of homosexual rights, and the use of educational materials that question traditional family roles). The New Right does not oppose an activist state. As feminist scholar Zillah Eisenstein (1982) explains, the New Right shares the neoconservative opposition to the expansion of the welfare state but departs from the neoconservative position in its enthusiastic support of a state that seeks to assert its influence over the social and sexual mores of its citizens. The New Right encourages the state to engage in moral leadership but certainly in ways that would pressure or reestablish the breadwinner system that Kingsley Davis describes in Chapter 4.

This is one important distinction between the New Right exponents such as Schlafly or Gilder, and neoconservatives, such as the Bergers, Nathan Glazer, and Irving Kristol. While the former exhort the state to actively exercise moral authority, the latter generally eschew such espectations. The Bergers, for example, go to some lengths to distinguish themselves from moral majority activists. They aver that they are not part of the chorus arguing for the dismantling of the welfare state, and they indict those who would use the state to "influence or control behavior within the family" (1983, p. 207). They thus do not share the New Right's enthusiasm for patrolling antifamily educational materials; they also do not display anything like the almost ecclesiastical tone of George Gilder's case for returning to the era of the male breadwinner. Nevertheless, the Bergers' search for the middle ground lands them closer to the New Right than to feminism. Although they support a (restricted) version of legalized abortion, they insist that abortion has nothing to do with famly policy. They therefore refuse to make a case for abortion in their discussion of policies needed to "strengthen" the family; nor do they give even a mention to the desirability of legislation for programs to extend child care or reduce domestic violence. Homosexual rights, they argue, are in no way related to family policy. They write: "It is not a function of the state, at least in a democracy to regulate the arrangements by which 'consenting adults' arrange their private lives—AS LONG AS THEY ARE UNENCUMBERED BY CHILDREN" (1983, p. 206). Hence the neoconservative position, at least as espoused by the Bergers, appears to reject expanded day care, additional funding of services for victims of battering, abortion, or homosexual rights, as long as any of those claims are related to the needs of family members. The position is strongly suggestive of John Stuart Mill's 19th-century argument (progressive for its time) that women should have rights similar to men—except when they choose to marry and have children. In the course of his long essay otherwise decrying the subjection of women, Mill wrote:

> Like a man when he chooses a profession, so, when a woman marries it may in general be understood that she makes choice of the management of a household and the upbringing of a family, as the first call upon her exertions . . . and that she renounces not all other objects and occupations, but all which are not consistent with the requirements of this. (Mill, 1859/1970, p. 179)

The policies that the Bergers say would help to strengthen the bourgeois family—redressing the heavier tax burden on married couples; providing child allowances; furnishing special allowances for the care of the sick, handicapped, and aged family members; offering vouchers that would empower families to make educational choices for their children—are also policies that the New Right would find easy to support because they in no way threaten the gender-based traditional division of labor. In their common belief that public policy has no place in facilitating the abilities of men and women to depart from their traditional roles within and outside the family, both neoconservative and New Right perspectives stand in direct opposition to the position of most feminists. It is to feminist views on the family—and the roles of men and women—that we now turn.

THE REAL DEBATE OVER THE FAMILY: FEMINISM AND THE AUTONOMY OF WOMEN WITHIN THE FAMILY

According to the Right, feminists are against the family. This antifamily charge is basically a slogan that muddles rather than clarifies the true political issue. The real debate is over women's autonomy within and outside the family.

While the Right idealizes the traditional nuclear family in which the man works for wages and the woman stays home to raise the children, feminists reject the claim that this particular version of family life is the only acceptable form. As Barrie Thorne says in her introduction to *Rethinking the Family*, "Feminists have challenged beliefs that any specific family arrangement is natural, biological, or 'functional' in a timeless way" (1982, p. 2). Thus if one is asking who is for the family and who against it, one must also ask, "Which family?"

A profound disagreement between the Right and feminists does exist—one that focuses on the relationship of women to the family. It is this, rather than the debate over the needs and interests of children, that has fueled the feminist-Right conflagrations. Feminism has been the source of serious criticisms of the traditional family. Yet, in exploring feminist critiques of the traditional family, it is at once apparent that feminist thought is anything but monolithic. At some level, all feminists have insisted that the traditional nuclear family has deprived women of autonomy and in so doing has been an oppressive force that must be altered. But the broad and widely divergent set of views within that position needs to be acknowledged.

A number of the early feminist writings of the late 1960s and early 1970s condemned the nuclear family as the institution centrally responsible for the denial of women's freedom. The writings of Shulamith Firestone (1970) and Kate Millet (1969) argue that the biological family is basic to women's oppression; thus for women to be free within a reconstituted nonbiological family, they must reject their biologically given childbearing role. A revolution in the technology of childbirth (test-tube babies) for Firestone and a separatist, lesbian politics for Millet were the necessary prerequisites of women's liberation from the traditional family.

Yet other feminists writing in the same period took a quite different view. Autonomy for women *could* occur within the biological/heterosexual family provided certain changes in the traditional family could be realized. According to the politics of the National Organization for Women (NOW) in the early 1970s, the demand for autonomy meant, among other things, the right to define and express a woman's own sexuality, economic independence, and a sense of identity not wholly dependent on relationships to other people (Freeman, 1975, p. 20). These views translated into demands for equal pay, equality of education and job opportunities, reproductive choice, and personal sexual choice. The thrust of NOW's politics was quite different, however, from the radicalism of Firestone and Millet. For the latter, autonomy was impossible without women divorcing themselves from the biological and heterosexual family. For many NOW members, gay sexuality was an option women might choose, but it was not the *sine qua non* of female autonomy. For some groups within NOW, the issue was how to realize greater autonomy for women within rather than apart from the heterosexual and biological family. For others it was how to constitute a family, but one not defined by traditional heterosexual/biological norms.

The writings of other feminists made it clear that a critique of heterosexuality was not identical with the rejection of motherhood. Adrienne Rich, like Millet, protested the tyranny of traditional gender roles and the fact that heterosexuality occupied the exalted status of an "institution," instead of being one of many legitimate sexual choices. Yet Rich found much to celebrate in the mother-knot, unlike Firestone, whose negative view of motherhood suffuses the pages of her writings. There is a resonant image in *Of Woman Born* (Rich, 1976) of what the abolition of motherhood as an institution might mean: Rich and her three young sons, alone in a summer house in Vermont, living temporarily joyous and anarchic lives. "We were conspirators, outlaws from the institution of motherhood; I felt enormously in charge of my life" (p. 193). The picture is one of attentive love, but love freed of compulsion and the incessant guilt that comes of not being the perfect mother mythologized by the institution of motherhood. Clearly Rich believes that restructuring motherhood to be free of all vestiges of patriarchal control is both necessary and possible.

Nancy Chodorow explores the issue of autonomy at considerable depth in the *Reproduction of Mothering* (1978). She argues that the subordination of women derives from a pattern of upbringing in which women are the primary caregivers—a pattern that prohibits young girls from experiencing a necessary independence, just as it forces young boys into an excessive independence that deprives them of the capacity for nurturance. What is needed to break this cycle is a new mode of childrearing in which both parents play a substantial role. The fruits of such an arrangement would be more autonomy for mothers, as well as for their female children. Both male and female children would become more whole and ultimately more capable of satisfying relationships than their parents were.

More recent feminist writings (mistakenly characterized by some as feminist capitulation to the Right [Barber, 1983]) echo the earlier sentiments of Chodorow and others that autonomy for women is ultimately possible within the biological and heterosexual family. Betty Friedan's *The Second Stage* (1981) makes an argument that is hardly new to feminism, although it has been seen by the media as a redirection of contemporary feminist thinking. In the early years of women's movement, she says (castigating herself along with others), feminists believed that work alone could make for a meaningful life. But this was a mistaken, unbalanced view since all people need love as well as work. Based on this insight, *The Second Stage* is above all a reaffirmation of the family. While Friedan tries to encourage the growth of new kinds of family ties, it is clear that she still sees the heterosexual biological family as the norm, the major change from old patterns being the sharing of child care and household tasks.

Friedan's argument is not explicitly an argument for autonomy, but it is highly individualistic in character, and it clearly rests on the assumption that the vision of family life presented is compatible with autonomy for both men and women. Demands such as flex-time (flexible working hours), reproductive rights, and quality day-care can be seen as mechanisms by which women's range of choices is expanded.

Like Friedan, Jean Elshtain believes that family life is extremely important and that women can be autonomous within the blood-tied family, or at least autonomous enough that one can say that they are not oppressed. At the same time, much of what Elshtain writes appears to echo the Right's view of the family: Her rejection of androgyny, her suggestion that women are particularly suited to mothering, her inattention to abortion and homosexuality, and her insistence on the separation of private and public spheres (see also Rossi, 1977). And although she writes of the importance of parenting (close child–parent bonding) in gender-neutral terms, she caps her discussion by calling on not all men and women but rather the feminist thinker, to "ask at what price she would gain the world for herself or other women, utterly rejecting those victories that come at the cost of the bodies and spirits of human infants" (1981, p. 331).

How close is the affinity between Elshtain and the Right? Parallels with the Bergers, for example, are striking: Even as all three allow for variations on the traditional theme, their highest praise is reserved for families where women are responsible for the care of their children. And yet, there are serious differences. Elshtain's work is self-consciously feminist. It is interesting to contrast her concern with the political resonance of language, and the language she herself uses (e.g., her references to the "isolation and debasement of women under terms of male-dominated ideology and social structures" [1982, p. 333]) to the Bergers' sarcastic discussion of "Femspeak" (i.e., nonsexist language).

Elshtain can be seen as traditional in her stress on the private sphere (Stacey, 1986). Yet she wants to revitalize the private, not only for its own sake but also for its potential to change public values and structural arrangements. In this Elshtain is linked to 19th-century feminists, as well as to contemporary feminist thinkers like Carol Gilligan. The Bergers praise the traditional (bourgeois) family for producing the sort of people who do well in a liberal capitalist order; Elshtain sees the family as a place from which to challenge that order.

Finally, it is important to recognize that Elshtain is not without objections to the traditional family. She speaks of a need to "articulate a *particular ideal* of family life that does not repeat the earlier terms of female oppression and exploitation" (1982, p. 323). She repeatedly expresses a concern that women be viewed as autonomous subjects, and that the voices that relate women's experience of their lives not be silenced. Unlike the Right, she does not simply evoke the past; instead she asks people to forge links with it through traditions that do not oppress women. The point here is that even that part of feminist thinking that is closest to the Right's view of the family and women's role within it rejects those conceptualizations of the family that give little attention to the value of women's autonomy.

The policy demands that stem from feminist conceptions of women's autonomy include quality day care, reproductive rights and rights of sexual preference, shelters for battered women, programs for displaced homemakers, incentives for industry to make available parental leaves and flex-time, and the Equal Rights Amendment (ERA). Various feminist writings reveal, of course, different emphases. Elshtain hardly talks about policy at all. Friedan says most women "do not want impersonal 'government day care'" (1981, p. 260); she urges the widespread adoption of flex-time and job sharing and speculates on new forms of domestic architecture that would be conducive to communal cooking, housework, and child care. Adrienne Rich warns against looking to public day care or communal living arrangements for an easy solution to the problem of women's oppression; what is needed, she says, is a transfiguration of society for which there is no exact blueprint. Firestone writes of the need for a technological revolution in reproductive biology. However diverse the policy issues addressed, the basic idea underlying feminist discourse is to give women greater autonomy than that provided by the family in which husband is breadwinner and wife homemaker.

THE DEBATE OVER CHILDREN'S INTERESTS

Feminist views do, then, stand in clear opposition to the perceptions of the Right about the relationship of women to the family and to society. These views of women in family roles are separated by a deep ideological chasm from those of the Right. The argument of this section, however, is that there is no such vast divide between the views of feminism and the Right over the interests and needs of children.

The views of the Right are well known. Children's interests are met best in a heterosexual, two-parent family where the mother stays home to raise her children. This is the optimal situation, at least. If it were also the absolute requisite of decent childbearing, then the views of the Right and of feminism would be entirely uncongenial. But in fact the views of the Right and, as we shall see later, those of feminism are neither monolithic nor unbending.

Most conservative exponents are prepared to recognize the exigency of some variations on the theme of full-time mother's care. Phyllis Schlafly makes it as clear as anyone on the Right that a child is best brought up by the biological mother. Having recently become a grandmother, Schlafly says, she has been able to observe first hand that babies' needs "are the same now as they always have been."[3] Babies are constantly demanding and need the love, care, and attention of someone who will be a steadfast part of their lives. But as Schlafly recognizes, the presence of a biological mother as the chief caretaker is not always possible. She acknowledges the mothering capacities of the nonbiological mother who has adopted a child; and she observes that there are occasions when the mother may need to work outside the home, where families "must accommodate themselves to such situations." In that case, the person caring for the child may be, best, "a grandmother, an aunt, a relative or some other person." What is harmful to a child, she says, is government-funded day care, because staff is constantly changing, as well as situations where "women, the feminists, argue for day care simply out of a desire to justify their own life styles."

Schlafly's arguments about the needs and interests of children insist on children being raised by a devoted and constant caretaker. Her emphatic view that a child suffers in the hands of government-funded day care or feminists out to justify their own life-styles may have at least as much to do with her antipathy towards government intrusion and feminist ideologies as it does with the needs and interests of children. If these needs and interests were her sole or even primary concern, she would presumably be more interested in whether the "bonding between mother and child" can occur alongside government day care settings or within feminist households. The argument here is as much about society and the place of men and women as it is about the needs and interests of children.

The Bergers' preference for the mother assuming the primary task of infant and child care is only somewhat less explicit. They write, however, that "the anthropological evidence suggests that the precise form [of the family] does not matter for the infant as long as the minimal imperatives are not violated—most important as long as the structure is stable and allows for the expression of love toward the infant" (1983, p. 152).

The Bergers then go on to note that the evidence leaves open the possibility that a female need not play the role of mother figure (they do not address the analogous possibility that the male need not play the role of father figure). But their speculation ends there. Because arrangements where males predominate as childrearers have not been known historically, they conclude that it is unlikely that alternate family forms would be equally viable. The Bergers' preference for the biological mother as childrearer[4] does at least leave open the possibility of a less than always-present mother, and even of some other gender-structured arrangement as long as it could be demonstrated to be stable and loving.

An enormous body of feminist writing on the family focuses on the importance of mothering, but from the primary perspective of its impact on women. Adrienne Rich's *Of Woman Born* (1976) is one such work whose principal concern is the experience of mothering for women. But her description of children's needs, like Schlafly's comment about the unrelenting demands of her new grandchild, evokes the passion of small children for unconditional love ("from dawn to dark, and often in the middle of the night" [1976, p. 4]). Rich's book is largely about the way in which mothering in a patriarchal society imprisons women, and about the need to release mothering from patriarchal burdens, although not from children. This is closely connected to her argument about children's needs: Mothering, she argues, when it is imbedded in patriarchal society, cannot meet children's needs—daughters learn to resent the powerlessness of their mothers, sons grow to be sent either literally or figuratively into the fields of battle.

Throughout Rich's analysis of mothering, there is little discussion, however, of the needs of children apart from the adults they will become. What needs infants or children may have, independent of their gender socialization is hardly addressed.[5]

Chodorow's book on mothering is similarly structured to address the question of how sex roles get reproduced through the mothering process; children "mothered" within patriarchal society grow up less than whole. Girls emerge as dependent women; boys grow into adults who experience difficulty in their ability to relate to others. Children thus need the parenting of both male and female—parenting that provides "consistency of care and the ability to relate to a small number of people stably over time" (1978, p. 217).

More recent feminist writing critical of "first stage" feminism—allegedly preoccupied with the emancipation of women—makes an explicit case for the primacy of children's needs. And yet even this writing has little to say about what actually constitutes the needs and interests of children. This brand of feminism is represented by Jean Elshtain, who comes closer than most feminists to associating the traditional family structure with the capacity of the adult world to meet the needs of infant and child. Elshtain asserts (and there would be many feminists and conservatives who would agree) that children need "strong early attachment to specific adult others" (p. 320). She continues,

> Not every neglected and abused child becomes a Charles Manson but every Charles Manson was an abused and neglected child. "The jailhouse was my father," Charles Manson cried. (1981, p. 329)

In sketching a feminist theory that calls for a newly strengthened but nonoppressive family, Elshtain says, "Responsibilities for children are paramount . . . social feminist of the sort I propose places children in the center of its concern" (1982, p. 448). Elshtain's argument does not require women to take on the primary task of childrearing, nor does she explicitly, as do the Bergers, hail the success of the traditional bourgeois family. Rather abstractly, however, she insists on the preservation of the "[private] sphere that makes [such] a morality of responsibility possible" (1982, p. 336). Traditional feminine virtues of nurturance and compassion must be maintained, both for the sake of children and for the construction of a moral society. This restructuring of the private sphere (whatever it may look like—and

Elshtain is less than clear on this) will have enormous ramifications. The rediscovery of "maternal" values will serve women because, by strengthening the private, the public life that has excluded and debased women (and the poor) will be challenged. Children will benefit from the love and compassion now surrounding them, and society will be altered in desirable ways by the infusion of feminine values.[6]

The isomorphism of children's, family's, women's, and societal needs in feminist writings—writings as different as those of Chodorow, Rich, and Elshtain—is extraordinary. Perhaps this coincidence of interests can be explained by the possibility that views concerning the interests of children are derivations of an idealization about the lives of the adults that these children are to become. Children's needs are not identified independent of the adult qualities (autonomy, sensitivity, compassion—all strikingly adult in sound) that these authors hope children will acquire. In most feminist writings, there is little concerted attempt to explore the needs of children apart from the models of adulthood it is hoped that children will later fulfill.

The failure of feminist theory to properly address ideas of children's needs and interests is recognized in an essay by Chodorow and Contratto. They exhort feminists to rethink ideas about mothering and the family based on a more fully elaborated exploration of child development. They call for theories that are:

> interactive and that accord the infant and child agency and intentionality, rather than characterize it as a passive reactor to drives or environmental pressures. We need to build theories that recognize collaboration and compromise as well as conflict, theories in which needs to not equal wants; in which separation is not equivalent to deprivation and in which autonomy is different from abandonment. We must begin to look at times other than infancy in the developmental life span and relationships over time to people other than the mother to get a more accurate picture of what growing up is about. (1982, p. 71)

In an article titled "Re-visioning Women and Social Change: Where Are the Children?" (1986), Barrie Thorne undertakes the beginning of such an analysis. She observes that feminists have seen children largely as threats to an ordered society, as victims of a disordered society, or as learners of adult culture. She argues instead for a conceptualization that attributes agency to children.

Most feminists and conservatives would agree on a "bottom line" of childrearing—that infants and young children need constant, committed devotion from a stable cast of adults. Nor does there appear to be an irremediable polarization over how such basic children's needs are to be met. The right prefers the full-time presence of the biological mother but is not implacably opposed to at least a limited array of alternative arrangements. Some feminists are deeply opposed to the institution of full-time motherhood under conditions of patriarchy (e.g., Rich and Chodorow). Others, such as Elshtain, celebrate the possibility of the reconsecration of mothering in a domestic setting that may or may not involve shared parenting (Elshtain is unclear). Some feminist theories appear to prefer dual, heterosexual parenting; others reject or do not require such arrangements.

Kristin Luker's (1983) fascinating study of pro-life and pro-choice activists lends support to the claim that the usual pro- and antifamily slogans applied to the Right and to feminism are not useful labels. Almost counterintuitively, pro-choice activists, Luker observes, are often *preoccupied* with planning for the care and education of their children. They insist that parenting must be purposeful, designed to give the child maximum parental guidance and every possible advantage. Pro-life activists, by contrast, tend to be laissez-faire individualists in their attitude towards child upbringing. Advocates of large families, pro-life activists assert that the individual qualities of the particular child, rather than parental planning, or material advantage, will determine the child's destiny.[7]

But the beliefs of such activists aside, what is most remarkable about the *writings* of both the Right and of feminism on the family is the scarcity of attention paid to the identification of children's needs. Common to both is the tendency to derive conceptions about children's needs from assumptions about desirable gender arrangements to which those children are expected later to conform. There appears to be a dual agenda for both feminists and conservative writings on the family. In the construction of this agenda, children's needs seem all too readily subsumed by the eagerness to win acceptance for a particular preferred arrangement of men's and women's place in adult society.

AUTONOMY, COMMUNITY, AND SOCIETY

In their writings about the kind of society in which children attain adulthood, both conservatives and feminists struggle to reconcile the often conflicting goals of autonomy and community. The fostering of individualism and the creation of community are themes that preoccupy both feminism and the Right, and the tensions between these dual goals are a constant source of problems for both theoretical perspectives.

The Bergers' *The War over the Family* (1983) treats these themes at some length. Their defense of the bourgeois family rests on what they believe to be the particular strength of that institution: its capacity to provide community and a sense of belonging while at the same time creating in its members the spirit of individualism. "Human beings," they write, "can not live without community any more than they can live without institutions" (1983, p. 146) The family, better than other institutions, can create sharing, trust, and identity. At the same time, they argue, the great contribution of the bourgeois family has been the promotion of individualism. The bourgeois famly fosters self-assertion, the belief in the individual's ability to control the world through rational calculations. They write: "Put simply, the bourgeois family socialized individuals with personalities and values conducive to entrepreneurial capitalism on the one hand and democracy on the other" (1983, p. 157).

It would be surprising if a single institution that bred moral harmony and community on the one hand and individualism on the other were not to experience the tension that derives from reconciling these potentially conflicting values. And indeed, as the Bergers ackowledge, the family as the locale where both harmony and individualism are to be nurtured does find itself under seige. Although they accede explicitly to the importance of this problem, they do no more than acknowledge it:

> Also the very values of the bourgeois family ethos from the beginning, had within them the seeds of their own destruction. Individualism brought forth within the family, would turn against it. (1983, p. 103)

They acknowledge that individualism bred in the bourgeois family has led to educational institutions that can challenge the family and to a middle class that is far more skeptical than lower-income populations about reigning values. The efflorescence of individualism, by this argument, may be at the very root of feminist discontent with the family. They acknowledge this idea in a single flippant observation:

> Perhaps it should not surprise us that some women become disenchanted with this role [within the household] quite apart from the feminist movement as such. Civilization building is a weary-making task, with its own psychic costs. In the (somewhat misleading) language of the critics; it can become tiresome to be "on a pedestal." (1983, p. 103)

Beyond this passing acknowledgement, there is little discussion by the Bergers of how the inculcation of individualism in the family may affect male and female members differently. Self-assertion and rational calculation are mentioned as qualities that families breed in their members, presumably without regard to gender. There is absolutely no discussion of battering or incest, experiences that curtail the "autonomy" of male and female family members in quite different ways.

The potential tension between individualism spawned within the bourgeois family and the sense of community that the family is also expected to transmit is reconciled only when the range of individualist aspirations is limited. Individualism that promotes, as the Bergers describe it, "the ideal of the 'swinging single,' with no ties on his or her project of endless self-realization; the idealization of abortion, once and for all eliminating the vestigial risk of pregnancy, the insistence that a 'gay life style' is as socially legitimate as heterosexual marriage" (1983, p. 135) is individualism that cannot be reconciled with the harmony of the bourgeois family. The possibility of reconciling community and autonomy within the bourgeois family is, then, entirely dependent on the creation of individualist values that conform to standards that do not fundamentally undermine the traditional nuclear, heterosexual family.

A central motif in feminist discussion is, likewise, the idea of autonomy. Most of the changes sought by feminists can be understood as means toward, or aspects of, this end. But the idea of autonomy has some problematic implications in spite of its pivotal role in feminist theory.

Autonomy can take different shapes. One involves "the right of all individuals to develop their highest potential" (Gordon, 1982, p. 50). A classic presentation of this notion of autonomy can be found in John Stuart Mill's 1859 essay, *On Liberty*. Going further back in time, to the philosophical origins of liberalism, one finds a somewhat different version of autonomy: In Hobbes and Locke the emphasis is on acquisitions and competition. This egoistic and often aggressive type of autonomy is a *modus operandi* that many feminists explicitly reject, and that they perceive as a serious threat to another feminist goal—egalitarian communities.

Liberal feminists are prone to overlook the issue of community and instead tend to portray feminism in almost wholly individualistic terms. Betty Friedan writes,

> feminism is threatening to despots of fascism, communism, or religious fundamentalism, Third World or American brand, because it is an expression of individualism, human autonomy, personal freedom, which once freely experienced, can never be erased or completely controlled. (1981, p. 329)

The primary concern of *The Second Stage* is the needs of the individual. While it is true that Friedan gives much attention to our needs for connectedness, her focus remains on the individual. Moreover, she sees the need for connection being met primarily within the nuclear family. Friedan seems to attach little importance to the notion of political community, or to communities of women.

Many feminists write about individualism in a more guarded way than does Friedan. Linda Gordon, in her essay in *Rethinking the Family*, expresses an "ambivalence between individualism and its critique" (1982, p. 50). The task of feminism, she says, is

> to develop a feminist program and philosophy that defends individual rights and also builds constructive bonds between individuals to defend all the gains of bourgeois individualism and liberal feminism, while transcending the capitalist-competitive aspects of individualism with a vision of loving, egalitarian communities. (1982, pp. 51–52)

Many feminist writers would find themselves in accord with this formulation of feminist goals. However, the uncomfortable question arises as to whether the transcendence that Gordon envisions can ever actually be achieved.

Jean Elshtain has written on this issue in a sobering if not pessimistic way. She makes a case for the primacy of community over individualism, arguing that much of feminism rejects the possibility of community within the bonds of traditional ethnic family life that provided a basic identity to women like her grandmother. She goes on to argue that, in this world at least, it is impossible to establish both individual autonomy and strong communal ties: "Feminism of the sort I propose recognizes that there is no final resolution to the twin goals of individual and social good" (1982, p. 448).

Many radical, Marxist, and social feminists would dispute Elshtain's claim, or grant that while it may be true now, it will not be so after the revolution (of whatever sort). Unfortunately this issue is addressed directly far too infrequently by feminists of the Left. Instead of explicit discussion, there is often an underlying assumption that once the revolution takes place, each person will have the freedom to realize her- or himself fully and at the same time will naturally join others in creating egalitarian communities.

Among less revolutionary feminists there is a tendency to see the tension between individual freedom and social good as an inevitable, if unfortunate, aspect of the human condition. According to this view, political life is an arena in which compromises are always necessary. Decisions must be made as to how much freedom one is willing to give up for the sake of a strong community, and how far one is willing to weaken communal authority for the sake of individual freedom.

Elshtain's argument, though, is not merely that these two important ends are contradictory, but also that they are in a fundamental sense dependent on one another. In a discussion of Dostoyevsky's "Grand Inquisitor," she comments,

> In the Inquisitor's world, there is *neither* freedom *nor* community. Dostoyevsky's mass are "pitiful" and "childlike" in the worst sense—hardly a community, hardly exemplars of mutuality. They have security but the price they pay is the loss of *both* community and liberty. (1983a, pp. 251–252)

> Freedom requires roots and roots involve communities and no community has ever existed without constraints of some kind. (1983a, p. 253)

It is thus not just that perfect freedom and perfect community are impossible. Freedom paradoxically requires constraints, including the constraints that are inevitably an aspect of family life. While Elshtain clearly doesn't equate community with family—she stresses the importance of political participation and a sense of political purpose beyond the family—she does see strong families as an essential element of communal life: " There is no way to create real communities out of an aggregate of 'freely' choosing adults" (1982, p. 442). Not only is community impossible without families, freedom (paradoxically) is impossible without families; as she states above, "Freedom requires roots." Roots are composed of family, ethnic, and religious ties, ties that are largely involuntary.

One way in which families nourish freedom, says Elshtain, is by fulfilling our needs for intimacy, security, and a sense of purpose that, if unmet by the family, will be met elsewhere, in ways that may prove disastrous.

> Cults moved into the vacuum created by the "thinning-out" of community and family ties, even as they further eroded those ties to preclude any outside locus for human relations. In an argument that eerily replicates radical claims that attachment to the family vitiates commitment to "the Cause," Jim Jones rejected a request by two members of his doomed cult for a Thanksgiving visit to the family of one of them in these words: "It's time for you to cut your family ties. . . . Blood ties are dangerous because they prevent people from being totally dedicated to the Cause." (1982, pp. 444–445)

Yet many feminists would reject Elshtain's contention that freedom and community require the blood-tie of the family. Her argument about the threat from cults might well be met with the response that some families are cult-like in the way they treat individual members. Linda Gordon states:

> Feminism has undermined the family as it once existed faster than it has been able to substitute more egalitarian communities. This is not a criticism of the women's movement. Perhaps families held together by domination, fear, violence, squelched talents, and resignation should not survive. (1982, p. 50)

Elshtain recognizes that families have often restricted freedom for women and says this must be changed (1981, pp. 144, 323). However, she disagrees with many feminists on the extent to which "domination, fear, violence, squelched talents, and resignation" have marked family life.

Elshtain makes another argument as to why families are essential to freedom, and it rests on a particular conception of freedom. Her understanding of freedom is not the classical liberal one centering around an absence of restraint, nor is it freedom to fulfill one's potential, although it includes elements of both these ideas. Elshtain's conception of freedom includes the idea of moral responsibility. For her, to be free is above all to be free to act morally. Here the family is crucial, as a place where moral responsibility is taught to children, and is part of the experience of family members in their relations with one another.

> My vision holds that if we are to learn to care for others, we must first learn to care for those we find ourselves joined to by *accident* of birth. Such commitments are essential to a social order grounded in the image of a social compact or convenant rather than in contract and self-interest. (1983b, p. 108)

She says,

> The social compact is a different notion from that of contract. It is inseparable
> from ideals of civic virtue and retains a hold on working-class, religious, and
> rural culture. A compact is no contingent agreement but a solemn commitment
> to create something "new" out of disparate elements—a family, a community, a
> polity—whose individual members do not remain "as before" once they become
> part of this social mode of existence. Within the social compact, community
> members, ideally, share values that are sustained by moral suasion, not en-
> forced by coercion. (1982, p. 446)

This is a vision that involves both freedom and morality. "Morality" is a
term rarely used by feminists of the Left, except in a negative way. Moral
systems are frequently portrayed as part of the array of tools men have used
to deprive women of their autonomy. There is little discussion of possibilities for creating a new morality to replace the codes that in the past have
been so oppressive to women. Rather, there seems to be an underlying
assumption that if people—especially women—are finally allowed the autonomy that is their right, moral behavior will somehow flow from that.
Women allowed autonomy will bring into the public sphere values of caring
and nurturance. What sanctions will be needed, which moral precepts will
define the rules governing who is "cared for," how, by whom, and why, are
less fully examined.[8] Thus we return to the view that individual autonomy
and social good are not in tension, that genuine autonomy for all entails the
social good.

Clearly, this debate over the relation between autonomy and community is of utmost importance for feminist theory. Further exploration of this
issue—both for what it can tell us about how to view the family and for its
overall implications for feminism—is essential.

It is of no less importance for the Right. Both perspectives are troubled
by the problems of creating an institutional setting (the "family" or some
alternative structure) in which children can be raised and that can foster the
qualities of individualism within the supportive parameters of community.

CONCLUSION

In the struggle between feminists and the Right the family has been a
battleground, but it is not, in fact, the real source of conflict. Feminism is
not antifamily; the Right is not simply pro-family. To recognize that there
has been a misnaming of the issue is, we hope, to introduce a note of calm
into the conflict, a conflict that has frequently been tinged with hysteria.
There *are* serious, deep differences between feminism and the Right. These
cannot be minimized. However, there are differences not primarily over
what children need or whether the family ought to be abolished, but over the
place of men and women in society. Looking past the turmoil, one finds this

common ground: an acceptance of the family as an arrangement that is, at least potentially, productive for the human spirit as well as the body, and a recognition that all children need stable affectionate care.

Where feminists and conservatives part ways, often bitterly, is over the traditional sexual division of labor. In a fundamental sense this question of gender roles is a question about autonomy.

"Autonomy" is a term often heard in liberal democracies, and in this country both feminism and the Right claim to value it highly. But it is a protean word. One finds widely varying notions about what it means, who has a right to it, in what ways, and what it has to do with public policy. Conservatives, many of whom are in reality laissez-faire liberals, tend to think in terms of "being left alone." Feminists, on the other hand, are far more likely to hold government responsible for giving people *tools* for autonomy; public policy is to increase life-options.

The central question today, of course, is autonomy for women. Recognizing that neither feminism nor the Right represents monolithic entities, we generalize in the following way: The New Right sees a natural sexual order outside the realm of autonomy; in it, biology determines how we live. What it mandates for women is not only the physical act of giving birth but a female essence, a female place in society, flowing almost entirely from that physical act (or the capacity for it) and from the rearing that follows childbirth. The neoconservative Right avoids the implication that biology is destiny. Women and men are said to choose their destiny, to affect through individual effort and talent the course of their own life careers. Yet both implicitly and explicitly, neoconservatives express their expectations that men and women will choose differently.

Feminists, with the exception of those such as Firestone, gracefully, often joyfully, accept the gift of biology, but respond to it so as to preserve women's autonomy as much as possible. The capacity to bear children is seen as a gift to be used when motherhood is genuinely desired; it should not mean an unwanted child. Most feminists are reluctant to draw neobiological conclusions from biological facts. That is to say, having the capacity for childbirth says little about who one is or how one is to find meaning in life or what sort of freedom one has or should have. Although feminists such as Elshtain are exceptions, most feminists assiduously avoid the advocacy of a social or moral division of labor lest it appear to evoke the traditional strictures of biological destiny.

With the exception of radical thinkers like Millet and Firestone, most feminists believe that a large measure of autonomy is possible for women, whether they are mothers or not, within the confines of the nuclear (not necessarily heterosexual or dual-parenting) family. The traditional family has to be rethought and refashioned. Feminist visions of the family are far more varied than the vision of the family that is idealized by the Right (in which the woman meets her destiny by channeling all energy into motherhood). Feminism calls on people to give up such cherished but mistaken notions as: all women have a vocation in motherhood; a child needs constant care from her or his biological mother; lesbians are morally inferior mothers; men aren't suited to be the nurturers of small children. A sharing of child care and household tasks, and day care arrangements in which there is stable, affectionate attention, are two ways in which family life can be reshaped so as to make it possible to be both a woman and a person who is economically, politically, psychologically, and spiritually autonomous.

While insisting on autonomy as perhaps the most essential of feminist goals, most feminists recognize other important goals, including that of community. The family, in fact, represents one attempt to achieve both of these. But there is widespread criticism both external to and within feminism that denies the easy possibility of reconciling autonomy and community within a restructured family institution. Autonomy and community are in constant tension, this criticism claims, even as they might nourish each other in certain ways.

The Right also endorses the twin goals of individuality and community, though their definitions and arguments are quite different from those of feminists. Individualism, for the Right, is encouraged by the family even as it must be, in another sense, sacrificed to the family. The Right maintains that the family is uniquely qualified to instill norms of independence and freedom in its young. Yet the exercise of this individualism is to happen outside, not within, the family. Within the family, community supersedes individuality. The choices men and women make inside the family are to be curtailed by the parameters of biology and tradition. Outside the family, however, individualism may flourish—but an individualism (feminist critics charge) that embraces only men. The Right, then, seeks to reconcile the goals of community and autonomy by assigning community to the family and individuality to society; such an equation, its critics maintain, aggravates rather than reconciles the tension between individualist and community values.

Much more work needs to be done by feminists as well as conservatives about what individualism and community mean, about the complicated ways they relate to each other, and about how people try to realize them in daily life. In the meantime, we must recognize the debate over the family for what it is: true discordance about the roles and values of men and women— rather than a contest over the needs and interests of children.

ACKNOWLEDGMENTS

The authors thank Gretchen Ritter for her bibliographic help and ever insistent questioning, as well as Diana Meyers and Helene Silverberg for their comments on an earlier draft. Mary Katzenstein is grateful to the Jonathan Meigs Fund and to the Ford Foundation funding of the Stanford project which provided research support.

NOTES

1. For a particularly helpful discussion of the New Right and neoconservatism, see Zilah Eisenstein (1982, Spring), "The Sexual Politics of the New Right: Understanding the 'Crisis of Liberalism' for the 1980s," *Signs*, 7(3). Her focus on the antifeminism of the Right adds an absolutely crucial dimension to existing analyses. Her description of neoconservatism as bent on conservatizing as opposed to dismantling the welfare state (as the New Right intends) does however, raise the question of how neoconservatism can be distinguished from Carter liberalism, which also wanted to restrict the "excesses" of the welfare state.

2. Robert Coles' review of the Bergers' book questions whether the causal order might be the other way around: *New York Times Book Review*, May 15, 1983, p. 7.

3. The quotations in this paragraph are from a telephone interview Mary Katzenstein had with Mrs. Schlafly, Nov. 8, 1983.

4. The Bergers do not state this explicitly but the idea comes through clearly when they state that women, not men, should give priority to the family.

5. She discusses the liberating experience of living during a Vermont vacation without rules and without her husband, who was then in Europe, an experience liberating both for herself and her sons. But Rich does not generalize from this to children's needs in ordinary times.

6. This is similar but not identical to the 19th-century argument that women's entrance into the *public sphere* would enhance domestic and public life.

7. The laissez-faire view of the pro-life activists was described by the author to Mary Katzenstein in a separate conversation and does not appear in the book.

8. See Jessie Bernard's discussion of the difference that women's participation in the public sphere could make (1981, pp. 546–557).

REFERENCES

Barber, B. R. (1983, July 11). Beyond the feminist mystique. *The New Republic*, 26–32.

Berger, B., & Berger, P. L. (1983). *The war over the family: Capturing the middle ground.* New York: Anchor Press/Doubleday.

Bernard, J. (1981). *The female world.* New York: The Free Press.

Chodorow, N. (1978). *The reproduction of mothering: Psychoanalysis and the sociology of gender.* Berkeley: University of California Press.

Chodorow, N., & Contratto, S. (1982). The fantasy of the perfect mother. In B. Thorne & M. Yalom (Eds.), *Rethinking the family: Some feminist questions.* New York: Longman.

Christensen, H. T. (1977). Relationship between differentiation and equality in the sex role structure. In L. Lenevo-Otevo (Ed.), *Beyond the nuclear family model.* Beverly Hills: Sage.

Coles, R. (1983, May 15). Honoring fathers and mothers. *New York Times Book Review*, 7.

Eisenstein, Z. (1982). The sexual politics of the New Right: Understanding the "crisis of liberalism" for the 1980s. *Signs*, 7(3), 567–588.

Elshtain, J. B. (1981). *Public man, private woman: Women in social and political thought.* Princeton: Princeton University Press.

Elshtain, J. B. (1982). Feminism, family, and community. *Dissent*, 29(4), 442–449.

Elshtain, J. B. (1983a). Feminism, community, freedom. *Dissent*, 30(2), 247–255.

Elshtain, J. B. (1983b). Feminism, family, and community. *Dissent*, 30(1), 103–109.

Falwell, J. (1980). *Listen America.* New York: Doubleday.

Firestone, S. (1970). *The dialectic of sex: The case for feminist revolution.* New York: Bantam Books.

Freeman, J. (1975). *Politics of women's liberation*. New York: Longman.

Friedan, B. (1981). *The second stage*. New York: Summit Books.

Gilder, G. (1981). *Wealth and poverty*. New York: Basic Books.

Gordon, L. (1982). Why nineteenth-century feminists did not support "birth control" and twentieth-century feminists do: Feminism, reproduction, and the famly. In B. Thorne & M. Yalom (Eds.), *Rethinking the family: Some feminist questions*. New York: Longman.

Katzenstein, M. (1983, November 8). Telephone interview with Mrs. Schlafly from the Schlaflys' home in Illinois.

Kramer, R. (1983). *In defense of the family: Raising children in America today*. New York: Basic Books.

Luker, K. (1983). *Abortion and the politics of motherhood*. Berkeley: University of California Press.

Mill, J. S. (1869/1970). On liberty. In A. S. Rossi (Ed.), *Essays on sex equality*. Chicago: University of Chicago Press.

Mill, J. S. (1869/1970). The subjection of women. In A. S. Rossi (Ed.), *Essays on sex equality*. Chicago: University of Chicago Press.

Millet, K. (1970). *Sexual politics*. New York: Avon Books. (*Sexual Politics* was revised a year after its original publication.)

Rich, A. (1976). *Of woman born: Motherhood as experience and institution*. New York: W. W. Norton.

Rossi, A. (1977). A biosocial perspective on parenting. *Daedalus*, *106*(2), 1–27.

Schlafly, P. (1978). *The power of the positive woman*. New York: Jove Publications.

Schlafly, P. (1981). *The power of the Christian woman*. Cincinnati: Stanford Publications.

Stacey, J. (1986). Are feminists afraid to leave home? The challenge of conservative pro-family feminism. In J. Mitchell and A. Oakley (Eds.), *What is Feminism?* New York: Pantheon.

Thorne, B. (1987). Re-visioning women and social change: Where are the children? *Gender and Society*, *19*(1), 85–109.

Thorne, B., & Yalom, M. (Eds.). (1982). *Rethinking the family: Some feminist questions*. New York: Longman.

3

Public Opinion on Change in Women's Rights and Roles

JEANNE J. FLEMING

INTRODUCTION

Attitudes about women's rights and roles have changed dramatically over the past 20 years. The women's liberation movement, reborn in the mid-1960s after a 40-year hiatus, successfully fought for reforms such as affirmative action and the legalization of abortion. The feminist movement seemed to articulate the needs of growing numbers of women in an era of changing patterns of employment, marriage, and fertility.

In recent years, however, a variety of groups have challenged the "new feminists'" claim to represent the interests of American women. One interpretation of the growth of the so-called pro-family movement is that views about women's issues are now becoming more conservative, with reappraisals of sex roles and of the relationship between the sexes going the way of so much of the radicalism of the '60s.

This chapter begins with a description of changes over time in the American public's support for the philosophy and goals of the women's liberation movement. Is public sentiment in fact increasingly leaning away from feminism? The chapter then highlights some of the variables associated with attitudes toward feminism, with special attention to gender.

Unraveling what constitutes feminism is a difficult task. If it can be said with certainty that feminism fundamentally concerns itself with analyzing women's place in society and developing an agenda for change that aims to expand women's autonomy and power, it must also be added that beyond this basic concern the ideologies self-identified as feminist differ extraordinarily in scope, content, and goals (see Chapter 2). Here, pro- and antifeminist positions are defined according to the explicit ideologies and stated goals of social movement organizations seeking either to further change in women's rights and roles or to reverse the direction of change.

Jeanne J. Fleming, Ph.D. Public Response Associates, San Francisco, California.

PUBLIC SUPPORT FOR THE GOALS
OF THE WOMEN'S LIBERATION MOVEMENT

Attitudes toward women held by both women and men have changed considerably, especially in the past 2 decades, and that change has consistently been in the direction of increased support for expanding women's rights and minimizing sex role differentiation. The trend holds in a variety of arenas, including women's political, domestic, and labor-market roles; the women's rights movement; and abortion rights. Today, as in the past, however, a substantial proportion of both women and men surveyed hold traditional views of women's rights and roles.

One question pollsters have asked over a long period to determine attitudes toward women has been some variant of the query "Would you vote for a qualified woman for president of the United States?" Erskine (1971) compiled the Gallup polls asking this question, and found a substantial change in attitudes from the mid 1930s to the late 1960s. In 1937, 27% of male respondents and 40% of female respondents said they would vote for a qualified woman for president. In 1955, the figures were 47% and 57% respectively, while in 1969, the last year on which Erskine reports, 58% of men and 43% of women agreed that they would vote for a qualified woman for president.

Ferree (1974) looked at the polls on the same question and found 69% of respondents of both sexes agreeing with the statement in 1978. Lipset and Schneider (in press) reported that 78% of all respondents in a 1975 National Opinion Research Center (NORC) survey said they would vote for a qualified woman for president. More recent surveys show similar results. Gallup, for example, reported 78% of respondents ready to vote for a woman for president in 1984 (Gallup, 1984), and a 1986 General Social Surveys poll found 84% of respondents willing to vote for a woman (NORC, 1986). Overall, then, the trend has been an increased receptivity toward a woman holding the highest elective office in the United States, so that today by far the majority of the population says it would be willing to vote for a woman for president.

Lipset and Schneider (in press) reviewed polling data on attitudes toward women working outside of the home, women's roles in politics, affirmative action, the "basic nature" of women and men, and the extent of discrimination against women. They concluded that attitudes in these areas have become steadily more egalitarian over the past decade. For example, in 1978, 56% of respondents in a Center for Political Studies (CPS) survey agreed that "By nature, women are happiest when they are making a home and caring for children," while 4 years later in 1976, only 40% of respondents agreed with the statement. Similarly, 44 % of those responding to the 1972 CPS survey concurred with the statement that "Our society, not nature, teaches women to prefer homemaking to work outside the home," but in 1976 three fifths (60%) shared this opinion (Lipset & Schneider, in press).

With regard to women's involvement in politics, between 1970 and 1975 the percentage of respondents disagreeing with the Harris poll statement, "The country would be better off if women had more to say about politics," decreased dramatically. In 1970, 46% of women and 51% of men thought that the country would not be better off if women were more involved with politics, while only 5 years later 29% of women and 42% of men held that same view (Lipset & Schneider, in press). In 1986, only 23% of respondents to a General Social Surveys poll agreed with the statement "Women should take care of running their homes and leave running the country up to men" (NORC, 1986).

Attitudes toward the women's movement and toward movement strategy similarly are becoming more rather than less favorable. Harris asked the question, "Do you favor or oppose most of the efforts to strengthen and change women's status in society today?" In 1970, 41% of respondents said they were not in favor of such efforts, while in 1975 28% of respondents continued to look with disfavor on efforts to change women's status in society. The percentage of respondents supporting such efforts increased from 59% to 65% (Harris, 1981).

A Newspaper Readership Project poll (1979) in the same year showed a similar pattern of support for the women's movement. Twenty-three percent of female respondents said they opposed organized efforts to strengthen women's rights, while 41% favored them. In 1981, a Harris poll found 67% of respondents of both sexes favoring attempts to strengthen and change women's status, and 29% opposed (Harris, 1981).

Over the 1970 to 1979 period, public assessment of feminist organizations also grew more approving. In 1970, 34% of those surveyed responded "most" or "some" to the query "How many organizations trying to change women's rights in society are helping the cause of women," while in 1975 47% said "most" or "some," and in 1979 more than half of those polled (53%) gave these responses (Harris, 1979a).

Thornton and Freeman (1980) reported ". . . a dramatic increase in the number of women who have liberal attitudes about appropriate roles for men and women in the home and at work" over the period between 1962 and 1977. When asked to respond to statements about whether certain jobs were best done by one sex or the other, 75% of women in 1977 did not agree that jobs should be sex differentiated, compared to slightly over 50% who held that view in 1962.

Duncan and Duncan (1978) looked at survey data from 1953 to 1959 and 1971 that tapped attitudes with regard to many different dimensions of sex roles at work and in the home (e.g., the work motives of women, political activism, division of labor in the family, socialization of girls and boys). While carefully pointing out that they had little behavioral evidence for a revolution in sex roles, Duncan and Duncan concluded that the liberalization of attitudes about sex roles that began in the 1960s did continue through the middle 1970s. Similarly, Fultz (1980), in analyzing Harris data collected between 1970 and 1975, found that over that period "a trend toward less traditional attitudes occurred among both women and men" (p. 4).

The principal goal of a number of women's liberation organizations has been the passage of the Equal Rights Amendment (ERA). The level of opposition to the ERA among the population as a whole was fairly constant throughout the 1970s. Harris (1978b) reported that in 1975, 36% of those surveyed said they opposed the amendment, while the proportion opposing it was 23% in 1976, 35% in 1977, and 38% in 1978. A 1981 Harris survey reported that 46% of those polled opposed ratification of the ERA in 1980, and 44% opposed it in August of 1981 (Harris, 1981).

Gallup polls of individuals who said they had "heard or read about the Equal Rights amendment" found 24% opposing it in 1976 and 31% in 1978, 1980, and 1984. This represents a small increase. The percentage of respondents who said they favored passage of the amendment also increased slightly over that period, however, from 57% in 1976 to 63% in 1984 (Gallup, 1981a, 1984). Thus on this issue, as on that of women in politics, opinion at variance with the feminist view has either not been growing or has been offset by an increase in profeminist sentiment.

Abortion has been a central concern of both feminist social movement organizations and organizations with explicitly antifeminist goals. For the contemporary women's movement in the United States, maintaining the lawful status of abortion is a key issue (although, as Willis (1981) pointed out, there is a small but vocal group of self-identified feminist antiabortionists). And for the contemporary far Right in American politics, an antiabortionist stance has served as a powerful symbol of moral rectitude. Evangelicals, for example, whose roles in the 1980 election and in shaping the social policies of the last days of the Reagan administration have generated much discussion, are more united in their opposition to abortion than they are on any other issue except school prayer (Fleming & Marks, 1980). Similarly, Phyllis Schlafly's powerful "Stop ERA" organization focuses on abortion as a crucial issue, second only to the ERA itself and the conscription of women.

Despite the growing organized opposition to legalized abortion, and despite the challenges to legalized abortion in the courts and in Congress, public opinion on this issue has in fact become increasingly favorable over the past 2 decades.[1] Blake traced changes in public opinion on abortion over the 1960 to 1970 period, and found that while support for "discretionary" abortion (i.e., abortion sought because a woman does not want to have a child) was still relatively small, it nevertheless was growing rapidly (Blake, 1971).

Tedrow and Mahoney (1979) analyzed trends in attitudes toward abortion over the 1972 to 1976 period, using data from the National Opinion Research Center's General Social Surveys conducted in each of those 5 years. The General Social Survey queried each year:

> Please tell me whether or not you think it should be possible for a pregnant woman to obtain a legal abortion 1. if there is a strong chance of serious defect in the baby, 2. if she is married and does not want any more children, 3. if the woman's own health is seriously endangered by the pregnancy, 4. if the family has a very low income and cannot afford any more children, 5. if she became pregnant as a result of rape, and 6. if she is not married and does not want to marry the man?

Tedrow and Mahoney (1979) found growth in support for each of the six reasons for an abortion offered in the survey. They reported that "between 1972 and 1976 there was an increase in approval of three percentage points for each of the traditionally "hard" reasons (health, rape and defect) and an increase of 3, 6, and 6 percentage points respectively for the "soft" reasons (poor, single, and no more children wanted)" (p. 183).

Other polls also indicate increased support for legalized abortion. According to a series of Harris polls, the percentage of Americans favoring the 1973 Supreme Court ruling that made abortion legal during the first trimester of pregnancy has grown. While in April 1975, 54% of respondents in a Harris survey favored the ruling, 60% favored it in 1979 (Harris, 1979b). On the other hand, Gallup reported that 47% of respondents favored the ruling in 1974, compared to 45%—a small drop—in 1981. Five years later, Gallup reported again that 45% of respondents favored the ruling (Gallup, 1986). An August, 1980 CBS News/*New York Times* poll found 62% of respondents agreeing with the statement, "If a woman wants to have an abortion, and her doctor agrees to it, [she should] be allowed to have an abortion." Nineteen percent of those polled said "should not," and 15% volunteered the response that it depended on the specific situation. Attitudes toward abortion, like attitudes toward the ERA and toward change in women's rights and roles generally, have become increasingly favorable or—depending on the way the question was asked—have remained stable.

It appears that attitudes toward women's rights and roles have changed steadily over the past 10 years, with opinion on the whole becoming increasingly liberal. A substantial proportion of the population today rejects change in women's rights and roles, as it has in the past, but the growing activism and increased successes of organized antifeminists do not appear to be mirroring a groundswell of opinion among the American people. Overall, the trend is one of steadily (if slowly) increasing support for passage of the ERA and for preserving legal abortion, issues that are considered central by both feminist activists and pro-family groups.

In addition, people are more and more inclined to favor an active political role for women, and to support the efforts of women's liberation organizations. They are more likely to express egalitarian views with regard to women's domestic and work roles as well. While the antifeminist movement is increasingly visible and successful, and a fair proportion of the population today as in the past holds opinions in line with that movement's goals, the percentage sharing the antifeminists' sentiments does not appear to be growing. The victories of the antifeminist movement do not stem, it appears, from a growing constituent base.

THE SOCIAL BASES OF SUPPORT FOR FEMINISM

What groups are most likely to have attitudes favorable toward change in women's rights and roles? Opinion on political and social issues traditionally has been affected by such characteristics as age, income, and education, as well as by general conservatism or liberalism (political philosophy). In this section, these factors are related to women's opinions (among both the general public and movement activists) concerning change in sex roles and women's legal/political rights.

A number of other potentially important variables are also considered. Since the movement of women into the labor market is often cited to explain the emergence of the new feminism, employment status—or more broadly, labor-market participation—may well influence views on women's issues. Similarly, level of domestic commitment (e.g., marital status and number of children) may also be important.

Section IV addresses the question of how the bases of support for feminist goals may vary depending on the particular issue at stake. Opinion on abortion, for example, appears to be associated with different factors than does opinion on the ERA.

Feminism as a social movement explicitly casts its efforts in terms of promoting women's interests. Consequently, men are likely to respond quite differently from women on issues such as the ERA and division of labor between the sexes, and male support or opposition to feminist causes may be associated with different factors. Gender differences are discussed in a later section.

Age and Education

Studies polling attitudes toward women among women find that a traditional view of women's rights and roles is correlated with a number of social characteristics. Antifeminist attitudes appear to be, first, negatively related to respondents' education, especially when college-educated and non-college-educated groups are contrasted. Second, antifeminism is positively associated with age, although the relationship is less powerful than with education. These relationships hold when looking at opinions on a variety of issues relevant to feminism (e.g., abortion, division of labor between women and men, women's political participation), as well as different populations (e.g., students, national samples).[2] However, the association between antifeminism and age varies depending on the particular topic considered. Blake (1971), for example, found young women more opposed to abortion than older women, a finding that Bardes (1972) replicates.

Labor Market and Domestic Sphere

One plausible explanation for differences in women's opinion on changes in women's rights and roles emphasizes women's differential participation in the labor market and in the domestic sphere, stressing the interrelatedness of the two and their linkage to class, family structure, and the structure of sex roles. Briefly, women who have a high level of participation in the labor market and a low level of activity in the domestic sphere are thought to tend to support feminism and its goal of legal identity and social parity of women and men. In contrast, women who have a high investment in the institution of marriage and a lower investment and level of activity in paid labor are thought to tend to oppose feminism. They seek instead to retain laws and reinforce customs and norms that recognize and protect the special domestic roles that women play.

Since women's experiences are divided along the critical dimension of location and conditions of work, women do not constitute a unified class with unified interests. Women whose primary domain is the family are lodged within a patriarchal system, so that they strive to legislate the patriarch's beneficence. Job security issues for domestic work such as alimony and child support and wage guarantees (i.e., husbands' legal responsibility for family financial support) are key concerns. Housewives, women who are not employed in the market at all, are the clearest subcategory of women with a high involvement in family work. Women working at low-paying jobs may be in an analogous position, however. Since they, like housewives, are likely to be significantly dependent on the shared resources of marriage, it is imperative that the security of marriage (whether through a husband's or a divorced spouse's legal responsibility to support) be maintained. Opponents of feminism stress this concern.

In sharp contrast to the concerns of women primarily engaged in family work, the principal objective for women with a minimal domestic investment and high participation in paid labor is achieving parity with male workers in the labor force. This group is likely to look favorably on the feminist movement and to hold views in line with the movement's goals. While housewives' interests (again, to single out a particularly vulnerable group of women) tend to lie in stressing their differences from males and their dependent position, the interests of women who are active in the labor market lie in stressing their identity with males, thereby enhancing their chances for success in the market. The struggle between profeminist and antifeminist women is thus political, a conflict over definition by the state of the rights, privileges, and obligations of female citizens. A major concern is whether the state will treat women as legally and socially identical to men, or as different from and dependent on men (see Chapter 7).

In short, an important determinant of women's attitudes toward feminism may well be whether they perceive that over the life span their work— and therefore their life chances—is located primarily in the sphere of paid labor or primarily in the institution of the family.

This line of reasoning suggests that employment status, marital status, and fecundity will be associated with opinion on women's issues. Employment status is of particular interest since, as Davis notes in this volume (Chapter 4), by 1997 the employment rate for women will be equal to that for men. Huber, Rexroat, and Spitze (1978), however, failed to find a relationship between employment status and women's attitudes toward feminism. The Huber *et al.* study explicitly asked whether people respond to the ERA "more on the basis of social characteristics which enable them to benefit from women's labor market opportunities (e.g., education, employment status) or more on the basis of other sex role attitudes which have a random relation to background variables" (p. 551). They found that employment status, as well as education, age, income, and marital status had surprisingly little effect on attitudes toward the ERA, while the perceived consequences of the amendment had a powerful effect on attitudes toward it. Both men and women who believed the ERA would take jobs away from men tended to oppose it. Huber *et al.* argued that this finding demonstrates the centrality of employment concerns, despite the fact that working women were not more apt to support passage of the ERA.

Other studies do report a direct relationship between employment and attitudes toward change in women's rights and roles, however. The Newspaper Readership Project poll (1979), for example, found a link between employment status and women's views on feminism, as did Stewart's 1980 study of women's opinion with respect to equal employment opportunity, and the work of Thornton, Alwin, & Conburn (1983).

Ferree (1980) also found a direct relationship between employment status and feminism among working-class women. Employed women in Ferree's small (N=135) sample, whether working full- or part-time, were more likely to support change in women's rights and roles than were housewives. Ferree attributed this to the role that the social networks of each group play in either facilitating feminism or encouraging resistance to it.

Scott (1982, 1985) reported a relationship between labor-force participation and opinion on the ERA, interpreting it as evidence that the clash over the legislation is rooted in a struggle for prestige and status. The strongest predictors of opposition to the ERA were (1) what Scott termed "value threat," (2) the perceived importance of having children, (3) the perceived conflict between motherhood and work roles, and (4) age. When these factors are considered, Scott found that the effect of employment status evaporated.

Fleming (1982) found that employment status and opinion on women's issues were related. Women working full-time were consistently the most feminist in their views, women not working at all outside of the home were least likely to share the feminist perspective, and those employed part-time fell in between. This relationship held across income and education groups.

On the other hand, work commitment ("Do you plan to make your job a life-time career, or is it just something temporary?") was not related to opinion on women's issues, Fleming (1982) found. For example, 70% of women who responded "temporary" to this query also said they favored the women's movement, compared to 72% of women who responded "lifetime career." Moreover, professional versus nonprofessional employment also did not appear to be related significantly to attitudes on feminism. For example, 76% of women employed in professional occupations favored the women's movement, compared to 70% of those otherwise employed.

The association between "domestic sphere" factors such as marital status and number of children and opinion regarding women's rights and roles is rather weak. Huber *et al.* (1978) found that marital status (except for the divorced/separated category) did not appear to have an appreciable effect on attitudes toward women's issues by women. Huber *et al.* attributed this to the simple fact that virtually all women are, have been, or will be married.

Welch (1975) reported a moderate effect of marital status on female opinion, however. And Fleming (1982) found that divorced women were most likely to hold feminist views, followed by single women, with married women bringing up the rear. For example, 73% of single and divorced women said that change in women's roles should continue, while only 57% of currently married women shared that opinion. At the highest education level (4 years of college or more), however, marital status was a less salient factor than at other education levels.

Fleming (1982) also found that, except for opinion on the ERA, women with a larger number of children showed less sympathy for the feminist point of view. The average gap on four measures of opinion concerning women's rights and roles between women with one child and women with six children was approximately 15 points. So, for example, 70% of women with only one child said they favored feminist organizations' efforts, compared to 53% of women with six children. Women with no children were only slightly more likely than women with one child to support feminist goals. As with marital status, controlling for education slightly tempered the effect of number of children. Thornton *et al.* (1983) found only a small and inconsistent association between number of children and sex-role attitudes, however, and Mason and Bumpass (1975) found none.

In sum, factors related to labor market and domestic sphere involvement appear to play a role in shaping women's opinions on change in women's rights and roles. But the associations between these variables and feminism are relatively small, and some studies do not find any association at all.

Political Philosophy and Religion

Another variable associated with opinion on women's issues is general political philosophy. Welch (1975) reported, for example, that women with conservative political ideologies were more likely to oppose change in women's status than were women with liberal ideologies, a relationship Lipset and Schneider (in press) stressed. Bowker (1981) argued that a general conservatism underlies both sexism and racism.

Fleming (1982) found that increasing liberalism was associated with increasing feminism. For example, 87% of the women who identified themselves as "very liberal" said they supported feminist organizations' efforts, compared to 67% of "middle-of-the-road" women and 52% of self-identified "very conservative" women. Age and education interacted with political views to affect attitudes toward feminism, however. Young self-identified conservatives and old self-identified liberals held about the same views, as did conservatives with a college degree or more, and liberals with less than a high school diploma.

One measure of social conservatism—rights for homosexuals—is very strongly associated with opinion on women's rights and roles. Fleming (1982) found, for example, that 73% of women opposed to discrimination against homosexuals favored feminist social movement efforts, but only 18% of those who thought such discrimination should be legitimate favored the women's movement.

Religion and religiosity are also related to negative attitudes toward changes in women's rights and roles, as Henley and Pincus (1978), Huber et al. (1978), Thornton and Freeman (1980), Thornton et al. (1983), and Welch (1975) document. Fundamentalist Protestants (Thornton et al., 1983) are most apt to hold traditional sex-role attitudes, and Fleming and Marks (1980), Granberg (1978; Granberg & Denney, 1982), and Tedrow and Mahoney (1979), among others, have found a link between religion or religiosity and a negative opinion on legalization of abortion.

Biology versus Socialization

One tenet of feminist ideology is that most of the differences in womens' and mens' roles are socially rather than biologically determined. Are women opposed to change in women's rights and roles more likely to attribute those social roles to physical, innate differences than are feminists? Fleming (1982) reported that women who hold a biological explanation for sex roles are somewhat less likely than those who agree with the socialization view to support changes in women's rights and roles. For example, of those who said physical differences primarily account for sex-role differences, 60% favored the women's movement, while 67% of those who cited socialization favored the movement. The percentages of the ERA and legalized abortion were, respectively, 45% versus 54%, and 41% versus 53%. These differences are surprisingly small, considering the fundamental difference in ideology they presumably represent.[3]

Characteristics of Activists

A variety of factors are associated with women's views on change in women's rights and roles: age, education, income, marital status, employment status, religion, political philosophy, and views on other political and social issues. While the strength of the associations between these variables and views on women's issues are not particularly large, the associations are stronger for activists than for the general public. Let us now analyze the data for activists.

A number of researchers have investigated the sources of support for antifeminist activism, especially the social characteristics of participants in anti-ERA activity. Tedin, Brady, Buxton, Gorman, & Thompson (1977) contrasted female pro- and anti-ERA activists in the 1975 Texas debate over ratification of the amendment. They looked at social background, political ideology, liberal/conservative bent, sense of political efficacy, and religion.

Tedin et al. found that supporters of the ERA fit the general profile for political activists. According to Milbrath (1965), activists tend to be middle-aged, white, married, professionally employed, highly educated, and well paid. Tedin et al. reported that amendment supporters tended to be younger, more likely to have an urban residence, more secular, and more likely to enjoy higher social status than individuals opposed to the amendment. Anti-ERA activists, on the other hand, were more likely to be religious and to be active on only the single issue of the ERA. The general political philosophy of women supporting the amendment tended to be liberal, while that of its opponents tended to be conservative.

In a later analysis, Brady and Tedin (1976) compared the characteristics of women active in opposing the ERA amendment to those of right-wing activists generally. Distinguishing among three rightist orientations—religious (with middle- and upper-class, relatively well-to-do members); secular (with essentially the same membership base as the religious Right, but with goals formulated in nonreligious terms); and segregationist (lower- and working-class membership)—they concluded that anti-ERA women fit the pattern of the religious Right.

The anti-ERA activists shared the political views of right-wing activists generally (e.g., viewing Communism as an imminent threat, opposing "big government," and seeing rapid moral decline in the United States) and were similar in social characteristics to members of the religious and secular Right. Importantly, 70% of the female anti-ERA activists in the sample were housewives with no employment in the market, and 98% were church members. Two thirds of all the anti-ERA women were members of a fundamentalist religious organization.

Arrington and Kyle (1978) also tried to determine whether ERA activists were similar to other political activists. Anti-ERA women deviated from the political activist profile more than pro-ERA women and men or anti-ERA men. The anti-ERA women were likely to be housewives, to be somewhat less educated than their opponents (though more educated than average), were more likely to belong to a fundamentalist Protestant religion, and more likely to be active on the single issue of the ERA.[4]

Studies of antiabortion activists point to similar factors. Using the 1975 NORC survey, Granberg (1978) found that background characteristics (e.g., age and education), political conservatism, conservatism with regard to other women's issues, religious beliefs, and traditional morality were each somewhat related to opposition to abortion. The last factor, traditional morality, was the most powerful. Tedrow and Mahoney (1979) found some support for the relationship between educational level, occupational prestige, religion or religiosity, and antiabortion sentiment. Ebaugh and Haney's 1978 study found that for members of fundamentalist churches, frequency of church attendance was positively related to disapproval of legalized abortion, but that this association did not hold for members of nonfundamentalist denominations.

Granberg and Denney (1982) reported that the memberships of the National Abortion Rights Action League (NARAL) and the National Right to Life Committee (NRLC) were different in a number of respects. NRLC members were much more likely to be conservative (56% vs. 6%), Republican (41% vs. 14%), Catholic (70% vs. 4%), attend church once a week or more (86% vs. 9%), come from a small town or medium-sized city (53% vs. 31%), have more children (an average of 3.4 versus an average of 1.3), to be housewives (81% vs. 28%), and married (87% vs. 55%). NRLC members were also more likely to be male. Sixty-three percent of the NRLC membership was female, compared to 78% of NARAL.

Summary

Two types of studies, those polling the public's attitudes on women's issues and those exploring the characteristics of activists on either side of the ERA and abortion, have both found a relationship between age, education, political ideology, and religion and views with regard to women's rights and roles.

Thus, on the whole, increasing age is associated with antifeminism, although Blake (1971) found this was not so with regard to opinion on legalized abortion, and Arrington and Kyle (1978) reported that the median age of anti-ERA women was in fact about 3 years lower than that of pro-ERA women (33 vs. 36). Education is negatively related to conservatism on women's issues. Individuals with less education tend to be more antifeminist.

Political ideology is a factor in views about change in women's rights and roles, as both attitude studies and studies of movement participants have shown. Liberals are more likely to be profeminist, conservatives to be antifeminist. Religion weighs heavily in all of the studies. Fundamentalist Protestants are likely to make up the membership base of antifeminist organizations, though Catholics are especially active in antiabortion groups. Most of the studies reported correlations of these factors with views of women's rights and roles, although the relationships are rather weak.

The studies of activists especially support the hypothesis that employment status plays a role in women's attitudes toward feminism. While Huber et al. (1978) found virtually no relationship between labor force participation and women's views on women's issues, Ferree (1980), Fleming (1982), and Thornton et al. (1983), among others, reported a moderate association. Tedin et al. (1977) and Arrington and Kyle (1978) found employment status to be a critical factor in participation in pro- and anti-ERA organizations, and Granberg and Denney (1982) noted its importance in antiabortion membership. Thus Arrington and Kyle reported that 62% of the women working against the amendment desribed themselves as housekeepers or homemakers, while only 13% of women for the ERA had that occupation. Tedin et al. (1977) reported that 72% of the anti-ERA women in their sample were housewives, while only 24% of the pro-ERA women were housewives.

DIMENSIONS OF FEMINISM

It is difficult to assess the relative weight of the various predictors of opinion on women's issues because feminist ideology and goals have numerous dimensions (see Chapter 2). The association between opinion with respect to women's issues and such factors as education and political philosophy depends on the dimension considered.

The ERA and legalization of abortion in particular appear to represent different facets of feminism with potentially different constituencies. For example, while one issue focuses on equality, the other focuses on autonomy; while one is concerned with public roles, the other is concerned with private behavior. Other potentially meaningful dimensions along which feminist issues vary include action versus heightened consciousness, and individual rights versus community welfare.

The dimension of economic versus "cultural" import is also potentially meaningful. Is the ERA related primarily to economic interests, for example, and legalization of abortion to religious beliefs, or can support for each position be accounted for equally well by both economic and cultural factors?

Fleming (1982) examined the degree of consistency in respondents' replies to questions about four women's issues: efforts to change women's status in society, role change per se, the ERA, and legalized abortion. She argued that if respondents reacted very differently to each issue, it may indicate that the public does not view the four as part of one ideological package, and furthermore that opinion on each may well have a unique social base.

While the four measures of feminism were to some degree intercorrelated, responses to each were by no means wholly overlapping. Opinion on the women's movement was correlated .59 with attitudes vis-à-vis role change and .47 with the ERA, and views of role change correlated .40 with opinion on the ERA. The correlation between each of these three measures and attitudes toward abortion never exceeded .20, however. The highest correlation was between attitudes toward the women's movement and toward change in women's roles, the lowest between opinion on the ERA and abortion.

Twenty-one percent of the total sample were consistent feminists. This group uniformly gave the most "feminist" response on each of the four measures (they favored the women's movement, said that change in women's roles should continue, supported the ERA, and opposed abortion repeal). Only 4.3% of the sample of females were consistent antifeminists. Seventy-five percent of the female respondents—the overwhelming majority—were inconsistent in their responses.

Moreover, the four measures of opinion on women's rights and roles were not related in the same way to such factors as age. For example, age was much more strongly associated with views on role change than on abortion, and self-identified political philosophy was associated with all of the variables at about the same level except for abortion. Marital status, in contrast, was related at roughly the same level to all four opinions.

These analyses suggest that conceptualizing "women's issues" as a coherent whole can be misleading. People respond differently to different women's issues (and not merely along a conservative/liberal dimension), and factors associated with support for one are not necessarily associated with support for another. Abortion, in particular, is an issue that appears to have a different ideological basis when compared to other feminist issues.

GENDER AS A BASE OF SUPPORT FOR CHANGE IN WOMEN'S RIGHTS AND ROLES

Counter to what might be expected, the polls show that on women's issues such as the ERA and legal abortion, women and men are about equally likely to oppose or support the feminist stand. Harris (1978a), for example, reported that 33% of women and 34% of men said they opposed passage of the ERA. A 1984 Gallup poll (Gallup, 1984) reported about the same proportions of women and men opposing the amendment: 31% of male respondents and 32% of female respondents.

On abortion, another issue associated with feminism, women's and men's views were also similar. Tedrow and Mahoney (1979) found that males were slightly more approving of abortion than females in 1972 on all six abortion items, with the gap between the sexes smaller for the hard reasons of health, rape, and birth defects than for the soft reasons of poverty, being single, or not wanting more children. This pattern shifted slightly over the 5-year period they examined, but at no point did the opinions of women and men differ widely. A 1986 Gallup poll reported that 45% of female respondents and 45% of male respondents favored the Supreme Court ruling that legalized abortion during the first 3 months of pregnancy (Gallup, 1986). A 1980 Gallup poll reported that 26% of females and 24% of males said they thought abortion should be legal under any circumstances, while the percentages, respectively, were 54 versus 51 for legal abortion under some circumstances, and 16 versus 20 wanted abortion to be illegal under all circumstances (Gallup, 1980).

Responding to the 1980 Virginia Slims poll question "There has been much talk recently about changing women's status in society today. On the whole, do you favor or oppose most of the efforts to strengthen and change women's status in society today," 64% of both women and men said they favored such change (Fleming, 1982). Men's and women's views on the issue of continued change in women's roles were also very similar. Asked "Do you think women's roles should continue to change in the years to come, or that change in women's roles has gone as far as it should, or that the change has already gone too far," 13% of men responded "too far," 21% "far enough," and 59% "should continue." The percentages for women were, respectively, 15%, 23%, and 57% (Fleming, 1982).

Numerous other studies of attitudes about women's issues similarly report that gender does not seem to distinguish pro- and antifeminists. Men and women are just about equally likely to oppose or support feminist views. In fact, when there is a difference between the sexes, men as often as not tend to be somewhat more liberal than women (see Huber *et al.* [1978] and Lipset and Schneider [in press], for example).

The association between men's attitudes on women's issues and variables such as age and education in most respects parallels the pattern of relationships between women's attitudes and these factors. So, for example, education, age, and increasing income are all associated with greater support for both women and men for the feminist point of view. Likewise, both women and men who are conservative on other social issues such as rights for homosexuals are more likely to oppose feminism than women and men who are liberal. The relationship between men's attitudes on feminism and each of these variables tends, however, to be weaker than the same relationship for women (Fleming, 1982).

Labor-market participation and domestic roles, however, do not affect men's and women's attitudes in the same way. Fleming (1982) found that the more children a female respondent had, the less likely she was to support issues such as the ERA or legal abortion. There does not appear to be any relationship between men's views and the number of children they have, however.

This difference between the sexes undoubtedly lies in the fact that men do not have a "stake" in the domestic sphere parallel to that of women. Although men also marry and have children, these events do not in the main determine either men's daily activity or the course of their work lives. In short, domestic activity for men does not constitute a form of employment (and a way of life) that competes with the market.

Marital status also appears to be related differently to men's and women's attitudes. Divorced and single women support change in women's rights and roles at roughly the same level, and the two groups are considerably more feminist than are married women. For men, divorced and married individuals share about the same views on women's issues, and they are less favorable than single men. This pattern does not hold for opinion on the continued lawful status of abortion, however. Divorced men are more likely than either single or married men to say they support legal abortion.

For women, then, divorce is a liberalizing experience with regard to women's rights and roles, while for men divorce tends to be a conservatizing force. The finding that divorced men are most likely to favor abortion, when they are least likely to take the feminist point of view on the other measures, again suggests that the configuration of interests on this issue is quite distinct.

The absence of a predominantly female constituency supporting feminist goals and a predominantly male constituency supporting antifeminist goals is counterintuitive. While some differences exist in the level of opposition of men and women to change in women's rights and roles, and some differences in how (or whether) men's and women's attitudes are linked to factors such as marital status, on the whole the picture for each sex is remarkably similar. This can in part be attributed to the inadequacies of survey research; the method does not often get at very deeply held beliefs. Another explanation is that for men, a general tendency to hold liberal views pushes their pro-feminist sentiment up, despite their economic interests and their behavior, while for women, their tendency to hold conservative views pushes pro-feminist feeling down, despite their economic interests.

Huber *et al.* (1978) attributed the similarity between the sexes on women's issues to the relatively greater salience of the issues for women. For example, they argue with regard to the breakdown of opinion on the ERA, that ". . . since the Equal Rights amendment is a more salient issue for women than men, we expect more men to respond favorably to the Equal

Rights amendment after less serious consideration, primarily because this is perceived to be an acceptable response" (p. 552).

It cannot be emphasized too strongly, however, that activists on either side of women's issues do, in fact, break down more nearly by gender. Just as many men as women may agree with feminist views, but much more rarely do men act on those beliefs. Certainly feminist social movement organizations have a primarily female membership, and it is doubtful that this imbalance is entirely, or even mostly, the result of exclusionary policies. Conversely, the organizations with antifeminist goals do not lack for men.

CONCLUSION

Since the early 1970s, active opposition to the feminist movement has emerged both from organizations focused exclusively on women's issues and from groups with more sweeping conservative aims. Contrary to what might be inferred from this phenomenon, however, the available survey data show overwhelmingly that opposition or resistance to change in women's rights and roles has not been growing. In fact, the American public has become increasingly favorable over the past 10 years on issues ranging from such narrowly political questions as the suitability of a woman for president of the United States and whether or not women should take a more active role in politics, to the more philosophically and morally complex issues of legal abortion and sex-role equalization.

Although their numbers do not seem to be growing, many people today as in the past hold traditional ideas about sex roles and do not agree with feminist objectives. The second goal of this paper was to review the social bases of support for and of opposition to feminism. Numerous studies have shown that factors such as increasing age and education, labor-market participation, and liberal political philosophy are associated with support for the feminist point of view.

At least two important caveats are in order regarding these findings, however. First, the associations between variables such as age and employment and *attitudes* toward feminism are rather modest. The variables are considerably more powerfully linked to *activism* on feminist issues, though, as the studies of anti- and profeminist participants in social movements have shown. Second, women's issues are not necessarily perceived by the public as a coherent whole. Feminism appears to contain different dimensions with different bases of support. Recall, for example, the finding that age and political philosophy were much more strongly associated with views on role change than with views on abortion (Fleming, 1982).

One variable that seems likely to be associated with opinion on change in women's rights and roles—gender—is not. Numerous studies report that gender does not distinguish those who hold pro- and antifeminist attitudes (although pro- and antifeminist activism is related to gender). Just as the gap between men and women on a wide range of political and social issues has traditionally been rather small, so too the gap on feminist issues—which seem so polarizing—is small as well.

To sum up: (1) the increasing visibility of the antifeminist movement does not appear to be due to a growing constituent base; (2) attitudes about feminism are related to a number of background characteristics, but not very strongly and not uniformly across issues; and (3) attitudes about feminism are decidedly not associated with gender, although activism is.

NOTES

1. Gallup found that the percentage of respondents agreeing that abortion should be illegal in all circumstances was 21% in 1981 and 18% in 1980, not much different from the 22% recorded in 1975 (Gallup, 1980, 1981b). But an August 1981 ABC News/ *Washington Post* poll reported that only 10% of respondents would make abortion illegal in all circumstances.

2. See, for example, Bernard (1974), Blake (1971), Duncan and Duncan (1978), Ferree (1974), Fultz (1980), Huber et al. (1978), Lipset and Schneider (in press), Mason, Czajka, & Arber (1976), Roper and Labeff (1971), Scott (1985), Shepard and Hess (1975), Thornton et al. (1983), Thornton and Freeman (1980), and Welch (1975) for the association of lower education and higher age with opposition to feminist ideology and goals.

3. One explanation perhaps lies in the ambiguity of the question. Some respondents may connect males' relative physical strength to an historical seizure of the dominant position, yet not believe that biological differences between men and women account for current sex-role differentiation.

4. Handberg and Lowery (1980) tried to establish correlates of support for the ERA among women legislators. They found that education and political party were important factors. Republicans were less likely to favor the amendment than were Democrats, and education was positively related to support for the amendment. The legislator's occupation, age, and region of the country were not related to views on the amendment, however.

REFERENCES

ABC News-Washington Post Poll. (1981, August). *Abortion has become an American fact of life* (Study #0034, p. 1).

Arrington, T., & Kyle, P. (1978). Equal Rights Amendment activists in North Carolina. *Signs*, 3, 666–680.

Bardes, P. (1972). Abortion and public opinion: a research note. *Journal of Marriage and the Family*, 34(3), 111.

Bernard, J. (1974, September). Age, sex, and feminism. *Annals of the American Academy of Political and Social Sciences*, 120–137.

Blake, J. (1971). Abortion and public opinion: The 1960–1970 decade. *Science*, 171, 540–549.

Bowker, L. (1981). Racism and sexism: Hints toward a theory of the causal structure of attitudes toward women. *International Journal of Women's Studies*, 4, 277–288.

Brady, D., & Tedin, K. (1976). Ladies in pink: Religion and political ideology in the anti ERA movement. *Social Science Quarterly*, 56, 564–575.

CBS News/New York Times Poll, The. (1980, August). *Abortion vs. pro-life*. p. 7.

Duncan, B., & Duncan, O. (1978). *Sex typing and social roles: A research report*. New York: Academic Press.

Ebaugh, H. R. F., & Haney, C. A. (1980). Shifts in abortion attitudes: 1972–1978. *Journal of Marriage and the Family*, *42*(3), 491–499.

Erskine, H. (1971). The polls: Women's role. *Public Opinion Quarterly*, *35*(2), 275–290.

Ferree, M. (1974). A woman for president? Changing responses 1958–1972. *Public Opinion Quarterly*, *38*(3), 390–399.

Ferree, M. (1980). Working class feminism: A consideration of the consequences of employment. *The Sociological Quarterly*, *21*, 173–184.

Fleming, J. (1982). *Women against feminism: The social bases of women's attitudes toward change in women's rights and roles*. Unpublished doctoral dissertation, Stanford University, CA.

Fleming, J., & Marks, G. (1980, Fall). Mobilizing for Jesus: Evangelicals and the 1980 election. *The Toqueville Review*, pp. 195–208.

Fultz, N. (1980). Changing image of women, 1970–1975. *University of North Carolina Newsletter*, *65*(3), 1–4.

Gallup Opinion Index, The. (1980, June). *Legality of abortion*, (Vol. 178, p. 7).

Gallup Poll, The. (1981a, August). *Public support for ERA reaches new high*, (pp. 4–5).

Gallup Poll, The. (1981b, May). *Public evenly divided on court ruling on abortion*, (p. 3).

Gallup Poll, The. (1984, August–September). *Women in politics*.

Gallup Poll, The. (1986, January–February). *Public remains divided in 1972 abortion ruling*.

Granberg, D. (1978). Pro-life or reflection of conservative ideology? An analysis of opposition to legalized abortion. *Sociology and Social Research*, *62*, 415–429.

Granberg, D., & Denney, D. (1982, May). The coathanger and the rose: Comparison of pro-choice and pro-life activists in contemporary U.S. *Transaction/SOCIETY*.

Handberg, R., & Lowery, W. (1980, January). Women state legislators and support for the Equal Rights amendment. *The Social Science Journal*, *17*, 65–71.

Harris Survey, The. (1978a, Feburary 13). *The women's conference resolutions have support*, (pp. 1–2).

Harris Survey, The. (1978b, July 17). *ERA campaign paying off*, (pp. 1–3).

Harris Survey, The. (1979a, March). *Women's organizations are helping*.

Harris Survey, The. (1979b, March). *Supreme court abortion ruling*.

Harris Survey, The. (1981, August). *Support increasing for strengthening women's status in society*, (pp. 1–3).

Henley, N., & Pincus, R. (1978). Interrelationship of sexist, racist, and anti-homosexual attitudes. *Psychological Reports*, *42*, 83–90.

Huber, J., Rexroat, E., & Spitze, G. (1978). A crucible of opinion on women's status: ERA in Illinois. *Social Forces*, *57*, 549–565.

Lipset, S. M., & Schneider, W. (in press). *From discrimination to affirmative action: Public attitudes 1935–1980*. Washington, DC: American Enterprise Institute.

Mason, K., & Bumpass, L. (1975, March). U.S. women's sex-role ideology, 1970. *American Journal of Sociology*, *80*, 1212–1219.

Mason, K., Czajka, J., & Arber, S. (1976). Change in U.S. women's sex-role attitudes 1964–1974. *American Sociological Review*, *41*, 573–596.

Milbrath, L. (1965). *Political participation*. Chicago, IL: Rand McNally.

National Opinion Research Center. (1986). General Social Surveys 1972–1986. Chicago: NORC.

Newspaper Readership Project. (1979). *Women and Newspapers in the 1970's*. New York: Newspaper Advertising Bureau Incorporated.

Roper, B., & Labeff, E. (1976). Sex roles and feminism revisited: An intergenerational attitude comparison. *Journal of Marriage and the Family*, *39*(1), 113–119.

Scott, W. (1982, March). *Status politics and the Equal Rights Amendment: A struggle over how women should spend their days*. Paper presented in the Southwestern Sociological Association meetings, San Antonio, TX.

Scott, W. (1985). The Equal Rights Amendment and Status Politics. *Social Forces, 64,* 499–506.

Shepard, W., & Hess, D. (1975). Attitudes in four age groups toward sex role division in adult occupations. *Journal of Vocational Behavior, 6*(1), 27–29.

Tedin, K. L., Brady, D. W., Buxton, M. E., Gorman, B. M., & Thompson, J. L. (1977). Social background and political differences between pro and anti-ERA activists. *American Politics Quarterly 5*(3), 395–408.

Tedrow, L., & Mahoney, E. (1979). Trends in attitudes toward abortion: 1972–1976. *Public Opinion Quarterly, 43*(2), 181–189.

Thornton, A., Alwin, D., & Conburn, D. (1983). Cause and consequences of sex-role attitudes and attitude change. *American Journal of Sociology, 48,* 211–227.

Thornton, A., & Freeman, D. (1980). *Consistency of sex role attitudes of women 1962–1977.* Ann Arbor, MI: Institute for Social Research Working Paper.

Welch, S. (1975, Spring). Support among women for the issues of the women's movement. *The Sociological Quarterly,* 216–227.

Willis, (1981). Abortion, which side are you on? *Feminist Studies, 7,* 89–91.

4

Wives and Work: A Theory of the Sex-Role Revolution and Its Consequences

KINGSLEY DAVIS

In industrialized societies it used to be that a woman would be asked what her husband did for a living. Now, increasingly, men are being asked what their wives do. Behind that small switch lies an important social revolution, a revolution in sex roles.

My goal here is to explain that revolution and to assess its consequences—not an easy task, since the change is still in progress, but one that is too important to ignore. For good or ill, the massive shift of wives from home to workplace is altering parental and marital relations and, through these, the fabric of society. Almost all policies dealing with men and women, with children and families, will have to reckon with this shift and its effects, as subsequent chapters in the present volume indicate.

Let us begin by getting the essential facts before us, in order to be clear about what is being interpreted.

THE RECORD OF A REVOLUTION

The main fact is that in virtually every industrialized country in the world the proportion of married women in paid employment has risen dramatically. In the United States, for example, in 1890 only some 4.6% of wives were in the labor force; by 1950 the figure had risen to 23.8%; by 1970 it was 40.8%; and by 1985 it was well over half—54.2%.

This chapter, in somewhat fuller form, was given as the Sixth Paul F. Lazarsfeld Lecture at Columbia University, April 6, 1984, and was published in *Population and Development Review*, *9* (3), (September 1984).

Kingsley Davis, Ph.D. Department of Sociology, University of Southern California, Los Angeles, California; Hoover Institution, Stanford University, Stanford, California.

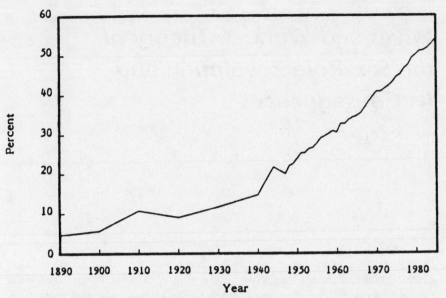

Figure 4.1. Percent of married women in the U.S. labor force, 1890–1985. *Source.* Adapted from U.S. Bureau of the Census (1975, 1986).

For nearly a century the increase has been remarkably steady, as depicted in Figure 4.1. It ran right through the Great Depression, two world wars, the postwar baby boom, and the youth revolt of the 1960s and 1970s. The average annual increase in the proportion was 2.8% between 1890 and 1950, 2.7% between 1950 and 1970, and 1.9% between 1970 and 1985. A surge did occur in World War II, but the basic trend was resumed soon after that and was not stopped by the baby boom of the 1950s.

Although other industrial countries have shown a similar upward trend, the level so far reached varies considerably. Some countries fall below and some exceed the U.S. rate. If we count wives of working age only—20–59—the proportion in the labor force was 47.8% in France and 62.9% in Sweden in 1975, 57.0% in England and Wales in 1981, and 60% in the U.S. in 1984. In general, the more highly developed the country and the longer it has been developed, the higher the proportion of married women in the labor force. The exceptions are the Communist countries, where the proportion is high regardless of the degree of development.

In the case of the United States, we are clearly dealing with a revolution that is still unfinished. The question immediately arises as to how long the trend will continue and what will be its final shape. The speed of the trend is shown by the fact that from 1940 to 1985 the proportion of wives (of all ages) in the labor force rose from 14.7 to 54.2%—a gain of 39.5 percentage points, or 269% of the starting figure. If this rate of change should continue, the employment of married women would reach 100% in the year 2006, only 21 years from 1985. Of course, there is no reason to expect wives to reach 100% participation, for no group ever does. A more realistic limit is the rate for married men, which in 1985 was 93% in the working ages. At the 1960–1985 pace of change, married women's labor-force participation will equal that of married men in the year 2000, only 15 years from 1985.

But it is unwise to expect the past rate of change to continue unabated. It seems more likely that the relative increase will slacken as the base (the proportion of married women already in the labor force) grows larger. If so, the labor-force rate for married women will approach the rate for married men as an upper asymptote, perhaps never quite reaching it. In fact, a slowdown in relative gain has already been occurring. The average increase in wives' participation was 3.3% in 1920–1950, 2.5% in 1950–1980, and 1.6 % in 1980–1985. If this deceleration is taken into account, the proportion of married women who are economically active will approximate that of married men by the year 2030, or 45 years from 1985. Thus the entry of married women into full economic activity should be complete sometime between 2010 and 2030.

At ages above 55, the growing employment of married women has been colliding with an opposite trend, a lessening of employment among the elderly as they depend increasingly on social security and transfer payments rather than work. The effect is to dampen slightly the female gain in labor-force participation. When we look at the data by age, we find that the wives most committed to the labor market are those in the prime reproductive stage (U.S. Statistical Abstract, 1986; see Table 4.1). This suggests that in the future the labor-force trend will be strongly reinforced.

All told, the massive movement of wives into paid employment is closer to being complete than most analysts realize. Although its consequences may take much longer to spin themselves out, the essential revolution will be over by the end of the century.

Table 4.1. Labor-Force Participation Rates of Married Women, by Age

Year	Ages of married women				
	15–19	20–24	25–34	35–44	45–64
	Percent in labor force				
1960	25.3	30.0	27.7	36.2	34.2
1985	64.9	65.6	68.1	50.6	49.2
	Percent increase				
1960–1985	94.5	116.3	136.8	88.1	48.0

Source. U.S. Statistical Abstract, 1982–1983 and 1984, pp. 382 and 412 respectively.

Evidently in 1890 there was extreme prejudice against married women's employment. How else could it be that only 2 to 3% of native white married women were working? Even among foreign-born wives, no age-group achieved as much as a 5% participation rate (Durand, 1948, pp. 216–217).

Yet at the same time the employment of unmarried women (single, widowed, and divorced) was substantial. For native white women aged 14–54, it was 30.9% in 1890, compared to 2.4% for married women. As the years went by, although the gap was never completely closed, the employment of married women increased much faster than that of unmarried women. By 1940 the proportion was 48% for the unmarried and 15.2% for the married. By 1984 there was little difference: For women aged 20–64, nearly 60% of those married were in the labor force or compared to 76% for single women and 65% for widowed and divorced women (U.S. Statistical Abstract, 1986, p. 398). It seems that it will be only a short time (10–15 years) before women in the working ages will be as fully employed when married as when unmarried.

Of particular significance is the fact, noted already, that the greatest increase has occurred among wives under 35 years of age, precisely the group most likely to be burdened with children. Indeed, mothers with young children have increased their labor-force participation at an amazing rate. In 1960 only 16.6% of married women with children under age 6 were in the labor force. By 1985, the proportion had risen to an astounding 53.4%. Note that these were not single parents; they were married women with husbands present. It used to be that when employed wives had young children, they dropped out of the labor market, at least temporarily. No longer is this the case. In fact, among the nation's wives, children seem to be less of a deterrent to employment than advancing age. The rise in labor-force participation has been greater for those women who in the past were normatively ruled out: married versus single women, women with children versus those with no children, and women with young children versus those with older children.

In sum, the facts are clear. Beginning at an extremely low level in 1890, the first date for which we have good information, U.S. wives under age 60 have steadily increased their participation in the labor force, regardless of age, race, or parenthood. Today, over half of them are employed, and within 15 to 30 years their employment rate, age for age, seems likely to approximate that of married men.

This remarkable transformation characterizes not only the United States but virtually all other industrialized countries, some of which have higher rates of wives' employment than in the United States. How, then, do we explain the change?

THE RISE AND FALL OF THE BREADWINNER SYSTEM

This question is often answered in an off-hand way, by vague reference to such developments as the feminist movement, the rise of service industries, the invention of modern contraception, or the growth of individualism. Such intuitive leaps remind us that in social science we usually know more about what happens than why it happens. Ironically, great precision often goes into describing a trend, while the explanation is either ignored or treated casually. In the present case, the spectacular rise in the proportion of married women in the labor force is about as clear and definite a social change as one can find. It therefore offers a challenge to our explanatory prowess.

I propose to adopt a combined sociological and historical, or evolutionary, approach. I want to place the change we are discussing in a wider analytical framework and to analyze it by trying to understand what went before. In so doing, I prefer to start with the Industrial Revolution, because this is, by all odds, the greatest technological change that ever occurred in human society. Interpreting this change to mean the use of science and machinery to harness inanimate energy, thus increasing productivity per worker by hundreds or even thousands of times—a transformation that is still advancing and spreading with further application of science to all human goals—we can begin by asking how this change has affected the division of labor between men and women.

The Emergence of a Separate Workplace

The phrase "division of labor" ordinarily suggests interdependent *kinds* of work, but there is also a spatial, or geographical, side to it that should not be neglected. In my estimation, the first and greatest impact on sex roles made by the Industrial Revolution was the shift of the locus of work to outside the home. In the industrializing countries of the 19th and early 20th centuries, with the decline of agriculture and handicraft and the organization of other activities in factories, firms, and shops, the home was gradually replaced as the locus of work. The new technology required a division of labor more complex than that found in the household, and a site that minimized the costs of energy, raw materials, transport, and distribution.

The shift, however, did not come quickly or easily. To work where one lived was convenient, and to work with family members was to enjoy cheap and dedicated labor. Neil Smelser has shown that in the English cotton industry of the late 18th and early 19th century, whole families were frequently employed in factories together; child labor was trained and supervised by parents on factory premises (Smelser, 1959, Chs. 9–11). In addition, despite the march of industrialism in towns and cities, agriculture (in which, of course, family members worked together) long continued to be a major activity. In Great Britain as late as 1830 (Mitchell & Deane, 1962, p. 60), and in the United States as late as 1907 (U.S. Bureau of the Census, 1975, Vol. 1, p. 138), approximately a third of the labor force was still employed in agriculture. In Japan, as late as 1955, "unpaid family labor" still absorbed some 54.7% of female workers and 14.3% of male workers

(United Nations, 1964, p. 264). Only a few decades ago, then, depending on the stage of industrialism reached, did the household and its immediate environs cease to be an important locus of work, as is still the case in most of the Third World.

The Novelty of a Separate Workplace

When it did come, the switch to a nonhome workplace had great significance. In certain occupations, such as fishing, shipping, warfare, and distant trade, work had always been done elsewhere than at home, but throughout history the main workplace, and hence the seat of the division of labor between the sexes, had been the household and surrounding land. Even in nomadic herding societies, the family tended to travel together as a productive unit.

In the technological regime under which 98% of human history has occurred—that is, a hunting and gathering regime—the division of labor was based mainly on sex and age, but in a rudimentary fashion. Although males made some economic contribution to the family and the band through hunting (especially of large game), most of the actual calories consumed were obtained by women. Women did most of the gathering, hunted small animals, and tended to food preparation.[1] Since their young were helpless and had to be carried, mothers could not go far away from the base camp to find food, and they naturally performed necessary food processing at home. Thus, in contrast to other primates, the human species came to depend on a home base for food sharing and subsistence activities.[2] The male was presumably drawn into the family unit by sexual need and the availability of food, companionship, and familiar surroundings; but from an economic standpoint the family was essentially a mother-child unit, with the mother gathering food for both herself and her young.

The domestication of plants and animals tended to make the household more stable and tightly integrated, with a greater participation of the male and a clearer and more complex face-to-face division of labor based on gender and age. Both male and female work centered on the household and the land near it. The man was thus further assimilated into the family, and his work, like the woman's, was compatible with a parental role. Although agrarian civilizations ultimately developed structures that took some men away from their native locales, most men in these societies resided in rural villages and were attached to rural households and plots of land. For this reason I call this the "household economy" system.

What the Industrial Revolution Did

The Industrial Revolution, by systematically separating the workplace from the home, destroyed for the first time in human history the direct division of labor between husband and wife. Male and female roles remained distinct, as they had always been, but they assumed a radically new character. The man's work, instead of being directly integrated with that of wife and children in the home or on the surrounding land, was integrated with that of nonkin in factories, shops, and firms. The man's economic role became in one sense more important to the family, for he was the link between the family and the wider market economy; but at the same time his personal participation in the household diminished. His wife, relegated to the home as her sphere, still performed the parental and domestic duties that women had always performed. She bore and reared children, cooked meals, washed clothes, and cared for her husband's personal needs, but to an unprecedented degree her economic role became restricted. She could not produce what the family consumed, because production had been moved from the home. She could not sell goods and services or her labor in the market place, because her domestic duties precluded that. She could not enter the wider economy except indirectly through her husband. The burgeoning industrial economy produced a surplus great enough to maintain her at home. Thus an unprecedented social order arose in which the two facets of existence— economic production and familial regeneration—were organized in two separate systems distinct in location, institutions, and personnel.

Although the husband's occupation took him away from home during most of his waking hours, he was the "breadwinner." The wife, in turn, became the "homemaker," devoting full time to the household. For brevity I call this the "breadwinner" system.

The Breadwinner System as an Anomaly

This arrangement is often called "traditional," but actually it is unusual and, I think, ephemeral. It is associated with a particular stage of development: the process of industrialization from the time when agriculture first loses predominance to the time when it uses only a fourth of the manpower. The breadwinner system develops slowly in the early phase, characterizing the burgeoning but small middle class rather than the peasantry or the proletariat. Then, after reaching a climax in which virtually no married women are employed, it declines as more and more wives enter white collar employment in offices, schools, hospitals, stores, and government agencies. In the United States the heyday of the breadwinner system would be from about 1860 to 1920. In Britain it flourished somewhat earlier. In Russia the breadwinner system apparently never prevailed. Under the Tsars the country was still too agricultural to exclude most wives from productive activity, although the sparse bourgeoisie did so; and under the Communists, at least in Slavic regions, the frightful losses of males in a violent revolution and two world wars drove married women into the labor market. Japan today has more than a fourth of its married women in nonagricultural employment. This level is similar to that of the United States in the 1950s, and a sizable proportion of these women are still unpaid family workers; nevertheless, the employment of Japanese married women in nonagricultural and nondomestic activities has been rising rapidly (Hashimoto, 1983). The breadwinner system is on the way out there as well as in the rest of the industrial world.

When development is hastened by the overnight transfer of modern technology to a backward country, the breadwinner system emerges correspondingly. For instance, although the oil-rich countries of the Arab world are using their wealth to modernize their economies rapidly, their social institutions are still extremely conventional. The response is to bring in foreign workers while keeping married women at home. In Kuwait, where half the population lives in cities of 100,000 or more, where per capita income is among the highest in the world, where economic modernization is occurring at a dizzying pace, in 1975 only 12.6% of married women were in the labor force, and of these the overwhelming majority (91%) were employed in social and personal services (and most of these probably foreigners).[3] Despite their desire to keep women at home, however, these countries are frightened by such an importation of labor that a fourth to three fourths of their populations is foreign (see United Nations, 1981). The socially more advanced Arab countries—Bahrain, Jordan, Kuwait, and Egypt—are beginning to employ their own women—a movement that will probably grow.

Clearly, the division of labor between husband and wife that arose historically from the separation of the workplace and the home is not the "normal" or "traditional" pattern. Rather, it is a recent aberration that arose in a particular stage of development and tends to recur in countries now undergoing development.

But why did the separation of home and workplace lead to this system? One can imagine other responses. For instance, married women could have been employed outside the home but under the authority or supervision of the husband. Or from the very start they could have been employed autonomously, just as they are today in advanced nations. Why instead were they left at home?

The answer, I think, is that wives had or were expected to have too many children to engage in outside work. With a gradual decline in mortality and yet a continuance of old mores favoring numerous births, the size of family households reached its zenith. As late as 1890 in the United States, 34.6% of households had 6 or more members.[4] Caring for numerous children was particularly burdensome as urbanization and mobility increased. Accordingly, as the workplace became separated from the home, a new division of labor emerged. Wives did, on a full-time basis, what they had always done on a part-time basis; they tended to duties concerned with the house, children, and husband, but they lost their role in economic production. Single women, not burdened with children, always participated substantially in the labor market. Widows (many of whom still had young children) did so to a lesser extent, while wives hardly participated at all. The husband not only worked in the outside world but was paid as an individual with no reference to his family role. Although his wife and children had a claim on his income, it was still *his* income, and they had no control over its amount or its source.

At its zenith, in about 1890 when only 2.3% of native-born American wives were in the labor force (Duvand, 1948, p. 51), the breadwinner system was remarkably complete, and it held on in policy and ideology long after it had been eroded in fact. Welfare legislation after the 1930s assumed that the breadwinner pattern was normal, its absence abnormal. For instance, the Aid to Families with Dependent Children (AFDC) program in the United States was designed to help families in which the husband, through injury, unemployment, or other calamity, was temporarily unable to support his family. Women receiving AFDC were discouraged from working because they were supposed to be at home taking care of the children. Aid would be given only so long as the breadwinner was incapacitated. Similarly, the social security system arranged for the worker (assumed to be male) to receive benefits not only for himself but for his wife as well. If he died before she did, she was entitled to widow's benefits based on his employment. The legal system viewed husbands as obliged to support a family and wives as obligated to care for home and children.

Why did the breadwinner system become so deeply embedded in thought and policy? Doubtless social policy and ideology lagged behind events. But in addition, the system seemed "natural" because it involved two features that had been true in the preceding household economy: first, the dominance of the husband (now translated into control of the family purse), and second, the devotion of women to children and child care. Given the salience of these two features, the novelty introduced in the breadwinner system—transfer of economic production out of the home and out of female hands—tended to pass unnoticed or at least unchallenged. Indeed, the idea prevailed that the employment of mothers outside the home was deleterious for children.

THE EMERGENCE OF THE EGALITARIAN SYSTEM

Now we have to ask why, despite its strength and tenacity, the breadwinner system in the industrial nations has been rapidly disappearing. Note that this is the same as asking why the egalitarian system has been rapidly growing. My answer is twofold: First, the breadwinner system has, as the Marxists would say, internal contradictions that make its ultimate demise a foregone conclusion. Second, demographic and social changes peculiar to mature industrialization are undermining the system and hastening its demise.

Internal Contradictions in the Breadwinner System

Simply to describe the system is to suggest its major weakness. It involved two interrelated dichotomies: that between the workplace and the home and that between the breadwinner and the homemaker. Never before had the roles of husband and wife been so distinct. The income of wife and children was determined by forces over which they had no control, and it was funneled to them through the husband, giving him an iron grip on the family's economic destiny while involving him in minimal personal contact with the family members. For a woman, picking the right man was the most crucial step in her life, yet as Talcott Parsons pointed out years ago, in attracting a man she had to rely heavily on her sexual appeal, which normally declined with age, and on other considerations over which she had little control. From a man's standpoint, being the sole support in perpetuity for an entire family was a heavy responsibility.

In view of this structural weakness, the system could not operate without strong normative controls. The husband's obligation to support his family even after his death had to be enforced by law and public opinion; illicit sexual relations and out-of-wedlock reproduction had to be condemned, divorce had to be punished, and marriage had to be encouraged by making the lot of the "spinster" seem a pitiful one.

With the subsequent history of this system behind us, we know that these normative controls collapsed, causing the internal contradictions to surface. This collapse was due to a great extent to the demographic and social changes brought by advanced industrialism. In other words, the breadwinner system was brought down by the same process (modernization) that had created the system in the first place.

Lending credence to this view is the extent to which all of the developments capable of undermining the system occurred together and began well before the actual demise of the system, like a house whose hidden termite infestation goes on for years before producing observable disintegration.

Postponement and Rejection of Marriage

An early sign of weakness in the breadwinner system was the number of men and women who delayed marriage or remained permanently single. Postponement of marriage had long been practiced in the agrarian societies of Western Europe, where access to land was regarded as necessary for family formation, but it came to characterize the industrial sector as well. In Sweden, by 1920, the proportion of the population aged 30–34 who had never married was 37.2% for men and 34.9% for women. For persons aged 45–49, the two percentages were 16.2 and 22.5 respectively. In a study of native white women in Massachusetts, Uhlenberg found that among women reaching age 50, the proportion of those who were single rose from 14.5% in the cohort born in 1830 to 22.7% in the cohort born in 1870. For cohorts born after 1890, however, the proportion fell until it was only 10.7% for women born in 1920 (Uhlenberg, 1969, pp. 411, 419). Thus the flowering of the breadwinner system in the late 19th century was associated with delayed or foregone marriage, and its subsequent decline was signalled by a reversal of that trend.

Postponement of marriage was a high price to pay for keeping wives at home. For biological reasons people tend to marry early if they get an opportunity, and one way to get that opportunity is to have the wife employed. This helps explain why, once it started, the fastest rise in employment was among young wives. The rise in the U.S. for wives aged 15–19 is particularly impressive, because many women of this age have become wives because of premarital pregnancy and hence have high fertility (see Table 4.2).

Since young wives are so motivated to be married, their rising labor force participation must also be strongly motivated. One motive, I suggest, is precisely a chance to marry early afforded by the additional income the prospective wife could bring in. True, since the 1950s the marriage trend has reversed itself. The age at first marriage has risen sharply. This marital postponement, however, differs from that of the previous century. Today, many young couples are living together without marriage, and both are working. They are often waiting until they decide either to split or to get married. If and when they do marry, an important factor in the decision will probably be the woman's prospect of continued employment. Her ability to work facilitates marriage as well as cohabitation.

DIMINISHED MARITAL FERTILITY

The breadwinner system, by making domestic duties the full-time occupation of the wife, was ideally suited to producing many children. And so it did, until the second half of the 19th century, when changes occurring in industrializing societies steadily reduced marital fertility, ultimately weakening the breadwinner system itself. In the U.S. white population, for example, ever-married women whose main reproductive years were in the 1880s bore an average of 4.9 children; those of the 1930s an average of 2.4 (U.S. Bureau of the Census, 1975, p. 54); and those of the 1970s an average of only 1.8, well below the stable replacement rate. To be sure, a baby boom intervened, but during that period (1940–1959) with the exception of one year (1947) the birth rate never climbed to the level of 1924 or any preceding year.

Significantly, the decline in fertility began long before married women entered the labor force. Motivated by a desire to retain or advance one's own and one's children's status in a rapidly evolving industrial society, reduced fertility probably paved the way for wives' employment, but not until a triggering level was reached (see Davis, 1963, pp. 345–366).

Table 4.2. Crude Birth Rate by Age of Wife

Age of wives	Births per 1000 wives, 1983
15–17	471
18–19	327
20–24	180
25–29	146
30–34	79
35–39	25

Source. Calculated from data in National Center for Health Statistics, "Advance Report of Final Natality Statistics, 1983," *Monthly Vital Statistics Report*, Vol. 34, No. 6, Supplement (September 20, 1985).

This conclusion derives partly from the logic of the situation. A woman who is at home full-time and yet has only one to three children who are at school most of the day, has less than a full-time vocation. She can, of course, find plenty to do at home, but in economic terms, the opportunity costs of her nonemployment are very high in relation to the familial needs being satisfied.

It was not only low fertility per se that released wives for employment, but also the way it was achieved. Women did not cut their reproduction by a wider spacing of births but by stopping reproduction sooner. Although early U.S. data are lacking, we do know that in preindustrial France and Germany the mother's average age at last birth was around 39 to 41 years (van de Walle & Knodel, 1980, p. 11; see also 1979, p. 233). If this pattern characterized early America as well, the transition in age at last birth would be approximately as shown in Table 4.3 (Glick, 1977, p. 6; Norton, 1983, p. 268; van de Walle & Knodel, 1979, p. 233).

THE AMAZING EXTENSION OF LIFE

To understand the impact of these reproductive changes, one has to see how they interacted with another revolutionary development: the extension of the average length of life. Back when women (if still surviving) bore their last child around age 40, the average life expectancy after getting married was about 38 years. Since the mean age at marriage was around 22, this meant that the average mother had an even chance of being dead by the time her last child left home. A bride could therefore expect to spend her entire married life with children in the house. Today, however, both because of longer life (57.4 years after marriage for women in 1983) and because of earlier termination of childbearing (at approximately age 28), a bride can expect to live about 33 years after her last child has left home. This is more than half of her whole life expectancy following marriage.

Table 4.3. Median Age of Mother at Last Birth, by Mother's
Birth Date

Cohort born	Median age of mother at last birth
1800–1850	40.0
1880–1889	32.9
1910–1919	31.6
1930–1939	29.6
1940–1949	27.3

Not only has child care come to occupy a more limited portion of women's lives, but so has marriage. Although dissolution through death has decreased, dissolution through divorce has risen (see Chapter 10). Further, the widening difference in mortality between men and women has distorted the sex ratio at older ages. In the white population of the United States, for example, the difference in life expectancy at age 20 was only 1.6 years in 1900; by 1983 it was nearly 7 years. Under the conditions of 1900, if the bride were 3 years younger than the groom, she could expect to outlive him by 5 years. By 1980 that figure had grown to 10 years, or about 18% of her lifetime after marriage. Of course, she might remarry, but this has been made improbable by the distorted sex ratio above age 45 and by the tendency for men to marry young women.

Divorce and the Employed Wife

Despite fluctuations associated with wars and depressions, the increase in the U.S. divorce rate was remarkably consistent from the 1860s (the first years for which information is readily available) until the 1980s. In 1983 the rate was 18 times what it had been in 1860, and 2.4 times what it had been in 1940. A similar upsurge has occurred in nearly all other industrial countries, although the U.S. trend has remained about 20 years ahead of the average for other advanced nations (Davis, 1983, pp. 33–37). Based on recent U.S. dissolution rates for couples marrying today, the chance of a first marriage ending in divorce is above 50%.

Reasons for the Increase in Divorce

Doubtless changes in the conditions of life such as urbanization and greater mobility were ultimately responsible for the long-term rise in the divorce rate. But more specifically, I think the rise can be traced to the development that created the breadwinner system of sex roles in the first place—namely, the shift of economic production out of the home. With this shift, husband

and wife, parents and children, were no longer bound together in a close face-to-face division of labor in a common enterprise. They were bound, rather, by a weaker and less direct mutuality: the husband's ability to draw income from a wider economy and the wife's willingness to make a home and rear children. The husband's work not only took him out of the home but also frequently put him into contact with other people, including young unmarried women, who were strangers to his family. Freed from the social controls characteristic of rural areas and small towns, many husbands either sought divorce or, by their behavior, caused their wives to do so.

Regardless of its causes, the exploding divorce rate struck at the heart of the 19th-century sex-role pattern. If a young wife could not count on her husband remaining married to her, she could not count on his economic support either. Divorce thus broke the central bargain of marriage by which a woman traded her services as wife and mother for the financial support of the husband. Her best hedge against the disaster of divorce was to earn her own money by outside employment (see Chapter 10).

But why did the onset of the climb in divorce rates precede the entry of wives into the labor force by 3 to 4 decades? The answer, I believe, is similar to that regarding fertility decline: A threshold had to be reached before this factor could enter the calculations of married women. With a divorce probability below 10%, most young women would take a chance; but with the rate rising to above 20%, as it did in the 1920s in the U.S. (Cherlin, 1981, p. 23), they would seriously consider employment after marriage.

A further question about the effect of divorce on employment is posed by the high remarriage rate. About three fourths of divorced women remarry, and they do so, on average, within 3 years (Cherlin, 1981, p. 29). They therefore have a relatively short time to worry about finances, and court-ordered alimony payments partially provide support for the children (see Chapter 10). Furthermore, the probability of widowhood is low. In 1901 the chance of a 25-year-old white male reaching age 60 was only 63%; by 1983 it had risen to 85%. As a result of these counterweights to the divorce increase, the proportion of ever-married women who at any given time are divorced or widowed has remained remarkably stable (see Table 4.4). For women aged 15–44, in 1890 this proportion was 6.5%; by 1970 it was still only 7.1%; only after 1970 did it advance, reaching 13.9% in 1984.

To the extent that improved male longevity and frequent remarriage compensate for rising divorce, they explain (along with the threshold argument) why the divorce trend did not immediately push wives into the labor force. However, to avoid underestimating divorce as a factor, we should recall that death and divorce dissolve marriages in quite different ways. Death, being normally involuntary, can be predicted on an actuarial basis and can therefore be insured against. Divorce, on the other hand, involves a contest of wills; it cannot be insured against. Also, a divorce tends to occur early in the marital career, while death most often occurs late. Consequently,

Table 4.4. Proportion Currently Divorced or Widowed
Among Ever-Married U.S. Women Aged 15–44, Selected
Years, 1890–1984

Year	Percent currently unmarried
1890	6.5
1900	6.9
1910	6.2
1930	6.7
1950	5.6
1960	5.3
1970	7.1
1984	13.9

Sources. Calculated from U.S. Bureau of the Census (1975, pp. 20–21; 1986, p. 36).

a bride staying at home rather than working risks a far greater loss from divorce than from bereavement, even though the eventual chance of one or the other is about equal. Finally, death leaves the children orphans, clearly attached to the surviving parent, while divorce leaves them in an ambiguous and often unsatisfactory relationship with two surviving but estranged parents (see Chapter 11).

Given the uncertainty of support from the ex-husband and the meagerness of support from the government, ex-wives can be expected to be in the labor force even when they have young children. The data in Table 4.5 confirm this. In 1985, 67.5% of divorced women with children under 6 years of age were in the labor force. This being true, the best protection for a young woman is to have a job while married that will continue when she is no longer married.

Table 4.5. Labor Force Participation of Separated and Divorced
Women with Children, United States, 1970 and 1985

	Percent in labor force	
	1970	1985
Separated women		
With children under 6 years	45.4%	53.2%
With children 6–17 years only	60.6	70.9
Divorced women		
With children under 6 years	63.3	67.5
With children 6–17 years only	82.4	83.4

Source. U.S. Bureau of the Census (1986, p. 399).

SUPPLY VERSUS DEMAND FOR MARRIED WOMEN'S LABOR

I have so far stressed the supply side of the married female labor force. I have said that the inherent weaknesses of the breadwinner system and its erosion by demographic and social changes pushed married women into the labor market. At first glance this appears to compete with explanations from the demand side. The structure of the labor force has changed. A higher proportion of jobs are in service and clerical occupations traditionally considered to be particularly suited to women.[5] With the falling age at marriage, the number of *single* women declined, thus creating a demand for *married* women in the labor force (Oppenheimer, 1970). Real wages rose, thus making it more costly for women to stay at home.

These propositions, however, do not refute the analysis made here. We have assumed all along that the Industrial Revolution continues to produce higher real income, to substitute skilled and sedentary jobs for physical labor, to foster urbanization and social mobility, and to expand the total size of the labor force. But these changes enlarge the *opportunity* to work, not the motivation; they seem either too broad to account for wives in particular, or too narrow to explain the timing and speed of wives' century-long rising participation in the labor market.

CONSEQUENCES OF THE EGALITARIAN SYSTEM

The difficulties of demand-side theory become more evident when the consequences of the labor force transition are discussed. Since the opportunities to work are available, the significant question is not only why so many wives work but also why so few of them do. Why are nearly 40% of young adult wives still at home? The answer is not that they have calculated the dollar costs and benefits and found that employment does not pay. Rather, it is that they have calculated the human costs and benefits, and found employment deficient.

If this is true, it is not only the breadwinner system but also this egalitarian system that has problems. In analyzing these problems, one finds it hard to separate those that are due to the newness of the system from those that are inherent. A century may seem a long time, but it is a short time to alter the basic structure of human institutions. The new egalitarian system of sex roles still lacks normative guidelines. It is not clear what ex-wives and ex-husbands, children, cohabitants, friends, or neighbors should expect. Each couple has to work out its own arrangement, which means in practice a great deal of experimentation and frustration.

The main inherent weakness of the egalitarian system is that although it brings the wife back into economic production, it does so outside the home, and thus in a way incompatible with child rearing. This incompatibility characterizes the husband's situation as well as the wife's, but because the wife in both previous systems (the household production system and the breadwinner system) was the one especially charged with domestic duties, it is ordinarily seen as her problem.

The obvious remedy for this weakness is to equalize the rights and obligations of the two sexes in both the workplace and the home. Women would achieve a higher position in the workplace than they now have, and men would share half the burdens at home. This prescription, so simple in theory, is difficult to carry out in practice. In the workplace, for instance, it is doubtless possible to equalize the position of women in general compared to that of men in general, but it is less possible to do so for the position of a particular man and a particular woman. How can a female lawyer and a male filing clerk be made equal to each other simply by marriage? As long as husband and wife are unequal in the labor market, they will be unequal at home; on the average, the one who contributes less in the labor market is expected to contribute more at home. Even apart from this workplace influence, biological specialization makes equalization of home duties difficult. Since men cannot bear and breastfeed children, they must do something equivalent; but how can one measure equivalence? It has to be measured in terms of time and energy, but the final determination may be more a matter of the personalities of the two partners than of the physics and physiology of the workload.

Doubtless the aim of public policy in the future will be to lessen the conflicts between work and child care. At the workplace, such devices as day-care centers, pregnancy leaves, seniority retention, shorter hours, and part-time work will be encouraged. At home, greater efficiency in housing design, culinary activity, health service, shopping, and commuting will be achieved. Also, an effort will be made to reduce the economic cost of parenthood, by providing child allowances and more free services for children. Most of the mutual accommodations between workplace and home will be thought of as applying to women, but some will also apply to men, as in contemporary Sweden.

If accommodation policies succeed and this egalitarian system becomes fully operable, what will be the long-run consequences? Will the new order, like the preceding one, carry the seeds of its own destruction? No one can say for sure, because the question relates to the future and is therefore speculative, but it is possible to generate a few hypotheses.

One possibility is that a continuance of voluntary factors that undermined the breadwinner system will ultimately militate against the egalitarian system as well, or at least against the survival of societies that have that system. Two factors in particular—the rising divorce rate and the declining birth rate—could together have this effect. Although the increase in divorce may taper off, there is no guarantee that it will. In the breadwinner system the husband's life in a separate workplace increases the risk of divorce. The egalitarian system make this worse: It puts both husband and wife in the labor market and does so not together, as in the household economy, but separately. Each thus interacts with people who are strangers to the family. Marital partners are in three worlds, only one of which they share.

The risk of divorce exacerbates the low fertility of the egalitarian system, because unstable unions weaken the long-run and dedicated commitment required for child care. A woman can, of course, have a child and forget the father, relying on the government or her own work to bear the monetary costs, but she is not likely under these circumstances to have many children, because she has the worst of all arrangements: separation of workplace and home and no husband to help her at home.

Since some women, mainly for reasons beyond their control, have only one child or none at all, the rest must have substantially more than two each to replace the population. Among women aged 40–44 in the United States in 1984, the proportion childless was 11.1% and the proportion having borne only one child was 12.2% (U.S. Bureau of the Census, 1985, p. 7). To provide an average of 2.1 children per woman for all women, the rest would have had to have an average of 2.58 births each, whereas in fact young women of the time anticipated a life-time average of only 2.03 births. Such findings raise doubts that societies with this egalitarian system will survive.

Another possibility is that husband–wife activities may be combined in the workplace, but this would encounter the same difficulties that led to the separation of workplace and home in the first place. A more likely prospect is the return of the workplace to the home, a reversal that is said to be fostered by computer technology, but, given the fantastically complex division of labor in a modern economy, a return to household production seems unlikely.

Whatever develops with respect to sex roles and fertility, it may be part of a broader moral reform. As things stand now in advanced democracies, there is little relation between the moral standards of home and work. An employee may have his or her wages garnisheed for nonpayment of alimony or support, but in general, family morals are not enforced in the place where the highest penalty could be imposed—the workplace. It thus appears that egalitarian sex roles are associated with a lack of enforcement of sexual norms and with low fertility.

It seems possible that, rather than return to either the household production system or the breadwinner system, societies will modify the egalitarian system by political and moral controls designed to determine the birth rate, as appears to be happening in China. Speculation about the future, however, should take into account human resistance to regimentation. For all but a brief period of human history, women have rivaled men in economic production, are now returning to that condition, and would understandably be reluctant to give it up. Further, although the separation of workplace and home has created two forces in life, they are not equally valued. Many people regard the workplace as an instrumentality, marriage and the family as goals in themselves. It follows that people seek some system of sex roles that will work for them. Under modern conditions they cannot revive old patterns, but neither can they eliminate sex roles altogether. It is for this reason that a modified egalitarian system that recognizes a division of labor between husband and wife but minimizes the effect on sex roles by equalizing rewards both at home and in the marketplace seems the most likely path in the future.

NOTES

1. "Among !Kung hunters and gatherers in southwestern Africa, women "provide two to three times as much food by weight as the men" (Lee, 1968, p. 33).

2. Concentrations of artifacts over a million and a half years old "seem to indicate that the movements of Plio-Pleistocene hominids were organized around a home base . . . a distinctive feature of human behavior vis-à-vis other hominids" (Isaac, 1976, p. 500). For a useful summary of comparative evidence on food sharing and the family, see Passingham (1982, Ch. 9).

3. United Nations (1979a, pp. 1010–1011, 1096; 1979b, p. 1036–1037; 1980, p. 237). On female labor force participation in Arabic and Latin American countries, see Yousef (1974).

4. U.S. Bureau of the Census (1975, p. 42). In 1790, the figure was 49%.

5. Bancroft (1958, p. 37) states: "The growth in white-collar jobs, particularly clerical jobs, is an important reason for the vast increase in employment of women."

REFERENCES

Bancroft, G. (1958). *The American labor force.* New York: Wiley.
Cherlin, A. J. (1981). *Marriage, divorce, remarriage.* Cambridge, MA: Harvard University Press.
Davis, K. (1963). This theory of change and response in modern demographic history. *Population Index, 29*(4), 345–366.
Davis, K. (1983, May). The future of marriage. *Bulletin of the American Academy of Arts & Sciences, 36,* 33–37.
Durand, J. D. (1948). *The labor force in the United States 1890–1960.* New York: Social Science Research Council.
Glick, P. C. (1977). Updating the life cycle of the family. *Journal of Marriage and the Family, 39*(1), 6.
Hashimoto. (1983). Unpublished raw data. University of Washington, Seattle.
Isaac, G. L. (1976). The activities of early African hominids. In G. L. Isaac & E. R. McCown (Eds.), *Human origins: Louis Leakey and the East African evidence.* Menlo Park, CA: W. A. Benjamin, Inc.
Lee, R. B. (1968). What hunters do for a living. In R. B. Lee & I. Devore (Eds.), *Man the hunter.* Chicago: Aldine.
Mitchell, B. R., & Deane, P. (1962). *Abstract of British historical statistics.* Cambridge, England: Cambridge University Press.
Norton, J. (1983). Family life cycle: 1980. *Journal of Marriage and the Family, 45*(2), 268.
Oppenheimer, V. K. (1970). *The female labor force in the United States.* Westport, CT: Greenwood Press.
Passingham, R. E. (1982). *The human primate.* San Francisco: Freeman.
Smelser, N. J. (1959). *Social change in the Industrial Revolution* (Chs. 9–11). Chicago: University of Chicago Press.

Uhlenberg, P. R. (1969, November). A study of cohort life cycles: Cohorts of native born Massachusetts women, 1830–1920. *Population Studies, 23,* 411, 419.
United Nations. (1964). *Demographic Yearbook.* New York: United Nations.
United Nations. (1979a). *Demographic Yearbook.* New York: United Nations.
United Nations. (1979b). *Historical Supplement.* New York: United Nations.
United Nations. (1980). *Demographic Yearbook.* New York: United Nations.
United Nations. (1981, May). *International migration in the Arab world.* Proceedings of an ECWA Population Conference, Nicosia, Cyprus.
U.S. Bureau of the Census. (1975). *Historical statistics of the United States, colonial times to 1970* (Vol. 1). Washington, DC: Government Printing Office.
U.S. Bureau of the Census. (1985). *Fertility of American women, June, 1984.* (Current Population Reports, Series P-20, No. 401). Washington, DC: U.S. Government Printing Office.
U.S. Bureau of the Census. (1986). *Statistical Abstract of the U.S.* Washington, DC: U.S. Government Printing Office.
van de Walle, E., & Knodel, J. (1979). Lessons from the past: Policy implications of historical fertility. *Population and Development Review, 5*(2).
van de Walle, E., & Knodel, J. (1980). Europe's fertility transition. *Population Bulletin of the Population Reference Bureau, 34*(6).
Yousef, N. H. (1974). *Women and work in developing societies.* Westport, CT: Greenwood Press.

SUPPLEMENTARY BIBLIOGRAPHY*

Bernhardt, E. M. (1985). Women's home attachment at first birth: The case of Sweden. *Stockholm Research Reports in Demography, 28,* 34.
Bielby, D., & Bielby, W. T. (1984). Work commitment, sex-role attitudes, and women's employment. *American Sociological Review, 49,* 234–237.
Cain, G. (1984). *Women and work: Trends in time spent in homework.* Institute for Research on Poverty Discussion Paper 747-84.
Cherfas, J., & Cribbin, J. (1984). *The redundant male.* New York: Pantheon.
Davis, K. (Ed.). (1985). *Contemporary Marriage.* New York: Russell Sage Foundation.
Espenshade, T. J. (1982). Collaborative paper: Marriage, divorce, and remarriage from retrospective data: A multi-regional approach. Population Association of America, San Diego, CA.
Fleming, A. T. (1986). The American wife. *New York Times Magazine.*
Joshi, H. (1985). *Motherhoood and employment: Change and continuity in post-war Britain.* University of Sussex. Conference papers, 70–87.
Keyfitz, N. (1981). Paradoxes of work and consumption in late twentieth century America. *Research and Human Development, 2,* 31–54.
Lowenstein, H. (1986). A special section on the time we spend working. *Monthly Labor Review, 109*(11).
Newell, M. L., & Joshi, H. (1986). *The next job after the first baby: Occupational transition among women born in 1946.* CPS Research Paper, University of London, No. 86-3, p. 68.
O'Connell, M., & Bloom, D. E. (1987). *Cutting the apron strings: Women in the labor force in the 1980's.* Center for Population Studies Discussion Paper, No. 87-1.
Popenoe, D. (1987). Beyond the nuclear family: a statistical portrait of the changing family in Sweden. *Journal of Marriage and the Family, 49,* 173–188.
Presser, H. B. (1987). Work shifts of full-time dual-earner couples: Patterns and contrasts by sex of spouse. *Demography, 24,* 99–112.
Rabier, J. R., Riffault, H., & Inglehart, R. (1984). Euro-barometer 19: Gender roles in the European community. ICPSR, April 1984.

*As could be expected, the sex-role revolution has given rise to an enormous literature, only a tiny fraction of which could be used in this chapter. Some additional references, relevant but not cited, are thus included.

5

Black–White Differences in Marriage and Family Patterns

HENRY A. WALKER

INTRODUCTION

The black American family is alternately a perplexing problem and an embarrassment to social researchers and policymakers alike. The patterns of family formation and maintenance exhibited by black Americans are different from those found among the white majority. Moynihan (1965) described the situation clearly: Compared to whites, blacks are less likely to marry, less likely to remain married, more likely to bear children while unmarried, and more likely to reside in households headed by women. Social scientists have offered several general explanations for the differences that exist and policy makers have created programs to reduce or eliminate them. Yet there is no satisfactory general explanation of why the family patterns of black Americans are so different from those of the white majority, and social programs have not reduced the growing divergence between the two groups.

Interracial differences have often been the object of social research but have not always become an issue on the public agenda. Differences in the family patterns of blacks and whites have received public attention because a large number of black families do not conform to the traditional patterns of marriage and family formation. This is alarming because it is widely assumed that life in the "traditional" nuclear family is an important prerequisite of social and economic success in American society. As a consequence, it has been argued that "deviant" family patterns are largely responsible for the social and economic disadvantages that have plagued black Americans (cf. McLanahan, 1985). Public debate has focused on the sources of black–white differences in family relations and on the appropriate strategies for eliminating them.

There are some striking parallels between the debate about the consequences of racial differences in family formation and maintenance and the debate over the implications that differences in the "feminist" and traditional conceptions of the family have for life in American society. First, just as nontraditional family forms are assumed to be responsible for the disad-

Henry A. Walker, Ph.D. Department of Sociology, Stanford University, Stanford, California.

vantaged position of black Americans, it is assumed by some that the women's movement will result in the demise of the American way of life. One of the principal tenets of the conservative position (see Cohen & Katzenstein, Chapter 2 in this volume) is that progress toward women's equality is made at the expense of the traditional family. Consequently, the women's movement threatens the basic social and economic fabric of American society.

A second parallel is found in the arguments advanced to account for the emergence of nontraditional family life. Racial differences in family patterns are often attributed to a black cultural system that neither promotes nor sustains the traditional family. Similarly, it is argued that the contemporary family is being undermined by a system of values and beliefs—what might be called a "feminist culture"—that, if not openly hostile to the traditional family, does not support or sustain it.

The remainder of this paper provides a detailed historical examination of patterns of family formation and maintenance among black and white Americans. Census data will be used to demonstrate that: (1) until recently blacks and whites have exhibited patterns of marriage and family formation that are remarkably similar, (2) historical data are generally inconsistent with arguments that attribute existing racial differences to differences in culture, and (3) historical patterns are consistent with an exchange or "marriage market" argument. The paper concludes with a discussion of the public policy implications of the analysis.

BLACK FAMILIES VERSUS WHITE FAMILIES: THE CONTROVERSY

There has been serious sociological research on the black family for at least 80 years. Dubois (1899) devoted several chapters to discussions of marital status and family living in his pioneering sociological investigation, *The Philadelphia Negro*. A decade later, he published *The Negro American Family* (Dubois, 1908) as part of the Atlanta University series. Other important landmarks of scholarship on the black family include the works of Frazier (1932, 1939), Billingsley (1968), and Gutman (1976). But research and writing on the black family virtually exploded during the decade that began in 1970, when more than 50 books and 500 articles on the black family and family life were published. The research published in that period represented a more than five-fold increase in the then existing literature on black family life (Staples & Mirandé, 1980).

A significant portion of the recent literature has appeared as a direct response to the Moynihan Report (Moynihan, 1965). When simplified, the report offered two principal theses:

1. Patterns of marriage and family maintenance among black Americans are fundamentally different than those found among the white majority.

2. The basic patterns of marriage and family maintenance observed among black Americans are, in large part, root causes of the serious social and economic dislocation which blacks suffer.

While the first thesis has not gone unchallenged, it is the second thesis that has generated a firestorm of controversy. The residue of the debate—and the public policy concerns it raised—remains with us today. There is no consistent support for the proposition that growing up in a nontraditional family has serious social and economic consequences. Nevertheless, the fact that blacks exhibit marriage and family patterns that are significantly different from those of the white majority and also experience a disproportionate share of social and economic problems has been cited as evidence of a causal link between family life and social and economic success.

Moynihan pointed to higher rates of (1) marital dissolution, (2) illegitimacy, (3) households with female heads, and (4) women's labor-force participation among blacks as evidence for the first thesis. While the Moynihan report noted that racial differences in patterns of marriage and family maintenance were growing, it was suggested that contemporary patterns reflected relatively long-standing differences. What follows is an assessment of the extent to which Moynihan's first thesis has been true historically and an examination of the more general issue of why traditional patterns of marriage and family are changing.

MARRIAGE AND FAMILY DISRUPTION: 1890–1980

Much of the literature that appeared as a response to Moynihan's work is stridently ideological, and its scientific and practical utility is questionable (on this point see Allen, 1978; Staples, 1974). Moynihan's ideas were based primarily on data collected for the census of 1960, and current data are consistent with his argument that the traditional black family was "crumbling." In 1980, 58.6% of black men and 65.5% of black women 15 years and older were ever married. Those figures are substantially lower than the comparable figures for white men and women and represent a dramatic decline from levels reported in 1960. In 1980, 29.5% of ever-married black women and 22.7% of ever-married black men were either separated or divorced. Among ever-married white women, 10.7% were either separated or divorced while only 9.2% of ever-married white males were separated or divorced. As a consequence of a reduced likelihood of marriage and a greater likelihood of marital disruption, the proportion of all black persons who were married and living with their spouses had plummeted. In addition, although the fertility of black women had fallen, the proportion of births that were illegitimate approached 50% and the proportion of black households headed by women nearly doubled from 1960 to 1980.

The differences reflected in these data are substantial and important. There is little wonder that some students of the family have suggested that patterns of black family life should be considered separately from those of the majority (cf. Cherlin, 1981). But a reliance on cross-sectional data may obscure the processes that produce the patterns. Researchers have tended to devote considerable attention to racial differences while neglecting important similarities. As a result, separate consideration of the patterns that exist among black and white Americans has impeded understanding of more general changes in patterns of marriage and family maintenance.

Much of the controversy that surrounds the Moynihan Report concerns the language he used to characterize the dramatic changes he observed. He reported that the black family was "crumbling" and characterized the black family of that era as a "tangle of pathology." Whether justified or not, Moynihan's characterization was interpreted as an attack on black family life and predictably, debate on the issue has been ideological and acrimonious. I agree with Cherlin (1981) and others who suggest that recent changes in patterns of marriage and family maintenance have resulted in greater differences between black and white families than were true historically. But the discussion that follows suggests an even stronger statement: Recent changes in patterns of marriage and family maintenance have established significant racial differences where few or none existed.

Patterns of Marriage and Family: 1890–1980

It is generally assumed that "successful" family experiences are important for success in other societal institutions, and that unsuccessful family experiences have deleterious consequences. While these assumptions—which comprise the second of Moynihan's theses—have been challenged on several fronts (cf. the collection of papers in Rainwater & Yancey, 1967; but also Heiss, 1975; Hill, 1971; Jackson, 1973), it would appear that Moynihan's first thesis has been generally accepted. That is, the patterns of family living among blacks and whites are fundamentally different and have been for some time.

The nuclear family consisting of a heterosexual couple and their children is the prototypical American family (see Davis, Chapter 4 in this volume). Nuclear families are generally created through marriage—a social-sexual bond that is recognized and/or legitimized by a society, some subgroup of society or by a public institution such as the state or church. All known societies have some form of family system (Goode, 1963), but it has generally been assumed that the underpinnings of African family life were destroyed during slavery. During that historical period, blacks were usually not permitted to marry or to establish stable families. Hence, it is argued that blacks had no tradition of marriage and family living at emancipation. Several investigators (Blassingame, 1972; Furstenberg, Hershbert, & Modell, 1975; Gutman, 1976) have called that thesis into question by using historical records to demonstrate that substantial numbers of black slaves lived in intact, stable families. However, the extent to which such families existed is not known.

This general set of assumptions about the black family has informed much of the research on black family life. For example, one of the principal concerns of the Moynihan Report was the extent to which the black family—which was presumed to be historically different from the white family in America—was becoming more different, that is, "crumbling." But Moynihan generally compared conditions in 1960 with conditions that existed in 1950. It is important to examine family patterns in broad historical perspective in order to understand general patterns of change in family organization and to determine how present differences in black and white family patterns have evolved over time.

Patterns of Marriage and Family Formation

The U. S. Bureau of the Census did not ask questions about marital status prior to the census of 1880 and the answers were not recorded until the census of 1890. This examination of patterns of marriage and family maintenance begins with data collected in 1890 and concludes with data from the census of 1980. It is assumed that an examination of data collected over this period will permit an assessment of the extent to which current differences are a continuation of historical patterns, and provide some insight into general trends of family living over the past century.

A couple's decision to marry can be taken as one indicator of their intention to adopt conventional patterns of family life. Because marriage plays a central role in the formation of traditional families, the extent to which group members participate in marriage is an indicator of the group's commitment to traditional family values. It has been suggested that blacks do not exhibit "typical" patterns of marriage and family formation. Hence, one important piece of information is the extent to which blacks participate in the institution of marriage. The data in Table 5.1 are the percentage distributions of ever-married and currently married persons by race and sex for the period 1890–1980.[1]

The data for the period 1950–1980 support Moynihan's basic observations. Since 1950, blacks have been less likely to report being ever-married than whites and the differences between the two groups have increased dramatically since 1960. In 1980 the difference between the groups was 12.9% for women and 13.3% for men. But the data also indicate that the differences that existed in 1950 were atypical when compared to data from earlier historical periods.

As the data reveal, the percentages of ever-married black women and men are *higher* than the figures for whites at every census from 1890 through 1940.[2] The mean differences in percentages (black minus white) for the period are 1.33% for men and 2.42% for women. Any reasonable interpretation of the data for the period 1890–1940 would suggest that the patterns of

Table 5.1. Percentage Distribution of Persons 15 and Older Ever-Married and Married by Race and Sex, 1890–1980

Marital status, race, and sex	Year									
	1890*	1900*	1910*	1920*	1930*	1940#	1950#	1960#	1970	1980
Ever-married women										
Black	69.8%	69.9%	73.1%	75.6%	76.3%	75.9%	80.5%	79.1%	72.7%	65.5%
White	69.3	68.9	70.0	71.4	72.6	73.9	81.1	82.6	79.5	78.4
White##	(65.0)	(65.3)	(67.4)	(69.1)	(70.9)	(70.7)	(78.4)	(80.5)	(76.3)	(73.8)
Black-White	.5	1.0	3.1	4.2	3.7	2.0	−0.6	−3.5	−6.8	−12.9
Ever-married men										
Black	60.1	60.4	64.4	67.3	67.7	66.5	72.4	70.3	66.0	58.6
White	60.0	60.0	61.7	64.4	65.5	66.8	75.2	76.9	74.0	71.9
White##	(55.1)	(56.0)	(59.6)	(63.6)	(64.6)	(63.8)	(71.8)	(73.8)	(69.4)	(65.7)
Black-White	.1	.4	2.7	2.9	2.2	−0.3	−2.8	−6.6	−8.0	−13.3
Currently married women										
Black	54.7	53.8	57.5	59.7	58.6	58.5	62.5	60.7	53.4	43.5
White	58.3	57.9	59.5	60.5	61.6	61.2	67.0	67.4	63.1	60.0
White##	(56.2)	(56.6)	(59.3)	(60.6)	(62.3)	(59.1)	(67.1)	(68.3)	(62.8)	(58.6)
Black-White	−3.6	−4.1	−2.0	−0.8	−3.0	−2.7	−4.4	−6.7	−9.8	−16.5
Currently married men										
Black	55.6	54.2	57.5	60.6	60.0	60.0	64.8	62.7	57.8	47.5
White	55.7	55.1	56.7	59.1	60.1	61.3	67.7	71.3	68.2	64.5
White##	(51.5)	(51.8)	(55.2)	(58.9)	(59.9)	(59.1)	(65.7)	(68.9)	(64.3)	(59.1)
Black-White	−0.1	−0.9	0.8	1.5	−0.1	−1.3	−2.9	−8.6	−10.4	−17.0

*White = Native born of native parents;

#White = All whites and Mexican; black = nonwhite;

##Age standardized against the black population

marriage and family formation exhibited by blacks and whites were essentially the same. But more importantly, the data indicate important changes in marriage patterns. The proportion of both populations that had married at least once increased from 1890 until the period after World War II when it began to decline. The peak year for blacks was 1950 when 72.4% of men and 80.5% of women were ever married. The peak in marriages in the white and 80.5% of women were ever married. The peak in marriages in the white population is reflected in the 1960 census when 76.9% of men and 82.6% of women reported having been married at least once. Racial differences in the timing and magnitude of the recent trend toward fewer marriages are indicated by data for the period 1950–1980. Blacks are significantly less likely to be ever married and the mean differences are 7.68 for men and 5.95 for women.

A similar pattern is revealed by an examination of data for persons who are currently married.[3] From 1890 through 1950 there was a general increase in the percentages of men and women who were currently married, although the percentages for blacks are generally lower than those for whites. The percentage married among blacks reached its modern zenith in 1950 when 64.8% of black men and 62.6% of black women were married. The percentage of whites who were married continued to rise until 1960 when 71.3% of men and 67.4% of women were married.

Racial differences in the percentage married during the period 1890–1940, when the percentage of those ever married was increasing, are not large. Black women are consistently less likely to report being currently married than white women, although the mean percentage difference for the period 1890–1940 is only 2.70. After 1950 there is much greater divergence in the percentage of women reporting that they are married. The mean difference for the period 1950–1980 is 9.35% with a difference of 16.5% reported in 1980.

There is a similar pattern for men. Prior to the 1950 census the differences in percentages of white and black men who report that they are currently married are small. For the period 1890–1940 the mean difference in percentages is 0.78%. Furthermore, there is no consistent pattern of differences between the two groups of men. Some censuses report proportionately more black men who are married while other censuses report more married white men. After 1950 there is a consistent pattern of proportionately fewer black men being married. The mean difference in percentages for the period 1950–1980 is 9.73% with the difference standing at 17.0% in 1980.

The difference between the percentage ever married and the percentage currently married is one indicator of marital disruption. The fact that there were proportionately more ever-married blacks than whites from 1890 through 1940, while proportionately fewer blacks were married is an indicator of greater dissolution among black families. While the greater post-war decline in the percentage ever married among blacks would tend to reduce the numbers of families which can be disrupted, the even sharper decline in percentage currently married indicates significant changes in patterns of marriage and family maintenance during the post-World War II period.

Marital Instability

Marital instability, the extent to which couple-headed families are disrupted or dissolved, is another aspect of family life on which there are significant racial differences. It has been supposed, at least since Frazier (1932, 1939), that blacks had a higher incidence of separations and divorces than whites. Frazier attributed this to several causes, including the absence of a tradition of stable family life, and family dislocation associated with large-scale migration, that is, rural to urban migration in the early part of this century and large-scale migration from south to north. Because the majority of children remain with their mothers after family disruption, significant variation in family breakups is associated with increased numbers of families headed by women. It is argued that the destabilizing effects of those factors have been buttressed by a matriarchal tradition—an artifact of African kinship systems that has survived to the present—that facilitates the formation of female-headed households.

Marriages may end in a number of ways but not all marital disruption is due to family instability. For example, one member of a couple may die and leave the partner widowed. The problem of widowhood is not generally thought of as marital instability, even though it has significant impact on the family profiles of social groups. The more usual indicators of family breakups are numbers or percentages of families that have experienced desertion, separation, or divorce.

The data in Table 5.2 are the differences in percentages ever married and currently married by race and sex for the period 1890–1980. These data indicate the percentages of persons whose marriages are legally dissolved. It is important to note that the percentage differences between the races are relatively small over the entire period of observation. However, there is a consistent pattern of more dissolution among blacks of both sexes than among whites. There are also consistent sex differences. Nevertheless, there is no consistent pattern for the magnitude of racial differences when data for the sexes are examined separately. The differences for men are slightly higher in more recent years than in the period 1890–1940, but exactly the opposite is true of women. What accounts for the differences that are observed?

The data in Table 5.3 are the percentages of all men and women who are widowed or divorced by race and sex. There are several general tendencies exhibited in these data:

1. Despite fluctuation from one measurement period to another, the percentage of persons who are widowed in 1980 is slightly lower than the comparable figure for 1890. The only exception is among white women where the percentage reported in 1980 (11.98%) is higher than the 1890 figure (10.64%).

2. There has been a significant increase in the percentage of persons who are divorced.

3. Black women are more likely to have been widowed or divorced than white women throughout the period. The single exception is found in the data for 1940 when proportionately fewer black women were divorced than white women.

Table 5.2. Difference in Percentages of Persons 15 and Older Ever-Married and Married by Race and Sex, 1890–1980

Sex and race	Year									
	1890*	1900*	1910*	1920*	1930*	1940#	1950#	1960#	1970	1980
Women										
Black	15.09	16.03	15.70	15.90	17.73	17.37	17.95	18.38	19.31	22.02
White	11.02	11.07	10.40	10.92	10.96	12.64	14.13	15.11	16.42	18.37
Black-White	4.07	4.96	5.30	4.98	6.77	4.73	3.82	3.27	2.89	3.65
Men										
Black	4.57	6.18	6.89	6.72	7.71	6.52	7.57	7.48	8.18	11.07
White	4.25	4.87	5.05	5.30	5.38	5.52	7.46	5.56	5.73	7.43
Black-White	0.32	1.31	1.84	1.42	2.33	1.00	0.11	1.92	2.45	3.64

*White = Native born of native parents;

#White = All whites and Mexican; black = nonwhite

4. Black men are consistently more likely to be either widowed or divorced than white men throughout the period of observation. The exceptions to this generalization are the figures for divorce in 1890 and 1950. In 1890, when relatively few men of either race were divorced, the percentage difference is small. The percentage difference in 1950 is 1.35.

The data in Table 5.3 are important to an understanding of the racial differences found in Table 5.2. The likelihood of divorce has increased dramatically for women of both groups since 1890, and the gap between black and white women increased by 2.77 percentage points. But at the same time the gap between the percentages of women widowed decreased by 3.81 percentage points. Hence, among women the racial difference in marital dissolution is slightly less in 1980 than it was in 1890.

The tendencies among men are different from those observed among women. Although black men were slightly less likely to be divorced than white men in 1890, they were generally more likely to be divorced for the remainder of the period studied. The gap between the two groups increased by 2.23 percentage points from 1890 to 1980. But while the data indicate a general decline in the proportion of men who are widowed, the decline has not been as great for black men. As a consequence, the percentage difference increased by 1.11 points and among men the racial gap in marital dissolution is greater in 1980 than in 1890.[4]

On balance, the racial differences in marital dissolutions are not very great. The differences in 1980 were 3.65 percentage points for men and 3.64 points for women. But marriage is a social and legal status that may not accurately reflect living patterns. It has been argued that black marriages are

Table 5.3. Percentage Distribution of Persons 15 and Older Widowed and Divorced by Race and Sex, 1890–1980

Sex, race, and marital status	Year									
	1890*	1900*	1910*	1920*	1930*	1940#	1950#	1960#	1970	1980
Women										
Black										
Widowed	14.67	15.35	14.81	14.83	15.93	15.83	15.36	14.70	14.17	12.83
Divorced	0.42	0.67	0.89	1.07	1.80	1.53	2.59	3.66	5.13	9.20
Total	15.09	16.02	15.70	15.90	17.73	17.36	17.95	18.36	19.30	22.03
White										
Widowed	10.64	10.62	9.83	10.18	9.70	11.09	11.85	12.40	12.82	11.98
Divorced	0.38	0.45	0.58	0.74	1.25	1.56	2.28	2.71	3.60	6.39
Total	11.02	11.07	10.41	10.92	10.95	12.65	14.13	15.11	16.42	18.37
Men										
Black										
Widowed	4.33	5.76	6.23	5.93	6.29	5.49	5.59	4.88	4.67	3.70
Divorced	0.24	0.42	0.66	0.79	1.42	1.53	1.99	2.60	3.51	7.38
Total	4.57	6.18	6.89	6.72	7.71	7.02	7.58	7.48	8.18	11.08
White										
Widowed	3.98	4.50	4.51	4.59	4.18	4.23	3.33	3.38	2.97	2.24
Divorced	0.28	0.37	0.54	0.71	1.40	1.29	3.34	2.17	2.76	5.19
Total	4.26	4.87	5.05	5.30	5.58	5.52	6.67	5.55	5.73	7.43

*White = Native born of native parents;

#White = All whites and Mexican; black = nonwhite

more susceptible to disruption than white marriages. It is also argued that economic considerations might lead proportionately more black couples to separate rather than divorce. The costs of attorneys and legal procedures are prohibitive for the poor, and blacks are more likely to be poor than whites. Blacks are more likely to divorce than whites but the magnitudes of racial differences are not large. Hence, a study that examines differences in percentages of families that are legally terminated, that is, families that have experienced divorce or widowhood, but neglects separations may understate the numbers of black families that have experienced serious disruption.

Good data on separation are not available prior to the census of 1940. But the data displayed in Table 5.4 indicate that throughout the period 1940–1980 far more blacks than whites reported being married and living apart from their spouses.[5] The difference for women was 5.75% in 1940 and rose to 8.23% in 1980, when of all black women 15 and older, 10.27% reported that they were married but separated while only 2.04% of white women were married but separated. While black males are generally more likely to be separated than white males, the differences between the races are

Table 5.4. Percentage of Persons 15 Years and Older Married but Separated by Race and Sex, 1940–1980

	Female			Male		
	Black	White	Difference	Black	White	Difference
1940*	8.38	2.63	5.75	7.25	2.68	4.57
1950	9.06	1.37	7.69	6.34	1.11	5.23
1960	8.95	1.32	7.63	5.78	1.01	4.77
1970	9.54	1.51	8.03	5.67	1.09	4.58
1980	10.27	2.04	8.23	5.91	1.44	4.47

*Data for 1940 are married, spouse not present. These data include separations, desertion, and other instances in which one spouse did not live at home at enumeration.

not as large as those for women. In 1980 the difference (4.47%) was slightly more than half the difference for women.

Families Headed by Women

The importance of the data on marital instability is reflected in the percentages of families that are headed by women. As Sweet (1978) has pointed out, female-headed families can be formed in either of two general ways. The first path is represented by the woman who marries, has a child, and loses a spouse through separation, widowhood, or divorce and does not remarry. We have pointed out that black women are more likely to be widowed, divorced, and separated than their white counterparts; they are also less likely to remarry. The second path to female-headed families is typified by the woman who bears a child out of wedlock, keeps the child, and either maintains or creates a separate household. The data in Table 5.5 are the percentages of all births that are illegitimate for the period 1920–1980 by race.

Rates of illegitimacy are higher for blacks than for whites throughout the period. The proportion of all births that are illegitimate has climbed steadily for both groups since 1920, when 1.2% of white births and 11.2% of black births were illegitimate. The increase has been very sharp since 1960. In 1980 11.9% of all white births were illegitimate and nearly one half (48.9%) of black babies were born to unmarried women. To some extent, these data reflect a decline in fertility among married women of both races. But despite a ten-fold increase in the percentage of illegitimate births to white women since 1920, a black child born in 1980 was four times as likely to be illegitimate as a white child.

Table 5.6 depicts the data on female-headed households for the period 1930–1980. Throughout the period a greater proportion of black than white families are headed by women. From 1930 through 1960 about 20% of all

Table 5.5. Illegitimate Births as a Percentage of All Births
by Race, 1920–1980

Year	Black	White
1920	11.2%	1.2%
1930	9.9	1.4
1940	13.6	1.8
1950	16.8	1.7
1960	21.2	2.3
1970	37.3	5.7
1980	48.9	11.9

black families (the average is 20.5%) and 11% of all white families (the average is 10.8%) were headed by women. But while the figures for whites have remained relatively stable since 1960—11.6% in 1980—the figure for black families has doubled to 40.2%.

Sweet has suggested that, in the past, the modal path to female-headed households has been through widowhood. But there is evidence that suggests that this is changing. In 1940, 75.5% of all white females who headed households were 45 years of age or older. The comparable figure for black women was 52.2%. Hence, in 1940 the majority of female heads of households in both races were beyond normal childbearing age. By 1980 the tendency for female heads of families to be older women had been reversed in both groups. In that year, 65.3% of all black female heads of families were 44 years of age of younger and fully 42% were younger than 35. Over half of all white female heads of families (54.6%) were younger than 45 and 31.7% were 34 years of age or younger. In 1980 female heads of families were generally younger than they had been historically, and that was especially true of those who were black.

Table 5.6. Families Headed by Women as a Percentage
of All Families by Race, 1930–1980

Year	Black	White
1930	19.3%	11.2%
1940	22.6	14.5
1950	19.1	8.4
1960	20.9	8.1
1970	27.4	9.0
1980	40.2	11.6

All these data support Moynihan's general observations. In contemporary America, blacks are more likely to experience marital disruption than whites, and black families are significantly more likely to be headed by women than are white families. But patterns of family life have changed in both groups. In the period prior to 1950, black women were somewhat more likely to have been widowed than white women but racial differences have diminished since 1950. In addition, while the proportions of women who are separated or divorced have increased in both groups, black women are more often separated from their husbands than white women, and the difference has been increasing. Rates of illegitimacy have also increased for both groups over the period of observation—with gradual increases from 1920 through 1960 and very sharp increases since 1960—but black illegitimacy has always been very high when compared to whites. When taken together, the changes in patterns of divorce and separation, and dramatic increases in illegitimacy have helped to create a change in the age structure of the population of women heads of families and to create dramatic racial differences in the proportions of families headed by women.

Explaining the Differences

The historical patterns expressed in these data suggest a different set of questions than those raised by cross-sectional examinations of differences between the races. It is clear from the data presented here that blacks and whites experienced similar rates of marriage and marital disruption until relatively recently. It appears that beginning about one generation after the Civil War and continuing until World War II, blacks were as likely to marry as were whites. And even though black and white marriages experienced different rates of dissolution during that period, death was the primary cause of "failed" marriages. The racial differences that existed were due, in large part, to racial and sex differences in mortality and particularly to the higher mortality of black men compared to that of women and white males.

But patterns in the two groups have diverged since World War II and the rate of divergence has increased with time. This is true even though patterns of family living are changing in both groups and in simliar ways. Fewer men and women were ever-married in 1980 than in 1940. Divorce has become more common among both groups and in 1980 was a more likely occurrence among men than widowhood. In addition, black couples are more likely to experience divorce than are white couples even though the percentage differences are not large. Blacks are substantially more likely to separate than are whites and, although there are no good data before 1940, it is plausible to assume that some differences in rates of separation existed prior to that time. These observations raise important issues: First, what factors account for the long-term changes in family patterns? Second, what factors account for the differences in *rates* of change experienced by black and white families? I will offer some observations and attempt to answer those questions, but first it is important to assess the utility of the current theories that have been applied to the problem of differences in the patterns of marriage and family maintenance exhibited by blacks and whites.

Current Theories

Allen (1978) argues that literature on the black family generally fits one of three distinct ideological perspectives. Each of those perspectives can be linked to a general set of ideas that is used to account for black and white differences in family patterns. I have collapsed the three perspectives into two general categories, one of which has two variants.

The Black Family as Culturally Different

Writers who take this view argue that blacks exhibit family patterns that differ from those of whites because blacks have a different culture than the white majority. However, there are important disagreements with respect to the origins of that culture. The disagreements are expressed in two variants of the general argument:

The black family as culturally deviant. Those who take this approach, suggest that the typical family consists of a married couple and their offspring. The male is presumed to be the primary breadwinner and is expected to exert considerable power and influence over family affairs. Black family life is assumed to deviate from this pattern, in large part, because blacks have created a different culture—as an adaptation to the black experience in America—than that of the white majority. The two factors most often called upon to account for the "deviant" nature of the black family are the experiences of slavery and large scale migration. Slavery is assumed to have had a catastrophic effect on black family life. African traditions of marriage and family were assumed to have been destroyed. The ideas of family stability and permanence were presumed to be alien to slaves because biological families could be dismembered by slaveholders at any time. In addition, children of separated parents were more likely to remain with their mothers, thereby creating a tradition of slave families headed by women. Finally, the prohibition against marriage was presumed to facilitate promiscuous sexual relations and "illegitimacy."

Large-scale migration of blacks was also assumed to play a significant role in the evolution of a cultural form that is different from that of white Americans. Because the typical migrant is a young male, the effects of migration are important and immediate. Large-scale migration of males contributes to an oversupply of males in the location of destination, and families are often left behind when married men migrate for economic reasons. Hence, there are fewer opportunities for marriages to form in both area of origin (due to a large outflow of men) and in the area of destination (due to an undersupply of women). In addition, many families in the area of origin are disrupted. The net result is that populations that have high rates of migration are likely to have somewhat different patterns of family life than populations that have lower rates of migration. But it should be noted that while large-scale migration may contribute to an exaggeration of a pattern based on cultural differences, the effects of migration usually diminish with the passage of time.

The black family as culturally variant. Like those who adopt the view that the black family is culturally deviant, writers who espouse this perspective argue that the beliefs, values, and behaviors that blacks exhibit with respect to family life are different from those of the majority. But it is argued that those differences are "natural" because blacks possess a different culture than the general populace. The beliefs, values, and behaviors of blacks are assumed to be products of African cultural and kinship systems that have been slightly modified by the experience of slavery. There is strong emphasis in this perspective on the "strengths" of the family forms exhibited by blacks. The belief is that while black family forms may be different from those of the majority, they are not negative or deviant; they are as functional, as facilitative of success, for blacks as the family forms exhibited by Americans of European descent are for members of those groups.

The Black Family as Culturally Equivalent

This second perspective suggests that, in the main, black values and beliefs about family life, and the families they create are similar to those of the white majority. Those who hold this perspective assume that there are social class and regional (e.g., urban–rural or south–north) differences in values, beliefs, and behaviors. The major differences between black patterns of family behavior and those exhibited by the white majority are presumed to result from the fact that blacks are predominantly members of the lower and working classes and have different regional backgrounds than whites. An implication of this view is that the marriage and family maintenance patterns of blacks and whites will become more similar as differences in the social class and regional backgrounds of the two groups are reduced.

In brief, the three arguments suggest that black family patterns differ from family patterns found among whites because (1) black family patterns are the result of cultural adaptation to the unique experience of blacks in America (i.e., the experiences of slavery and large-scale internal migration since the Civil War); (2) black family patterns are "survivals" (cf. Herskovits, 1941) of African cultural traditions; or (3) blacks differ from whites in terms of socioeconomic status and/or demographic conditions (e.g., region of residence).

Assessment of the Arguments

Black families differ from white or majority families in that: (1) Black families are less likely to be headed by married couples than white families, and black couples who head families are more likely to experience marital disruption and dissolution than are white couples; (2) women are more likely to play a dominant role in black families than in white families; and (3) black families are more likely to experience illegitimate births than white families. It is these differences in black and white families that are implicated as factors in the "disadvantaged" status of blacks in America. How well do the arguments advanced above account for the observed differences?

The argument that the patterns of family living exhibited by black Americans are cultural adaptations to the slave experience and to large-scale migration is not as credible today as it might have been in an earlier period. Even though there are differences in rates of marriage in data taken from the census of 1890, the first census for which such information was recorded, the differences are not large and blacks were more likely to marry than whites. As Dubois (1899) reports of Philadelphia blacks, the differences in marital patterns exhibited by northern-born blacks versus southern-born blacks—those most likely to have been directly affected by the experience of slavery—are not compelling. In addition, one would expect that the longer the interval from slavery to the point of observation, the less powerful the effects on behavior. Yet the data suggest that the condition of black families has "worsened" since emancipation, and particularly so since World War II (Cherlin, 1981).

The second component of this argument, that the great migration of blacks that began after World War I resulted in significant family disruption, is certainly consistent with historical and current thinking about the effects of mobility and migration on family patterns. There are both urban–rural, and regional differences in the marital experiences of blacks (cf. Dubois, 1908; Frazier, 1939). But the pattern of large-scale black migration shifted during the 1960s. Blacks, as did other Americans, began to move from the Northeast and Midwest to the West and South. In addition, the migration of blacks has subsided significantly when compared to earlier periods in this century. Finally, black migration has not been completely unlike migrations of other groups: While the early migrants were typically young males, later waves included whole families and, sometimes, substantial portions of whole communities (Price, 1969). Hence, one would hypothesize that members of the early migrations would experience somewhat greater family disruption and instability than those who participated in later waves. The effect on the group as a whole would be relatively dramatic changes during the early and middle periods of migration, with diminishing effects as migration slowed or ceased. Longitudinal data are not consistent with that hypothesis.

A second view, that racial differences are due largely to long-standing differences in culture, is also inconsistent with historical patterns of behavior. While there are differences in the patterns of values and beliefs of blacks and whites that might be construed as cultural in a broad sense of the term, the available evidence suggests that those differences are diminishing rather than increasing. This is true among even the poorest segment of the population—those who were believed to have been susceptible to the "culture of poverty" (Lewis, 1965)—as well as among blacks and whites who are better off economically (Irelan, Moles, & O'Shea, 1969; Wilson, 1978). But the differences in family patterns of the two groups are diverging rather than converging.

A third perspective, that the major differences that exist between blacks and whites are due to differences in social class, regional differences in residence, and other social factors has received some support in the literature. In fact, one of the more important contributions of Frazier's early work (cf. Frazier, 1932, 1939) was his demonstration that changes in socioeconomic status, consequent to movement to different residential areas in cities, had similar effects on social problems, including marital instability, among blacks as among whites. Moynihan (1965) noted important differences in the behavior of middle- and lower-class blacks and pointed to a relation between male unemployment and marital disruption. Both Dubois (1908) and Frazier (1939) pointed out the relation of regional differences and differences in tenancy (i.e., whether persons rented or owned their residences) to family patterns. There is a growing body of evidence (cf. Hannan, Tuma, & Groeneveld, 1977; Heiss, 1975; Jackson, 1971; Rodman, 1965; Scanzoni, 1971) that suggests that demographic, social, and economic factors play a more important role in determining aggregate patterns of family living than "cultural" factors.

Black Families versus White Families: Another Look

One of the central features of the contemporary profile of American family life is the increasing divergence in the proportions of blacks and whites who are single, that is, never married. While Cherlin (1981) suggests that this phenomenon can be explained in part by a declining age at first marriage for white females, that factor alone cannot account for the patterns expressed in the data. An examination of age-specific rates of marital status demonstrates that substantial differences persist well into the late 30s. Indeed, age-group data from the 1980 census suggest that there are proportionately fewer single white women than black women in every age category with the exception of those women 65 and older. There are important implications of such a trend.

One of the major effects is on rates of illegitimacy. Given an increased likelihood that women of childbearing age are single, and a concomitant increase in sexual activity among younger women, more women are at risk of becoming unwed mothers. Hence, even though fertility is declining among both blacks and whites, the proportion of all births that are illegitimate has increased. One consequence of changes in the ratio of illegitimate to legitimate births is an increase in the proportion of families headed by women. Historically, black women have been more likely than white women to keep their illegitimate children (Hill, 1971; Jackson, 1973). In turn, children who are members of single-parent households are at greater risk of themselves bearing illegitimate children than are those who live with both parents (cf. Hogan & Kitagawa, 1985). The net result is that single-parent families tend to produce more single-parent families, although the reasons for this would appear to be related more to the degree of adult monitoring of behavior than to differences in personal morality (cf. Frazier, 1939, 1962; Hogan & Kitagawa, 1985).

Finally, because an overwhelming majority of single-parent families are headed by women, and women tend to be disproportionately poor, the net effect is a significant increase in the ranks of families living below the poverty line (Glick, 1981).

Explaining Changes in the Likelihood of Marriage

If there is a central issue for contemporary research on differences in black and white patterns of famly relations it is determining the factors that promote the creation and dissolution of pair relations. Some of the old answers—that contemporary black family organization is a cultural adaptation to the institution of slavery and/or the disruption of massive migration (cf. Frazier, 1932, 1939; Moynihan, 1965) or that black culture is essentially African and different from that of white Americans—is contradicted by the evidence I have presented. But more importantly, those arguments fail to address the issue of why general patterns of marriage and family maintenance are changing.

Many of the observed differences in patterns of black and white family organization are of relatively recent vintage (Cherlin, 1981). There appear to have been significant changes in black family patterns since World War II, with similar, although not nearly as dramatic, changes occurring among the white majority. Indeed, there are much greater differences in the family profiles of black and white Americans in 1980 than there were in 1890. One would suppose that the effects of traditional African culture (Herskovits, 1941), of the slave experience, or of internal migration would have been more immediate and certainly would not have waited for many decades to appear. What is left are arguments that place a major emphasis on elements of the social context as explanatory factors (cf. Heiss, 1975; Jackson, 1971; Lieberson, 1980).

The Marriage Market
It is useful to think of marriages as market transactions. That is, potential mates enter the market with a set of attributes that they would bring to a

marriage and with some preferences for attributes they would like in a mate. It is reasonable to suggest that the "market conditions" that blacks and whites encounter are different, that the market conditions are dynamic, and that the rates at which those conditions change are different for the two groups.

One of the important features of the market is the supply and demand of potential spouses. Over time, women, and black women in particular, have encountered a market that is increasingly disadvantageous for them. Since 1890, among blacks 15 and older, the sex ratio—the number of males per 100 females—has fallen precipitously from approximately 97.4 to below 81.9 (cf. Guttentag & Secord, 1983; Jackson, 1971). There has been similar, but not as dramatic, change for native-born whites of native parents. Within that group the sex ratio has fallen from 103 (an oversupply of men) to 91.2. The current sex ratios in the prime marriageable ages 20–44 are more disparate. In 1980, the sex ratio for blacks in that age group was 82.6 compared to 98.5 for whites. Hence, for today's women of marriageable age, there are fewer men available as potential mates than in earlier times. Although interracial marriages comprise only a small proportion of all marriages, there has been a dramatic increase in such marriages over the past decade, and they are much more likely to involve black grooms than black brides (U. S. Bureau of Census, 1983a). As a consequence, the "marriage squeeze" (Glick, Heer, & Beresford, 1963) that has disadvantaged black women for decades is even more critical today.

Other Market Conditions

An exchange conception suggests that a low (male to female) sex ratio would result in a lower likelihood of women marrying or remarrying, but that fact alone does not account for the growing tendency of men to remain unmarried.[6] We must look to other factors to explain this growing trend.

In a society that places high value on work status, many black men and women bring little to the marriage marketplace. Black unemployment has been consistently double that of whites since World War II. As a result, a large proportion of black men and women are less attractive from an economic perspective as potential mates. It might be expected that black men and women would be more reluctant to enter into long-term relations if they believed that those who are economically disadvantaged are less attractive as potential mates and that they could not provide for the families that they would create.

In general, aggregate data support such expectations. During the prewar year 1930, 32.3% of black men and 34.5% of white men aged 15 and older were single. In 1980, only 28.1% of white men in this age group were single while 41.4%, over two fifths, of black men were single. During that period labor-force participation rates for black men have fallen below those of white males and unemployment among black males has risen from figures equal to or lower than that of white men to figures that are consistently double those experienced by white males.

In the same vein, until very recently, black women were less likely to rely on men as their sole support than were white women. In 1940, 37.8% of black women were in the labor force and 32.3% were employed, compared to only 24.1% of white women in the labor force and 21% employed. By 1980, the two groups were about equal in labor-force participation and employment with 51.3% of white women and 53.4% of black women in the labor force and 47.7% and 46.3%, respectively, having been employed.

There are important consequences of the increased labor-force participation of American women and particularly that of married women with young children. Women need not rely on men as their sole source of support and as a consequence need not tolerate less than satisfactory relations with men. This is especially true of black women, for over the period from 1940 to 1980 there has been a general decline in the labor-force participation of black men and a dramatic increase in the proportions of males who are unemployed. While chronic unemployment undoubtedly plays an important role in rates of marital dissolution (cf. recent data on experiments with income maintenance, e.g., Hannan et al., 1977; as well as Moynihan, 1965), it is also likely that it is an important factor in the rising age at first marriage among black men and women.

Finally, even though neither women nor black men earn as much as white males, there have been important changes in the wage structure of our society. The wages paid to women and to black men entering the labor force, when expressed as a percentage of the wages paid to white men have increased over the past 2 decades. This development has been especially important for the most highly educated blacks. College-educated blacks of both sexes often earn *starting* salaries that are equal to, and in some instances higher than, those paid to whites with comparable levels of education and training. However, the relative improvement for black women has been greater than the relative improvement for either black men or white women. As a consequence, there has been a greater reduction in the male to female disparity in wages among blacks than among whites.[7]

These changes in the wage structure can affect the marriage market and marital behavior in two ways: First, a reduction in the male to female wage ratio has the effect of further reducing women's dependence on men (Scanzoni & Szinovacz, 1980). Such an alteration in dependency relations would suggest both a lower incidence of marital bonding and less tolerance (on the part of women) of unsatisfactory pair relations. Those tendencies should be greater among blacks than whites due to the lower disparity in wages. Second, the mean wage for all women is less than the mean wage earned by men. But it is likely that the "costs" of leaving a relationship are perceived differently by black and white women. Because average black earnings are lower than those of whites, the combined earnings of a black couple are likely to be considerably less than the earnings of a white couple with a similar background. As a consequence, even though a black woman may "fall" into poverty if she is separated or divorced (and the likelihood is that she will), in all probability she will not have as far to fall as her white counterpart. Hence, differences in the standards of living experienced by the two groups are likely to have important effects on marital stability, and those differences are heightened by the lower wage disparity among black couples. In addition, some investigators (cf. Ladner, 1971; Stack, 1974) suggest that black women who head families have more social and economic support available to them from other family, kin, and their communities than do members of the white majority. If such findings are generally true, black women should be less likely to continue in unsatisfactory marital relationships than white women.

POLICY IMPLICATIONS

There has been considerable attention paid to the role of black family instability in creating the lower educational and occupational attainments of blacks and the high rates of crime and delinquency experienced by the black community. It has been supposed that an attack on these problems could be made on two fronts. First, the black family could be "strengthened." That is, some strategy could be devised to stabilize black marriage and family relations. Such programs would, it is presumed, encourage single blacks to marry and help married couples to remain married.

Second, deficits that blacks suffer due to the current "instability" of black family life could be reduced. This philosophy spawned a number of programs in the 1960s, such as Project Head Start and massive bussing for school integration. It was assumed that black families could not give their children the preschool training necessary for success in schools, nor could they successfuly compete for homes in "better" school districts. The limited success of such programs, in either limited implementation or in production of results, need not be detailed here.

An examination of historical data suggests a different approach. Such data clearly demonstrate that racial patterns of marriage and family maintenance were highly similar from 1890 to 1950. Blacks formed stable pairing relations, at times against seemingly insurmountable difficulties (Blassingame, 1972; Gutman, 1976). The proportion of persons ever married rose in both groups until after World War II. The major differences that exist today (with the possible exception of differences in rates of separation) have generally appeared in the post-war period. There is no credible evidence that suggests that cultural differences have widened since 1890. In addition, while the black population changed from predominantly rural and southern in 1890 to urban and northern by 1950, one would expect that migration enhanced rather than harmed their economic circumstances. If that is the case, an exchange interpretation is consistent with the fact that the proportion ever married rose until 1950.

But other social conditions have changed dramatically. Furthermore, some changes in social, demographic, and economic factors that might influence changes in traditional patterns of marriage and family formation have occurred at different rates in the black and white communities. The sex ratio has declined significantly since 1890. The decline has been substantially greater among blacks than among whites. Hence, there was less of a marriage squeeze for black women in 1890 than there is today (Guttentag & Secord, 1983; Jackson, 1971).

The population has become more urbanized since 1890 and the black population is among the most urbanized in the United States. Blacks are overwhelmingly concentrated in the largest urban centers. Urbanization would appear to have played an important role in reducing the level of women's economic dependency on men. Urban areas offer improved job opportunities for women as well as for men. But there have been important changes in the occupational structure since World War II.

While black women have always participated more fully in paid employment than white women, there has been a continuing increase in the labor force participation of black women. In addition, the wage disparity between black women and men has been reduced significantly. Finally, black males who had a history of high labor-force participation and high employment prior to World War II, have had lower labor-force participation and dramatically lower rates of employment since that time. Since 1947, black males have consistently had rates of unemployment twice that of white males. The decline of blue-collar industry in large urban centers and the expansion of service and white-collar industry has had positive effects on the economic position of all women. But they would appear to have more effects on blacks than on whites.

The substantial demographic, social, and economic changes that the black population has experienced since the end of the Civil War have undoubtedly had their effects on the alteration of the "traditional" black family. It is clear from the data that compared to whites, patterns of marriage and family formation among blacks *are* different. But it is important to recognize that the major differences have emerged only recently, and that the rate of differentiation is accelerating. It is also important to note that many of the changes that black families have experienced are also observed among whites. Fewer white men and women are marrying, and those who marry are doing so at later ages. The illegitimacy rate for whites has also risen. None of these tendencies are exhibited to the same degree as they are in the black population. Similarly, the white population has experienced many of the same social, demographic, and economic changes as blacks, even though the magnitude of those changes has not been as dramatic as that experienced by blacks.

If the patterns we observe in contemporary black families have emerged due to changes in conditions in the marriage market, as my argument suggests, the family can only be "strengthened" by strengthening the individuals who join together to create them. Black men and women are victims of the vestiges of racism that persist in our society. In addition, black women are further disadvantaged by the subordinate status of women. There are several steps that might be taken to correct these deficiencies.

It would appear that creating racial parity in the workplace is a critical first step toward improving the economic strength of the black family. That is, a significant reduction in the rates of unemployment and underemployment of blacks—and particularly of black males—and of women is crucial to making black men and women more attractive as potential marriage partners. Wage parity (i.e., equal pay for equal work) is just as important. Despite recent improvement in the wages and salaries paid to black workers, the average wage of full-time black workers lags behind that of the average white worker. But this issue is of interest to women as well as to blacks. Two fifths of all black families are headed by women, and the majority of such families are poor. And while only 12% of white families are headed by women, those families are also inordinately impoverished. Families headed by women are poor primarily as a result of the lower wages paid to women who earn their living in the marketplace.

Many problems that are associated with families headed by women (e.g., illegitimacy, lower educational and occupational attainments, and delinquency) are more correctly attributed to their poverty than to the gender of the family head. That is, children of such families are more likely to encounter difficulty in school and with authorities due to problems associated with poverty than they are to get into difficulty because a woman is the family head.

There is no guarantee that strengthening the economic positions of blacks and women will reverse the trend toward fewer couple-headed families. A marriage-market argument would suggest that further reduction of women's dependence on men would result in more not fewer one-parent households. The "conventional marriage" has not generally been advantageous to women. It is quite likely that the incidence of couple-headed families will increase only after men and women have renegotiated family roles so that women are equal partners in such relationships. That is, the traditional role of woman as housewife that is currently undergoing redefinition (see Davis, Chapter 4 this volume) will probably have to become less central in the pairing relation. Tanner (1974) has noted, as have others, the extent to which black women have deemphasized the housewife role and the similarities that black women share with women in societies in which women enjoy more advantaged social positions. A marriage-market argument suggests that the increasing economic independence of women should enhance their ability to redefine the role.

Reducing the wage disparity between men and women should make conventional marriages less likely. One effect of women's declining economic dependence on men has been to provide them the option of creating lives independently of men. Similarly, rates of illegitimacy may continue to rise. There are small but growing numbers of women who opt to give birth and to raise children without having a long-term relationship with a man. While single-parent families may not be "normative," neither are they inherently bad. The evidence suggests that it is predominantly their poverty that creates disadvantage for their members. But whatever their effects on the formation and maintenance of couple-headed families, the conditions of blacks and women in American society require material improvement. The social and economic subordination of women would appear to be buttressed by the traditional couple-headed, male-dominated family. Ironically, the twin disadvantages of racial subordination and a low sex ratio would appear to have forced black women to become somewhat more independent of men earlier than white women. A marriage-market argument implicates these factors, in the "deterioration" of black families. But the growing independence of the majority of women and the assessment of historical tendencies suggests that white families are following similar trends. Others (c.f. Clark, 1983; Jackson, 1973) have suggested that white family patterns are simply lagging behind those of blacks. That notion is also consistent with the marriage-market argument. Some will make the inference from this discussion that women's inexorable drive for social and economic equality with men portends the end of the couple-headed family. Others, this author among them, see that movement as the dawn of a new era in which women and men can live together in more stable and egalitarian relationships.

NOTES

1. The age distributions of the black and white populations have been and continue to be different. One could argue that the differences in patterns of marriage are due to differences in the age distributions of the populations. Age-standardized data are included in Table 5.1 to demonstrate that this is not the case. The standardized data can be interpreted to suggest what the black population would "look like" if it had the same age distribution as the white population; or alternatively, what the white population would look like if it had the same age-specific distribution of marital status as blacks.

The data were standardized by multiplying the age-specific white population by the proportion that was black in each age-specific marital status. The standardized age-specific distribution was divided by the total white population to yield the standardized percentages reported in Table 5.1.

2. When age-standardized data are used for comparison, blacks are more likely to have been ever married through the 1950 census.

3. Beginning with 1940, the datum "married" included only those persons who were married *and* residing with their spouse. To facilitate comparisons, the data in Table 5.1 have been modified to include all married persons whether or not the spouse is present.

4. A recent paper by Watkins, Menken, & Bongaarts (1987) describes the effects that changes in mortality have on marital status. Substantial reductions in mortality since the turn of the 19th century have raised the average number of years that marriage cohorts can expect to spend in a marriage by approximately 8 years. This improvement exists despite significant changes in rates of divorce and separation.

5. Data for 1940 are "spouse absent," which includes desertions, persons in prison, and other "separations," as well as those technically separated. An examination of the data for later years suggests that the data are comparable within rounding error.

6. Guttentag and Secord (1983) argue that an oversupply of women should reduce the marriage rates for men. They argue that men can acquire a number of women partners under such conditions and are reluctant to marry. They attribute this development to the greater "structural" power of men. But the argument is incomplete. Men have traditionally had the option of multiple relations, whether married or not. A decline in the proportions of men who marry would suggest a change in men's preferences for marriage when compared to remaining single. While such changes in preferences might occur, it is just as plausible to argue that men would be more likely to marry since the likelihood of their finding a more desirable mate is enhanced when there is an abundance of women.

7. There has been a substantial increase in the real incomes of full-time workers over the past 2 decades. The relative magnitudes of the increases can be compared by examining mean earnings in 1960 with earnings reported in 1981 (all figures are constant 1981 dollars). Mean incomes for 1960 (1981) are $17,631 ($23,875) for white men, $10,615 ($17,395) for black men, $9,770 ($14,079) for white women, and $6,788 ($12,627) for black women.

It is women's income as a percentage of men's income that is important to the arguments presented here. In 1960, the figure was 63.9% for black women and 55.4% for white women. In 1981, the figures had risen for women of both groups, but the improvement was substantially greater for black women who were earning 72.6% of the wages earned by black men while white women only earned 59% of the wages paid to white men.

REFERENCES

Allen, W. (1978). The search for applicable theories of black family life. *Journal of Marriage and the Family, 40*: 111–129.

Billingsley, A. (1968). *Black families in white America*. Englewood Cliffs, NJ: Prentice-Hall.

Blassingame, J. W. (1972). *The slave community: Plantation life in the antebellum South*. New York: Oxford University Press.

Cherlin, A. (1981). *Marriage, divorce, remarriage*. Cambridge, MA: Harvard University Press.

Clark, R. (1983). *Family life and school achievement*. Chicago: University of Chicago Press.

Dubois, W. E. B. (1899). *The Philadelphia Negro*. Boston: Ginn & Co.

Dubois, W. E. B. (1908). *The Negro American family*. Atlanta: Atlanta University Press.

Frazier, E. F. (1932). *The Negro family in Chicago*. Chicago: University of Chicago Press.

Frazier, E. F. (1939). *The Negro family in the United States*. Chicago: University of Chicago Press.

Frazier, E. F. (1962). *Black bourgeoisie*. New York: Collier Books.

Furstenberg, F., Hershbert, T., & Modell, J. (1975). The origins of the female-headed black family: The impact of the urban experience. *Journal of Interdisciplinary History, 6*, 211–233.

Glick, P. C. (1981). A demographic picture of black families. In H. P. McAdoo (Ed.), *Black families* (pp. 106–126). Beverly Hills, CA: Sage Publications.

Glick, P. C., Heer, D. M., & Beresford, J. C. (1963). Family formation and family composition: Trends and prospects. In M. B. Sussman (Ed.), *Sourcebook in Marriage and the Family* (2nd ed., pp. 30–40). Boston: Houghton-Mifflin.

Goode, W. J. (1963). *World revolution and family patterns*. New York: Free Press.

Gutman, H. G. (1976). *The black family in slavery and freedom*. New York: Random House.

Guttentag, M., & Secord, P. F. (1983). *Too many women.* Beverly Hills, CA: Sage Publications.

Hannan, M. T., Tuma, N. B., & Groeneveld, L. P. (1977). Income and marital events: Evidence from an income-maintenance experiment. *American Journal of Sociology, 82,* 1186–1211.

Heiss, J. (1975). *The case of the black family: A sociological inquiry.* New York: Columbia University Press.

Herskovits, M. J. (1941). *The myth of the Negro past.* Boston: Beacon Press.

Hill, R. B. (1971). *The strength of black families.* New York: National Urban League.

Hogan, D. P., & Kitagawa, E. M. (1985). The impact of social status, family structure and neighborhood on the fertility of black adolescents. *American Journal of Sociology, 90,* 825–55.

Irelan, L. M., Moles, O. C., & O'Shea, R. M. (1969). Ethnicity, poverty, and selected attitudes: A test of the culture of poverty hypothesis. *Social Forces, 47,* 405–13.

Jackson, J. J. (1971). But where are the men? *Black Scholar, 3,* 34–41.

Jackson, J. J. (1973). Family organization and ideology. In K. S. Miller & R. M. Dreger (Eds.), *Comparative studies of blacks and whites in the United States* (pp. 405–445). New York: Seminar Press.

Ladner, J. (1971). *Tomorrow's tomorrow.* Garden City, NY: Doubleday.

Lewis, O. (1965). *La Vida: A Puerto Rican family in the culture of poverty.* New York: Random House.

Lieberson, S. (1980). *A piece of the pie: Black and white immigrants since 1880.* Berkeley: University of California Press.

McLanahan, S. (1985). Family Structure and the Reproduction of Poverty. *American Journal of Sociology, 90,* 873–901.

Moynihan, D. P. (1965). *The Negro family: The case for national action.* Washington, DC: Office of Policy Planning and Research, U.S. Department of Labor.

Price, D. O. (1969). *Changing characteristics of the Negro population.* Washington, DC: U.S. Bureau of the Census.

Rainwater, L., & Yancey, W. (1967). *The Moynihan report and the politics of controversy.* Cambridge, MA: MIT Press.

Rodman, H. (1964). Middle-class misconceptions about lower-class families. In A. B. Shostak & W. Gomber (Eds.), *Blue-collar world: Studies of the American worker* (pp. 65–68). Englewood Cliffs, NJ: Prentice-Hall.

Scanzoni, J. H. (1971). *The black family in modern society.* Chicago: University of Chicago Press.

Scanzoni, J. H., & Szinovacz, M. (1980). *Family decision-making.* Beverly Hills, CA: Sage Publications.

Stack, C. B. (1974). *All our kin: Strategies for survival in a black community.* New York: Harper & Row.

Staples, R. (1974). The black family revisited: A review and a preview. *Journal of Social and Behavioral Sciences, 20,* 65–78.

Staples, R., & Mirandé, A. (1980). Racial and cultural variations among American families: A decennial review of the literature on minority families. *Journal of Marriage and Family, 42,* 887–903.

Sweet, J. A. (1978). Indicators of family and household structure of racial and ethnic minorities in the United States. In F. D. Bean & W. P. Frisbie (Eds.), *The demography of racial and ethnic groups* (pp. 221–259). New York: Academic Press.

U.S. Bureau of the Census. (1983a). *Statistical abstract of the United States: National data book and guide to sources: 1981–82.* Washington, DC: Department of Commerce.

U.S. Bureau of the Census. (1983b). *1980 census of population. Detailed Characteristics of the Population, Part 1. U.S. Summary.* Washington DC: U.S. Government Printing Office.

Watkins, S. C., Menken, J. A., & Bongaarts, J. (1987). Demographic Foundations of Family Change. *American Sociological Review, 52* 346–58.

Wilson, W. J. (1978). *The declining significance of race.* Chicago: University of Chicago Press.

6

The Interests of Feminists and Children in Child Care

KAREN SKOLD

PUBLIC POLICY AND CHILD CARE: DO THE INTERESTS OF FEMINISTS AND CHILDREN CONFLICT?

In recent American history, child care has periodically emerged as a public issue demanding a policy response. For example, during World War II, concern over the increased employment of married women led to the creation of government-subsidized child-care centers "for the duration." Similarly, in the 1960s, concern over the impact of poverty on children led to the development of programs such as Head Start.

Today child care is again becoming an important issue for public attention. One reason is that never before have so many mothers of such young children been in the labor force. In 1985, more than half of all mothers with children under age 1 were employed (Hayghe, 1986; also see Chapter 4 by Davis and Chapter 8 by Strober). The most dramatic change in women's employment in recent years has occurred among mothers of young children for whom the cultural prescription to stay home has been the strongest. Part of the growing concern about child care reflects unease about the wisdom of this trend.

Another change has been the entry into employment of middle-class mothers. Before World War II, it was unusual for middle-class married women to work outside the home, whether they had children or not. By the 1950s, the typical working woman was married and middle class, rather than young, single, and poor. In 1980, middle-income families were the most likely to have mothers in the labor force. Because of this, the perception of child care as an issue linked with poverty is beginning to change. The difficulties of making adequate arrangements for child care are experienced by families across the economic spectrum.

Part of the renewed concern with child care is prompted by public response, both positive and negative, to issues raised by the women's movement in the 1970s. While feminists have sought equality both in the public

Karen Skold, Ph.D. Institute for Research on Women and Gender, Stanford University, Stanford, California.

113

arena and in the private domain of the family, critics have questioned whether women's freedom would be won at the expense of their children. Questions regarding the social cost of child care have been raised by commentators across the political spectrum. For example, Valerie Suransky, who describes herself as both a child advocate and feminist, claims that "one of the painful paradoxes of the women's liberation movement is that the quest for human rights has resulted in the oppression of children, for the pursuit of liberation has often been waged at the cost of the early 'containment' of children" (1982, p. 191). These are serious charges. Are they true?

The perception of a conflict of interest between feminists and children with respect to child care is a product of two basic assumptions. First, it is assumed to be in the interests of children to be cared for within their families, primarily by the mother, until they are ready for school. From this perspective, any form of substitute care (with the possible exception of part-day nursery school) is less desirable and possibly damaging to the child. The second assumption is that in order for women to gain equality with men, they must participate in work and public life in the same way men do, that is, with little accommodation to the demands of family life. From this perspective, children become a barrier to women's equal participation in society in the absence of widely available forms of substitute child care. If both these assumptions are accepted, then women are faced with the stark dilemma of sacrificing their own economic and personal interests for the sake of their children, or sacrificing the quality of their children's lives in order to meet their own needs.

Most women do not challenge these assumptions, and thus experience this dilemma in an acutely personal way. Mothers who are employed experience guilt and anxiety about leaving their children, even when they enjoy their work and have made good child-care arrangements. Mothers who are caring for their children full-time feel defensive about "not working" and resentful of the lack of respect they receive even when they are staying home by choice. An instance of our cultural ambivalence about mothers' employment is experienced by women on welfare, denounced for their dependence on society if they stay home to care for their children, but criticized as bad mothers for leaving their children if they do find work. (The irony of this is that AFDC was originally designed to allow poor women to stay home with their children.)

What is the feminist interest in child care? Feminists believe women should be able to participate fully in all aspects of society and that the fact of motherhood should not be a constraint on women's activities beyond the home. At its best, feminist thought advocates not only the integration of women into the public sphere, but also its transformation, so that neither women nor men must sacrifice family involvement for participation in the larger society (Hoffman, 1985). Feminists have also challenged the validity of the assumption that children need full-time mothering. This argument, they point out, has been used to justify a system that suppressed women's individuality within the constraints of one role. Such a system was based not on children's real needs but on the power of men as a group to define women in such narrow terms.

What, then, are children's interests? The essential fact about children is that they are completely dependent on adult care and protection for their survival, and that emotional as well as physical sustenance is required for their healthy development. The issues around which there are disagreements concern the determining of which adults should provide the care children need and under what circumstances. Feminists do not want a social system in which children's needs can be met only at the expense of women's freedom. Child advocates are concerned that the issue of equality between the sexes not take precedence over meeting children's needs for high quality care.

An additional problem in the debate is that children are not in a position to articulate their own needs and interests. Thus children's interests are always defined by adults and, as Cohen and Katzenstein have shown in Chapter 2, adult agendas often hide behind the presumed concern with children. With this caution in mind, children's interests may be defined as responsible, responsive adult care that includes a relationship with at least one adult based on love and long-term commitment. When parents are working, the child's interests would be best served by high quality care complementary to parental care. Defining high quality care is complex, but some agreed-upon components are adult–child ratio, group size, caregiver training, stability over time, as well as nonmeasurable factors such as caregiver warmth (Ruopp & Travers, 1982).

The feminist interest in child care can be summarized as an interest in equality, and the child's as an interest in quality. Conflicts between them result from the way in which work and family life are structured in our society. Despite the fact that four of every ten workers are women, work is still organized as if all workers were men with no family duties other than bringing home a paycheck. Thus work schedules and time demands take no account of the needs of young children for parental care. For example, work shifts that begin before schools open, compulsory overtime, and rotating shifts, common in many occupations, all place burdens on a worker who is also responsible for the care of young children. Professionals and managers are expected to work unlimited hours when necessary, and commitment is defined as the ability to put all other life activities aside.

Such demands assume that there is a wife at home who is responsible for the children. Since mothers of young children are the fastest growing group in the labor force, this assumption is no longer accurate. The trend for women's labor-force participation pattern increasingly to resemble that of men suggests a future where it is normal for adults of both sexes to work full-time most of their lives, with women taking only a brief leave for childbirth. In this situation, the amount of time children can spend with either parent is drastically limited. Concerns about the impact of prolonged and early separation on the bond between parent and child are felt both by working parents and child development professionals. As long as work continues to be organized without regard for the time demands of parenting, it may seem that a mother's decision to work outside the home conflicts with her child's need for a close bond with at least one parent.

The way in which family life is organized also contributes to conflicts between the interests of mothers and children. Despite the rise of the two-earner family, now more common than the breadwinner–homemaker pattern, the belief that household and children are women's responsibilities remains strong. (See Strober, Chapter 8 for a current picture of the two-earner family.) Even when wives work full-time, the ultimate responsibility for running the household and organizing family life remains with the wife. Employed mothers face time and energy demands that are not shared by men or childless women. A woman in this situation can feel that meeting the needs of her children must come at the expense of her own basic needs, such as the need for adequate sleep. As long as family life is organized with little regard to women's extra-family responsibilities, the needs of children can seem to conflict with their mothers' economic activity beyond the home.

If the source of the conflict lies in the inflexibility of work organization and the inequity of family organization, the implication is that conflict is not inevitable. Changes in the structure of work and family, some of which have already begun to appear, could reduce the strains of a situation where children are seen as barriers to women's equality and women's departure from full-time motherhood is seen as harmful to children. In order to think about structural change and how it might be influenced by public policy, it is helpful to remember that the structures that we now see as "traditional" are of relatively recent historical origin. As Davis has shown in Chapter 4, the radical separation of work and family life that we now experience as normal was one of the most dramatic changes brought about by the Industrial Revolution over the past 2 centuries (see also Zaretsky, 1976). Throughout most of human history, the notion of a conflict between the demands of work and those of family would have been incomprehensible, since for the most part families were economic units working together to produce at a subsistence level.

The conflict between the values of individualism and autonomy versus those of community and nurturance, which Cohen and Katzenstein in Chapter 2 identify in both feminist and conservative writing on the family, is also rooted in the changes brought about by industrialization. The rise of industrial capitalism coincided with political changes that emphasized individual rights and freedoms. As the competitive values of the marketplace became dominant in the public sphere, the values of nurturance and affective relationships in general were assigned to the private sphere of the family, and specifically to women. The mother–child bond was seen as symbolic of all ties based on love rather than money, which was coming to dominate relationships between men in the public sphere. The history of this dichotomy of values helps explain the intensity of reaction to subsequent social changes that altered the relationship of women to the public sphere and the mother–child tie. For example, women's long struggle for the vote was perceived by opponents as an attack on the family. More recently, the increased employment of mothers of young children and the consequent growth of nonfamily child-care arrangements has appeared to some as a threat to the continued existence of nurturance in society.

Understanding the historical and structural roots of these conflicts can help frame questions for public policy. Have alternative forms of child care developed in such a way as to adequately meet the needs of both children and working parents? Should the government, employers, and other institutions of the public sphere formulate policies that will aid in reducing the structural conflicts between work and family life? The remainder of this chapter will examine the current child-care arrangements made by working parents, point out problems and gaps in services, and analyze the strengths and weaknesses of some public policies that address the issue of child care.

CHILD-CARE ARRANGEMENTS

What are the child-care arrangements made by families when the mothers of young children are employed? To what extent do they meet the child's interest in good quality care and the feminist interest in equality? The most recent and comprehensive information on child-care arrangements comes from a Census Bureau study of the primary and secondary child-care arrangements made by employed mothers for their children under age 15, based on data from Winter, 1984–1985 (U.S. Bureau of the Census, 1987). This discussion will refer only to data on the care of preschool children. According to the 1984–1985 Survey, the most common child-care arrangement for preschool children is for the child to be cared for by a relative. Almost half (48%) of all employed mothers managed child care by keeping it within the family. The relative may be a grandparent (16%), father (16%), other relative (8%), or the mother may care for the child while she works (8%).

The most obvious advantage of parental care for the child, whether by the mother or father, is that it involves no extra expense. In addition, some families feel it is essential in order to preserve their childrearing values and avoid any weakening of parent–child bonds. When the father is the primary caretaker while the mother works, the situation potentially encourages an equal sharing of responsibility for daily care of the child. However, there are limitations to this arrangement. Mothers employed full-time, and thus sharing the breadwinner responsibility, are only half as likely as those employed part-time to rely on father care for their children under 5 (11% compared to 24%). Fathers cared for 19% of the children of married women, but for only 2% of the children of unmarried women. Among mothers who worked full-time and used father care as their primary care arrangement for their preschool child, about one quarter also used a secondary arrangement.

There are many families where the husband and wife work different shifts in order that the children be cared for by their parents. The most serious cost of this arrangement is that the couple has little or no time together. This stress may lead to marital dissatisfaction and breakup, though we do not know the extent to which this occurs. Studies of the impact of shift work on families have mostly focused on men's occupations, but shift work is considered a significant source of family stress. Shift work as a child-care strategy has only recently begun to be studied. Presser and Cain (1983) found that among couples with children who both worked full-time, 10% had no overlap in their work hours. Clearly, such an arrangement is limited to occupations where shift work is common, and is not a strategy that most families could use. For example, among fathers whose wives were waitresses and practical nurses, over 30% were the primary caretakers of their children while their wives worked (Presser, 1982, 1986).

The other form of parental care, where the mother cares for her preschool child while working, is also, not surprisingly, used more by women working part-time (13%) than full-time (5%). This arrangement too is limited by the mother's occupation. It is used most frequently by women in service sector jobs (20%). Nearly half (47%) of these mothers working and caring for their children at the same time are private domestic workers or child-care workers. Women in this situation have multiple responsibilities and no break from the demands of children while they work. They also may not benefit from the chance to socialize with other adults outside the family, an aspect of their jobs that many employed women value. However, this arrangement does facilitate nursing an infant for as long as desired, a choice that is difficult for women working in most settings. The relative costs and benefits depend on the age of the child, and whether other adults and children are present.

Another way of keeping child care within the family and minimizing costs is for grandparents or other relatives to care for the preschool child, an arrangement used by 24% of employed mothers. Many of these relatives accepted a nonmonetary payment or no payment at all for child care. Those who received monetary payment may have charged less than a nonrelative. The sex of these grandparents and other relatives is not recorded in the data, but most probably they are female. The major limitation on this form of care, then, is that it depends on the availability of female relatives who do not need or want to work outside the home and who are willing and able to care for children. Both the increased labor-force participation of women throughout the life cycle and the geographical mobility of families place limits on this arrangement. While shared values may be one advantage of this type of care, it cannot be assumed. For example, a grandmother who disapproves of mothers of young children working may not be a good choice as a caretaker, at least from the mother's point of view. These arrangements may not be stable over a long period of time, either. A grandmother who enjoyed caring for a young infant may find caring for an active toddler too tiring. An aunt may go back to work when her own children reach school age.

Single mothers are especially likely to rely on the child's grandparents or other relatives for the primary child-care arrangement for preschool children (40%). Among those who work part-time, an extraordinary 56% rely on such arrangements. This, in part, simply reflects the absence of a father to share child care but also represents a survival strategy of single mothers. Many women in that situation move back into a relative's home in order to benefit from the emotional and economic support the extended family can offer, though this practice can place a real strain on family ties.

The extent to which preschool children of employed mothers are cared for by family members as opposed by nonrelatives depends in large part on the occupation of the parents. While the average for all families was 39% for all types of care by relatives, in families where the mother was in a managerial or professional job, only 23% used such care. In contrast, 61% of families where the mother was a service worker kept child care within the family. The greater use of family-based child care by working-class families reflects the greater incidence of shift work, home-based work for the mother, and greater likelihood of living near relatives. It may also reflect the need to minimize the cost of child care (though occupation rather than income level accounted for a more pronounced difference in use of family care) and perhaps a value preference for relatives caring for their children.

Slightly over half of all preschool children are cared for by nonrelatives while their mothers work. It is these extrafamily arrangements that have most often been the subject of public awareness and debate. The 1984–1985 census data show that for the first time, care in a group setting (nursery school or day-care center) was used as often as family day-care homes as the primary child-care arrangement for preschoolers while their mothers worked. Twenty-three percent of these children are in group care, while 22% are in family day care (care in the home of a nonrelative). In-home care by a nonrelative (a "babysitter" or "nanny") is the third alternative outside the family, but it is used by only 6% of mothers.

Child care in a center-based program may be either in day-care centers (used by 14% of mothers) or in nursery or preschools (9%). Because nursery schools are usually part-time programs, mothers who work full-time often have to use a secondary child-care arrangement (32%). However, some of those who use day care also need secondary care arrangements (12%), if the center's hours do not coincide with the mother's work hours. The use of both day-care centers and nursery schools for care of the youngest child of employed mothers has increased dramatically since 1982, from 16 to 25%.[1]

A major advantage of a center is its stability as an institution. If one teacher is sick or on vacation, there are other teachers to fill in. When parents must depend on a single individual as a care provider, they have to make back-up arrangements for those times the provider is unable to care for the child. A center is also socially visible, in comparison to a family day-care home, and thus is easier to locate, and potentially easier to monitor in terms of quality. A center can offer a child the benefits of a group experience, preparation for school, facilities and equipment not usually found in a home setting, and an environment designed for children rather than adults.

Disadvantages are that children may get sick more often when exposed to children from many other families, and few centers have any provision for the care of a sick child. In addition, the stability of the institution may not be matched by stability of staff. Many child-care centers have a very high rate of turnover among teachers, due to low wages and difficult working conditions, such as having to work overtime for no pay. Other disadvantages are that many of the educationally oriented nursery schools offer only part-day programs, and are often very expensive.

The other commonly used nonfamily child-care arrangement is the family day-care home, used by 22% of working mothers. The family day-care provider is usually a woman (though occasionally a couple) who provides care for a small group of children, often including her own, in her home. Caregivers who are young and well-educated tend to be providers only briefly, while their own children are young. Those who are older and less well-educated tend to have a more sustained "career orientation" to family day care. These women often have raised their own children and find caring for the children of others their most satisfying employment option. The advantages of this form of care are that children have an opportunity to play with other children while remaining in a family-like environment. Family day-care homes are more likely to care for very young infants, toddlers, and sick children, and may be less expensive than group care centers. Disadvantages are that since the vast majority of such care is informal and unregulated, it can be difficult for parents first to locate such homes and then to evaluate and monitor their quality.

Another child-care arrangement that employed mothers use is to hire someone to come into their homes to care for their child. The main advantage is that the parents do not have to transport a small child to and from the caregiver and the child remains in a familiar environment. The main disadvantage is that it is expensive, since the children of only one family are being cared for. Cost is the main reason why this type of care is used by only 6% of employed mothers. It is also difficult to find someone to do this work. Sitters work in isolation from other adults, like family day-care providers, but they are also in someone else's home. This type of work also has overtones of a servant relationship, and women have been leaving domestic work for other jobs for a long time. The quality of care the child receives depends on how much the parents are willing and able to pay to find and keep someone who is both qualified and enjoys the work. It is an option that is most feasible for higher income families.

How well are feminist interests in equality and children's interests in quality care met by the child-care arrangements that are currently used? Overall, the most important critique from a feminist point of view is that child care is still being done almost exclusively by women, for little or no pay. The only child-care arrangement that promotes an equal sharing of child-care responsibility between women and men is when the father cares for the child while the mother works. However, this advantage must be weighed against the potential cost to the couple of time with each other. When a grandmother or other female relative looks after the child, the mother's option to work is dependent on the availability of other women to take over what is still considered the job of the mother. Such arrangements neither enhance the autonomy of women as a group nor equalize childrearing responsibilities between men and women. From a feminist point of view, the low cost of family day care is of concern because it represents a situation where women are being paid less than the real cost of their work (Kamerman, 1985). Family day-care providers usually charge what working parents can afford, not what their services actually cost (e.g. the cost to their homes of caring for others' children). Women working in isolation from other adults, as is often the case with these providers, can experience the same stress feminists have pointed out for mothers who are alone at home with their young children. This work is largely invisible and unrecognized, and family day-care providers may be seen by others as "not really working." Child-care centers potentially offer the benefits of socially recognized work, employee benefits, the chance to work with other adults, and decent pay. However, the reality for most child-care center teachers is that they are poorly paid for work which often is stressful due to poor working conditions (Whitebook, Howes, Darrah, & Friedman, 1981).

The most important critique from the child's point of view is that we know little about the quality of care most children are receiving, regardless of setting. Most of the debate on whether child care is good or bad for children has focused on the child-care center. Most of the research on this topic has been conducted at centers that meet high standards of quality care. What we now know is that good quality centers have no detrimental effects on children, and that children from deprived backgrounds may experience some benefits in their development from such programs. (Berrueta-Clement Schweinhart, Epstein, & Weikart, 1984; Ruopp & Travers, 1982).[2] But what about the child in an average center? Many children are cared for in impersonal institutional environments by staff who are overworked, ill-trained, and underpaid.[3]

Most children are not cared for in centers, however, and there is much less known about the quality of care received in family day-care homes, or in the child's own home, where the caretaker may be a relative or a sitter. In the late seventies, researchers began including family day care in their studies of the effects of day care on children, and the National Day Care Home study provided descriptive data on family day care (Ruopp & Travers, 1982). In general, it was found that caregivers provided a positive and supportive environment for children. However, a study of British child minders found that the quality of care was quite variable, with some of it clearly inadequate (Rutter, 1982). While research has shown that both center and home-based day care can provide adequate care for children, it is not clear that we know how many children are receiving excellent, fair, or poor quality care.

When children are cared for by relatives, it is often assumed that quality of care is not at issue, because of the presumed emotional bond between the child and the relative. However, it is important not to romanticize family ties when considering the possible benefits of relative care. While most families may provide children with a basic sense of security and love, families are also settings where children are sometimes abused and neglected. These are extreme cases, but there are other factors that may limit the extent to which relatives can provide high quality care for the child. For example, what else is the adult in question responsible for while caring for the child? Mothers who combine their paid work with caring for the child, fathers who do shift work and need to sleep, unemployed relatives who are looking for work, all have needs and concerns that may interfere with their ability to provide good quality child care.

ISSUES, PROBLEMS, AND GAPS IN SERVICES

What is wrong with this picture? While the wide range of alternatives and the combinations of different types of care testify to the creativity of parents and the resilience of children, the system as a whole has not been responsive to the increased need for child care. The "market" has not worked to provide the requisite services because the services are very costly and most parents cannot afford to pay what would be required for a provider to make a profit.

Child care is a major expense for working families, and it is one of the factors that affects choice of child-care arrangements and even the decision of the mother to work. Nearly three quarters (72%) of all working families with children under 5 pay cash for child care. In 1984–1985, the median cost of full-time, preschool child care was $41 per week ($2,132 per year). Thirteen percent of families with a preschool child paid $70 and over per week ($3,640 per year) (U.S. Bureau of the Census, 1987). However, Friedman (1985) cites cost data for seven major cities for January, 1985 that are considerably higher. Weekly costs for full-time care ranged from a low of $30 to $55 for family day care in Atlanta for children aged 2 to 5, to a high of $90 to $150 for infant care in child-care centers in Boston. As these figures illustrate, costs vary greatly depending on geographical location, type of care, and age of child. More recently, Friedman (1986b) estimated that most families pay about $3,000 per year for full-time care for each preschool child. Child care is the fourth largest expense for working families, after food, housing, and taxes. Families with one preschool child typically spend 10% of their income on child care, while those with two preschoolers often spend as much as 30%.

A survey of child-care information and referral agencies in one California county found that affordability was the first concern of parents who called seeking child care. Questions concerning quality of care were a luxury that only middle- and upper-income families could consider (Skold, Siegel, & Lawrence, 1983). Nearly one quarter of all working families have incomes so low that they "cannot afford anything more than a nominal payment for child care" (Winget, 1982, p. 357). Unless government or other subsidies are available, these families have severely limited options regarding child care.

The cost of child care is also a barrier to many women who would like to be working, but are not. The Census Bureau's 1982 survey found that one fourth of the 6.5 million nonworking mothers with children under 5 would look for work if they could afford child care. The percentage is higher for women in families with incomes below $15,000 (36%), and highest for single mothers (49%). While these women may face additional barriers to employment, such as lack of training, the absence of child care they can afford prevents them from even looking for work (U.S. Bureau of the Census, 1983). The high cost of child care creates a financial burden for working families, restricts the range of choices available to families using child care, and prevents many women who really need to work from seeking employment.

The main cost factor in child care is labor, comprising about 75% of all costs (Nelson, 1982). Costs could be reduced in two ways: by paying child-care workers less, or by increasing the staff–child ratio. The former simply exacerbates an already problematic situation. Child-care workers are already extremely poorly paid, given the level of responsibility, skill, and education that they have. Many who work in child-care centers are college-educated, with degrees in child development, and yet work at rates close to the minimum wage (Friedman, 1986b). This situation leads to such problems as "burnout" and high staff turnover (Whitebook et al., 1981). This, in turn, affects the quality of care that the children receive, especially their security in knowing that their teachers will continue to be there.

Increasing the staff–child ratio also would affect the quality of care that children receive. The National Day Care Study found that both group size and staff–child ratio affected the quality of interaction between adults and children (Ruopp & Travers, 1982). Children have an interest in being cared for by caretakers not overburdened by too many children. Are feminist interests and children's interests in conflict over the problem of cost? One example from the debate on federal day-care regulations in the late 1970s suggests that this may sometimes be the case. Feminists who want to encourage women's labor-force participation have an interest in promoting low-cost child care. In the debate over regulation, proprietary child-care centers argued that enforcement of child–staff ratios lower than current state requirements would drastically increase costs, and many working mothers would be priced out of the market. Some feminist organizations joined them in lobbying against federal day-care regulations (Nelson, 1982).

On the other hand, feminists also have an interest in promoting better pay for occupations that have traditionally been filled by women. The issue of "comparable worth" has raised consciousness about the extent to which female-dominated jobs are underpaid relative to male-dominated jobs that require the same level of skill or education. The occupation of child-care worker is a clear example of a job that is low paying because it is "women's work." Feminist child-care workers have also challenged the way in which job skills are defined. For example, in the *Dictionary of Occupational Titles*, the job of child-care worker was given the same skill rating as the job of a parking lot attendant. The low pay and prestige of working with children reflects the lack of value placed on this work, traditionally done by women at home for no pay.

Thus while children's interests would be best served by changes that would increase the cost of child care (better pay, better staff–child ratios, and training child-care workers), feminist interests are split between the desire to make low-cost child care available to all working women, and the desire to upgrade the rewards and prestige of occupations typically filled by women.

A second problem area concerns availability of care for certain age groups. Most child-care services that exist are for preschoolers, ages 3 to 5. Finding child care for younger children, and for school-aged children during the time they are not in school is very difficult. A study of child-care needs in Santa Clara County, California, based on inquiries to information and referral agencies, found that after affordable care, the greatest unmet needs were for infant-toddler care, followed by care for school-aged children (Skold et al., 1983). These would probably be the major unmet needs in any area of the country, given the lack of services for these age groups.

The problems of infant-toddler care (defined as children under age 2) are threefold: availability, locating such care, and affordability. Child-care centers and nursery schools traditionally serve only the older preschooler, and while more are accepting children from age 2 to 3, toilet training is often a prerequisite. Child-care centers that will accept children under age 2 are rare, and those that do have very long waiting lists. In order to be assured of space in such a center, mothers often register their children for child care before they are born. Because of the lack of center care, and because many parents prefer that their very young children be in a home environment, family day care has become the most common out-of-home care arrangement for children under 3. But not all family day-care homes are willing to take very young children, especially those under 1 year. And finding a family day-care home can be difficult and frustrating. Parents must rely on informal networks to find out about family day-care homes; and while talking to other parents may be one of the best ways to find out if a caretaker will meet one's needs, not everyone has access to such a network. In addition, infant care is more expensive than care for older preschool children. For example, in 1985, infant care in San Francisco cost $90 to $120 per week, compared to $65 to $90 per week for children aged 2 to 5 (Friedman, 1985). Centers have to charge more for infants because more staff are required to care for them than for the same number of older children. Family day-care homes, however, did not typically charge much more for infants in any of the seven major cities Friedman surveyed.

The other group for whom care is difficult to find is school-age children. These children are in school about 6 hours a day. This may not be a problem in families where the mother wants to work only part-time, or in families where the parents can arrange work schedules so that one parent can be home at the time school gets out. However, even these families may have difficulty with school holidays and vacations, which do not usually coincide with parental holidays and vacations. For families where both parents work during "normal" working hours, and for single-parent families where the mother must work full-time to make ends meet, school-age child care is needed. In recent years, services have begun to be developed for school-age children, though they are not yet sufficient to meet the needs of working families (School-Age Care Project, 1982; for policy recommendations on school-age child care see Strober and Dornbusch, Chapter 14).

Another set of problems concerns care for the sick child. Young children are often sick, usually with minor ailments. Adults in the constant presence of young children (parents, child-care workers) are also exposed to illness more often than the average adult. What do parents do when their children are sick and they have to work? A child who normally attends a day care center may not be admitted if he or she shows any signs of illness. Sometimes this leads to deception, where the parent does not inform the caretaker of the child's symptoms. This can lead to a difficult situation between the parent and child-care provider. Parents sometimes lose their child-care situations because they bring a sick child too many times. Family day-care providers are also concerned about exposure to illness. If the adult caregiver gets sick, there is no backup.

The alternative is for a parent to stay home with the sick child, but this may lead to problems with the parent's employer. Most employers allow sick leave only for the employee's illness. Parents may face a dilemma of having to fake an illness of their own in order to stay home with a sick child. A growing minority of employers now provide "personal leave," which is to be used for any purpose by the employee, including child-related leave. While this is an advance, the total number of days allowed may still be inadequate for parents of young children, who may need more days off to care for sick children and more sick leave for themselves than, perhaps, the "average" employee with no children or older children.

While parents may prefer to stay home when a child is very ill, they may feel that once the child is recovering, parental care is not needed. What is best for the parent, child, and child-care center or home, under these conditions? A handful of programs across the country provide care for mildly ill or recovering children either by providing a trained caregiver to go into the child's home or by accepting the child in a "get well" room at a child-care center or in free-standing sick-child-care centers. Very recently, there has been a flurry of growth in hospital-based sick-child-care centers. However, most parents still have no access to such services, and it is not clear which model of sick care best meets the needs of children and their parents. If such programs are to be developed more widely, the issue of cost must be addressed. Sick child care is more expensive to provide than well child care, and funds from government, employers, and the voluntary sector will probably be necessary for any expansion of such services to take place (Skold, 1985; Fredericks, Hardman, Morgan, & Rodgers, 1986).

From a feminist perspective, an additional problem is that, when a parent must stay home with a sick child, that parent is usually the mother. This reinforces the notion held by many employers that women always have to put family demands ahead of work, and are thus not reliable employees, or not suited for responsible positions. In a family in which both parents work, the message conveyed to the children is that the father's work is more important than the mother's work. Feminists would like to see care of the sick child equally shared by fathers and mothers. However, men may face even more negative sanctions than women for absences related to family needs, since men would then violate beliefs about appropriate sex roles. The willingness of individual men to share this parenting responsibility may thus be tempered by the societal response.

This raises the larger issue of the feminist interest in child care. The problem that feminists perceive is that child care is defined as the responsibility of individual women, and that neither men, nor society as a whole, take responsibility for raising the next generation. Women care for the children when they are at home, and they are also responsible for making alternative care arrangements when they are at work. It is mothers who locate child care, and coordinate the logistics of parental schedules and the often varied child-care arrangements. And, as noted above, it is usually mothers who stay home with a sick child. The difficulties of making child-care arrangements are exacerbated by the problem of finding affordable care, the lack of services for infants, school-age children, sick children, and the overall lack of coordination of the child-care service delivery system. As columnist Ellen Goodman points out, each mother is left on her own to find a child care solution, "not from a range of enhanced and attractive possibilities, but from limited options and chaos" (Goodman, 1984). The employed mother pays a price in exhaustion, stress, and lack of job advancement simply for having a job and a child, a burden not shared by working fathers, or by childless female workers.

The current child-care system in this country also leaves much to be desired in terms of the child's interest in quality care. This issue is usually framed in such a way that studies of quality in child care compare center-based care with home (maternal) care. What is lacking is information about all other types of child care that serve the majority of children. What type of child-care arrangements and parental work schedules give children the best quality time with their parents? What is the impact of multiple alternative care arrangements on children? Or of frequent changes in child-care arrangements? Research that began with the question of how best to create good quality environments for children, regardless of the setting, might prove more useful for promoting children's interests than studies comparing mother care to other care. Children need time with their mothers and with their fathers. Children also need to be cared for by adults who are doing so by choice, and who do not feel overburdened, resentful, overworked, or underpaid. Children need stability in child-care arrangements, and many features of the current child-care picture in this country promote instability. They also need care when they are sick, when school is not in session, and increasingly, when they are too young for child-care centers. Too much of the public policy debate over child care has been concerned with the desirability of mothers working, while year after year the proportion of mothers in the labor force continues to grow. It is time for public policy to recognize the economic reality of working mothers and fathers and begin concentrating on promoting the well-being of children in all care settings.

The next section suggests directions in which child care can develop to serve feminists' interests in equality at work and in the family as well as the interests of children in quality care at home and in other arrangements.

TOWARD POSSIBLE SOLUTIONS

I have argued that there is no inherent conflict between the feminist interest in equality and the child's interest in quality care; I have also argued that the current child-care situation in this country does not adequately meet either set of interests. In order to improve the quality of childen's care while enhancing equality between the sexes, two basic directions for social change are necessary: men and women (fathers and mothers) must move toward a more equal sharing of child-care responsibilities, with the ultimate goal being equal involvement with children; and society must recognize its interest in supporting and supplementing the resources of parents in fulfilling childrearing responsibilities. When the entire society looks upon children not as the private problems of parents, nor as "life-style options" chosen by some adults, but as the embodiment of the future of the society, then the societal interest in the quality of child care can be seen.

The social changes required to bring about such a broadening of responsibility for children's well-being are deep and far-reaching, but their potential benefits are great. If men are more involved in child care, women will be less often faced with the choice of sacrificing their own goals or their children's need for parental attention. The exhaustion and lack of time faced by working mothers will be alleviated when working fathers share the double burden. Children may benefit from closer involvement with their fathers, and from less dependence on mothers as the only source of attachment. Men may also benefit by sharing the provider role more equally with women, and by sharing the close involvement with children that women have enjoyed.

Greater public commitment to children will be of special benefit to women rearing children alone, helping to ease their work load and isolation. Societal involvement will also benefit women in two-parent families, so that greater paternal involvement in child care does not have to come at the expense of the couple's time together, as in the case with shift work families. And children will certainly benefit from greater societal responsibility for their welfare, so that they are not so entirely dependent on the one or two adults who happen to be their parents, and who may be more or less prepared, emotionally and financially, for the demands of parenthood. The public interest would be served by such changes, which would enable women to contribute more fully to public life without sacrificing family life, and which would help ensure that the next generation would be well cared for, regardless of the particular circumstances of their parents.

Involvement by federal, state, and local government in licensing, regulating, funding, and providing child-care services is potentially the most wide-ranging form of societal responsibility for children's care. Government is, of course, involved in all of the above activities. However, the extent of government support for child care is much less in the United States than in most European countries (Kamerman, 1981) and the current trend is toward indirect forms of support rather than direct provision of services. For example, the major federal child-care expenditure today is the child-care tax credit, which benefits primarily the middle class, while funds for providing child-care services to low-income families have been cut back. Efforts to affect quality of care through government regulation have been hampered by a political climate hostile to any kind of regulation. For example, the Federal Interagency Day Care Regulations, developed after much research and debate, have never been implemented (Nelson, 1982). State licensing requirements do not fill the gap left by this abdication of responsibility on the federal level. Young and Zigler (1986) found that state regulations vary widely, and often permit conditions promoting very poor quality care to exist. The 1985 Model Child Care Standards Act, established in response to public concern over child abuse scandals, failed to establish minimum standards of quality care (Phillips, 1986). Prospects for a comprehensive federally funded child-care system, which exists in some European countries, have not approached political feasibility since the 1971 Nixon veto of the Comprehensive Child Development Act. Subsequent efforts in the 1970s did not pass Congress.[4] Some child-care advocates are now working to make the child-care tax credit refundable and to raise the level of reimbursement to 50% so that it benefits low-income families. Already the tax credit has been changed from a flat rate to a sliding scale, and beginning in 1983, the short form for federal taxes contained a line for the child-care tax deduction, so that families who did not itemize deductions could take advantage of it (Children's Defense Fund Reports, March 1984).

Two types of policies that would help broaden social responsibility for children are the development of support systems to aid parents in taking care of their own children, especially in early infancy, and of child-care services as a supplement to parental care. In the past, and to some extent today, the extended family provided a framework of support for parents raising children. But as families have become smaller and more fragile, additional support systems are needed.

If men and women are to share childrearing, changes in the structure of both work and family life are necessary. One possible model has been suggested by Strober (1981), who proposed that we move toward a reallocation of work and leisure (or family) time over the life cycle. In this schema, parents would trade part-time work during the early childhood years for part-time work after the normal retirement age. (Or, to put it another way, fewer work hours when children are young in exchange for more work hours when the parents are old.) This arrangement would be coupled with government-backed low-interest loans to parents of young children, who otherwise would not be able to afford to take reduced work hours at a time when their expenses are high and their earning power is frequently low. For those in professional and managerial occupations, career paths would require redefinition. In contrast to the "fast track" model, where the greatest time commitment is expected from people between about ages 25–35, Bailyn (1982) proposes an "apprenticeship" model of organizational careers. This model provides for less intense time commitment during the childrearing years, with peak involvement coming later, perhaps between ages 35–45.

In order for these proposals to effect equality in men's and women's work and family roles, men would need to be as committed to changing the distribution of work and family time as women apparently are. Otherwise, these ideas might be another way to help women "combine career and family" by solidifying a female ghetto of part-time "working mothers" who accept limited careers in exchange for flexibility. The case of Sweden illustrates both the possibilities and limitations of policies designed to enable both men and women to work and share parenting. Sweden has a policy of parental leave, where either parent can take time off to care for a new baby. Parental insurance provides 90% of the parent's earned income for 6 months. An additional special allowance is available if either parent wishes to stay home full-time or part-time for an additional 6 months. Parents also have the right to work 6 hours a day instead of 8 while their children are young. Approximately 25% of Swedish fathers take some time off when a child is born (usually 1 month), a substantial increase since the policy was first introduced. Nevertheless, it is still a minority of fathers. The typical work pattern for Swedish women is to work full-time until they have children and then to work part-time. Most Swedish men continue to work full-time for most of their lives (Kindland, 1984; Rollin, 1984). Apparently there are additional barriers to equality in work and family life that have not been fully addressed by current policies.

Another danger has been pointed out by Hunt and Hunt (1982): The "dual career couple" might succeed in creating equality between men and women who choose to combine work and family, leaving the old "male" career model to both men and women who choose to be childless. They warn of a new "class" distinction between parents and nonparents, whereby privileges, advancement, and economic rewards would go to the childless, while parents become second-class citizens with less opportunity. Without social policy that supports parenting as valuable for society as a whole, this new polarization might be the result of what otherwise appears as a move toward greater equality.

Additional specific policies to help parents care for their own children include paid maternity leave with job protection and the possibility of gradual reentry into full-time work (or, pro-rated time off). As Kamerman, Kahn, & Kingston (1983) have documented, only 40% of women in the United States are covered by disability insurance for maternity leave. Current federal law requires only that where disability insurance is provided, childbirth be treated as any other temporary disability. Most European countries provide at least 3 months paid maternity leave, in contrast to the more usual 6 weeks of leave in this country.

In order for improved maternity leave to avoid solidifying infant care as a "women's problem," paternity leaves are needed as well. The Swedish example cited above, however, shows that making fathers eligible for parental leave is a necessary but not sufficient condition for promoting shared parenting. What would it take for men to be willing to spend more time with their young children? Both structural (policy) changes and changes in sex-role attitudes must take place if men and women are to share more equally in child care. As it stands now, men in the United States suffer more negative repercussions than women do for decisions to take time off from work to care for their children. At the very least, fathers could be encouraged to use accrued sick leave or vacation time to stay home when a child was born. This would help build a relationship between father and infant and establish father's competence and confidence in caring for the child right from the start. In addition, new mothers can recover faster from the physical stress of childbearing when there is another pair of hands available.

Another way to help parents care for their own children is to encourage the use of more flexible personnel policies by employers. A number of employers have introduced policies to allow personal leave to be used to care for sick children; flex-time schedules where employees choose their hours of work within a set of guidelines; flex-place, where employees work at home, often at a computer; and job-sharing, where two people fill one full-time job in coordination with each other. Although proponents of work-place flexibility claim employers benefit from these options in terms of greater productivity and employee satisfaction, more statistical documentation is needed (McGuire, 1984). The most widely adopted of these policies is flex-time, which has clear benefits in reducing traffic congestion. However, it is not a practical option for manufacturing industries where workers in the production process must be present at the same time.

The development of additional child-care services that supplement parental care is another way in which societal responsibility for children's well-being can be expanded. One approach is to begin with existing child-care arrangements and introduce improvements in the quality of care and the coordination of the system. A promising development is information and referral services that link parents needing child care with providers who have openings.

Information and referral is an important addition to the current array of child-care services that have evolved in a haphazard and uncoordinated way. In particular, it is most useful for linking parents with family day care homes, which often do not have the means to advertise their services. Other services have grown out of the initial provider–consumer link, such as training and information for child-care providers, recruitment of additional family day care homes, and links with other child-related services. One recent example of the latter is the child abuse prevention program sponsored by the California Child Care Resource and Referral Network. Child care information and referral also plays a key role in monitoring changes in the child care supply and demand, thus providing a ready base of information for developing additional services based on expressed need (Siegel & Lawrence, 1984).

In recent years, interest has revived in the idea of employer-supported child care, with child care providers, parents, and government increasingly looking to employers as a possible source of funds for the expansion of child-care services. This turning toward the private sector is a result in part of cost-cutting on the part of the government as advocates of government-funded social programs find themselves lobbying against cuts in spending, rather than for any new programs.

Employer involvement in supporting child care is still very small, though there has been growth in recent years. In 1985, there were about 2500 employers nation-wide who provided some form of support for the child-care needs of their employees. Half of the employers are hospitals; the rest are primarily high-growth service industries, such as banks and insurance companies, plus some high technology firms. What these employers have in common is rapid growth, high levels of female employment, and a shortage of labor, particularly skilled and professional/technical employees (Friedman, 1986b). For example, it was the shortage of registered nurses during the 1970s that prompted a number of hospitals to set up child-care centers as an incentive for nurses with young children to return to work.

On-site child-care centers are what most people think of when they envision employer-supported child care. Most of the hospitals with child care have chosen this option since it best meets the need for night and weekend child care, which is not readily available in most communities. In addition, the "caring" function of hospitals has seemed compatible with on-site child care. Among corporations, however, only a few programs involve on-site centers. On-site care is the most expensive option to implement, and is not always the most appropriate. The trend is toward other forms of support.

Currently, employers are more interested in helping employees use existing child-care services than in creating new ones. Most new employer programs focus on providing information or financial assistance. Information may be in the form of a contract with a local child-care information and referral service, which will help employees find care that meets their needs, or parents seminars on how to choose child care. Since the Economic Recovery Tax Act of 1981 made Dependent Care Assistance Plans a non-taxable benefit, an estimated 1000 employers have adopted such plans as an option in flexible benefits. They are usually financed by salary reduction, which allows employees to pay for child care with pre-tax dollars (Friedman, 1986a). Employer costs are minimal with this form of support, while employee savings consist of the amount they would have paid in taxes on child-care expenses up to $5,000 dollars, the limit set by the new tax law in 1986.

There are dangers in the tendency of both government and child-care advocates to look to employers for a solution to the problem of funding child care. The vast majority of parents work for small employers who are unlikely to offer child-care benefits and services. Those unemployed, looking for work, or in training are likewise left out of any benefits tied to employment. Employer involvement so far has been in high-growth industries, usually large companies that already provide good benefits. Government clearly has a role to play in creating a better system of child-care services that private employers can invest in, as well as providing for those parents who are unlikely to be covered by workplace benefits (Friedman, 1986b).

Involvement by labor unions in child care is another way in which societal responsibility for children could be broadened. During the 1970s women unionists and labor organizers raised this issue, and pointed to its potential for attracting new members. However, union involvement has never been great. The Amalgamated Clothing and Textile Workers Union (ACTWU) established six on-site centers, most jointly funded by union and management, but all but one of these centers have now closed. Interest in the issue of child care has been expressed by public employee (AFSCME) and service employee (SEIU) unions, because of their large female memberships. However, successful bargaining on this issue has been rare. One exception is a recent SEIU contract with a Kaiser Hospital in Los Angeles, which resulted in the establishment of child-care information and referral services for employees.

The major barrier to union involvement is that unions have been strongest in the traditionally male-dominated heavy industries, and have lagged behind in organizing women, office workers, and workers employed in service industries. Those unions that may have been interested in including child-care services as part of their collective bargaining efforts have been stymied by an economic and political climate in which they have had to defend wages and benefits from employers anxious to reduce labor costs. Union involvement in child care as a benefit to be included in bargaining will depend on unions moving out of their current defensive position and successfully organizing workers in high-growth industries.

One social change that would advance both feminist and children's interests would be equal pay for work of comparable worth. Most working women today do not earn enough to pay for good quality care for their children. The feminization of poverty literature has emphasized that the poor are increasingly made up of women and children, and single mothers are poor even when they are working full-time. Paying child-care workers on the basis of comparable worth would also raise their wages. If employed women earned more, they could pay more for child care, and this might improve the quality of care available.

Equality between men and women at work and in the family, and societal commitment to provide high quality care for children in both the family and other settings—these are visionary goals, and perhaps not ones upon which all Americans would agree. Nevertheless, to the extent that Americans are committed to the principle of fairness and to the idea that children represent our best hopes for the future of our country, support may be built for a number of specific programs and policies that would further these values.

The future of quality care for children, as is clearly the case with equality for women, will ultimately depend on grass-roots involvement in public policy development. Feminists have begun to develop political clout and to support candidates and legislation to promote equality for women. Children, however, must depend on adults to represent their interests in the larger society. While it is necessary for men ultimately to become more involved with children if equality between the sexes is to be achieved, it is now crucial that feminists adopt children's needs as congruent with their own. (Kamerman, 1985, makes a similar argument.) Feminists must not only seek equality in the public sphere, but promote the transformation of that sphere so that conflicts between the structure of work and family life do not continue to impose hardships on women and children.

ACKNOWLEDGMENT

I would like to thank the following for their comments on earlier drafts of this chapter: Kendyll Stansbury, Sheila Kamerman, Birte Siim, Dana Friedman, and the IRWG Affiliated and Visiting Scholars Group. Sorca O'Conner and Carol Muller provided research assistance and ideas in the early stage of writing. Editors of this volume Myra Strober and Sandy Dornbusch deserve special thanks for their comments and encouragement on several drafts of the chapter.

NOTES

1. The 1984–1985 survey covered the three youngest children, while the 1982 data included only the youngest child. Thus when data were compared, the total percentage of mothers using group care changed from 23% to 25% for 1984–1985.

2. Controversy has arisen recently among researchers who study the effects of day-care on children regarding whether children who begin care before age 1 are at some risk of developing negative reactions (Belsky, 1986, 1987). Other researchers argue that this conclusion cannot be drawn and that negative outcomes are usually associated with poor quality care, rather than age at which the child began care (Phillips, McCartney, Scarr, & Howes, 1987). A nonspecialist can only conclude that the research results are not clear.

3. See Suransky (1982) for a critical ethnographic description of life in several child-care centers from the point of view of the child.

4. See Joffe (1983) for an analysis of why the United States has no child-care policy.

REFERENCES

Bailyn, L. (1982). The apprenticeship model of organizational careers: A response to changes in the relation between work and family. In P. Wallace (Ed.), *Women in the workplace.* Boston: Auburn House.

Belsky, J. (1988, September). Infant day care: A cause for concern? *Zero to Three: Bulletin of the National Center for Clinical Infant Programs, 6,* 1–7.

Belsky, J. (1987, February). Risks remain. *Zero to Three: Bulletin of the National Center for Clinical Infant Programs, 7,* 22–24.

Berrueta-Clement, J. S., Schweinhart, W. S. B., Epstein, A. S., & Weikart, D. P. (1984). *Changed lives: The effects of the Perry preschool program on youths through age nineteen.* Ypsilanti, MI: High Scope Press.

Children's Defense Fund. (1984, March). CDF Reports.

Fredericks, B., Hardman, R., Morgan, G., & Rodgers, F. (1986). A little bit under the weather, a look at care for mildly ill children. Boston, MA: Work/Family Directions.

Friedman, D. (1985). *Corporate financial assistance for child care.* New York: The Conference Board, Research Bulletin 177.

Friedman, D. (1986a, March–April). Child care for employees' kids. *Harvard Business Review*, 28–34.

Friedman, D. (1986b). Painting the child care landscape: A palette of inadequacy and innovation. In S. Hewlett, A. Ilchman, & J. Sweeney (Eds.), *Family and work: Bridging the gap.* Cambridge, MA: Ballinger.

Goodman, E. (1984, November 27). Child-care: The constant crisis of working mothers. *San Jose Mercury-News*, p. 7b.

Hayghe, H. (1986). Rise in mothers' labor force activity includes those with infants. *Monthly Labor Review*, *109*(2), 43–45.

Hoffman, F. (1985). Serving the needs of children: Child care in the voluntary sector. In Gary Tobin (Ed.), *Planning and social service delivery in the voluntary sector.* Westport, CT: Greenwood Press.

Hunt, J., & Hunt, L. (1982). The dualities of careers and families: New integration or new polarizations. *Social Problems*, *29*(5), 499–510.

Joffe, C. (1983). Why the United States has no child care policy. In I. Diamond (Ed.), *Families, politics and public policy: A feminist dialogue on women and the state.* New York: Longman.

Kamerman, S. (1981). *Child care, family benefits, and working parents: A study in comparative policy.* New York: Columbia University Press.

Kamerman, S. (1985). Child care: An issue for gender equity and women's solidarity. *Child Welfare*, *64*(3), 259–270.

Kamerman, S., Kahn, A., & Kingston, P. (1983). *Maternity policies and working women.* New York: Columbia University Press.

Kindland, S. (1984, May). *Family support in Sweden.* Paper presented at a conference on "The working family: Perspectives and prospects in the United States and Sweden," San Francisco. (Available from the Swedish Consulate, San Francisco, CA).

McGuire, N. (1984, May). *Time options: How they can resolve workplace/family conflicts.* Paper presented at a conference on "The working family: Perspectives and prospects in the United States and Sweden," San Francisco. (Available from the Swedish Consulate, San Francisco, CA).

Nelson, J. R. (1982). The politics of federal day care regulation. In E. Zigler & E. Gordon (Eds.), *Day care: Scientific and social policy issues.* Boston: Auburn House.

Phillips, D. (1986). The federal Model Child Care Standards Act of 1986: Step in the right direction or hollow gesture? *American Journal of Orthopsychiatry*, *56*(1), 56–64.

Phillips, D., McCartney, K., Scarr, S., & Howes, C. (1987, February). Selective review of infant day care research: A cause for concern! *Zero to Three: Bulletin of the National Center for Clinical Infant Programs*, *7*, 18–23.

Presser, H. (1982). Working women and child care. In P. W. Berman & E. R. Ramey (Eds.), *Women: A developmental perspective* (NIH Publication No. 82-2298). Washington, DC: U.S. Department of Health and Human Services.

Presser, H. (1986). Shift work among American women and child care. *Journal of Marriage and the Family*, *48*, 551–553.

Presser, H., & Cain, V. (1983). Shift work among dual-earner couples with children. *Science*, *219*, 876–879.

Rollin, B. (1984, May). *Work and family patterns in Sweden.* Paper presented at a conference on "The working family: Perspectives and prospects in the United States and Sweden," San Francisco. (Available from the Swedish Consulate, San Francisco, CA).

Ruopp, R., & Travers, J. (1982). Janus faces day care: Perspectives on quality and cost. In E. Zigler & E. Gordon (Eds.), *Day care: Scientific and social policy issues.* Boston: Auburn House.

Rutter, M. (1982). Social-emotional consequences of day care for preschool children. In E. Zigler & E. Gordon (Eds.), *Day care: Scientific and social policy issues.* Boston: Auburn House.

School-Age Child Care Project. (1982). School-age child care. In E. Zigler & E. Gordon (Eds.), *Day care: Scientific and social policy issues.* Boston: Auburn House.

Siegel, P., & Lawrence, M. (1984). Information, referral, and resource centers. In J. Greenman & R. Fuqua (Eds.), *Making day care better.* New York: Teachers College Press.

Skold, K. (1985). *Working parents and the problem of sick child care: A report on the issue for local grant makers.* (Available from the Institute for Research on Women and Gender, Stanford University, Stanford, CA.)

Skold, K., Siegel, P., & Lawrence, M. (1983). *Child care in Santa Clara County.* (Available from the Institute for Research on Women and Gender, Stanford University, Stanford, CA.)

Strober, M. (1981). Market work, house work, and child care: Burying archaic tenets, building new arrangements. In National Institute of Mental Health (Ed.), *Women, a developmental perspective: A conference on research.* Washington, DC: U.S. Government Printing Office.

Suransky, V. (1982). *The erosion of childhood.* Chicago: University of Chicago Press.

U.S. Bureau of the Census. (1983). *Child Care Arrangements of Working Mothers: June, 1982.* (Series P-23, No. 129.) Washington, DC: U.S. Government Printing Office.

U.S. Bureau of the Census. (1987). *Who's Minding the Kids? Child Care Arrangements: Winter, 1984–85* (Series P-70, No. 9). Washington, DC: U.S. Government Printing Office.

U.S. Department of Labor, Employment and Training Administration. (1977). *Dictionary of Occupational Titles* (4th ed.). Washington, DC: U.S. Government Printing Office.

Whitebook, M., Howes, C., Darrah, R., & Friedman, J. (1981). Who's minding the child care workers?: A look at staff burnout. *Children Today, 10,* 2–6.

Winget, W. G. (1982). The dilemma of affordable child care. In E. Zigler & E. Gordon (Eds.), *Day care: Scientific and social policy issues.* Boston: Auburn House.

Young, K., & Zigler, E. (1986). Infant and toddler day care: Regulations and policy implications. *American Journal of Orthopsychiatry, 56*(1), 43–55.

Zaretsky, E. (1976). *Capitalism, the family, and personal life.* New York: Harper and Row.

7

The State and the Institutionalization of the Relations between Women and Children

JOHN W. MEYER, FRANCISCO O. RAMIREZ, HENRY A. WALKER, NANCY LANGTON, AND SORCA M. O'CONNOR

In what has been dramatically called "the dark side of families" (Finkelhor, Gelles, Hotaling, & Straus, 1983), no set of conflicts or strains has commanded more public attention than those that characterize the relations between women and their children. Legislative bodies and the courts are faced with new and difficult issues. The right of a woman to abort a fetus is contrasted with the rights of the unborn child. A mother's right to determine where the child shall reside is weighed against the child's freedom of choice. The right of a mother to pursue a career autonomously is contrasted with the right of the child to maternal care and supervision. And a wide range of socialization prerogatives and disciplinary practices are increasingly scrutinized to determine whether children are being subjected to physical, psychological, and sexual abuse. Some of these clashes apply to fathers as well, but because the mother–child relationship has been sentimentalized in modern Western history (see Illich, 1983), mother–child conflicts seem especially salient.

When the present state of mother–child relations is compared to an idealized past, one might argue that relations in the modern period are characterized by: (1) higher levels of conflict, (2) a greater variety of conflicts, and (3) a greater likelihood that conflicts will appear on the public agenda. But there is no evidence that indicates an actual increase in conflicts between mothers and children, just as there is no evidence showing an overall increase in conflict and violence within families (Brines & Gordon, 1983; Gelles, 1979). The historical record is painfully clear: Parents have abandoned, sold into marriage, apprenticeship, or slavery, and murdered

John W. Meyer, Ph.D., Francisco O. Ramirez, Ph.D., and Henry A. Walker, Ph.D. Department of Sociology (Meyer and Walker) and School of Education (Ramirez), Stanford University, Stanford, California.

Nancy Langton, Ph.D. School of Business, University of Toronto, Toronto, Canada.

Sorca M. O'Connor, Ph.D. Department of Education, Washington University, St. Louis, Missouri.

untold numbers of children (Aries, 1962; DeMause, 1974; Sommerville, 1982). Conversely, children have plotted against their parents and administered "retirement powder" to them (Held, Ramirez, & Meyer, 1983). Some present-day conflicts are novel, such as child custody disputes in which the rights of older children to make choices may be at odds with presumptions favoring mothers over fathers. But many traditional practices—infanticide, the exploitation of child labor, abandonment, vagrancy, or the neglect of impoverished older parents—have either disappeared or become unusual. Many of these practices were common in the Western past and authorities reacted to them with a half-forgiving legitimation, viewing them as unfortunate but understandable (see Langer, 1974, for a historical survey of infanticide). Clearly, by contemporary standards of harmony and conflict, the present status of mother–child relations is actually better than in the historical past.

What seems most different about the contemporary period is that mother–child conflicts that were once the substance of folklore and common gossip have become items for public discussion and political regulation (see Chapter 2 by Cohen and Katzenstein and Chapter 3 by Fleming in this volume). Scientific expertise and intellectual authority are brought to bear on debates about legal standards and public policies (e.g., who will determine the best interests of the child and how those interests will be safeguarded (Wald, 1979; Zelizer, 1986). Officers of the state debate the issues and adjudicate them in legislatures and the courts. What were once private troubles have increasingly become public issues. Thus, there is extended local, national, and in some cases international discussion (Gelles & Cornell, 1982; Kamerman, 1975) of many of the issues involved: the role of parents in abortion decisions of teenagers, the regulation of children's sexuality, the reciprocal legal obligations of children and parents, and the boundaries of those obligations, such as their terminability in the instance of "neglect." We are convinced that it is the increasingly public nature of conflicts between women and children that has led to the perception of a general increase in conflict.

Many of the clearly exploitative and conflictual features of traditional family life have been absorbed by the state: The extreme economic dependence of children on mothers and vice versa has been reduced. The relative financial advantages of killing or abandoning a child or aged parent are quite low in modern societies, when viewed in contrast to traditional societies. There has been a similar reduction in social dependency. A child's future depends on education (an institution that is state-controlled and almost universally compulsory) more than on his or her parents' status. From the parents' perspective, there is relatively little to be gained from the exploitation of a child's labor; and parents now depend on public institutions rather than on their children in retirement.

The transformation of private troubles into public issues also changes the shape of the issues: Modern public life has a peculiar coloration, making some issues central while others remain unrecognized. Thus many of the economic and educational obligations that linked mothers and children in premodern societies and that were at the forefront of their familial agendas are little discussed in modern times. The state, not the family, assumes primary responsibility for providing an education, managing employment, and providing protection to family members, while nonfamilial obligations, rather than filial duties, govern many welfare-related decisions. To illustrate, contemporary economic contingencies do not often require modern mothers to decide whether to sell their youngsters into apprenticeships. But were mothers to do so, the issue of whether their children would serve or not is more likely to be resolved in court than in a family discussion.[1]

One principal theme of this paper is that the expansion of the public domain and the associated increase in the authority of the nation-state has led to fundamental changes in the definition and regulation of mother–child relations. Contrary to the many popular accounts of widespread familial crisis, including images of deteriorating mother–child relations, there is no evidence that these relations are more strained today than in prior eras. Indeed, there is every reason to believe that they are less conflict ridden. But the increasingly public character of the ancient inconsistencies and tensions underlying these ties is conducive to the national, and perhaps even worldwide, fear of this presumed modern epidemic. We use cross-national data to describe some of the major ideological changes that have led to the present perception.

Modern societies differ in their construction of the "public," and in particular in the way in which the state becomes linked to private life. There are different forms of modern citizenship, and consequently different ways in which men, women, and children are seen as linked with one another. Put briefly, some political systems—notably the American one—have broadened their notions of what falls within the public domain by expanding a general definition of individual citizenship and the associated personal interests, rights, and obligations. Other societies conceive of the family as a corporate group, and as the main constituent group of modern society. Such societies may expand their general regulation and protection of the family as an entity, with men, women, and children seen as natural components of the family (rather than as autonomous individuals). Between these extremes, one can find modern societies in which age and sex roles, rather than the specific bounded family unit, are seen as natural units of society. In such cases modernization includes the extension of general social rights to men, women, and children as distinct groups with special needs and rights.

Such variation in the extension of citizenship—or the involvement of public authority and obligation in formerly private spheres—has considerable effect both on the degree to which potential conflicts of interest between mothers and children are seen and formulated, and on the kinds of conflicts that may be observed. This is the second principal theme of our paper.

THE EXPANSION OF PUBLIC LIFE,
AND THE PUBLIC ORGANIZATION OF THE PRIVATE

It is widely recognized that the centuries-long process of Western social and economic development has brought about dramatic expansion of the domain of public life (Anderson, 1974; Meyer, 1980). Nations and national cultures, world cultural ideas, and state organizations undergo enormous expansion with development and modernization. Public life incorporates and dominates much of everyday life and exercises great sovereignty over it. In a "modern" society, the private buying and selling of goods and services, raising children (and in some societies even having children), or personal sanitation, come under the scrutiny and standards of a public order—often the national state and its law. What were formerly private activities are regulated, often by individuals themselves, from the point of view of these collective standards.

Modernization is a long process that has reached its most advanced stages in richer and stronger societies. But modernization continues with time so that regardless of the extent to which they are developed, modern states and public orders penetrate much further into the private sphere than they did in earlier periods.

There are several aspects of this general process. The overall sovereignty and power of public orders and states increases. Unlike family and kinship groups, national states tend to be inclusive rather than exclusive. With the passage of time, more groups acquire citizenship and are subjected to the power and authority of the state. Furthermore, the process includes expansion of the state's jurisdiction over public life; many more aspects of life come under its authority. Women increasingly acquire the rights and obligations of citizenship (Milburn, 1976). As future citizens, children belong to the nation as well as to the family. Hence, notions of the family as a natural unit, protected by religious or private rights, weaken: public law takes precedence.

Interestingly, one can also view the long process of Western development as an important factor in the creation of the private, a point that is now much emphasized (e.g., Bell, 1976; Shorter, 1975). The subjective and interior space of the individual expands, self-awareness and self-consciousness expand. All this is highly legitimated, even obligatory, and modern literature, art, psychology, and political culture are filled with references to the tastes, needs, preferences, choices, and necessary strengths of the individual self and its perspectives. Peter Berger has suggested that the modern individual is trapped in the prison of the self (P. Berger, Berger, & Kellner, 1973). The image is apt: The modern self expands, but in a culturally standardized way (Meyer, 1986). Public life is filled with discussions of the needs of persons as selves (not simply as animals or objects of charity and protection). In other words, even the modern private sphere itself is associated with the rights and demands of citizenship and hence becomes part of the expanded public life and agenda.

From this point of view, the expansion, legitimation, and regulation of the private—one could call it obligatory personhood—has important implications. Women and children come to be seen as persons, not as components of a natural familial and religious order. They are seen, and are expected to see themselves, as individual personalities, with needs and choices that are ingredients of the public order and obligations that this order must protect.

Children, in short, come to be seen as a component of public society, and thus objects of protection and regulation by the state (Sommerville, 1982). This is a much-discussed process, and leads to some of the most dramatic changes in Western history. Massive schooling systems are created, so that children are removed from families at early ages, and exposed as individuals to the workings of the wider state and society (Boli-Bennett & Ramirez, 1986). Detailed health and labor regulations are enacted, with familial discretion removed. Parental obligations and child rights are spelled out in detail, and from the point of view of the requirements of the public order. Parents may no longer abuse, neglect, or interfere with the necessary socialization of a present or future citizen of the state—a person who is an individual member of society.

As individual citizens, men and women both become objects of societal protection and regulation. Family and community are undercut in an expansion of public sovereignty and jurisdiction (Donzelot, 1979). Men, then women, acquire more and more citizenship rights and capacities that are linked politically, economically, and culturally to the wider order. And they acquire the legitimated capacity for the private—for subjective choices, interests, and tastes. Family life becomes increasingly a negotiation of relationships among free individuals, operating under collective public constraints to be individual persons. Thus the work and child-bearing of women are increasingly matters of their own negotiated choice. So also with women's choices in childrearing—but here the problem arises.

Both women and children have public rights and obligations, among others the right and obligation to be free choosing individuals. As their needs and rights are perceived to conflict in modern societies, resolution is expected in the public arena. The women's right to freedom is seen to impinge on the child's right to care and attention (see Cohen & Katzenstein, Chapter 2 this volume). And correspondingly, the rights of the child constrain the mother's free expression of autonomous individuality.

None of these issues are new. The ancient inconsistencies of family life now come into the public domain—a modern domain demanding some sort of mythic integration and resolution. Hundreds of perceived "social problems" result throughout the modern period. They come in waves. An expansion of the rights of women or children as citizens makes public a whole new generation of social problems, discovered by the relevant professionals and organizations and debated through the public arena. Parental rights to obedience confront child rights to education and publicly approved medical care. Women's rights to occupational involvement are said to conflict with children's rights to parental (read maternal) rather than institutional care. (See, for example, the debate on whether mother's employment negatively affects children's educational achievement: Heyns & Catsambis, 1986; Milne, Meyers, Rosenthal, & Ginsberg, 1986.) Children's rights to make autonomous decisions abrogate parental rights to define and enforce orderly home lives.

It is, however, a new development that the conflicts are fought out in the press, courts, legislatures, and administrative agencies of public life, and that at every side arise professional and scientific judgments on the questions. The scientists who are our new theologians concern themselves with such questions as a child's right to an allowance.

Our arguments can be summarized in a few propositions:

> *Proposition 1.* With the world-wide expansion of Western modernity, and of the state and public life, there is an expansion of the citizenship rights of women and children.
>
> *Proposition 2.* As the rights of women and children expand, public regulation of the relations between women and children increases; more public attention is paid to conflicts between them.
>
> *Proposition 3.* Public discussion of the conflicts between women and children comes in waves, following periods of expansion in the membership rights of women or children.
>
> *Proposition 4.* Public attention to familial conflict is greatest in those societies that are most highly "developed."

One may suppose that the introduction of personhood increases some kinds of interpersonal conflicts. But it seems likely that many of the classic conflicts of interest between women and children are weakened by the modern system. Economic dependence—the root of many of the classic conflicts over control of children's labor and income and over parental rights to support—is greatly weakened. So are conflicts over, (1) the unilateral political authority of parents, or (2) all the issues of inheritance, or (3) the inconsistency between parental interests in children's work and children's interest in training and advancement. The long-term dependence of both parties on what was the same restricted set of resources builds into premodern family life a good many potential conflicts, some of which are clearly realized. But in the modern system, many of these are absorbed in the wider institutional machinery. For instance, political groups representing old women and children may conflict over state allocations or welfare or education. This is no longer an interpersonal or intrafamilial business.

We do not, thus, describe changes in mother–child conflict. Rather, we focus on the ways in which the power of the modern polity and state has reorganized and redefined them. We consider variations in the extent to which, in modified form, the ancient and private conflicts between mothers and their children are seen as public problems of modern life.

VARIATIONS IN FORMS OF INCORPORATION OF WOMEN AND CHILDREN INTO PUBLIC LIFE

Thus far we have discussed development as if all forms of Western modernization and expansion were equivalent. They are not, but indeed there is a very general tendency, described above, to extend social membership in public life to women and children as individuals. Modernization reifies the individual as a legal and cultural entity.

To a varying extent, and in varying ways, all forms of modernization extend public recognition to encompass basic human identities. But the identities that are elaborated and the ways people are linked to public life vary across modern systems, depending on political and cultural orders. We can conceive forms of modernization as being distributed along a continuum of national corporate structures with the endpoints corresponding in some sense to the classic model of Durkheim. At one end are more traditional communalistic societies, while located at the other are less traditional, more individualistic societies.

With modernization, the lives of people and societies are organized around wider and more inclusive social and cultural identities—large-scale ethnic or subnational groupings, the nation, the human race, and so on (Igra, 1976). People are tied to these larger identities as individual persons, but the exact mechanisms that accomplish this linkage may vary. At one extreme, there are liberal individualistic societies in which all persons, as individuals, have the same kinds of rights and obligations. Usually, the moral meaning and obligations that accompany this form of individualism are intense. At the other extreme, individuals are linked to wider collectivities through their membership in communal groups like age sets, kinship categories, or membership in nuclear families. In a sense, these constituent social forms are also individualistic in that they are built up from individual memberships. But societies that are organized on this basis differ from liberal individualistic societies in that various "natural" units, and indeed natural law, intervene to help accomplish the linkage between the individual and the state. We distinguish three forms of modernization.

Organic Corporatism

Latin countries are often discussed as models of this form of political incorporation (Stepan, 1978). Organic corporatist societies typically operate under the traditions of natural law and/or the church, and individualism takes more limited forms. Society is conceived as a system comprised of natural entities other than the individual—the family is one entity often given this preeminent status. As modernization proceeds, the family as a natural entity may come under extended public protection and incorporation. But there is very little penetration of the internal side of family life by public organizations, and thus limited public exposure of intrafamilial conflicts. The internal arrangements of familial life are determined by what is conceived to be natural or religious.

In organic corporatist systems—which often produce literature on intrafamilial strife—the conflicts between women and children as putative individuals are handled in more traditional ways. They are typically worked out in private and do not much enter the public agenda, which may concern itself with children such as orphans who are *not* in families, or with the rights of unmarried women. Thus we can isolate an additional proposition:

> *Proposition 5.* Organic corporatist political systems generate very low levels of public perception and discussion of intrafamilial conflicts; the state keeps out of this domain.

Familial life in organic corporatist systems has qualities that seem strange and inconsistent to those steeped in the tradition of American individualism. There is a rich set of literary and poetic (but not legal and organizational) images and accounts of the family as a corporate group with a history and structure all its own. The family is both the unit of unconditional commitment, and the arena of the most complete hostility. Incredibly romantic images of family history and meaning are mixed—in the same people and the same tales—with the most grim accounts of intrafamilial horror. Family members seem trapped within the legitimated structure, filled with alienation but unable to conceive of any alternative existence. Parents and children are tied together eternally, but are also engaged in the most extensive conflicts. The conflicts which exist are not matters of public discussion, nor are they concerns of the state and intellectuals. They appear only in literary and poetic images. The public order and its law remain relatively silent on issues arising within the family boundaries.

Communal Corporatism

North European countries are common models of communal corporatism (S. Berger, 1981). Modernization is built on a perception of the state as a national *community*, rather than as a nation of free individuals. Women, men, and children are natural parts of this community. They have rights and obligations in the public arena as *women, men, and children*—not just in the hidden world of the family but as members of the state. Hence, age and gender roles are important components of the conception of a national community.

In such systems, a good many issues between age and gender roles may come up for public discussion or resolution, and conflicts between women and children as groups may bear a superficial resemblance to conflicts between women and children as individual citizens. But there is a limited perception of conflict (although more than in organic corporatist societies) because conflicts between the age and gender roles are attributed to natural capacities and needs, which are incorporated as elements of the age and gender structure of the society. Public organizations recognize the natural character of conflicts between age and gender groups, and they may be periodically called upon to clarify or redefine mutual rights and obligations. But the resolution of conflicts between individual women and children is typically a private matter. This generates a further proposition:

> *Proposition 6.* Communal corporatist systems generate medium levels of public perception and discussion of conflicts between women and children.

In communal corporatist societies, conflicts between age and gender groups, as groups, enter the public discussion. Conflicts are not matters of individual rights, but of working out on a national basis what the standardized relations between "him," "her," and "children" should be. Conflict is recognized, but only between parties previously defined as possessing gender and generation, and thus the conflict is already partially managed. The age and sex statuses involved are viewed as natural elements of an organized system, rather than as prisons from which individuals in the liberal conception could escape. Interestingly, in the literature and poetry of such societies, images of persons trapped in age and sex roles are relatively common. There is a rich literature (perhaps best illustrated by Freud's work) describing the private tensions and repressions of individuals playing out their part in family life.

Liberal Individualism

American society is often seen as the model of a liberal individualistic society (Lipset, 1963), though this may be too restricted. Public society elaborates on a conception of individual citizenship and freedom. The economy (through market choices), the state (through citizen choice), and culture and religion all are rooted in a notion of free individual choice. Paralleling their choices, free individuals are conceived to have greatly expanded rights—*as individuals.*

Such a system naturally maximizes the public perception of a family life as filled with problems and conflict. No matter how much modernization proceeds, the daily lives of individuals are deeply involved in familial commitments that are beyond the notion of free individual choice. The commitments of marriage are weakened, but involve something more than

individual choice. The commitments of parenthood cannot easily be abro-
gated by individual choice and neither can children's obligations—obligations that are acquired at birth—to conformity with a given family system.

The inconsistencies, from the point of view of public authority, are
extreme. Children are supposed to be free-choosing, evolving individuals,
and yet are constrained. Women are free also, but the obligations of parenthood extend for decades. Thus we offer a general proposition:

> *Proposition 7.* Liberal individualist systems generate high levels
> of public discussion of conflicts between the interests of women and
> those of children.

Note again we do not argue that societies like the United States actually
generate higher levels of conflict. Our point is that the state's legitimation of
the freely choosing individual redefines conflicts between women and children as disputes about the rights of individual citizens—rights that are
guaranteed by the state. As a result, the public domain is in some sense the
only domain in which such conflicts *can* be worked out. The transfer of
individual interests to the public arena enhances the public's perception of
conflict.[2] The public resolution of conflict is part of the process of expansion
of citizenship—part of the process by which the public rights of the private
individual are secured.

We can conclude that it makes sense that the general public discussion
of intrafamilial conflicts is an ongoing part of American public, professional, and political life. A system that locates general political meaning in
the individual *qua* individual turns the special properties of its members into
public interests. Thus the special needs of children come to be professionally
and legally defined and articulated. So also with women and men. Once-
hidden dependencies become public problems. In the long run, such a
system probably provides more mechanisms for the resolution of the problems. But it does so precisely by parading them, in waves coming decade
after decade, on the pages of newspapers, on the television screen, and
everywhere on the public agenda.

The constant public discussion of supposedly private familial troubles
in liberal societies can be viewed as a form of penetration by public authority into private life. On the other hand, the process can be interpreted as a
manifestation of a national compulsion and narcissism in which individuals
inappropriately display private relations in public (Lasch, 1977). Neither of
these perspectives adequately captures the reality of the situation. Liberal
society is built on the myth of the individual who is free to choose and act—
free beyond age, gender and family relations. Such a perspective is available
to family members as they contemplate their lot, and almost inevitably,
many aspects of family life are seen as constraints. In one way or another,
people (or their professional agents and interpreters) use their rights in the
wider system to bring petition against their situations—fighting in individ-

ual cases, or more generally in cultural rhetoric, against the aspects of motherhood and childhood that, from an individualistic posture, seem to be imprisoning.

But the same perspective is held by agents of the public and the state, including various professionals. They also perceive an obligation to realize the general rights of free individual citizenship. They too see many of the constraints of childhood as having dubious legitimacy—for instance, as violating the general right to equal opportunity, or as involving assault or involuntary servitude. And they too perceive the obligations and constraints of motherhood as an interference with freedom. Thus, agents of the state are a constant source of energy for the creation or definition of family-related social problems and of social movements to repair them.

Pressures from all sides maintain the liberal system. It is a system in which it is deliberately made impossible for people to form what would in many societies be conceived of as a family—that is, irrevocable marriage and parenthood. Such commitment in liberal society has no legal standing and cannot be enforced in the courts.

CROSS-NATIONAL RESEARCH FINDINGS

We examine the theoretical themes developed in the previous sections with cross-national data. Our first argument presupposes long-term changes in the ideological status of national states, individual citizens, women, and children. We specify the direction of these long-term changes: There should be a general expansion of state authority; the rights of individual citizens should increase; the citizenship rights of women should increase, but so too should their responsibilities to the state; the status of children should increasingly become a national agenda topic; and state–family linkages— that is, support for as well as regulation of "the family" by the national state—should also increase.

National constitutional documents comprise our primary source of comparative data with which to measure these long-term changes (Blaustein & Flanz, 1971). We use indicators derived from a comprehensive coding of national constitutions (Boli-Bennett, 1976), taken at 20-year intervals from 1870 to 1970, to characterize *all* countries for which there are available data. The number of cases increases throughout this 100 year period, from 47 in 1870 to 142 in 1970, because the number of independent countries steadily increased during this era. For each reporting period the number of cases is almost equal to the total number of independent countries; the trends we report characterize the countries of the world.

The global trends described in Table 7.1 summarize findings from prior cross-national research (e.g., Boli-Bennett, 1980a, 1980b, 1981; Boli-Bennett & Meyer, 1978) and from ongoing related studies. Each row in Table 7.1 represents a pattern of change for a particular variable, either by computing

Table 7.1. Long-Term Cross-National Changes (1870–1970) in Constitutional Bases for Family-Related Rights and Responsibilities

	1870	1890	1910	1930	1950	1970
1. State Authority[a]	25.6	26.7	29.1	35.8	49.4	46.2
2. Citizen Rights[a]	16.5	17.0	17.3	19.8	24.6	27.9
3. Female Franchise[b]	0.0%	0.0%	4.0%	47.1%	74.1%	80.1%
4. Children: State Duty[b]	2.6%	2.3%	4.0%	11.0%	44.4%	66.7%
5. Motherhood: State Right[b]	2.6%	2.3%	4.0%	23.4%	56.8%	69.4%
6. Family: State Support[b]	0.0%	0.0%	0.0%	9.4%	49.4%	52.5%
Number of Cases	47	51	56	68	82	142

[a]Mean scores.
[b]Percentages of countries.
Source. Boli-Bennett (1976).

global mean scores for each of the time periods, or, with respect to dichotomous variables, by indicating the proportion of countries with the expected constitutional properties (e.g., affirming state responsibility for children, or extending the franchise to women). By examining these mean scores or percentage distributions over time, we can identify some worldwide trends that illustrate the empirical grounds for our theoretical premises. It is not our intent, however, to undertake more formal tests of the general argument.

The data in row 1 of Table 7.1 are scores on indicators of the constitutional powers of the state. This measure is created by adding the number of institutional areas assigned to the jurisdiction of the state, such as the regulation of currency and banking or public health, and the number of mechanisms set forth to facilitate the exercise of state jurisdiction. The score for any country may vary from 0 to 113. In 1870 the mean score for the 47 countries for which data were available was 25.6; by 1970 the mean score had increased dramatically to 46.2 ($n = 142$). This measure taps the symbolic authority of the national state and not necessarily its organizational clout. But indicators of the fiscal and administrative powers of the national state also show upward trends during the same period (Boli-Bennett, 1980a; Ramirez & Thomas, 1978). The expansion of the public sphere and legitimated jurisdiction of the national state is a central point in our argument regarding the modern rationalization of the social order. Clearly there is some comparative evidence, illustrated in Table 7.1, supporting this argument.

Closely related to this trend is one regarding the expansion of the rights of individual citizens. In the second row we focus on a citizenship rights index computed by adding the total number of civil, political, and social/economic rights enumerated in national constitutions. Countries may receive scores from 0 to 56. We find a mean score of 16.5 in 1870 and a much higher score of 27.9 in 1970. Indicators of state power and of the rights of citizens exhibit similar trends, and through this period the index of state power is positively correlated with the index of citizenship rights ($r = .36$; $n = 141$ in 1970). This finding may seem paradoxical to those who believe that the relationship between state and individual authority is a zero-sum game, with an increase in one invariably leading to a decrease in the other. But what we are examining is the very nature of modern citizenship and the incorporative national order. The rise and elaboration of the rights and of individuals is not merely freedom *from* the state but freedom that requires state action to guarantee it and more clearly links the interests of individuals to those of the national collectivity.

We turn now to changes in the public reclassification of women. Our first argument suggests that women will be increasingly defined as citizens throughout the world, despite variations in forms of political incorporation. The extension of citizenship status to women is a complex process and no single indicator adequately measures this variable. However, if one accepts the assumption that the acquisition of the franchise is a necessary —albeit insufficient—condition for the attainment of citizenship status, one may reasonably employ this indicator. In the third row we consider changes over the period from 1870 to 1970 in the percentage of countries that extended the full franchise to women. Note that, as of 1870, women did not have the right to vote or to seek office in a single country, although some form of franchise had been extended to men in many of these countries. But by 1970 women had acquired this basic membership right of modern polities in 80.1% of the countries of the world. This figure rises to over 90% if we restrict our examination to only those countries in which some form of suffrage has been granted to men. And since then, suffrage barriers have been broken in Switzerland, Portugal, and other similar countries.

To this finding one can add that there has also been an increase in the proportion of countries that have affirmed overall equality between men and women in their national constitutions, from 0% in 1910 to 22% in 1970. The political incorporation of women has clearly been supported by the broader world context that provides national states with a wide range of opportunities to declare egalitarian principles through the ratification of numerous conventions. The public reclassification of women as citizens is evidently an ongoing process in the modern world.

Children are also being incorporated politically, though not in the same way. From our perspective, what is critical is that the welfare of children increasingly becomes a matter of national interest. In turn, this frequently results in the broader collectivity assuming rights in and responsibilities over children. The fourth row allows us to see changes in the extent to which a "state responsibility for children" clause is invoked in national constitutions. In 1870 we find this provision linking children to the state in 2.6% of the cases; by 1970 this has become the modal pattern, with 66.7% of the national constitutions containing such a clause. At the organizational level children are further linked to the national order through the massive expansion of national educational systems (Meyer, Ramirez, Rubinson, & Boli-Bennett, 1977). The average primary enrollment rate for all countries jumped from 59.9% in 1950 to 86.5% in 1975 (Ramirez & Boli-Bennett, 1982); during the same period the enrollment rate at the secondary level increased from 11.5% to 40.7% while the average tertiary enrollment rate soared from 1.3% to 9.8%. Furthermore, even in the new frontier of pre-primary schooling, the enrollment rate grew from 8.7% in 1965 to 20.1% in 1980 (O'Connor, 1988). This general pattern of increased schooling is found in all regions of the world, for richer as well as for poorer countries, and is due largely to growth in the public educational sector. Even as more and more children are linked to the national order through the certification power of the educational system, so too are women. At all educational levels the female share of schooling has expanded in the last 3 decades: For tertiary education this upward movement is from 23.8% in 1950 to 31.5% in 1975 (Ramirez & Boli-Bennett, 1982).

But as we have argued, women and children are not politically incorporated solely as individuals. Motherhood, and the status of the child as a dependent member of the family unit, becomes the subject of national debates with many national policy implications. We address this issue by focusing on whether national constitutions give the state the right to regulate and protect the institution of motherhood. We do not treat the specific character of the constitutional provision in this paper; at issue is whether the regulation of motherhood falls under the jurisdiction of the state. In the fifth row we find that in 1870 some provision regarding the right of the state to regulate motherhood is found in 2.6% of the cases; by 1970 motherhood is under the jurisdiction of the state in 62.4% of the cases. And, in the last row, we see a parallel increase in the percentage of constitutions expressing state support for the institution of marriage and the family, from 0% in 1870 to 9.4% in 1930 to a high of 52.5% in 1970. We interpret this finding as evidence that the family domain as a whole has increasingly become a topic on the national agenda, receiving much more general publicity as well as specialized professional attention than in prior eras. As we asserted earlier, the proliferation of literature on conflicts between women's rights and children's rights tells us very little about actual increases in levels of conflict but a lot about the extent to which the identities, rights, and obligations of women and children are linked to national collective authority.

FORMS OF POLITICAL INCORPORATION

So far we have concentrated on assessing evidence regarding common patterns of change across the world. But a second component of our general argument suggests that there is some cross-national variation in forms of incorporation, and furthermore, that the level of perceived conflict is influenced by the form of incorporation. Where women and children are primarily incorporated as individuals, we expect high levels of public concern about the nature and limits of their rights to make choices in broad areas of decision making. We expect moderate levels of concern in polities where age and gender roles are the units incorporated into the national community, and lowest levels of public concern where the family as an entity is the unit of incorporation.

Many national and international debates focus on the conflicts between the rights of women to enter into the paid labor force and the rights of children to the time and energy of their mothers. Cross-national data suggest that, historically, the labor-force participation of married women has been lower than that of single women (Cook, 1974). One important premise of our second set of arguments is that the labor force participation of married women should vary with the type of polity and the form of political incorporation. We would expect to find higher labor force participation of married women (and a smaller difference in the participation rates of married and single women) in societies in which women are more fully incorporated as individual citizens. Ramirez (1981), using cross-national data, reported findings that suggest that married women have higher labor-force participation rates in societies in which women are politically incorporated as individual citizens. There is a negative association between the legal status of women as individuals and the degree to which marriage reduced participation in the labor force ($r = -.60$; $n = 36$; United Nations, 1968). The higher the legal status of women the narrower the difference in the participation rates of single and married women.

To illustrate differences in participation rates associated with different types of polities, consider the cases of Argentina (organic corporatist), Sweden (communal corporatist), and the United States (liberal individualist). The labor-force participation rates of single women in these countries are very similar (United Nations, 1968): 49% in Argentina, 51.9% in Sweden, and 51.2% in the United States. In contrast, the participation rates of married women are quite different: 11.4%, 33.2%, and 39.1% respectively. The married Argentinean woman appears to be more absorbed in the familial domain than her Swedish and American counterparts. And, we would expect that a comparative content analysis of mass media coverage of potential conflicts between women's rights and those of children would show least coverage in Argentina, more coverage in Sweden, and even higher levels of coverage in the United States. And yet, no one who has read the novels of Garcia-Marquez or seen the films of Bergman could convincingly argue that Latin American and Swedish familial life is necessarily less conflict-ridden than it is in the United States.

Note that the relatively greater market freedom of the married woman in the United States does not impose any special obligations on central authorities to create and finance alternative child-rearing arrangements or obligations to support families more directly. When the level of economic development is controlled, such obligations are more likely to be assumed by the more corporatist polities. Indeed, more favorable maternity leave arrangements and more generous family allowances are likely to be found in countries that have more corporatist polities. Participation rights that do not impose obligations on the larger society or the national state are maximized in the more liberal individualist polities.[3] Evidence in support of this point is found in O'Connor's (1988) analysis of the expansion of preschool enrollment between 1965 and 1980. She demonstrates that liberal individualist polities are more likely to expand preschool enrollments than corporatist polities. In addition, she finds that the level of female participation in higher education is only weakly related to growth in preschool enrollments. Preschool enrollments are more likely to increase in corporatist countries, where a greater percentage of social security spending goes to family allowances. In the polities, women are more likely to enjoy a legitimate status as an interest group (rather than as a collection of individuals) and families are more likely to be both more supported and regulated than in more liberal individualist polities.

Lastly, let us briefly consider some preliminary analyses undertaken by Langton (1983) that are relevant to the ideas discussed above. Langton was concerned with the kinds of empirical comparisons that could be made among countries that might illustrate implications of their different forms of modernization. Two variables were constructed to characterize nation-states by their location on the typology we discussed above. The first is an index of the constitutional status of women as citizens. This national characteristic may reflect the extension of the rules of liberal individualism to women. The second measure is an index of constitutional provisions for the political incorporation of *families*, rather than of individuals, in the national society. It includes indicators of state power to regulate and protect motherhood, childhood, marriage, and the family. It reflects the political incorporation of the family as a unit into the rules of the state.

The analysis is designed to indicate the effects of these two variables on five dependent variables of interest, under the following simple theory: The political incorporation of women as citizens should increase the likelihood that intrafamilial problems become defined as public issues, while the political incorporation of the family should increase the costs and difficulties of constructing families and therefore increase the likelihood that problems appear outside the family's jurisdiction.

The two independent variables were included in multiple regression analyses of five dependent variables. These variables reflect information available in various compendia of national characteristics. (The availability of data is a recurrent restriction on cross-national research.) The first two dependent variables are the proportions of men and women 45 and older who are never married. Our argument suggests that as the family becomes a more central *corporate* entity within society, lower proportions of men and women are able to form families. The costs of establishing families are too high and hence fewer families are formed for socioeconomic reasons. On the other hand, we expect no such effect of the extension of citizenship to women.

We also expect the two independent variables to have different effects on a third dependent variable: the rate of out-of-wedlock births. We expect the rate of such births to be higher in systems that treat the family as an important corporate group and to be unaffected by variations in the extension of citizenship to women. We also expect the number of national women's organizations to be much lower in societies in which the family is a politically incorporated group, but to be unaffected or positively affected by the extension of citizenship rights to women.

Finally, we expect that the divorce rate will be negatively affected by the incorporation of the family by the legal system, but it should be positively affected by the extension of citizenship to women. The divorce rate is the one indicator we have of the public expression of *internal* family problems.

Multiple repression analyses of the effects of the two crucial independent variables on each of the dependent variables are reported in Table 7.2. A series of control variables is held constant in each analysis in order to provide a more reasonable test and to eliminate the possibility that our results may reflect the general expansion of state authority rather than the particular variables in which we are interested. We control: (1) whether a state is primarily Catholic, (2) whether it is a communist state (both of these types of states tend to have distinct family-related patterns), (3) gross national product per capita, as an indicator of national economic development, and (4) a general index of the overall constitutional power of the state.

Each column in Table 7.2 represents a distinct multiple regression analysis showing the effects of six independent and control variables on a dependent variable. All of the variables were measured for the same time period, 1970. Given the cross-sectional nature of the research design, caution should be exercised in drawing causal inferences. The number of cases

Table 7.2. Cross-National Multiple Regression Analyses of the Effects of the Political Incorporation of the Family and of Women as Citizens

| | Dependent Variables | | | | |
Independent and Control Variables	Percent of Men 45 and Older Never Married	Percent of Women 45 and Older Never Married	Percent of Children Born Out of Wedlock	Number of National Women's Organizations	Divorce Rate
1. Index of Family Incorporation	.31[a]**	.24*	.28*	−.28**	−.31
2. Index of Incorporation of Women	.00	.08	−.20	−.07	.61**
3. GNP Per Capita	.13	.11	−.25*	.49**	.04
4. Catholic Country	.25**	.35**	.08	.15**	−.12
5. Communist Country	−.20	−.18	−.11	−.19**	−.05
6. Index of Constitutional Power of the State	−.21	.02	−.02	.32**	.05
R^2	.16	.24	.24	.47	.34
N	79	79	57	130	45

[a]Cell entries are standardized regression coefficients.

*p < .10.

**p < .05.

Source. Langton (1983).

154

varies from analysis to analysis because the number of countries with information on the relevant dependent variable varies, from a minimum of 45 cases in the analysis of the divorce rate to a maximum of 130 cases in the analysis of the number of national women's organizations. Our inspection of the data showed that no analysis was restricted to countries from a particular region or to a specific level of industrialization.

The results suggest the merit of our overall theoretical imagery. States in which the family is incorporated as a central structure have higher proportions of single persons, higher rates of out-of-wedlock births, and fewer national women's organizations. They also have, as we expected, lower divorce rates. The extension of citizenship rights to women, on the other hand, sharply increases the divorce rate, but leaves the other variables unaffected.

We conclude that our argument is worth further exploration. The incorporation of the family as a "natural" central building block of societies lowers the public exposure of intrafamilial problems, but also leaves more problems for individuals to handle outside family life (including out-of-wedlock births). The extension of citizenship rights to women, on the other hand, expands the national organizational representation of women and their issues, and increases the public recognition of divorce.

SUMMARY

A cursory examination of societal patterns of relations between women and children is consistent with the notion that the traditional family and traditional relations between women and children are breaking down. Conflicts between women and children appear to be on the increase. Our analysis suggests that the increased *perception* of conflict may be a consequence of development and modernization. We argue that the political incorporation of women and children—and the *pattern* of incorporation in particular—plays an important role in bringing what were historically private issues into the public arena.

Our arguments suggest that the expansion of state authority accompanies social and economic development, and with the expansion of the state, rights of citizenship are extended to women and children. But societies differ in the manner in which women and children are politically incorporated. Liberal individualist societies, those like our own, incorporate women and children as individual citizens and conflicts are more likely to reach the public arena in those societies. As a consequence, the perception of conflict is heightened in such societies, whether actual levels of conflict increase or not.

We have used cross-national data to demonstrate a number of changes that have occurred since 1870: There has been a general expansion of state power that has been accompanied by a general increase in the rights of citizens. With increasing frequency the ranks of the citizenry have been extended to include women. The notion that the state has a responsibility to secure the welfare of children has also become widespread. National states have also increasingly felt it necessary to take responsibility for the protection and regulation of motherhood and the institution of the family. Finally, our preliminary analysis suggests that there is variation by country in the forms of political incorporation of women and children and that the incorporation of women and children is associated with the general expansion of state power.

Our work suggests a need to reexamine what appears to be the emergence of new sets of family problems and a dramatic upswing in old ones such as child abuse. The sheer volume of such problems threatens to clog our legislative and court systems. The notion that they are growing dramatically or that they signal a society that "secretly hates children" (cf. Pogrebin, 1983) lends an air of crisis to the situation. We would argue that the problems are real, but that it is likely that they have existed for centuries; it is their appearance on the public agenda and the dependence on public agencies and institutions to resolve them that is new.

NOTES

1. In reality, large numbers of women who are single parents *and* are inordinately poor might find this an attractive option—if it existed. But the transfer of private family issues to the public domain makes the option "unthinkable." Whether a child—or any person—can be bought or sold, and the age at which family members can legitimately seek and accept employment are issues that are regulated by agents of the state. No family can effectively decide such issues because the state preempts family authority in those areas.

2. Our argument is dramatically illustrated by the issue of incest which is much in the news. Anthropologists and other social scientists have suggested that the incest taboo is a "cultural universal." But their ideas about incest were based largely on observations of societies that have the features of organic corporatist groups. Our arguments suggest that cases of incest would be resolved as a private family matter in such societies. Any family member subjected to incest could appeal to only one regulatory agency—the family—to resolve it. In contrast, today's victims of incest can seek recourse through civil *and* criminal proceedings, both of which are carried out in the public arena. Hence, the perception that there is a "dramatic increase" in incest is quite probably due to its increasing public nature rather than to any real increase in its incidence.

3. Marshall (1964) distinguished three forms of citizenship rights, civil, political, and social. Civil and political rights are rights to participate in society. National states do not normally incur obligations by granting such rights as the right of franchise. On the other hand, the granting of social rights such as the right of every person to an education typically creates obligations for the state (Bendix, 1964).

REFERENCES

Anderson, P. (1974). *Lineages of the absolutist state.* London: New Left Books.
Aries, P. (1962). *Centuries of childhood.* New York: Vintage.
Bell, D. (1976). *The cultural contradictions of capitalism.* New York: Basic Books.
Bendix, R. (1964). *Nation-building and citizenship.* New York: Wiley.
Berger, P., Berger, B., & Kellner, H. (1973). *The homeless mind.* New York: Random House.

Berger, S. (1981). *Organizing interests in Western Europe: Pluralism, corporatism, and the transformation of politics.* New York: Cambridge University Press.

Blaustein, A., & Flanz, G. (1971). *Constitutions of the countries of the world.* New York: Oceana.

Boli-Bennett, J. (1976). *The expansion of nation-states, 1870–1970.* Unpublished doctoral dissertation, Stanford University.

Boli-Bennett, J. (1980a). Global integration and the universal increase of state dominance. In A. Bergensen (Ed.), *Studies of the modern world system.* New York: Academic Press.

Boli-Bennett, J. (1980b). The ideology of expanding state authority in national constitutions, 1870–1979. In J. Meyer & M. T. Hannan (Eds.), *National development and the world system.* Chicago: University of Chicago Press.

Boli-Bennett, J. (1981). Human rights or state expansion. Cross-national definitions of constitutional rights, 1870–1970. In V. Nanda, J. Scarritt, & G. Shepherd (Eds.), *Global human rights: Public policies, comparative measures and NGO strategies.* Boulder, CO: Westview Press.

Boli-Bennett, J., & Meyer, J. (1978). The ideology of childhood and the state: Rules distinguishing children in national constitutions, 1870–1970. *American Sociological Review, 43*, 797–812.

Boli-Bennett, J., & Ramirez, F. O. (1986). World culture and the institutionalization of mass education. In J. Richardson (Eds.), *Handbook of theory and research in Education.* Westport, CT: Greenwood Press.

Brines, W., & Gordon, L. (1983). The new scholarship on family violence. *Signs, 8*, 490–531.

Cook, A. (1974). *The working mothers.* Ithaca, NY: Cornell University Press.

DeMause, L. (Ed.). (1974). *The history of childhood.* New York: Psychohistory.

Donzelot, J. (1979). *The policing of families.* New York: Pantheon.

Finkelhor, D., Gelles, R., Hotaling, G., & Straus, M. (Eds.). (1983). *The dark side of families.* Beverly Hills, CA: Sage Publications.

Gelles, R. (1979). *Family violence.* Beverly Hills, CA: Sage Publications.

Gelles, R., & Cornell, C. (1982). *International perspectives on family violence.* Paper presented at the annual meetings of the American Sociological Association, San Francisco.

Held, T., Ramirez, F. O., & Meyer, J. W. (1983, September). *Violence and abuse in the family.* Paper presented at the annual meetings of the American Sociological Association, Detroit.

Heyns, B., & Catsambis, S. (1986). Mother's employment and children's achievement: A critique. *Sociology of Education, 59*, 140–151.

Igra, A. (1976). *Social mobilization, national context, and political participation.* Unpublished doctoral dissertation, Stanford University.

Illich, I. (1983). *Gender.* New York: Pantheon.

Kamerman, S. (1975, May/June). Eight countries: Cross-national perspectives on child abuse and neglect. *Today*, pp. 34–37.

Langer, W. (1974). Infanticide: A historical survey. *History of Childhood Quarterly, 1*, 353–365.

Langton, N. (1983). *Constitutional incorporation of families and of women as citizens.* Unpublished paper, Stanford University, Department of Sociology.

Lasch, C. (1977). *Haven in a heartless world: The family besieged.* New York: Basic Books.

Lipset, S. M. (1963). *The first new nation.* New York: Basic Books.

Marshall, T. H. (1964). *Class, citizenship, and social development.* New York: Doubleday.

Meyer, J. W. (1980). The world polity and the authority of the nation-state. In A. Bergensen (Ed.), *Studies of the modern world system.* New York: Academic Press.

Meyer, J. W. (1986). *Myths of socialization and personality.* In T. Heller, M. Sosna, & D. Wellbery (Eds.), *Reconstructing individualism* (pp. 212–225). Stanford, CA: Stanford University Press.

Meyer, J. W., Ramirez, F. O., Rubinson, R., & Boli-Bennett, J. (1977). The world educational revolution, 1950–1970. *Sociology of Education, 50,* 242–258.

Milburn, J. F. (1976). *Women as citizens: A comparative review.* Beverly Hills, CA: Sage Publications.

Milne, A., Myers, D., Rosenthal, A., & Ginsburg, A. (1986). Single parents, working mothers, and the educational achievement of school children. *Sociology of Education, 59,* 125–139.

O'Connor, S. (1988). Women's labor force participation and preschool enrollment: A cross-national perspective, 1965–80. *Sociology of Education, 61,* 15–28.

Pogrebin, L. C. (1983). *Family politics.* New York: McGraw-Hill.

Ramirez, F. O. (1981). Statism, equality, and housewifery: A cross-national analysis. *Pacific Sociological Review, 24,* 175–195.

Ramirez, F. O., & Boli-Bennett, J. (1982). Global patterns of educational institutionalization. In P. Altbach, R. Arnove, & G. Kelly (Eds.), *Comparative education.* New York: Macmillan.

Ramirez, F. O., & Thomas, G. M. (1981). Structural antecedents and consequences of statism. In R. Rubinson (Ed.), *Dynamics of world development.* Beverly Hills, CA: Sage Publication.

Shorter, E. (1975). *The making of the modern family.* New York: Basic Books.

Sommerville, J. (1982). *The rise and fall of childhood.* Beverly Hills, CA: Sage Publications.

Stepan, A. (1978). *The state and society: Peru in comparative perspective.* Princeton, NJ: Princeton University Press.

United Nations. (1968). *Demographic yearbook.* New York: United Nations.

Wald, M. S. (1979). Children's rights: A framework for analysis. *University of California Davis Law Review, 129*(2), 255–282.

Zelizer, V. A. (1986). *Pricing the priceless child: The changing social value of children.* New York: Basic Books.

PART II

THE NEW FAMILIES

8

Two-Earner Families

MYRA H. STROBER

The rise in two-earner families is one of the most striking economic and social developments of the post-World War II period. Two-earner families now account for 42% of all families (U.S. Bureau of the Census, 1985b). Married women now comprise almost one fourth (23.4%) of the total labor force and more than half (54%) of the female labor force (Hayghe, 1986). In 1940, the labor-force participation rate for married women was about 15%; by 1985, it was 54%, more than three times the 1940 rate, and continuing to approach the male participation rate of 77%.

Even more extraordinary have been the increases in the labor-force participation rates of married women with young children. In 1985 half of all married women with infants under the age of 1 year, almost 60% of those with children 3 to 5, and more than two thirds of those with children 6 to 13 were in the workforce (see Table 8.1). More than two thirds of these employed mothers worked full time, and about 90% were married to husbands who were also employed. Among black women, the labor-force participation rates were even higher. About two thirds of black wives with infants under the age of 1 and almost three fourths of those with children 6 to 13 were in the labor force in 1985 (Hayghe, 1986).

Many lament these changes, assuming that the "best" sort of family—the one that policy ought to promote—is the two-parent, husband-only-earner family (termed the breadwinner family by Davis in Chapter 4) enshrined in Parsonian writing (Parsons, 1942, 1949, 1955) and portrayed in 1950s television sitcoms. The notion that there is some "best" sort of family structure is often explicitly voiced by policymakers who seek to "save" *the family* (meaning the two-parent, husband-only-earner family), by voting, for example, against legislation to foster the development of extrafamily child care. The notion is less explicit, but nonetheless powerful, among decision makers in schools and workplaces who have yet to adjust to the realities of two-earner families.

From one perspective, two-earner families are a necessary evil to be borne, either because the family's economic situation requires the mother's

Myra H. Strober, Ph.D. Stanford School of Education, Stanford University, Stanford, California.

Table 8.1. Labor-Force Participation Rates of Wives, Husband Present, 1985

	Total	White	Black
All wives	54.3	53.4	64.2
With children under 18 years	61.0	60.0	71.5
With children 6–13 years	68.1	67.7	73.5
With children under 6 years	53.7	52.3	69.3
With children 3–5 years	58.6	56.6	73.8
With children 2 years	54.0	52.7	69.9
With children 1 year or less	49.4	48.6	63.7

Source. Hayghe (1986, p. 44).

income, or because the mother is selfish enough to insist on fulfilling her career goals despite the negative effects on "the family" (i.e., other family members). The husband/father is presumed to suffer the loss of home production (including special meals, attentive soothing, and carefree child-rearing); the children experience the loss of constant mothering (including milk and cookies after school); and the wife/mother is plagued by both guilt and stress as she tries endlessly (and unsuccessfully) to balance her two full-time jobs.

This view of two-earner families is now being superseded by a new model. Women appear to be choosing two-earner families not as a second-best alternative but as a preferred life-style. The effects on other family members of this life-style appear to be positive (or at least benign) rather than pernicious; and the stresses faced by women appear to stem at least as much from discrimination and occupational segregation in the job market as from juggling family and work roles. Moreover, for many and perhaps most young families it is childrearing that is added on to work, rather than the other way around; the decision appears increasingly to be whether or not to have a child, rather than whether or not to work. All of this is not to say that two-earner families do not face difficulties, but that they also experience satisfactions.

This chapter looks at four aspects of the rise in two-earner families. The first section examines the explanations for women's increased employment and three salient characteristics of the market for women's labor: hours of work, unemployment, occupational segregation, and gender differences in earnings. The second section discusses the effects of wives' employment on the division of labor in the home. In the third section, some of the economic, demographic, and social effects of married women's employment are analyzed. The final section of the paper presents several public policies designed to increase the satisfactions and decrease the difficulties for members of two-earner families.

WOMEN'S WORK IN THE MARKET

Labor-Force Participation

In 1900, the labor-force participation rate for all women was 18% (Durand, 1948). For wives it was only 6% (U.S. Bureau of the Census, 1975). As indicated in the chapter by Davis, over the next several decades, unmarried women entered the labor force in increasing numbers; they were followed, in turn, by married women with children over 18.

During the 1940s and 1950s, married women with school-age children provided the largest single increase in labor-market participation of the entire 50-year period. Beginning in the early 1960s, the only remaining group—married women with preschoolers—moved en masse into the labor market. The unprecedented influx of women into the labor force, which consistently outpaced predictions made by the Bureau of Labor Statistics, occurred without the development of a child-care system, without a national maternity policy, and with relatively few changes in workplace norms or regulations.

The explanations given for women's entry into the workforce fall into three groups: supply-side, demand-side, and structural. Each tells a piece of the story; together they offer a reasonably complete exposition. Those who stress supply-side explanations argue that women came into the workforce as the imputed wages of their home production fell relative to the wages they could earn in the market (Becker, 1965; Mincer, 1962). Lowering the value of their home production were such factors as the decline in the birth rate and the development of labor-saving devices; increasing their market wage were their ever-increasing levels of education and the steady rise of productivity in the market economy. Thus, increasing numbers of women became eager for market employment.

The demand-side explanation focuses on the importance of the growth of traditionally female occupations, particularly clerical and service occupations, as a factor in women's increasing employment. As vacancies in these female-typed occupations occurred, it is argued, employers sought not simply labor but female labor in particular, thus pulling a readily available resource into the marketplace (Oppenheimer, 1969).

The structural explanation takes a somewhat broader view of the changes in women's employment, pointing to the salience of major structural changes in technology, demography, and the economy (Vickery, 1979; Vickery-Brown, 1982). The improvement in birth control technology made it possible for families to limit the number of their children and to plan their spacing. At the same time, the increase in women's lifespan meant that, after they had borne and reared their relatively small number of children, they would have numerous years remaining in which to be productive members of the workforce. As the economy became more industrialized and market-oriented, women found that they could serve their families best, not by providing home-produced goods and services, but by earning income so that these goods and services could be purchased in the market. For example, in the 19th century a "good" mother who stayed at home could educate her children and, if they were ill, provide them with nursing services. Today, as education and medicine have advanced and become more complex, mothers work to help pay for their children's college education or hospital care.

Once women's labor-force participation rates began to rise, there were probably snowball effects that contributed to their continued increase. The term "pioneer" aptly characterizes the first wives who entered the labor force in each group (those with grown children, those with school-age children, and finally those with preschool children). But once new lifestyles were established, community attitudes began to change to make it accept-able, indeed desirable, for women in similar situations to work. As families sought to emulate their friends' consumption patterns and as neighborhoods provided less daytime sociability, more women sought employment.

The most recent increases in labor-force participation are also related to the decline in real income that families have experienced. Between 1973 and 1986, real earnings declined about 14% ("The Average Guy," 1986). It is a correct perception that today two incomes are often required to maintain living standards of a decade ago, let alone to make major new purchases, like a home. In 1950 and 1960, wives were much more likely to be in the labor force if their husbands' income was relatively low and their children were adolescents (Bowen & Finegan, 1969; Cain, 1966). By 1970, the income of husband was no longer a significant determinant of wives' labor-force behavior (Fields, 1976). And the data for the mid-1980s suggest that age of child, too, has become a much less powerful predictor of which women will work.

For many women, labor-force participation provides a modest insur-ance policy in case of divorce. The probability of divorce has risen signifi-cantly in the postwar period and women know that if they are divorced, their economic well-being will decline significantly. As Weitzman points out in Chapter 10, under the new no-fault divorce laws, courts award women almost no alimony even if they have no recent labor-market experience. Women with children are particularly at risk in divorce. About 90% of all children of divorce are cared for by their mothers. Yet almost two thirds of these mothers do not receive child support payments (U.S. Bureau of Census, 1985a). Often, a woman's own earnings provide the only protection she has against the economic fallout of divorce. When she has a history of steady employment, those earnings are more likely to be assured.

The changes in women's labor-force participation were well underway by the time the women's movement began in the early 1960s. It is therefore not accurate to argue that the movement was a salient factor in initiating increases in women's labor-force participation. The movement did, however, have a significant effect on the types of jobs that women began to seek, on the pressures on government and business to include women in affirmative action orders and nondiscrimination legislation, and on the efforts in families to rethink the division of labor at home.

Based on surveys of the employment expectations of young women, it seems safe to predict that women's labor-force participation will continue to increase in the future. In the 1979 National Longitudinal Survey, over 6,000 women aged 14–21 were asked about work expectations for themselves at age 35. Seventy-two percent of white women and 86% of black women said they expected to work at age 35 (Council of Economic Advisors, 1987).

Women's educational decisions also appear to be increasingly geared toward high levels of labor-force participation. Between 1975–1976 and 1985–1986, the number of women receiving first professional degrees increased by 150% (from 10,000 to 25,000); the number receiving Ph.D. degrees increased by 50% (from 8,000 to 12,000). In 1975–1976, women were 16% of the recipients of first professional degrees and 24% of Ph.D. recipients. By 1985–1986, they were one third of the recipients of first professional degrees and 36% of Ph.D. recipients (U.S. Bureau of Education, 1987). Women who receive first professional and Ph.D. degrees generally have very high levels of labor-force participation.

Hours of Work and Unemployment

Most women in the labor force work full-time, that is at least 35 hours per week. Among white women, 72% work full-time, compared to 90% of white men. Among blacks, 88% of men and 80% of women work full-time (Nardone, 1986). Even among mothers with young children, full-time work is the norm; about two thirds of all mothers with children under 6 work full-time. Among all mothers with school-age children, 70% work full-time. As is true among all women, among mothers, blacks are more likely than whites to work full-time (Hayghe, 1986).

Most workers who are employed part-time are "voluntary" part-time workers, that is, they work part-time as a result of their own preferences. Among women 16 and over, 82% of part-time workers are voluntary. The other 18% are termed "economic" part-time workers; they would prefer to work full-time, but cannot find full-time employment. The percentage of men 16 and over who voluntarily work part-time is 74, considerably lower than the figure for women (Nardone, 1986).

If we look at the work experience of the population throughout the year, as opposed to their employment at a single point in time, we also find some important differences between men and women. Among those who worked at all during 1985, 32% of women worked part-time, as opposed to only 14% of men. Moreover, only half of all women who worked at some time during 1985 worked full-time for at least 48 weeks, as opposed to their

male counterparts two thirds of whom worked full-time for at least
48 weeks (Smith, 1987).

Part-time workers generally earn an hourly wage that is lower than the
hourly wage of full-time workers. In a recent study comparing women part-
time and full-time workers, Blank (1986) found that part of this wage
differential is due to the fact that part-time workers tend to have less
education and experience than full-time workers. But the differential also
results from the concentration of part-time workers in industries and occupations that pay low wages and from a lower return to education in part-
time jobs (Blank, 1986). This lower return may be explained partly from the
fact that employers are less likely to "invest" in part-time workers through
on-the-job training since they often view these workers as temporary and
uncommitted. The absence of well-paying part-time jobs is a serious problem for some two-earner couples who would like to combine work and
family by having at least one parent work only part-time.

In addition to low wage rates, part-time and temporary jobs generally
do not pay pro-rated fringe benefits. Legislation has recently been introduced in Congress to require employers to lower the number of annual
hours of work required for an employee to receive credit toward pension
vesting and to require employers to offer pro-rated health insurance to part-
time and temporary workers, if the employer offers such benefits to full-time
workers.

Unemployment rates for men and women are much more similar than
are labor-force participation rates. Men are more likely than are women to
face layoffs because men are more likely to be employed in industries and
jobs that are sensitive to the business cycle. On the other hand, women are
more likely than are men to be recent labor-force entrants and thus women
face higher unemployment as they search for a job or take the consequences
of a last-hired, first-fired seniority system. During the recession years 1982
and 1983, women's rates were slightly lower than men's, but from 1984 to
1986, women's rates slightly exceeded men's (*Monthly Labor Review*, April
1983–April 1987). For example, in 1986, the rate for women 16 and over was
7.1 %, the rate for men 16 and over was 6.9%.

For blacks, unemployment rates are more than double those for whites.
But there is not very much difference between the unemployment rates of
black men and women. In 1986, for example, the rate for black women over
20 was 12.4%; the rate for black men over 20 was 12.9% (*Monthly Labor
Review*, April 1987).

Occupational Segregation and Earnings

Although the labor-force participation rate for women during this century
has soared, the labor force has maintained its rigid segregation by gender.
The degree of occupational segregation is often measured by the index of

occupational segregation. Ranging from 0, indicating complete integration, to 100, indicating complete segregation, the index may be interpreted as the percentage of women (or men) that would have to be redistributed among occupations in order for there to be complete equality of occupational distribution by gender.

While changes in occupational categories over a long period make comparisons difficult to interpret, it is generally agreed that in the U.S. the index of segregation remained at about .66 between 1900 and 1970.[1] During the 1970s, the index fell somewhat to about .63 (Beller, 1984; Gross, 1968; Reskin & Hartmann, 1986). Nevertheless, in 1980 about 5 out of 8 women or 5 out of 8 men in the workforce would have had to change their occupations for there to have been gender parity in the occupational distribution.

Another common way of looking at occupational segregation is to array occupations according to their percentage of female incumbents and then calculate the percentage of the female workforce employed in predominantly female occupations. In 1980, about half of all women workers were in occupations that were at least 80% female. At the same time, about 70% of men worked in occupations that were at least 80% male (Reskin & Hartmann, 1986). For black women and men these proportions were somewhat lower (Malveaux, 1982). Occupational segregation by gender, by these measures, continues to be pervasive.

Occupational segregation is one of the major causes of the earnings differential between men and women. For example, in 1970, women who worked full-time, year-round earned approximately 60% of the earnings of men who worked full-time, year-round. Based on an analysis of 499 detailed occupational categories, Treiman and Hartmann (1981) concluded that about 35% to 40% of this earnings differential was the result of occupational segregation. The other 60% to 65% came from the fact that for diverse reasons within the same occupation, men earn more than women.

While the 1970s saw a slight decrease in occupational segregation, there was no corresponding improvement in the female/male earnings differential. Women who worked full-time, year-round continued to earn about 60% of the wage or salary of men who work full-time, year-round. However, during the early 1980s, women's position improved somewhat relative to men's. In 1985, women who worked full-time, year-round had median earnings equal to 64% of those of men who worked full-time, year-round (Council of Economic Advisors, 1987).[2]

Some of this differential results from employment discrimination—unequal financial returns to equal productive characteristics—but some also results from the fact that men have slightly more formal education than women (and are more likely to major in subjects that have a high payoff), more on-the-job training and more continuous work experience than do women. In general, if we divide the earnings differential into two parts, that due to differences in productive characteristics, including work experience, and the remainder (usually called employment discrimination), most studies find that about half of the differential results from differences in productive characteristics and half from employment discrimination (Corcoran & Duncan, 1979; Treiman & Hartmann, 1981).

The extent to which women's earnings suffer as a result of their discontinuous employment has been extensively debated in the economics literature. Women who leave the labor force have lower real earnings when they return than they did at the time they dropped out. But in the first few years back at work their wages tend to rise rapidly and the overall loss from having dropped out seems to be small (Corcoran, Duncan, & Ponza, 1984). In managerial and certain professional jobs, however, the penalty for dropping out can be quite large. For example, see Strober (1981) regarding the penalty for MBAs.

Married women's earnings are important to their families' well-being. In 1984, among white married couples, those with a wife in the labor force had median family earnings 25% higher than couples with a wife who was not in the labor force ($35,176 vs. $28,246). Among black married couples, the difference was even greater: black couples with two earners had a median family income almost double that of couples with a wife not in the paid labor force ($28,775 vs. $14,502) (U.S. Bureau of the Census, 1985b).

Wives' earnings also reduce the poverty rate for families and increase the income share of the poorest quintile of families. For 1984, Danziger and Gottschalk (1986) estimate that among two-parent families, wives' earnings decreased the poverty rate by 35% as compared to what it would have been had families not been able to draw on these earnings. Similarly, they estimate that the poorest quintile of families raised their share of total income by 15% as a result of wives' earnings.

An interesting study by Blackburn and Bloom (1986) investigated the effect of wives' labor-force participation on the income distribution across families (married couple families and all families) for the period 1968 to 1984. They compared the level of inequality actually observed with the inequality that would have been observed had all wives' earnings been zero. They found that wives' earnings was *not* a contributory factor to the slight increase in family income inequality over the period.

THE DIVISION OF LABOR AT HOME
IN TWO-EARNER FAMILIES

We have already noted that fundamental, long-term changes in the production of home goods and services were an important factor in married women's entry into the labor force. And, once married women were in the workforce, family goods and services produced at home changed still further. However, the effects of married women's labor-force participation on home production and the division of labor at home are generally overstated.

The entry of women into the labor market is often cast in terms such as the exchanging of aprons for typewriters. In fact married women have not substituted market work for home work. Estimates by Bergmann (1986) and Blau and Ferber (1986) based on compilations of several studies indicate that, depending on the definition of housework used, married women who are employed spend an average of about 22 to 23 hours per week on housework, fewer than the average of 40 to 48 hours per week spent by their sisters who are full-time homemakers, but far from zero, and far from the 8.5 to 12 hours per week spent by husbands. Women who work outside the home still keep their aprons handy.

Like housework itself, measuring housework is a nontrivial task. Simplistic techniques of measurement are inadequate and misleading. Measuring housework by counting the number of tasks performed is inadmissible because certain tasks are specified in great detail while others are defined very generally. For example, tasks falling under the general rubric of food preparation—shopping, preparing food for cooking, cooking, serving, washing dishes, and cleaning the kitchen—are often individually itemized, whereas so-called outdoor tasks may be specified only very broadly, as in "automobile repair." Because the tasks that are generally performed by women tend to be specified in much more detail than those typically performed by men, it is particularly inappropriate to use number of tasks completed to measure the differences between men's and women's housework contributions.

Asking people to estimate the quantity of another person's housework is also problematic, especially if the other person is their spouse. In a fascinating study, Berk and Shih (1980) have shown that each spouse, relative to the other, tends to overestimate their own housework and underestimate their partner's.

The most sophisticated studies of housework rely either on diaries where respondents are asked to keep track of their activities at short intervals, or on telephone interviews where respondents are asked to recall their activities on the previous day. Researchers at the Michigan Survey Research Center, the major source of studies on American time use, have found that recall interviews produce replicable and reliable results (Juster, 1985; Robinson, 1985). Of particular interest is their finding that the recall interviews produced reports of time use quite similar to those obtained from the much more expensive procedure of having subjects keep a random beeping device and record time use each time the beeper sounded.

Even more difficult than measurement problems are thorny conceptual issues. What should be included in the definition of housework? Is repair to the outside of one's house part of housework? Is taking one's child to the park housework (child care), leisure, or some combination of the two?

The fact that several housework tasks are often completed simultaneously also causes difficulties. If one is ironing, listening to the radio, and watching one's child, how does one report the use of one's time? Generally studies permit the respondent to determine what the "primary activity" is in such a situation. But is reporting of one's primary activity dependent upon one's education? Might not a more educated woman engaged in those three tasks view herself as primarily caring for her child despite the fact that she is doing nothing different from the less educated woman who views herself as primarily engaged in ironing?

Several questions about time use are of interest in understanding the gender division of labor in two-earner families. First, what is the division of labor in such families? Second, how has that division changed over time? Third, how does the division differ as between two-earner and single-earner couples? In answering these questions, conceptual difficulties must be borne in mind.

Four-time diary studies of family time use have been completed in recent years. A study by Walker and Woods (1976) surveyed approximately 1300 husband–wife families in Syracuse, New York, in 1968. Employed wives were defined as those gainfully employed 15 or more hours per week. Nonemployed wives were either not gainfully employed or employed less than 15 hours per week. Data were collected both by an interview, in which wives were asked to recall the use of time by family members on the previous day, and a time record chart broken into 10-minute intervals.

A second survey, carried out by the Michigan Survey Research Center (SRC) in 1965 to 1966 (Robinson & Converse, 1972; Robinson, 1977), analyzed the time diaries of 2,000 Americans, 18 to 65 years of age, who lived in metropolitan areas and in households where at least one member was in the labor force. The diaries were kept in late 1965 through the spring of 1966.

The Michigan SRC also ran a time-use survey in 1975 to 1976 for a national probability sample of U.S. households, and a small follow-up survey in 1981 to 1982 of the 1975 to 1976 respondents (Juster & Stafford, 1985).

In 1975, married men spent an average of 7.13 hours per day in market work (including travel to work) while married women spent an average of 4.60 hours per day in market work. On the other hand, married women spent an average of 3.98 hours per day on work at home (including house-work; household repairs, maintenance, and gardening; child care; and shop-ping and financial work) while married men spent an average of 1.58 hours per day on work at home. If we add time spent on market work to time spent on work at home, we find that married women spent 8.58 hours per day on work while married men spent 8.71 hours per day on work. Married men had about 41 minutes more per day of passive leisure than did married women, while married women spent about 43 minutes more per day in personal care than did married men.

Between 1965 and 1975, both married men and married women cut back on their hours of market work (about 23 minutes per day for men and almost 1 hour per day for women); also, married women cut back (about 26 minutes per day) on work at home. Men's time spent on work at home remained stable over the 10-year period. Both men and women increased their leisure time (about 24 minutes per day for men, about 38 minutes per day for women).

The 1981 to 1982 Michigan follow-up study looked at changes in time use among respondents to the 1975 to 1976 study. Although the sample size is small, the results indicate that among married men and women over 25, use of time has become more equal, although significant differences remain. Unfortunately, the study does not report data separately for employed and nonemployed women. Over the period, married men increased their weekly housework time by about 1 hour and decreased their market work by the same amount. Among married women, time allocated to housework and market work remained about the same. In 1981 to 1982, men did 14.7 hours per week of housework while women did 22.4.

Although employed wives at all income levels and life-cycle stages report a greater shortage of time than do nonemployed wives, there appear to be limited differences between the two groups in their use of strategies to relieve time pressures. Both types of wives are similar with respect to the substitution of other's labor for their own market time, although there may be some tendency for employed wives to use paid help more frequently than nonemployed wives (Robinson, 1977; Robinson & Coverse, 1972; Stafford & Duncan, 1980; Walker & Woods, 1976).

The amount of time that husbands spend on housework is virtually the same in families where the wife is employed and where she is not employed. Robinson (1977) concluded that, income and demographic variables held constant, wives' employment increased husbands' housework time by only 5 minutes per day.

In a series of studies Strober (1977) and Strober and Weinberg (1977, 1980) investigated the effect of wives' employment on the use of time-saving capital equipment in the home. They found that, holding constant total family income and life-cycle stage, wives' employment had no effect on either families' purchase decisions (whether a particular item was purchased) nor on families' expenditure decisions (if an item was purchased, how much was spent) for such items as washing machines, dryers, freezers, dishwashers, or microwave ovens. Looking solely at families with an employed wife, Stafford and Duncan (1980) concluded that when family income, husband's education and age of children were held constant, there was no significant relationship between wives' hourly wage rate and ownership of several time-saving durables.

Strober and Weinberg (1980) also found that holding constant income and life-cycle stage, employed wives and nonemployed wives were similar with respect to their method of food preparation and their shopping behavior. Despite popular belief, employed wives did not seem to use frozen foods more, or any less frequently preserve by canning or bake from scratch, than did nonemployed wives in the same income or life-style group. Neither did employed wives economize on their time by shopping less frequently for clothes or groceries or shopping more frequently by mail-order catalogue as compared to their nonemployed counterparts in the same income or life-cycle group.

Evidence thus far obtained indicates that employed wives deal with their increased time pressures by decreasing the time spent on household production, the time allocated to volunteer and community work, and the time allocated to leisure and sleep. It may also be that employed wives work more intensively on household production tasks than do nonemployed wives or that they have lower standards for household cleanliness or elegance of food preparation.

Recently some have argued that because women do more housework than men, they therefore work less intensely on their paid jobs and seek less demanding work (Becker, 1985). Indeed, they speculate that this lower intensity of work effort may be a cause of women's lower wages relative to men. The Michigan time-use data (Stafford & Duncan, 1980) as well as the 1977 Quality of Employment Survey (Quinn & Staines, 1979) demonstrate that such suppositions are incorrect. The time-use data show that, as compared to men, women spend less time in coffee breaks and regularly scheduled work breaks, less time relaxing at work and less time at lunch. Although the unadjusted female/male wage differential was .62 in the time-use study, after adjusting for time spent in breaks and relaxing, the differential was .59. That is, the wage differential usually quoted understates the actual differential because women's work intensity is greater than men's.

Bielby and Bielby's (1988) study using the Quality of Employment Survey (Quinn & Staines, 1979) corroborates the time-use findings. As compared to men, women respondents score higher on a scale measuring their reported work effort even after controlling for family situation, household responsibilities, education, and earnings.

ECONOMIC AND SOCIAL EFFECTS OF WIVES' EMPLOYMENT

Social scientists have spilled considerable ink documenting and explaining the remarkable increase in wives' employment in the postwar period. Far fewer pages, however, have been devoted to assessing the economic and social effects of this work revolution. There remain intriguing questions about effects within families, effects on work organizations, and effects on the economy/society as a whole.

Chapter 9 by Mischel and Fuhr discusses the effects of mothers' employment on children and on mothers themselves. In this chapter, we review some of the theoretical and empirical literature on how wives' employment affects family consumption and savings patterns, family formation and dissolution, and marital satisfaction. We also examine the effects of wives' employment in dual-career families.

Family Consumption and Savings Patterns

How do families use the income earned by wives? With total family income held constant, do two-earner families spend their incomes differently from families where only the husband earns income? Economic theory provides several theoretical perspectives on this issue, each yielding different predictions.

At all income and life-cycle stages, working wives face greater time pressures and have less leisure than do nonworking wives (Strober & Weinberg, 1980). Combining this fact with Becker's (1965) allocation of time theory, one would hypothesize that two-earner families would place a higher marginal utility on time-saving goods and services and hence spend more on such goods and services than similarly situated single-earner families. Thus, we might expect that, holding total family income constant, two-earner families would spend more than their single-earner counterparts on such items as microwave ovens, dishwashers, and convenience foods.

Galbraith (1973), however, draws the opposite conclusion about consumption from the fact that two-earner families face greater time pressures than do single-earner families. He suggests that families with two earners may be expected to own and purchase fewer durable goods than families with one earner because durable goods require considerable time spent arranging for purchases and repairs (consumption administration) and employed wives have less time for, and possibly less interest in, such administrative activities.

According to the framework of the permanent income theory (Friedman, 1957), families have a higher propensity to save transitory income than to save permanent income. Thus, if families consider wives' employment to be impermanent and treat wives' earnings as having a large transitory component, two-earner families should save more than single-earner families with the same total family income. The theory suggests that two-earner families will also spend more on consumer durables, since expenditures on durables are considered as saving by the permanent income theorists (Mincer, 1960a, 1960b).

Duesenberry's (1949) relative income theory, on the other hand, can be used to argue that wives enter the labor market in order to bring their family consumption into parity with the income of their life-cycle reference group (Strober, 1977). In that case, we would expect two-earner families to spend the same amount *in toto* and on durable goods as do single-earner families with the same total income.

If we focus not on time allocation or consumption theories, but rather on theories of saving, we might predict that two-earner families would save less than single-earner families with the same income since one of the motivations for saving—providing for a rainy day—is less pressing in two-earner families. Two-earner families would have a lower propensity to save than their single-earner family counterparts because in two-earner families each spouse's earnings would provide a cushion for the other in case of unemployment.

Theories that view saving as a residual process, determined only after consumption decisions have been made, would also predict that two-earner families would save less than similarly situated single-earner families. The additional required work-related expenditures for transportation, child care, and clothing leaves two-earner families less *available* for saving. That is, holding income constant, both types of families might have the same inherent propensity to save, but two-earner families would be prevented from achieving their desired saving level because of their higher work-related expenditures.

Empirical work indicates that if income (and other variables) are held constant, two-earner families save less (and spend more) than do single-earner families (Strober, 1977; Vickery, 1979). But two-earner and single-earner families with the same total income spend the same amount on durable goods (Strober, 1977; Strober & Weinberg, 1977, 1980). Holding income (and other variables) constant, two-earner families have higher work-related expenditures than do single-earner families (Vickery, 1979).

The empirical findings support neither the time-allocation theory that two-earner families spend more on time-saving goods and services than do similarly situated single-earner families, nor Galbraith's theory that they spend less on consumer durables. The findings also fail to support the transitory income theory, perhaps because wives' attachment to the labor force is now stronger than in the past. However, the data are consistent with the lower propensity to save theory and the observation that two-earner families have higher work-related expenditures.

Marriage, Childbearing, Divorce, and Marital Satisfaction

Like the theoretical literature on the effects of wives' employment on family expenditures, the theoretical literature on the effects of wives' employment on marriage, divorce, and marital satisfaction yields conflicting predictions. Parsons' (1942, 1949, 1955) role differentiation theory argues that marital stability is fostered by the extreme differentiation of husbands' and wives' roles in the family, the husband's focused on obtaining income outside of the family, the wife's concerned with child bearing, psychological and physical caring, and sustenance within the family. If wives for some reason did need to be employed outside of the home, Parsons thought it important that they work in occupations that posed no threat to their husband's status as the primary breadwinner; otherwise the solidarity of the marriage could be threatened.

Becker's (1981) economic theory of the family also focuses on the importance of complementarity of roles for husband and wife (he earning income, she providing household production), if both are to obtain the maximum gains from marriage. The theory suggests that the more similar in role and hence the more substitutable husbands and wives become, the less likely are men and women to marry, and the more likely are they to divorce.

The predicted effects of wives' employment made by resource theory (Blood & Wolfe, 1960) are more complex. Resource theory points out that each spouse brings into a marriage resources such as education, occupation, and income, and also those such as physical attractiveness and the adequate performance of various roles. Although wives' employment increases a couple's shared resources (so that both members of the couple benefit), it increases the relative bargaining power (and hence well-being) of the wife, but decreases the bargaining power and well-being of the husband.

Role homophily theory (Simpson & England, 1982) is the opposite of role differentiation theory and contends that role similarity among spouses, far from decreasing marital solidarity, in fact builds marital strength. In role homophily theory, similarity of spouse's roles fosters communication and companionship and brings an enhanced appreciation of one another's problems and triumphs. But again, wives' employment is seen as a double-edged sword. On the one hand, it contributes to marital interaction and pleasure; but on the other hand, by providing each with a sense of independence (neither relies on the other to perform a nonfamiliar role), role homophily makes it easier for either spouse to end the marriage.

The empirical literature is in agreement that although women's employment leads to a delay in marriage (i.e., the average age of first marriage is higher for employed women), women's employment does not result in a decline in the marriage rate (Hofferth & Moore, 1979). Between 1970 and 1982, while women's labor-force participation increased by about 10 percentage points, the proportion of those 40 years or older who had never married decreased from 6.2% to 4.7% (Blau & Ferber, 1986). However, during the 1990s, the proportion of never-marrieds in the population is expected to increase to about 7% (U.S. Bureau of the Census, 1983).

The same calculus of welfare maximization that economic theory ascribes to decisions about marriage and divorce are also imputed to childbearing (Schultz, 1973). Women's employment is said to have two opposing effects on their desire to bear and raise children. In the direction of reducing fertility is the increased opportunity cost that employed women face in contemplating a child. In effect, being employed increases the price of a woman's time and thus makes investing time in children more costly. Working in the other direction, however, is the increased family income obtained by the wife's employment, which makes raising children more affordable.

The data on fertility show quite clearly that women who are employed have fewer children than women who are not employed. But there are several possible reasons for this negative relationship. It may be, using the economic model, that on balance employed women's higher opportunity cost outweighs the enabling effect of their additional income. Employed women's income may well be used to increase the amount of resources parents invest per child rather than to increase their total number of children.

It is also possible, however, that the causal relationship between fertility and wives' employment goes in the other direction. It may be that women who have a large number of children are highly productive in the home (and also probably like rearing children) and thus are less likely to be in the labor force. Complicating the matter still further is the possibility that labor-force participation and childbearing decisions are affected by some mutual antecedent (e.g., the decision regarding how much education to obtain); or that the employment and fertility decisions are made simultaneously (Waite & Stolzenberg, 1976). Hout (1978) has suggested that over the long run women's employment affects their fertility but that in the short run fertility affects employment (see Blau & Ferber, 1986).

The relationship between women's employment and divorce is also untidy. Although the divorce rate and women's labor-force participation have both risen over the recent past, studies seeking a possible causal relationship between the two obtain conflicting results. To make sense of the evidence it is necessary to complicate the question, to look not simply at whether wives work but why they do so (from choice, necessity, or both); whether wives have sought employment expressly to end an unsatisfactory marriage; the share of the total family income that wives earn; wives' occupational status relative to their husbands'; and whether wives' income (and husbands' income) is stable or unstable (see Blau & Ferber, 1986; Hofferth & Moore, 1979).

The effects of wives' employment on marital satisfaction are even more difficult to sort out. As Mischel and Fuhr indicate in Chapter 9, the effects of employment on mothers and on their children tend to be positive or neutral in most instances. The effects on husbands are less clear. Some husbands are displeased by their wives' employment, although there is some evidence that it is the transition period (when wives first work) that is most difficult for husbands. In addition, some husbands report displeasure at their wives' employment because their wives have taken jobs in order to start the process of leaving an already unsatisfactory marriage.

A recent study by Simpson and England (1982) gives some indication of the complexity of studies on such matters as the relation between marital satisfaction and wives' employment. Using a large, nationally representative data set, the authors developed multiple indicators of marital solidarity and socioeconomic status. They controlled for life-cycle stage and for family income, and they looked not simply at whether the wife was employed but also at the occupations of both spouses.

The findings provide some support for the role homophily theory. Both husbands and wives had a higher score on marital solidarity (the mutuality of their marriage, their marital commitment and their marital satisfaction) when the wife was employed. Interestingly, wife's employment was more highly correlated with the husband's marital solidarity score than with the wife's score, especially when there were children under 18 living at home. With regard to the type of job each spouse has, the results differed for wives and husbands. For wives, marital solidarity was higher if either the wife or the husband had a high-status job. For husbands, however, marital solidarity was not significantly affected by either his own or his wife's occupational status.

The dynamics of power within marriages appear to be different in families where wives are employed. Several studies corroborate that employed wives have more decision-making power in their families (Hofferth & Moore, 1979). But once again, the direction of the causality is not clear. It may be that those wives who are likely to have more decision-making power in the home to begin with are also those who are more likely to work.

In summary, it is very difficult to determine definitively the effects of wives' employment on such matters as childbearing, divorce, marital solidarity, or internal family dynamics. Cross-sectional correlations abound, but disentangling causal directionality is an ongoing and difficult exercise.

Effects in Dual-Career Families

Dual-career families are those two-earner families where both spouses are in professional or managerial occupations. The literature indicates that when they have children, dual-career spouses often experience difficulty finding sufficient time and energy to devote to family life amid the unceasing pressures of their occupations. If the wife is in a traditional female profession (elementary or high school teaching, nursing, social work, or librarianship), the pressures are eased because these occupations to not demand exceedingly long days and weeks; nor do they require travel. But severe strains can arise if both spouses are in such occupations as medicine, law, academia, or management. These occupations require not only long hours, but also long periods of intense career "initiation" that usually fall during the years in which childbearing and childrearing normally take place.

The career patterns and demands of these occupations developed during a time when their male incumbents had wives at home to manage childrearing and other domestic tasks. These patterns and demands do not fit well with family life when both parents are trying to succeed at careers.

Empirical studies document the difficulties encountered by dual-career families and verify that it is generally the wife who "accommodates" her career to family responsibilities (see, e.g., Paloma, Pendleton, & Garland, 1982). Interesting insights into the dynamics of dual-career families is provided by O'Reilly's (1983) study based on in-depth interviews with 12 couples, the husband or wife in each of the couples working as a manager in a large corporation.

All of the couples in O'Reilly's sample professed an "egalitarian" ideology. Adherence to such an ideology was prerequisite to participating in the interview. Yet, despite the presence of a philosophy that affirmed the importance of both careers, their behavior as couples clearly furthered the husbands' careers at the expense of the wives'. O'Reilly attributes this outcome to a web of factors operating both at home and at work.

The web begins with Steihm's (1976) observations about "invidious intimacy": Even among highly educated men and women, marriage choices are made such that the man is older, often taller, and perceived to be "smarter." The edge in age, even if the men and women are in the same occupation with the same opportunities (which is frequently not the case) gives the husband more work experience and hence higher earnings than his wife has. If, in addition, the couple believes that the husband's opportunities for promotion are greater than the wife's, which is frequently a correct perception, the couple will seek to maximize their joint income by furthering the career of the husband.

O'Reilly found two behavior patterns that favored husbands' careers over wives'. First, in determining whether or not to accept promotions that required geographical moves, couples made decisions that favored husbands' careers, even at the expense of their wives' careers.[3] Second, the pattern of labor division in the home favored the husband's career, especially in families where there were children. Even when husbands participated in housework and child care, wives typically fulfilled the time- and energy-consuming role of home manager and also did more of those home tasks that tended to conflict with work.

Like the couples themselves, the corporation that employed at least one member of O'Reilly's couples professed an egalitarian ideology. Equal opportunity policies had long ago abolished formal barriers to women's career progress. But career structures and informal barriers remained. And of course, the more the wife's career progress was slowed, the more "sense" it made for the joint-maximizing couple to favor the husband's career.

The fast-track promotion model made it extremely difficult for women with children to be seen as successful. If they turned down promotion opportunities, which they indicated they would have been glad to accept after their children were less dependent, they were seen as unsuccessful and were rewarded accordingly, even if their job performance was excellent. In addition, women with children were seen as lacking career commitment because they could not (or would not) socialize with colleagues after work or routinely work in the office in the evening—both traditional "measures" of managerial commitment to the corporation.

O'Reilly's study points out in vivid detail the close interconnections between home and workplace. She calls the relationships feedback loops. Others have called them vicious circles (Lloyd & Niemi, 1979). No matter what the term, Kanter's (1977) observation that social science has been in error in divorcing the study of families from the study of work is particularly apt with respect to dual-career families.

PUBLIC POLICIES FOR TWO-EARNER FAMILIES

The rise of two-earner families is an economic and social "event" that has only begun to be played out. The changes wrought thus far have been profound. But there remain numerous unresolved issues.

By and large, as of the mid-1980s two-earner families are psychologically acceptable to families and individuals and socially acceptable to extended families, friends, neighbors, and co-workers, even where the two earners are parents of quite young children. Moreover, both families and work organizations have come to rely on the earnings and labor of wives and mothers.

Some women have moved into occupations that are demanding, prestigious, and well-paid, occupations that were virtually closed to women, and especially to married women, as recently as 20 years ago. Young women now expect to work for all or most of their adult lives and many make their education and initial job decisions accordingly. For their part, young men expect that the women they marry will work outside of the home, although many still hope that it will be possible for their wives to care "personally" for their young children. The reality is, however, that the number of young children cared for outside of their families for large parts of the day is growing continuously.

Yet despite all of this upheaval in social and economic custom, in certain respects little has changed. In two-earner families, men are still the primary breadwinners and women are still performing the vast bulk of housework and childrearing tasks. Family decisions are still generally made so as to maximize the husband's job and career prospects; and affordable, dependable, good quality child care is still difficult for parents to obtain. At the workplace, women are still highly segregated into female jobs and still earn only about 60% of what men earn. In professional and managerial jobs, parents of young children are still expected to conform to a career pattern that is ill-suited to rearing their offspring.

It is clear that the current state of affairs represents a disequilibrium, a way-station on the road to further change. What will that further change look like? And how might policy makers act to bring about that change? We concentrate here on the workplace, the child-care system and two aspects of the tax system.

The Workplace

For the most part, gender divisions in the workplace today reflect the assumptions and realities of the past, when men were the sole breadwinners in most families and most women who worked (although certainly not all) were single and not involved in supporting a family. Women who wished to get ahead economically did so, with relatively rare exceptions, by marrying a man who had wealth or would earn a large income, not by accumulating wealth and/or income on their own.

A new ideology has now begun to replace the old. Many women now wish to be economically successful in their own right, not simply as a result of being married to an economically successful husband. And for their part, many men see their wives' earning power as important to their own well-being and the well-being of their families; and many men experience great relief in not being the sole financial mainstay of the family.

But the rules of the workplace still often reflect the old ideology. Although men often see merit in their own wives earning an equitable return on their educational investments by being able to move into more lucrative positions, some men continue to protect their gender's place in the labor market by excluding women from competition on an equal footing. Employers also often play by the old rules, for example by providing married men with additional financial compensation above and beyond that based on productive characteristics (Hill, 1979). Public policy must change some of the old rules of the labor market so that workplaces provide for more gender equality and more fully reflect the realities of the new families.

Antidiscrimination legislation and affirmative action orders have thus far had only a modest effect on reducing occupational segregation or the gender gap in pay, largely because they have been so poorly enforced (Beller, 1979, 1982; Brown, 1982; Eberts & Stone, 1985; Heckman & Wolpin, 1976; Leonard, 1985; U.S. General Accounting Office, 1975). Congress needs to strengthen the enforcement procedures for both Title VII of the Civil Rights Act and the Executive Orders (the sources of most affirmative action). Congress should also appropriate additional funds to the Equal Employment Opportunities Commission, the agency that enforces Title VII, so that it can more effectively investigate cases; the agency also should be given the right to investigate without waiting for a complaint.

In addition, the Office of Federal Contract Compliance, the agency that administers the executive orders that require affirmative action plans, needs a wider variety of remedies for noncompliance. Currently, companies not in compliance with affirmative action can be disbarred from entering into contracts with government agencies. But this penalty is generally seen as too severe, and is thus almost never used. The OFCC needs the power to implement lesser remedies as well.

Because so much of the pay gap between men and women results from occupational segregation, a good deal of the effort to achieve pay equity has revolved around breaking down that segregation. However, because the system of occupational segregation is so widespread and has been so resistant to change (except in some of the professions and in management), a second, and more direct strategy to obtain pay equity has recently been initiated. Many are seeking to broaden the concept of nondiscrimination so as to include comparable worth, rewarding the skills required in female-dominated jobs according to the same criteria used to reward the skills required in male-dominated jobs.

Australian labor courts, as well as several public employers in the United States, have begun to set wages according to criteria that include rewarding the skills and responsibilities used in women's jobs in a "comparable" fashion to those used in men's jobs. These experiences suggest that a comparable worth strategy is often economically feasible ("Comparable Pay," 1986; Gregory & Duncan, 1981; Gregory & Ho, 1984). However, the notion of comparable worth remains highly controversial.

More work needs to be done to educate employers about comparable worth. In the public sector, hearings should continue to be held and job evaluation studies conducted. In both the public and private sectors, unions should continue to place comparable worth issues on their bargaining agenda. Also, we endorse Bergmann's (1986) suggestion that a prestigious national research organization prepare a document that illustrates for key occupations the relative wages that emerge when taking a set of comparable worth principles into account. Although we do not expect that the concept of comparable worth will gain a large following immediately, we do see it as a goal toward which there is likely to be sporadic movement.

In addition to issues of equity in occupational access and pay, the increase in the number of two-earner families raises important issues about how to balance work and family responsibilities. Despite much discussion about flexible scheduling of the workday (flextime), only about 12% of full-time wage and salary workers are able to vary the time they begin and end work (Mellor, 1986). And only about 27% of employed women (and 10% of employed men) work less than 35 hours per week (Nardone, 1986).

Most workers are satisfied with the number of hours they work. When asked if they would like to trade hours for income (keeping their hourly pay rate the same), only about 10% of women and 6% of men in the 25 to 54 age group (where childrearing responsibilities are greatest) reported that they would be willing to decrease their income if they could work fewer hours (Shank, 1986). Thus, it appears that part-time employment for parents, with concomitant declines in income, is unlikely to prove a popular means of balancing work and family demands.[4]

If we wished to adopt a major change in work hours for parents with young children, we would need to find a mechanism to replace parents' foregone income (Strober, 1981). It may be that we could adopt an intergenerational transfer system, that would transfer funds from older workers to workers in their childrearing years. Or, we might develop a capital market so that young parents could get publicly guaranteed loans and pay back interest and principal from incomes earned in the years after childrearing. However, it seems more likely that we will develop a child-care system to care for the children of working parents rather than seek to make it financially possible for parents to care for their own children.

Child Care

Child-care issues are emerging high on the agenda of policymakers, as they become aware of the importance of good child care for the well-being of future generations. There is now widespread recognition that present child-care arrangements are too *ad hoc*, often deficient in quality, and unable to offer adequate infant care, sick child care and after-school care.

Recent evidence on the effectiveness of preschool education in promoting school achievement has become more widely known (Berrueta-Clement, Schweinhart, Epstein, & Weikart, 1984; Lazar & Darlington, 1982) and although the federal government has been relatively quiescent on the matter of child care since the early 1970s, numerous states and localities have appointed task forces that are now reporting on needs, of crisis proportions, for additional state and local involvement in child care. (See, for example, *A Report to the Governor of California from the Child Care Task Force*, 1985, and "North Carolina Panel," 1985, on the North Carolina report.)

As a result, state and local governments have now begun to experiment with various forms of financial assistance and planning for child care. At the same time, employers are increasingly offering direct services or service vouchers to their employees, and profit-making companies as well as numerous nonprofit organizations have expanded their child-care operations.

Child care is labor intensive and very expensive. It will become even more expensive as child-care workers are paid in accordance with their skills and responsibilities. The challenge to policymakers is to design a child-care system that is cost effective and provides quality care. One promising possibility is to devise a "satellite system" that combines family day-care homes and child-care centers into an integrated network (see Strober, 1975).

As is discussed in Chapter 14, researchers need to provide policy makers with information about the costs and quality of various types of child-care delivery systems. Numerous "natural experiments" are taking place both in the United States and abroad. These need to be evaluated as we begin to develop and expand the nation's child-care system and make decisions about its degree of centralization, forms of management, and sources of funds.

One aspect of child care that has proved particularly difficult for policy-makers in the United States is care during the first few weeks or months of a child's life. Although other industrialized countries provide for paid maternity leave during the first months of a child's life (e.g., Swedish law gives either parent the option to take leave to care for an infant), and guarantee the right of the parents to return to their jobs after the child-care leave is completed, the United States does not have such legislation. Companies that provide sick-leave benefits for their employees are required by legislation to treat childbirth as an illness and pay "sickness" benefits. But most women who are employed do not have the right to a paid childbirth/childrearing leave; nor do they have a guarantee that their job will be available to them when they return from maternity leave. And very few companies provide fathers with an option to take paternity leave to care for a new-born child.

The importance of the first few months of a child's life, the difficulty and expense of caring for young infants in a group setting, and the desire so many parents have to care for their own child during early infancy all point to the wisdom of a public policy that permits either parent (or both *in seriatim*) to take a childrearing leave with their job protected for several months. The leave should be paid for by the three parties that benefit from them: the parent, the employer, and the public. The parent's share could be paid for through a form of insurance; the employer's share could be a fringe benefit chosen by the employee from a menu of several possible fringe benefits. The public share should be small. Public funds should be reserved for those who need child-care leaves but have not paid into an insurance fund and/or have no employer to provide the fringe benefit.

Income Taxation and Social Security

Like many workplace rules and customs, our income taxation system and social security benefit packages are vestiges of an era when most adult women did not play a significant role in the labor market. Both the income tax system and social security benefit packages favor families with full-time homemakers (alias housewives). Should this favorable treatment be ended?

Feminists are divided in their views toward homemaking as a full-time occupation. Some argue that it is important for every woman to be able to choose among the options of full-time employment, full-time homemaking, and all of the hybrid alternatives between them. These feminists, therefore, are interested in protecting, nourishing, and enhancing the occupation of full-time homemaker. Some argue that the occupation should be made so attractive that men as well as women would seek to pursue it. Feminists of this persuasion would like to see the tax and social security systems remain as they are. In addition, they would like to see homemakers' "work" publicly acknowledged so that they are eligible for workman's compensation benefits, unemployment benefits, health insurance, and severance pay, should the "employment relationship" terminate.

However, most feminists believe that public policy should not encourage people to choose homemaking as a full-time occupation. These feminists believe that both men and women should be encouraged to work for pay in the marketplace and that both should be involved in housework and, when relevant, in child care. Their strategy is to improve women's employment and earning opportunities rather than to improve the occupation of full-time homemaker.

Because the income tax system is progressive, and because it treats married couples as a single tax unit (even if they file separate returns), it operates to discourage married women from working. If the husband is already earning income and the wife is contemplating entering the workforce, she is faced with a higher marginal tax rate on her income than she would be if she were not married. At the same time, if a single employed man were to marry a woman who became a full-time homemaker, the man's tax payments would decrease even if his income remained the same. While it is true that on paper these tax provisions are gender neutral—that is, the husband of a wife who was already earning income would also be faced with a higher marginal tax rate than he would if he were single and a woman who married a full-time male homemaker would also find that her tax payments decreased—in practice, given the gender roles in the vast majority of families, the federal income tax code discourages married women from working.

In keeping with the notion that adult men and women are independent economic entities, we favor an income tax system such as the one in Sweden, where all persons are taxed as individuals, regardless of their marital status. If such a tax reform were adopted, couples where wives are full-time homemakers would pay more tax than they do at present; two-earner couples, however, would pay lower taxes. Since about half of all married couples have two earners and about half have a full-time homemaker, the potential for change is currently at a stalemate. It seems likely that as the percentage of two-earner married couples increases, the notion of taxing men and women as individuals, regardless of their marital status, will become a political reality.

The social security system also favors full-time homemakers at the expense of married women who have been employed. Despite the rhetoric about the social security system being simply an insurance system, it is in fact also a mechanism for redistributing income. The benefits per dollar of contribution are higher for those with low earnings than they are for those with high earnings. Moreover, the benefit structure permits married women, regardless of whether or not they have ever been employed or paid social security taxes, to receive a spousal benefit equal to one half of the benefit received by their husbands. A married woman who is entitled to social security benefits on her own, by dint of her own employment history, can choose the higher of the two benefits, her own benefit or the spousal benefit.

Two inequities result from this system. First, for many married women the spousal benefit is higher than their own employment-related benefit. Thus, they find that, in effect, they receive no return on the social security taxes they have paid over the years. Even those who do choose to receive their own benefit receive a relatively low return on the taxes they have paid. Second, holding total family earnings constant, in some cases the married couple with only one earner will receive a higher total benefit (including the spousal benefit) than the couple with two earners (see example in Bergmann, 1986, p. 223).

The inequities could be remedied if, for purposes of setting up social security credits, earnings by both members of a married couple were considered as community property. Half of the husband's earnings would be credited toward his social security account, half toward his wife's account, and vice versa if the wife earned income.

Such a remedy would remove the current disincentive to married women's employment implicit in the social security benefit structure. Financially, it would benefit two-earner couples at the expense of single-earner couples. But it would also reduce the risk of being a full-time homemaker, since the earnings credits of a divorced former homemaker would clearly be designated as her own, ensuring her access to social security benefits.

Like the reforms associated with the tax system, it seems probable that as two-earner couples replace single-earner couples, splitting earnings for purposes of determining social security credits will become more popular politically. However, because so many in the polity "contracted" their marriages and planned their labor-force behavior according to the norms of the single breadwinner family system, any new system of calculating social security credits would have to be phased in gradually, allowing numerous beneficiaries and prospective beneficiaries to collect their payments under the old system.

Indeed, in many respects the current debates about the inequities of the federal income tax and social security systems are symbolic of society's transition to a new era. The pace of change is uneven. Some families are "new" and some quite traditional. And even within so-called new families, some activities adapt more rapidly to change than others. As we have seen, for example, even in two-earner families, the division of labor at home remains quite traditional.

But in all cases, the direction of change is clear. We are moving toward a world where men and women are more equal, both at home and at the workplace. Despite the wishes of some, it seems unlikely that public policy can reverse the trend. The sensible role for public policy is to facilitate the transition.

NOTES

1. The level of aggregation of occupations affects the value of the index of occupational segregation. The more disaggregated the occupations, the higher the index (the more segregation is evident).

2. Black women earn 92% of what white women earn. Hispanic women earn 85% of what white women earn. For a discussion of the debate surrounding the "convergence" between the earnings of black and white women see Malveaux and Wallace, 1987.

3. The empirical evidence is unclear on whether two-earner couples are less likely to move than are one-earner couples, even when their occupations and incomes are relatively similar. See Markham (1987).

4. Presser (1986), however, has noted that parents in two-earner families increasingly are caring for their children by having mothers and fathers work different shifts. She speculates that this phenomenon may continue to increase since the occupations that are expanding most rapidly have a significant proportion of non-day-shift workers.

REFERENCES

Becker, G. S. (1965). A theory of the allocation of time. *Economic Journal, 75*, (299), 493–517.

Becker, G. S. (1981). *A treatise on the family.* Cambridge, MA: Harvard University Press.

Becker, G. S. (1985). Human capital, effort, and the sexual division of labor. *Journal of Labor Economics, 3* (Supplement), 33–58.

Beller, A. H. (1979). The impact of equal opportunity laws on the male/female earnings differential. In C. B. Lloyd, E. Andrews and C. L. Gilroy (Eds.), *Women in the labor market.* New York: Columbia University Press.

Beller, A. H. (1982). Occupational segregation by sex: Determinants and changes. *Journal of Human Resources, 17*(3), 317–392.

Beller, A. H. (1984). Tends in occupational segregation by sex and race: 1960–81. In B. F. Reskin (Ed.), *Sex segregation in the workplace: Trends, explanations and remedies.* Washington, DC: National Academy Press.

Bergmann, B. R. (1986). *The economic emergence of women.* New York: Basic Books.

Berk, S. F., & Shih, A. (1980). Contributions to household labor: Comparing wives' and husbands' reports. In S. F. Berk (Ed.), *Women and household labor.* Beverly Hills, CA: Sage Publications.

Berrueta-Clement, J. S., Schweinhart, W. S. B., Epstein, A. S., & Weikert, D. P. (1984). *Changed lives: The effects of the Perry Preschool Program on youths through age nineteen.* Ypsilanti, MI: High Scope Press.

Bielby, D. D., & Bielby, W. T. (1988). She works hard for the money: Household responsibilities and the allocation of work effort. *Social Problems, 35*(2).

Blackburn, M. L., & Bloom, D. E. (1986, December). *Family income inequality in the United States: 1967–84.* Proceedings of the Thirty-ninth Meeting of the Industrial Relations Research Association, New Orleans.

Blank, R. M. (1986, December). *Part-time work and wages among adult women.* Proceedings of the Thirty-ninth Meeting of the Industrial Relations Research Association, New Orleans.

Blau, F. D., & Ferber, M. A. (1986). *The economics of women, men, and work.* Englewood Cliffs, NJ: Prentice-Hall.

Blood, R. O., Jr., & Wolfe, D. M. (1960). *Husbands and wives: The dynamics of married living.* Glencoe, IL: Free Press.

Bowen, W., & Finegan, T. A. (1969). *The economics of labor force participation.* Princeton, NJ: Princeton University Press.

Brown, C. (1982). The federal attack on labor market discrimination: The mouse that roared. In R. Ehrenberg (Ed.), *Research in labor economics*. Greenwich, CT: JAI Press.

Cain, G. G. (1966). *Married women in the labor force*. Chicago, IL: University of Chicago Press.

Comparable pay for comparable work gains acceptance, if slowly. (1986, July 15). *Wall Street Journal*, p. 1.

Corcoran, M., & Duncan, G. J. (1979). Work history, labor force attachment, and earnings differences between the races and sexes. *Journal of Human Resources, 14*, 3–20.

Corcoran, M., Duncan, G. J., & Ponza, M. (1984). Work experience, job segregation, and wages. In B. F. Reskin (Ed.), *Sex segregation in the workplace: Trends, explanations and remedies*. Washington, DC: National Academy Press.

Council of Economic Advisors. (1987). *Economic Report of the President*. Washington, DC: U.S. Government Printing Office.

Danziger, S., & Gottschalk, P. (1986, January). *How Have Families with Children Been Faring?* University of Wisconsin, Madison: Institute for Poverty Research, Discussion Paper #801-86.

Duesenberry, J. S. (1949). *Income, saving and the theory of consumer behavior*. Cambridge, MA: Harvard University Press.

Durand, J. D. (1948). *The labor force in the U.S., 1890–1960*. New York: Social Research Council.

Eberts, R. W., & Stone, J. A. (1985). Male–female differences in promotions: EEO in public education. *Journal of Human Resources, 20*(4), 504–21.

Fields, J. M. (1976). A comparison of intercity differences in the labor force participation rates of married women in 1970 with 1940, 1950 and 1960. *Journal of Human Resources, 11*(4), 568–577.

Freidman, M. (1957). *A theory of the consumption function*. Princeton, NJ: Princeton University Press.

Galbraith, J. K. (1973). *Economics and the public purpose*. Boston: Houghton Mifflin.

Gregory, R., & Duncan, R. C. (1981). The relevance of segmented labor market theories: The Australian experience of the achievement of equal pay for women. *Journal of Post Keynesian Economics, 3*, 404–428.

Gregory, R., & Ho, V. (1984). *Equal pay and comparable worth: What can the U.S. learn from the Australian experience?* Unpublished Manuscript.

Gross, E. (1968). Plus ça change. . . ? The sexual structure of occupations over time. *Social Problems, 16*(1), 198–208.

Hayghe, H. (1986). Rise in mothers' labor force activity includes those with infants. *Monthly Labor Review, 109*(2), 43–45.

Heckman, J. J., & Wolpin, K. I. (1976). Does the contract compliance program work? An analysis of Chicago data. *Industrial and Labor Relations Review, 29*(4), 544–564.

Hill, M. S. (1979). The wage effects of marital status and children. *Journal of Human Resources, 14*(4), 579–594.

Hofferth, S. L., & Moore, K. A. (1979). Women and their children. In R. E. Smith (Ed.), *The subtle revolution: Women at work*. Washington, DC: The Urban Institute.

Hout, M. (1978). The determinants of marital fertility in the United States, 1968–70: Inferences from a dynamic model. *Demography, 15*(2), 139–160.

Juster, F. T. (1985). The validity and quality of time use estimates obtained from recall diaries. In F. T. Juster, & F. P. Stafford, *Time, goods, and well-being*. Ann Arbor, MI: Institute for Social Research, University of Michigan.

Juster, F. T., & Stafford, F. P. (Eds.). (1985). *Time, goods, and well-being*. Ann Arbor, MI: Institute for Social Research, University of Michigan.

Kanter, R. M. (1977). *Work and family in the United States: A critical review and agenda for research and policy*. New York: Russell Sage Foundation.

Lazar, I., & Darlington, R. (1982). *Lasting effects of early education: A report from the consortium for longitudinal studies.* Monographs of the Society for Research in Child Development 47 (2–3, no. 195).

Leonard, J. S. (1985). What promises are worth: The impact of affirmative action goals. *Journal of Human Resources, 20*(1), 3–20.

Lloyd, C. B., & Niemi, B. T. (1979). *The economics of sex differentials.* New York: Columbia University Press.

Malveaux, J. (1982, May). *Recent trends in occupational segregation by race and sex.* Paper presented to the Committee on Women's Employment and Related Social Issues, National Academy of Sciences, Washington, DC.

Malveaux, J., & Wallace, P. (1987). Minority women in the workforce. In K. S. Koziara, M. H. Moskow, & L. D. Tanner (Eds.), *Working women: Past, present, future.* Industrial Relations Research Association Series. Washington, DC: Bureau of National Affairs.

Markham, W. T. (1987). Sex, relocation and occupational advancement: The "real" cruncher for women. In A. H. Stromberg, L. Larwood, & B. A. Gutek (Eds.), *Women and work: An annual review 2.* Beverly Hills, CA: Sage Publications.

Mellor, E. F. (1986). Shift work and flexitime: How prevalent are they? *Monthly Labor Review, 109*(11), 14–21.

Mincer, J. (1960a). Employment and consumption. *Review of Economics and Statistics, 42,* 20–26.

Mincer, J. (1960b). Labor supply, family income and consumption. *American Economic Review, 50,* 574–583.

Mincer, J. (1962). Labor force participation of married women. In H. G. Lewis (Ed.), *Aspects of labor economics* (Universities National Bureau of Economic Research Conference Studies, No. 14). Princeton, NJ: Princeton University Press.

Monthly Labor Review. (1983–1987, April). Volumes 106–110.

Nardone, T. J. (1986). Part-time workers: Who are they? *Monthly Labor Review, 109*(2), 13–19.

North Carolina panel says schools should provide child care. (1985, June 5). *Education Week,* p. 3.

Oppenheimer, V. K. (1969). *The female labor force in the United States: Demographic and economic factors governing its growth and changing composition.* Berkeley, CA: University of California Population Monograph Series, No. 5.

O'Reilly, W. B. (1983). *Where equal opportunity fails: Corporate men and women in dual career families.* Unpublished Ph.D. dissertation, Stanford University, California.

Paloma, M. M., Pendleton, B. F., & Garland, T. N. (1982). Reconsidering the dual-career marriage: A longitudinal approach. In J. Aldous (Ed.), *Two paychecks: Life in dual-earner families.* Beverly Hills, CA: Sage Publications.

Parsons, T. (1942). Age and sex in the social structure of the United States. *American Sociological Review, 7,* 604–616.

Parsons, T. (1949). The social structure of the family. In R. Anshen (Ed.), *The family: Its function and destiny.* New York: Harper & Row.

Parsons, T. (1955). The American family: Its relations to personality and to the social structure. In T. Parsons & R. F. Bales (Eds.), *Family, socialization and interaction process.* New York: Macmillan.

Presser, H. B. (1986). Shift work among American women and child care. *Journal of Marriage and the Family, 48,* 551–563.

Quinn, R. P., & Staines, G. L. (1979). *Quality of employment survey, 1977: Cross Section.* Ann Arbor, MI: Interuniversity Consortium for Political and Social Research.

Report to the Governor of California from The Child Care Task Force. (1985, March 31). Sacramento, CA.

Reskin, B. F., & Hartmann, H. I. (Eds.). (1986). *Women's work, men's work: Sex segregation on the job*. Washington, DC: National Academy Press.

Robinson, J. P. (1977). *How Americans use time*. New York: Praeger Publications.

Robinson, J. P. (1985). The validity and reliability of diaries versus alternative time use measures. In F. T. Juster & F. P. Stafford (Eds.), *Time, goods, and well-being*. Ann Arbor, MI: Institute for Social Research, University of Michigan.

Robinson, J. P., & Converse, P. (1972). Social changes as reflected in the use of time. In A. Campbell & P. Converse (Eds.), *The human meaning of social change*. New York: Russell Sage Foundation.

Schultz, T. W. (1973). New economic approaches to fertility. *Journal of Political Economy, 81* (2, Part II).

Shank, S. E. (1986). Preferred hours of work and corresponding earnings. *Monthly Labor Review, 109*(11), 7–13.

Simpson, I. H., & England, P. (1982). Conjugal work roles and marital solidarity. In J. Aldous (Ed.), *Two paychecks: Life in dual-earner families*. Beverly Hills, CA: Sage Publications.

Smith, S. (1987). Work experience of the labor force during 1985. *Monthly Labor Review, 110*(4), 40–44.

Stafford, F. P., & Duncan, G. J. (1980). The use of time and technology by households in the United States. In R. G. Ehrenberg (Ed.), *Research in Labor Economics*, 3. Greenwich, CT: JAI Press.

Steihm, J. (1976). Invidious intimacy. *Social Policy, 6*(5), 12–16.

Strober, M. H. (1975). Formal extrafamily child care—Some economic observations. In C. B. Lloyd (Ed.), *Sex, discrimination, and the division of labor*. New York: Columbia University Press.

Strober, M. H. (1977, February). Wives' labor force behavior and family consumption patterns. *American Economic Review, 67*, 410–417.

Strober, M. H. (1981). Market work, housework and child care: Burying archaic tenets, building new arrangements. In National Institute of Mental Health (Ed.), *Women, a developmental perspective: A conference on research*. Washington, DC: U.S. Government Printing Office.

Strober, M. H. (1981). The MBA: Same passport to success for women and men? In P. A. Wallace (Ed.), *Women in the workplace*. Boston: Auburn House.

Strober, M. H., & Weinberg, C. B. (1980, March). Strategies used by working and nonworking wives to reduce time pressures. *Journal of Consumer Research, 6*, 338–348.

Strober, M. H., & Weinberg, C. G. (1977, December). Working wives and major family expenditures? *Journal of Consumer Research, 4*, 141–147.

The average guy takes it on the chin. (1986, July 13). *New York Times*, Section 3, p. 1.

Treiman, D. J., & Hartmann, H. I. (Eds.). (1981). *Women, work and wages: Equal pay for jobs of equal value*. Washington, DC: National Academy Press.

U.S. Bureau of the Census. (1975). *Historical statistics of the U.S., Colonial times to 1970*. Washington, DC: U.S. Government Printing Office.

U.S. Bureau of the Census. (1983). *Marital status and living arrangements: March 1982* (Current Population Reports, Series P-20, No. 380). Washington, DC: U.S. Government Printing Office.

U.S. Bureau of the Census. (1985a). *Child support and alimony* (Current Population Reports, Series P-23, No. 141). Washington, DC: U.S. Government Printing Office.

U.S. Bureau of the Census. (1985b). *Money income and poverty status of families and persons in the United States: 1984* (Current Population Reports, Series P-60, No. 149). Washington, DC: U.S. Government Printing Office.

U.S. Department of Education, Center for Education Statistics. (1987). *Trends in education: 1975-76 to 1995-96*. Washington, DC: U.S. Government Printing Office.

U.S. General Accounting Office. (1975). *The equal employment opportunity program for federal nonconstruction contractors can be improved.* Washington, DC: U.S. Government Printing Office.

Vickery, C. (1979). Women's economic contribution to the family. In R. E. Smith (Ed.), *The subtle revolution: Women at work.* Washington, DC: The Urban Institute.

Vickery-Brown, C. (1982). Home production for use in a market economy. In B. Thorne & M. Yalom (Eds.), *Rethinking the family: Some feminist questions.* New York: Longman.

Waite, L. J., & Stolzenberg, R. M. (1976). Intended childbearing and labor force participation of young women: Insights from nonrecursive models. *American Sociological Review, 41*(2), 235–252.

Walker, K., & Woods, M. (1976). *Time use: A measure of household production of family goods and services.* Washington, DC: American Home Economics Association.

9

Maternal Employment: Its Psychological Effects on Children and Their Families

HARRIET NERLOVE MISCHEL AND ROBERT FUHR

The dramatic rise in maternal employment has made it imperative to understand how it affects mothers, children, and families. A number of researchers have studied the impact of maternal employment on the cognitive and social development of children, on the well-being of the women who are combining the mother and worker roles, and on family interactions. The child's age and sex, social class, parental attitudes, and the father's involvement in the family are among the variables that have been found to modify the effects of maternal employment. The growing body of research on this topic provides a basis for understanding the processes by which maternal employment affects children and their employed mothers. This chapter outlines the major conclusions that can be drawn from research findings on maternal employment in intact families and discusses the policy implications of this research.

The effects of maternal employment on children cannot be understood without first considering children's needs at different points in their development and the changing goals of childrearing (Hoffman, 1979). How does maternal employment affect the way parents interact with their child and other aspects of the environment important to the child's changing developmental needs? How may children best be prepared for their adult roles in times when both wives and husbands will be breadwinners?

Work is often an economic necessity even in families where the father is present and an active wage-earner. Working has more than economic significance as women become more educated, have fewer children, and live longer. Jobs provide social support networks and stimulation. Working increases a woman's feelings of self-efficacy, which in turn enhances her well-being and may make her a better wife and mother.

Harriet Nerlove Mischel, Ph.D. Department of Psychology, Columbia University and New York State Psychiatric Institute, New York, New York.

Robert Fuhr, Ph.D. Adult and Child Guidance Center, San Jose, California; Bramer Medical Center, Palo Alto, California.

Contrary to the belief that children's development is best promoted by full-time mothering, recent research findings indicate some increases in the cognitive and social development of children of working mothers. These findings are often specific to particular age groups and can best be understood in a developmental framework that takes account of the child's needs at each stage of development.

INFANCY AND EARLY CHILDHOOD

Cognitive and Social Development

Studies of the effect of maternal employment on young children's cognitive and social development have used various measures or combinations of measures. Among those used are the Bayley Scales of Infant Development (which include measures of both mental and psychomotor development), the Stanford Binet or Wechsler Preschool and Primary Scale of Intelligence, and ratings of social adjustment by teachers and others. These studies have shown either positive or mixed effects of maternal employment on early development. For example, Gold and her colleagues (Gold & Andres, 1978c; Gold, Andres, & Glorieux, 1979) found that teachers rated children of employed mothers as better adjusted. Preschool sons and daughters of employed mothers have broader sex-role concepts than those whose mothers remain at home (Hoffman, 1979).

The effects of maternal employment may be transient, or actually due to factors other than the mother's employment status. Schachter (1981) found that children of employed mothers between 2 and 3 years of age were more independent and peer oriented but had lower Stanford Binet IQ scores than children whose mothers were not employed. However, early scores on this test are not predictive of later IQ, and previous research (Kagan & Moss, 1962) has shown that both independence and peer orientation are associated with rising IQs. In a large-scale study of kindergartners' social adjustment and academic competence (Farel, 1980), nine out of ten score differences were no longer significant after adjustments were made for the effects of mother's race, education, and family income. In a rare longitudinal study (Cherry & Eaton, 1977) maternal employment during the first 3 years of the child's life was found to be associated with higher IQ scores at ages 4, 7, and 8 in a sample of 200 lower-class black families. However, homes in which the mother is employed have fewer children and more adults per child than those of nonemployed mothers (Cherry & Eaton, 1977), and a higher adult/child ratio has been shown to be related to higher IQ scores (Zajonc & Markus, 1975).

Assessment of the effects of maternal employment on preschoolers is sometimes approached indirectly through studies of the effects of day care on children's development. These findings point to the need to compare substitute care with the quality of home care that the child of an employed mother might have received were the mother at home. Substitute care may provide more of the stimulation necessary for optimal development and thus be advantageous for some groups of young children (e.g., Golden & Birns, 1976).

There may be negative effects of maternal employment for particular groups of children. For example, Cohen (1978) reports lower scores on several measures for premature infants of employed mothers. These differences were still apparent after corrections were made for the lower birth weights and the higher incidence of father absence in the premature infant group. However, Hoffmann (1983) has questioned the adequacy of the sample size after these corrections were made.

There has been much concern about findings of negative effects of maternal employment on the cognitive development of young sons. For example, 4-year-old sons of employed mothers had significantly lower IQs than daughters of employed mothers and both sons and daughters of nonemployed mothers (Gold & Andres, 1978c). To explore whether fathers' greater participation in childrearing ameliorates the negative impact of maternal employment on young sons, Gold et al. (1979) studied a group of French-Canadian families with 4-year-old children. As anticipated, the Francophone fathers were more active in childrearing, whether or not their wives were employed, than were the English-speaking Canadian sample of the earlier study (Gold & Andres, 1978c). The results showed no IQ differences between boys and girls or between children of employed versus nonemployed mothers in the French-speaking sample, suggesting that fathers' greater participation can outweigh the negative impact of maternal employment on young sons. In several recent studies of American preschoolers, sex differences in the effect of maternal employment on cognitive development have not been found (Cohen, 1978; Schachter, 1981).

We are far from having definitive knowledge of the consequences of maternal employment for very young children. As more mothers of infants enter the labor force, we need increased research and knowledge of the impact of maternal employment and of diverse forms of substitute care.

Parent–Child Interactions

Two decades ago it was widely believed that exclusive maternal care was crucial to the establishment of the mother–infant bond, thought to be a cornerstone for the child's emotional, intellectual, and social development. Current research on parent–child interaction and attachment in employed-versus non-employed-mother families reflect some important changes. Employed mothers of infants are no longer the atypical group they were 20 years ago, making comparisons with nonemployed mothers more meaningful. Earlier studies relied on interview and questionnaire data. Recent

studies often include observational data and multiple measures of the behavior of the child, the mother, and the father as well. Thus, current findings
provide a more solid basis for drawing conclusions about how maternal
employment affects the relationship between parents and children and the
impact this has on the child's development.

National time-use studies (e.g., Hill & Stafford, 1980) have found that
employed mothers of children from infancy to high school age spend less
time in child care than do full-time homemakers. Several researchers have
looked closely at the quality of the interactions between employed mothers
and their infants and young children during the time they do spend together.
Mothers and children have been observed in both structured tasks and free-
play settings. Ratings have been made of visual contact, vocalization and
touch, responsiveness, maternal care giving during feeding, and the infants'
behavior during and after separation from the mother. Several recent
studies have included fathers as well as mothers in assessments of the quality
of parent–child interactions in employed-mother families.

The majority of studies have shown no clear overall negative effects of
maternal employment on the quality of mother–child interaction (e.g.,
Hock, 1980; Owen, Easterbrooks, Chase-Lansdale, & Goldberg, 1983).
Several studies suggest that the employed mother is more attentive to her
child when they are together. Employed mothers are more likely to include
direct one-to-one interaction and tend to be more intense in their verbal
interaction with and social stimulation of their child than nonemployed
mothers (Goldberg, 1977; Pederson, Cain, Zazlow, & Anderson, 1982).
Employed mothers, at least in the middle-class samples of these studies,
seem to compensate for their absence. The tendency toward greater maternal attentiveness during time spent with the child has been shown to be
situation specific. For example, employed mothers were found to be more
verbal than unemployed mothers in an unstructured situation, but less
verbal in a structured situation (Stuckey, McGhee, & Bell, 1982).

Fathers in employed-mother families spend more time with their infants and young children than men whose wives do not work. Although
previous time-use studies failed to find a substantial effect of maternal
employment on the husband's family role, a recent analysis of time-use data
(Pleck & Rustad, 1980) finds that husbands of employed women participate
more in household tasks and also spend more time with their children than
do husbands of nonemployed women. Men in both groups still spend less
time in these activities than do their wives.

The timing and type of interaction between children and their parents
may also differ in employed-mother families. Several observational studies
suggest that fathers in these families engage in less of the intense father–
infant interactions at the end of the work day that is characteristic of
families in which the mother is not employed (Pederson et al., 1983; Zasl-
kow, Pederson, Suwalsky, & Rabinovich, 1983). Pederson has suggested

that in dual-wage families, fathers may handle household demands during the return-from-work period, while mothers compensate for their absence during the day by using this time to interact with the child. In single-earner families this early evening weekday period is typically the father's time with the child. Thus, although fathers in employed-mother families report spending more time with their children over the course of a week, they seem to be engaging less in a particular kind of interaction with their child, one which may be important to the child's development.

Parents' Satisfaction with the Maternal Work Role

Several researchers have hypothesized that it is the congruence between the mothers' employment status and her attitudes or satisfaction with her work role, rather than her work role per se, that is the crucial variable in predicting the quality of mother–child interaction. The data are consistent with this hypothesis. For example, Hock (1980) found negative effects on mother–child interactions when the mother's employment status was not congruent with her attitudes toward maternal care, whether or not she was employed outside the home. Women who experienced role conflict as a result of either being employed and believing strongly in exclusive maternal care or being at home yet not believing that maternal care need be exclusive were less likely to have positive interactions with their infants. In a laboratory situation, infants of "incongruent" mothers were less likely to stay close to their mothers and greeted them with more negative responses when they were reunited after separation. Fathers' behavior has also been shown to vary with the congruence between attitudes and maternal employment status. Both fathers and mothers expressed significantly more negative feelings toward their children when their attitudes were not congruent with the mother's work role (Stuckey et al. 1982).

Maternal attitude congruence may have less effect on children when the mother is employed than when she is not. Farel (1980) found that congruence between mothers' work attitudes and behavior had no effect on measures of children's social adjustment and cognitive competence in a group of children whose mothers were employed. In the group whose mothers were not employed outside the home, maternal work-role satisfaction did have a significant effect. Mothers who stayed at home and who expressed the belief that their labor-force participation would be detrimental to their child had children who scored the highest on several measures of social and cognitive development. However, children of mothers who preferred to work but stayed at home scored the lowest.

The importance of maternal satisfaction in mediating any effects of employment on children's development has been found in older children as well (Altman & Grossman, 1977; Baruch, 1972; Pearlman, 1981). Hoffman (1983) notes that these findings do not necesssarily prove that it is satisfaction with the maternal work role that produces positive child characteristics. She points out that work-role satisfaction may instead reflect a positive parent–child relationship and the judgment that the child is thriving under the prevailing arrangement. Conversely, parental dissatisfaction could result from difficulties with the child.

Gender Differences

Several studies have shown that the child's gender mediates the effect of the mothers' work role on parent–child interactions. Dual-wage parents with young children seem to feel more positive toward their daughters than they do toward their sons. Sons of employed mothers receive lower rates of stimulation across a variety of measures (e.g., encouragement to pay attention to objects) than sons of nonemployed mothers (Zaslow *et al.*, 1983). As compared to daughters, preschool sons get less attention (both positive and negative) from both parents when mother is employed. In contrast, when the mother is not employed, both parents pay more attention to sons (Stuckey *et al.*, 1982).

Studies of 3-year-olds by Bronfenbrenner and his associates (Alvarez, Henderson, & Bronfenbrenner, 1982; Bronfenbrenner & Crouter, 1982) found that full-time employed mothers described their daughters in the most positive terms, in contrast to the nonemployed mothers who were more positive about sons than daughters. Hoffman (1983) has suggested a number of possible explanations for the apparent shift among dual-wage parents:

1. Employed-mother families, less likely to hold traditional sex-role attitudes, simply reverse the traditional pattern of preferring and interacting more with sons than with daughters.
2. When added to the stress of dual roles, boys' greater activity and low compliance may put an excessive strain on employed-mother families.
3. The stress produced by boys may be further increased by pre-school group experience, more likely for employed mother's children, which increases activity level and noncompliance in children of both sexes.

Attachment

Infant–mother attachment, the quality of the relationship of a very young child and its mother, has been a focus for research on the effects of maternal employment on early development. Early studies of institutionalized infants (Bowlby, 1952; Spitz, 1945) indicated that a relationship with a stable adult who provides the infant with emotional support is crucial to development. Much current research has assessed the security of the child's attachment by a standardized procedure (Ainsworth, Blehar, Waters, & Wall, 1978). The child is separated briefly from the mother, and observations of both the reaction to the mother's return and exploratory behavior before and after the separation form the basis for judging the quality of the attachment.

A number of studies have not found any indication of less secure infant–mother attachment when the mother is employed (Chase-Lansdale, 1981; Hock, 1980; Vaughn, Gove, & Egeland, 1980). A difference has been found, however, for fathers and sons. Sons of employed mothers have significantly less secure attachments to their fathers than sons whose mothers are not employed. Father–daughter attachment is virtually identical in both groups (Chase-Lansdale, 1981).

The Timing of Maternal Employment

The concept of attachment as a developmental process occurring during the child's first and second years highlights the importance of assessing the impact on the child of the timing of the mother's entry or re-entry into the labor force. Several recent studies suggest that maternal employment begun early may be less disruptive to the child's development. No difference in mother–infant attachment was found between mothers who returned to work during the first 3 months after their child's birth and nonemployed mothers (Chase-Lansdale, 1981; Hock, 1980). In contrast, when the employed-mother group included mothers who returned to work later, some negative effects of maternal employment were found (Schwartz, 1983; Vaughn et al., 1980).

The timing of the mother's employment may make a crucial difference in the effects of other events in the family life cycle. In a study of the impact of divorce on 4-year-olds, Hetherington (1979) found that the negative effects of divorce were diminished when the mother had been employed before the divorce. Maternal entry into the labor force at the time of divorce resulted in a particularly stressful situation for the child, further disruption in routines, and added to the child's losses.

MIDDLE CHILDHOOD AND ADOLESCENCE

Most current research about the effects of maternal employment studies infants and young children. Therefore, our review of effects on older children can be brief. Cognitive development and academic achievement are summarized first, followed by social development. The review concludes with examination of an area in which research findings appear to be particularly consistent, the effects of maternal employment on children's values.

Cognitive Development

Gold and Andres (1978b) studied academic achievement in a sample of 223 10-year-old children with employed or nonemployed middle-class or working-class mothers. Sons of employed mothers from middle-class families scored lower on the language tests and mathematics tests of the Canadian tests of basic skills (King, Linquist, & Hironymus, 1968). For middle-class children, maternal employment did not affect liking for school, grades, or educational aspirations. For lower-class boys, maternal employment was related to lower grades and greater dislike of school, but not to lower test scores. Finally, the authors found some evidence that greater paternal involvement was associated with better academic performance by sons.

In a similar study with 206 adolescent children, Gold and Andres (1978a) found no differences between children with employed or nonemployed mothers on the Canadian Tests of Basic Skills, on the Otis-Lennon Mental Ability Test (Otis & Lennon, 1967), on grades, or on educational aspirations and liking for school. Greater paternal involvement was again positively related to the son's academic performance. The authors conclude that maternal employment is much less salient for the cognitive development of adolescent children than for younger children.

Etaugh (1974), reviewing primarily the effects of maternal employment on cognitive development in older children from the 1960s, concludes that academic achievement for girls appears to be unaffected, while for boys, academic achievement is either unrelated or negatively affected by maternal employment. In a more recent assessment, Hoffman (1979) finds that a number of studies show positive effects on cognitive development for school-age sons and daughters of employed mothers from working-class families; she also adds that adolescent daughters of working mothers often score higher on academic achievement.

Social Development

While stimulation, love, and guidance are necessary for the school-age child, optimal social development in middle childhood and adolescence has additional requirements. Maternal employment may provide greater opportunity for the school-age child to develop independence, responsibility, and competence (Hoffman, 1979). For example, children with working mothers may have more household responsibilities, and this has been found to contribute to self-esteem (Smokler, 1975). Their mothers are also more likely to encourage independence.

Positive social effects of maternal employment for children of this age are more apparent for girls. School-age daughters of working mothers show greater admiration for their mothers, value the female role more, and see it as including more competence (Hoffman, 1979). Some of the positive effects of maternal employment for girls may derive from their fathers. Competence in females receives more encouragement from husbands of working wives (Hoffman, 1974). A closer relationship between a girl and her father may develop when her mother is employed, and that can result in better achievement and adjustment (Hoffman, 1979).

The effect of maternal employment on school-age boys is less clear, and may depend on parental attitudes and social class. Gold and Andres (1978b) found no overall differences in adjustment between sons of employed and nonemployed mothers, but did find a rather strong negative relationship between length of maternal employment and personality adjustment for middle-class sons. They also noted problems between fathers and sons in working-class families with employed mothers, a result also found by other investigators. As maternal employment becomes more common and social expectations continue to change, these effects may disappear, but more investigation is needed on factors that can prevent these negative effects. One factor to consider is mother's satisfaction with her role, which Etaugh (1974) concludes is crucial to school-age children's adjustment. Two others are paternal attitudes toward maternal employment, and paternal involvement with sons. The former may influence sons' perceptions of fathers, while the latter has been shown helpful for cognitive development.

During adolescence the beneficial effect of maternal employment on children's social development seems much more clear (Hoffman, 1979). Identity, autonomy, and self-esteem are central issues for the adolescent. Research indicates that maternal employment fosters independence and competence in adolescents. Daughters of working mothers are more sociable, autonomous, active, and motivated (Hoffman, 1979). Both sons and daughters can have higher self-esteem, more sense of belonging, and better interpersonal relations both at home and at school (Gold & Andres, 1978a; Moore, 1975). Adolescence may trigger the mother's concerns about her role after childrearing, concerns particularly severe for the nonworking woman. The mother's effectiveness as a parent is influenced by her morale. Employment can provide the mother with an extrafamilial sense of competence and identity that parallels and facilitates the adolescents' achievement of these goals. Although earlier reviews found mixed results, maternal employment is currently viewed by researchers as more beneficial to adolescents than is full-time mothering.

Children's Values

Research also consistently shows that maternal employment promotes a restructuring of children's values. For daughters of working mothers, this remodeling of the value system has obvious benefits; daughters of working mothers are more achievement oriented, more socially competent, and less defined in their social role. For sons of working mothers, the effects are elusive and less direct. Though there exists some recent evidence suggesting that sons of working mothers are more socially competent and more achievement oriented, these effects are relatively uninvestigated. Researchers have assumed the affected values for sons are primarily tangential, that they do not directly affect the sons' self-image, but involve increased tolerance and approval of a less rigid female role. However, sons may also derive direct advantages from maternal employment.

Changes in values are difficult to assess. Thus, indirect approaches are frequently used to measure a child's set of values. One such approach is the assessment of sex-role stereotyping; that is, of a child's sex-role perceptions. Hartley (1961) found that 5-, 8-, and 11-year-old children of working mothers are more likely to list a wide variety of adult activities as appropriate for and characteristic of both men and women. In particular, the daughters saw women as more active in the outside world and less confined to their home. Several more recent studies find maternal employment associated with this significant flexibility in sex-role perceptions (Jones & McBride, 1980; Marantz & Mansfield, 1977; Perloff, 1977; Miller, 1975). In these studies, adult recreation, work, and home-related activities are viewed as more similar for both men and women by children whose mothers work. Furthermore, this expansion of sex-role perceptions in children of working mothers is present as early as nursery school (Gold & Andres, 1978c).

The study by Jones & McBride (1980) suggests this well-documented sex-role flexibility extends to children's activities. Playing baseball, climbing trees, jumping rope, and playing with stuffed animals are more likely to be categorized as sex-neutral by children of working mothers. Hence, the adoption of various types of play, traditionally believed to be a product of the child's intrinsic interest, now appears to be the result of rigid sex-role proscriptions. The broadened sex-role stereotypes for children of working mothers may allow them to develop skills in areas otherwise off-limits for both the male and the female child. Thus, less stereotyping of sex-role activities, noted as early as 3 years of age (Gold & Andres, 1978c), leads to less sex-role stereotyping of play for children of working mothers, thereby broadening the range of activities a child may pursue.

A mother's work status, aside from determining her child's sex-role stereotyping of activities, broadens the child's stereotypes of masculine and feminine personality traits (Marantz & Mansfield, 1977). 5- to 11-year-old daughters of full-time employed mothers perceive women as significantly more competitive, more competent, more independent, and less emotional than do daughters of nonemployed mothers. Another study found that adolescents of employed mothers describe traits of boys and girls more similarly than do adolescents of nonemployed mothers (Gold & Andres, 1978a). The ramifications for female children of working mothers are clearly beneficial; some traditional "female" personality traits such as dependence and passivity may no longer handicap women who aspire to a career (Almquist & Angrist, 1971). For male children of working mothers, benefits also include expanded occupational options. Creativity for both sexes may be encouraged by a broader range of personality traits (Maccoby, 1966). In addition, male and female adolescent children of employed mothers, who show less rigid sex-role sterotyping, have been found to have better personality adjustment and total adjustment scores on standard personality tests (Gold & Andres, 1978a).

Not only does the working mother provide a role model more conducive to achievement for the female child and more tolerant of egalitarian ideology, the working mother strongly motivates her daughter to adopt a similar role, regardless of socioeconomic class. In a study by Smith (1969) involving 268 female high school subjects, daughters of working mothers expressed more favorable attitudes toward combining family and career than did daughters of nonworking mothers. Miller (1975) found that daughters of working mothers more often name their mother as the person they would want to be if they could be anyone; adolescent daughters of working mothers were more likely to name their mothers as the person they most admired (Douvan, 1963). This effect is also consistent among college-age women of working mothers (Baruch, 1972).

But do a broader range of more achievement-oriented personality traits (competence, independence, competitiveness) and motivation to imitate the working mother's role lead to the adoption of that role? A study by Douvan (1963) indicates that daughters of employed mothers are acting on these changing values. Douvan found that adolescent daughters of working mothers are relatively independent, autonomous, and active. Other studies suggest this may be true for younger girls as well (Hoffman, 1979).

Studies of college-age women confirm that more egalitarian occupational values, characteristic of daughters with working mothers, lead to successful achievement. Career-oriented college women are more likely to be the daughters of working women (Almquist & Angrist, 1971), as are college women desiring less conventionally feminine careers (Tangri, 1972). In studies of highly educated professional women, both Ginsberg (1971) and Birnbaum (1975) found maternal employment a significant background factor.

Sons of working mothers may derive similar advantages. Brown (1971) found that maternal employment was positively related to the occupational mobility of adult sons, particularly in white-collar families. Brown's conclusions are consistent with two earlier studies. Douvan (1963) found that upward mobility strivings were more often associated with part-time maternal employment than were nonmobility or downward mobility strivings among urban middle-class boys. Similarly, Banducci (1967) noted that maternal employment was associated with higher educational aspirations among sons and daughters of laborers and skilled workers. In Banducci's study, however, among children of professional fathers, a mothers' working was related to lower aspirations in boys and lower expectations in girls.

In terms of effects on values, then, maternal employment results in less stereotyping of masculine- and feminine-appropriate activities and personality traits. Furthermore, these modified views of male and female roles may influence daughters of working mothers to be more career and achievement oriented, and may result in positive occupational mobility for sons of working mothers. For both sons and daughters, broader sex-role conceptions may be associated with better social adjustment.

Summary of Effects of Maternal Employment on Children

Recent research on the effects of maternal employment on infants and young children has found few overall differences in children's development or in mother–child attachment and interaction. The experiences of children with working mothers do not differ significantly from those of children with nonworking mothers. Preschool boys and girls whose mothers are employed seem to adjust better to school and to have broader sex-role concepts than those whose mothers remain at home. Young children with working mothers may adapt more easily to parental supervision. A working mother provides even a very young child with parental role models who display a broader variety of behaviors. Maternal employment may make family events such as divorce less stressful for both mother and child.

The attitudes of both parents toward maternal employment and the extent of the fathers' involvement in childrearing seem to have greater effects on childrens' cognitive and social development than those of the mother's work role alone. Thus, any negative effects of maternal work-attitude incongruence may be ameliorated if mothers who wish to work are encouraged to do so and mothers who wish to remain at home are free to choose this option. Education, job availability, child care, and supplementary income for women who remain at home are among the supports that enable mothers to assume work roles that are congruent with their attitudes. Greater paternal involvement in childrearing may be particularly beneficial for young sons. Education, paternity leave, flexible working hours, and increased awareness of the beneficial effects of paternal involvement would promote increased participation by fathers in childrearing. More research is needed to further understand the processes by which parents' attitudes and childs' gender interact with the mother's employment status in affecting children's development.

EFFECTS OF MATERNAL EMPLOYMENT
ON THE MOTHER AND HER RELATIONSHIPS

How does being a working mother affect a woman's life: her health, the way she feels about herself, the way she spends her time, and her relationships with her husband and children? A number of studies suggest that if a woman is married and has a child she will feel healthier, happier, and more satisfied if she also has a job (Merikangas, 1985). However, it is not clear that a job produces better health or a higher degree of happiness; it may be that women who are healthier and less often depressed are simply more likely to be employed. A careful analysis by Verbrugge (1987) indicates that such selection factors account for only a small portion of the positive mental and physical health factors that have been found for employed mothers.

Maternal mental health studies have consistently shown that married women who are employed outside the home are no more depressed or are even in better mental health than married women who are at home full time. (See Gove & Geerken, 1977 for a review.) In a rare comparison of the effects of part- versus full-time employment, Northcott (1981) found that women employed full-time, including mothers of young children, rated themselves healthier and happier than both those employed part-time and those not employed.

Married women who work outside the home, even those who work full-time, continue to perform most of the household chores (Bahr, 1974; Hill & Stafford, 1980; Inkeles, 1980; Model, 1981). Working women who are mothers as well as wives may experience additional role strain and work overload. Hill and Stafford's analysis (1980) of time-budget data reveals that working mothers devote a great deal of time to child care, often at the expense of free time and even of sleep. Yet employed mothers report more positive feelings toward their children; nonemployed mothers describe parenthood as more restricting, burdensome, and demanding than do employed mothers (Gove & Geerken, 1977).

The presence of children creates additional stress for both employed and nonemployed women but has less impact on men, perhaps because their wives so often absorb the increased demands (Aldous, 1981; Degler, 1980; Kessler, Price, & Wortman, 1985). The stress of combining marriage and a job does not appear detrimental to mental health, but the addition of the type of demands associated with children does take a toll. However, these demands do not seem to be easier on the woman who is not employed. The finding that nonemployed mothers report both the most desire to be alone and the most loneliness (Gove & Geerken, 1977) suggests the frustration of the woman whose lack of a work role leaves her with only one social network for support and satisfaction. Nonemployed mothers may experience children-related pressures more intensely than employed mothers, and this may make them more vulnerable to mental distress.

Barnett and Baruch (1979) found high levels of self-esteem and role satisfaction for both employed and nonemployed middle-class mothers of preschool children. For both groups, self-esteem and role satisfaction were strongly related to perceptions of their own competence and of their husbands' approval of their role. Much may depend on the point in the woman's life-cycle at which her satisfaction is measured, as well as on the conditions of her employment.

Traditionally socialized, college-educated young women enjoy high self-esteem shortly after college graduation and during early motherhood, while the personal-achievement-oriented young woman is more troubled by self-doubt at this time (Rossi, 1968). However, Birnbaum (1975) hypothesized that it is traditionally socialized women who account for the finding that by the time they are in their 30s, married women are more unhappy than married men. She studied the experience of self-esteem, self-competence, and satisfaction in three groups of college-educated women: nonemployed married mothers, professional married mothers, and single professional women. Birnbaum found that the women who were not employed had lower self-esteem and felt less competent, even in child care and social skills, than the employed mothers. Women not employed expressed more concern about their mental health and self-identity, and reported feeling lonely and less attractive to men. They said that they lacked friends and that they missed a sense of challenge and creative opportunity. Professional mothers reported experiencing time pressure (as did single professionals) but they also felt competent, secure in their self-identity and friendships, and showed few signs of mental illness. Baruch and Barnett (1986, p. 584) point to the need for a multidimensional conceptualization of well-being: "If the sources of well-being differ for each dimension, involvement in multiple roles may be a prerequisite for well-being."

While marriage and work both contribute to happiness, and work seems to be especially important for educated women, we know little about how women cope with the role conflicts—the difficulties in meeting the obligations of wife, mother, and worker. Although role conflict or role strain has been clearly documented in varied samples (Johnson & Johnson, 1976; Parry & Warr, 1980), its impact on children has not been extensively studied.

In a study of single and married employed black mothers, Harrison and Minor (1982) found that each group coped differently with role conflicts. A majority of the single employed mothers coped by working harder at both roles to achieve satisfaction with their performance as mothers. A majority of married employed mothers, in contrast, chose to separate the two roles by, for example, establishing priorities and overlooking some role demands. Those married mothers who tried to cope by working harder at each role reported less satisfaction with the mother role. Overall, the single employed mothers were more satisfied with their performance in their work role than were the married, employed mothers.

Socialization and Later Adjustment

As described earlier, the daughters of employed mothers are strongly identified with them and are more likely to choose careers for themselves. Women whose mothers were not employed are more likely to be satisfied with their own nonemployed maternal roles (Barnett & Baruch, 1979).

Birnbaum (1975) found that professional women with children differed from nonemployed mothers in having parents with more graduate education and fathers with middle- or upper- level occupational status. They perceived their fathers as very intellectual, felt they resembled their fathers intellectually, and perceived their mothers as occupationally competitive.

How do women feel when they look back on the life patterns they have chosen? Sears and Barbee (1977) studied over 400 gifted women from the Terman study group. The women, whose average age at the time of the study was 62, were asked about the life pattern they would currently choose. Two thirds of the women who had stayed home with their children said that they would choose either a career or a career except when raising their family. When the women were asked how they evaluated their success in achieving their life goals, professional work as well as children and marriages were reported as contributing to satisfaction.

It should be remembered that this data is retrospective and may be biased toward the report of more congruence between actual and preferred choices than if the ratings had been made at the earlier choice points. Moreover, the Terman sample consists of the top 1% of the population in terms of IQ. A higher percentage of these women were employed outside the home, had higher incomes, and were more likely to be professionals than women in the general population. Also, as compared to the population as a whole, a higher percentage of women in the Terman study who stayed at home may have been dissatisfied with their earlier choices.

A survey of a broader sample of 600 older women (Campbell, Converse, & Rodgers, 1976) showed that married women with or without children were, in general, more satisfied than unmarried women. Both employed and nonemployed married women described themselves as satisfied with life as a whole. However, among college graduates, employment outside the home increased satisfaction: Seventy-nine percent of the employed group said they were highly satisfied while only 56% of the nonemployed group were highly satisfied. A national survey of women aged 18 to 71 also found that more educated married women are more satisfied if they work outside the home (Spreitzer, Snyder & Larson, 1975).

CONCLUSIONS AND POLICY IMPLICATIONS

Researchers have been reluctant to draw implications for social policy from their findings (e.g., Farel, 1980). Much of the research has been correlational in nature, precluding definitive statements regarding causation. Part-time and full-time work are often not clearly distinguished, with little attempt to note the reason for and exact nature and demands of jobs outside the home. Intactness and size of the family are sometimes not considered, and the preponderance of families studied are white and middle class. Measures of development vary from study to study and the type of supplementary care received by children is not carefully specified. Nevertheless, some conclusions are beginning to emerge. For infants and young children, the following statements seem to apply:

1. Maternal employment cannot be said to have overall negative effects on infants' development; mediating psychological factors, such as parental attitudes toward employment, need to be considered.

2. A number of studies point to possible temporary negative effects on cognitive development for young sons of working mothers. Greater parental, and especially paternal, attention and involvement with them can probably prevent these problems.

The nature of effects on school-age and adolescent children can be listed as well:

1. During school age and adolescence, the effects of maternal employment on cognitive and social development depend upon children's age, sex, and social class, as well as mediating factors such as parental involvement.

2. For school-age and adolescent daughters, cognitive effects in general are probably positive, especially in working-class families.

3. Effects on sons' cognitive development and academic achievement may be positive, neutral, or negative, depending upon factors such as paternal attitudes and encouragement. More research is needed in this area.

4. School-age and adolescent daughters of working mothers are more independent, achievement oriented, and socially competent, with more flexible sex-role perceptions, better family relations, and higher self-esteem. Positive effects on cognitive and social development for daughters often extend into adulthood.

5. Effects on sons' social development need to be monitored during middle childhood. Parental attitudes toward maternal employment and paternal involvement are important for sons' social development, especially for working-class families. Adolescent sons can benefit socially from maternal employment.

For the women themselves, the results are quite consistent. Working can provide a stable source of satisfaction, enhance self-esteem, and promote mental health. For college-educated women, work outside the home seems especially to promote a sense of well-being. This may be the result of the more satisfying work roles available to college-educated women. The nature and quality of a woman's experiences, not merely the number of roles she occupies, is crucial to understanding the processes affecting her well-being (Baruch et al., 1987).

Most studies have been cross-sectional and correlational; there is a clear need for longitudinal studies that will enable us to understand more definitively the effects of maternal employment at various ages. Also useful would be process studies that begin to trace the ways in which employment brings about various consequences or outcomes for the woman who works, her children, and her family. For example, we need further knowledge about how the father's behavior changes when the mother works.

Better measures are needed of important variables such as attitudes and satisfaction for both the working mother and members of her family. More precise definitions of employment are also needed. For example, when did the mother begin to work? Has her work pattern been continuous, full-time? We need to take into account the particular jobs and demands encountered by the working mother, for the effects of employment do vary with the kind of employment (Piotrkowski & Crits-Christoph, 1981). It seems unlikely, for example, that the effects of maternal employment are the same for a waitress and a psychiatrist, a factory worker and a judge.

In addition, we need to broaden the data base by studying the different racial and ethnic groups in our population. Moreover, many forms of substitute care have not been studied, and we need to understand the impact of supplementary care other than day care. We also need to understand the experiences of families who do not use supplemental care: "latch-key" children, for example, and children whose parents work different shifts.

How married women make the choice to combine work with children also requires more study. Fertility is negatively correlated with the level of a woman's education and her participation in the labor force. Fuchs (1983), however, argues that the causality in this relationship may be bidirectional: Women may choose first to limit their fertility and then continue their education towards a more rewarding career.

Finally, society needs to provide a range of choices for both men and women so that they can combine employment with parenting in a way that best suits their needs. Parents who wish to work need support networks and periodic relief from childcare to pursue activities that provide them with additional sources of satisfaction.

In sum, the employment of mothers is associated with numerous positive results for the well-being of the mother and with few negative results for the children of employed mothers. Female interests and the interests of children appear to be more in concert than in conflict.

REFERENCES

Ainsworth, M., Blehar, M., Waters, E., & Wall, S. (1978). *Patterns of attachment: A psychological study of the strange situation.* Hillsdale, N.J.: Erlbaum.

Aldous, J. (1981). From dual-earner to dual-career families and back again. *Journal of Family Issues, 2*(2), 115–125.

Almquist, E. M., & Angrist, S. S. (1971). Role model influence on college women's career aspirations. *Merrill-Palmer Quarterly, 17*, 263–279.

Altman, S. L., & Grossman, F.K. (1977). Women's career plans and maternal employment. *Psychology of Women Quarterly, 1*, 365.

Alvarez, W., Henderson, C., & Bronfenbrenner, R. (1982). Maternal employment and mothers' descriptions of their three year old children. In M. Cochran & C.R. Henderson, Jr. (Eds.), *The ecology of urban family life: A summary report to the National Institute of Education.* Unpublished manuscript, Cornell University.

Bahr, S. (1974). Effects on power and division of labor in the family. In L.W. Hoffman & F.I. Nye (Eds.) *Working mothers.* San Francisco: Jossey-Bass.

Banducci, R. (1967). The effect of mother's employment on the achievement, aspirations and expectations of the child. *Personnel and Guidance Journal, 46*, 263–276.

Barnett, R., & Baruch, G. (1979). *Multiple roles and well-being: A study of mothers of preschool age children* (Working paper no. 3). Wellesley College Center for Research on Women.

Baruch, G.K. (1972). Maternal influence upon college women's attitudes toward women and work. *Developmental Psychology, 6*, 32–37.

Baruch, G.K., & Barnett, R.C. (1986). Role quality, multiple role involvement and psychological well-being in mid-life women. *Journal of Personality and Social Psychology, 5*, 578–585.

Baruch, G.K., Biener, L., & Barnett, R.C. (1987). Women and gender in research on work and family stress. *American Psychologist, 42*, 130–136.

Birnbaum, J. (1975). Life patterns and self-esteem in gifted family-oriented and career-committed women. In M.S. Mednick, S. Tanyin, & C. Hoffman (Eds.), *Women and achievement.* Washington, DC: Hemisphere.

Bowlby, J. (1952). Maternal care and mental health. *World Health Organization Monograph Series*(2).

Bronfenbrenner, U., & Crouter, A. (1982). Work and family through time and space. In S.B. Kammerman & C.D. Hayes (Eds.), *Families that work: Children in a changing world.* Washington, DC: National Academy Press.

Brown, S.E. (1971). *Husbands' attitude toward and consequences of wife-mother employment.* (Doctoral dissertation, Florida State University) Ann Arbor, MI: University Microfilms, No. 71-23, 698.

Campbell, A., Converse, P.E., & Rodgers, W.L. (1976). *The quality of American life.* New York: Russell Sage Foundation.

Chase-Lansdale, P.L. (1981). Effects of maternal employment on mother–infant and father–infant attachment. *Dissertation Abstracts International, 42*(6), 2562. DEN 81-25083.

Cherry, F.F., & Eaton, E.L. (1977). Physical and cognitive development in children of low-income mothers working in the child's early years. *Child Development, 48*, 158–166.

Cohen, S.E. (1978). Maternal employment and mother–child interaction. *Merrill-Palmer Quarterly, 24* 189–197.

Degler, C.N. (1980). *At odds: Women and the family in America from the revolution to the present.* New York: Oxford University Press.

Douvan, E. (1963). Employment and the adolescent. In F.I. Nye & L.W. Hoffman (Eds.), *The employed mother in America.* Chicago: Rand McNally.

Etaugh, C. (1974). Effects of maternal employment in children: A review of recent research. *Merrill-Palmer Quarterly, 20*, 71–98.

Farel, A.M. (1980). Effects of preferred maternal roles, maternal employment, and sociodemographic status on school adjustment and competence. *Child Development, 51*, 1179–1186.

Fuchs, V.R. (1983). *How we live: Economic perspective on Americans from birth to death.* Cambridge, MA: Harvard University Press.

Ginsberg, E. (1971). *Educated American women: Lifestyles and self-portraits.* New York: Columbia University Press.

Gold, D., & Andres, D. (1978a). Comparisons of adolescent children with employed and non-employed mothers. *Merrill-Palmer Quarterly, 24*, 243–254.

Gold, D., & Andres, D. (1978b). Developmental comparison between 10-year-old children with employed and non-employed mothers. *Child Development, 49*, 75–84.

Gold, D., & Andres, D. (1978c). Relations between maternal employment and development of nursery school children. *Canadian Journal of Behavioral Science, 10*, 116–129.

Gold, D., Andres, D., & Glorieux, J. (1979). The development of Francophone nursery-school children with employed and non-employed mothers. *Canadian Journal of Behavioral Science, 11*, 169–173.

Goldberg, R.J. (1977, March). *Maternal time use and preschool performance.* Paper presented at the Meeting of the Society for Research in Child Development, New Orleans.

Golden, M., & Birns, B. (1976). Social class and infant intelligence. In M. Lewis (Ed.), *Origins of intelligence.* New York: Plenum Press.

Gove, W.R., & Geerken, M.R. (1977). The effect of children and employment on the mental health of married men and women. *Social Forces, 56* 66–76.

Harrison, A., & Minor, J. (1982). Interrole conflict, coping strategies, and role satisfaction among single and married employed mothers. *Psychology of Women Quarterly*, vol. 6, 354–360.

Hartley, R.E. (1961). What aspects of child behavior should be studied in relation to maternal employment? In A.E. Siegel (Ed.), *Research issues related to the effects of maternal employment on children.* University Park, PA: Social Science Research Center.

Hetherington, E.M. (1979). Divorce: A child's perspective. *American Psychologist, 34* 851–858.

Hill, C., & Stafford, F. (1980). Parental care of children: Time diary estimates of quantity, predictability and variety. *Journal of Human Resources, 15*, 219–239.

Hock, E. (1980). Working and non-working mothers and their infants: A comparative study of maternal caregiving characteristics and infant social behavior. *Merrill-Palmer Quarterly, 26*, 79–101.

Hoffman, L.W. (1963). Effects on children: Summary and discussion. In F.I. Nye & L. W. Hoffman (Eds.), *The employed mother in America.* Chicago: Rand McNally.

Hoffman, L.W. (1974). Effects of maternal employment on the child: A review of the research. *Developmental Psychology, 10*, 204–228.

Hoffman, L.W. (1979). Maternal employment: 1979. *American Psychologist, 34*, 859–865.

Hoffman, L.W. (1983, April). *Maternal employment in the infancy period: Impact on family relations.* Society for Research in Child Development, Detroit.

Hoffman, L.W. (1984). Maternal employment and the young child. In M. Perlmutter (Ed.), *Minnesota symposium in child psychology.* Hillsdale, NJ: Erlbaum.

Inkeles, A. (1980). Modernization and family patterns: A test of convergence theory. *Conspectus of History, 1*, 59–60.

Johnson, F.A., & Johnson, C.L. (1976). Role strain in high commitment career women. *Journal of the American Academy of Psychoanalysis, 4*(1), 13–36.

Jones, L.M., & McBride, J.L. (1980). Sex role stereotyping in children as a function of maternal employment. *The Journal of Social Psychology, 111*, 219–223.

Kagan, J., & Moss. H.A. (1962). *Birth to maturity.* New York: Wiley.

Kessler, R.C., Price, R.H., & Wortman, C.B. (1985). Social factors in psychopathology: Stress, social support, and coping processes. *Annual Review of Psychology, 36*, 531–572.

King, E.M., Lindquist, E.C., & Hironymus, A.N. (1968). *Manual for administrators, supervisors, and counselors: Canadian Tests of Basic Skills.* Toronto: Nelson.

Maccoby, E.E. (1966). Sex difference in intellectual functioning. In. E.E. Maccoby (Ed.), *The development of sex differences.* Stanford, CA: Stanford University Press.

Marantz, S.A., & Mansfield, A.F. (1977). Maternal employment and the development of sex-role stereotyping in five-to eleven-year-old girls. *Child Development, 48*, 668–673.

Merikangas, K. (1985). *Sex differences in depression.* Paper presented at the conference of Mental Health in Social Context, Radcliffe College, Cambridge, MA.

Miller, S.M. (1975). Effects of maternal employment on sex role perception, interests, and self-esteem in kindergarten girls. *Developmental Psychology, 11*, 405–406.

Model, S. (1981). Housework by husbands: Determinants and implications. *Journal of Family Issues, 2*(2), 225–237.

Moore, T. (1975). Exclusive early mothering and its alternatives. *Scandinavian Journal of Psychology, 16*, 256–272.

Northcott, H. (1981). Women, work, health, and happiness. *International Journal of Women's Studies, 4*, 268–276.

Otis, A.S., & Lennon, R.T. (1967). Otis-Lennon mental ability test. New York: Harcourt, Brace, & World.

Owen, M., Easterbrooks, M., Chase-Lansdale, L., & Goldberg, W. (1983). *Infancy into toddlerhood: Effects of maternal employment on infant–mother and infant–father attachments.* Detroit, MI: Society for Research in Child Development.

Parry, G., & Warr, P. (1980). The measurement of mothers' work attitudes. *Journal of Occupational Psychology, 53*, 245–252.

Pearlman, V.A. (1981). Influences of mothers' employment on career orientation and career choice of adolescent daughters. *Dissertation Abstracts International, 41*(11-A), 4657–4658.

Pedersen, F.A., Cain, R.L., Zaslow, M.J., & Anderson, B.J. (1983). Variation in infant experience associated with alternative family roles. In L. Laosa & I. Sigel (Eds.), *Families as learning environments for children.* New York: Plenum Press.

Perloff, R.M. (1977). Some antecedents of children's sex-role stereotypes. *Psychological Reports, 40*, 463–466.

Piotrkowski, C.S., & Crits-Christoph, P. (1981). Women's jobs and family adjustment. *Journal of Family Issues, 2*(2), 126–147.

Pleck, J., & Rustad, M. (1980). *Husbands' and wives' time in family work and paid work in the 1975–1976 study of time use.* Unpublished manuscript, Wellesley College, Center for Research on Women.

Rossi, A.S. (1968). Transition to parenthood. *Journal of Marriage and the Family, 30*, 26–39.

Schachter, F.F. (1981). Toddlers with employed mothers. *Child Development, 52*, 958–964.

Schwartz, P. (1983). Length of day care attendance and attachment behavior in 18-month-old infants. *Child Development, 54*, 1073–1078.

Sears, P.S., & Barbee, A.H. (1977). Career and life satisfaction among Terman's gifted women. In J.C. Stanley, W.C. George, & C.H. Solano (Eds.), *The gifted and the creative: A fifty year perspective.* Baltimore: John Hopkins Press.

Smith, H.C. (1969). *An investigation of the attitudes of adolescent girls toward combining marriage, motherhood and a career.* (Doctoral dissertation, Columbia University) Ann Arbor, MI: University Microfilms, No. 69–8089.

Smokler, C.S. (1975). *Self-esteem in pre-adolescent and adolescent females. Dissertation Abstracts International.* (Unpublished Doctoral Dissertation) University of Michigan, Ann Arbor, Ann Arbor, MI: 3599B university Microfilms No. TS275–00813.

Spitz, R.A. (1945). Hospitalism: An inquiry into the genesis of psychiatric conditions in early childhood. *The Psychoanalytic Study of the Child, 1*, 53–74.

Spreitzer, E., Snyder E., & Larson, D. (1975). Age, marital status, and labor force participation as related to life satisfaction. *Sex Roles, 1*, 235–247.

Stuckey, M., McGhee, P., & Bell, N. (1982). Parent–child interaction: The influence of maternal employment. *Developmental Psychology, 18*, 635–644.

Tangri, S.S. (1972). Determinants of occupational role innovation among college women. *Journal of Social Issues, 18*, 177–200.

Vaughn, B.E., Gove, F.L., & Egeland, B. (1980). The relationship between out-of-home care and the quality of infant–mother attachment in an economically disadvantaged population. *Child Development, 51*, 1203–1214.

Verbrugge, L.M. (1987). Role burdens and physical health of women and men. In F. Crosby (Ed.), *Spouse, parent, worker.* New Haven: Yale University Press.

Zajonc, R., & Markus, G. (1975). Birth order and intellectual development. *Psychological Review, 82,* 74–88.

Zaslow, M., Pedersen, F., Suwalsky, J., & Rabinovich, B. (1983, April). *The impact of maternal employment and parent interaction with one-year-olds.* Paper presented at the meeting of the Society for Research in Child Development, Detroit.

10

Women and Children Last: The Social and Economic Consequences of Divorce Law Reforms

LENORE J. WEITZMAN

In 1970, California launched a legal revolution by instituting the first no-fault divorce law in the United States. The new law not only changed the rules for divorce, it also changed the rules for dividing property and awarding support. Responding to the widespread dissatisfaction with the abuses of the old law, and recognizing the "emerging equality" of women, the reformers tried to fashion a fair and equitable divorce law that treated wives as full and equal partners in the marital partnership.

But the consequences of these reforms have extended far beyond the intent of the drafters. Ends may influence beginnings. In a society where one half of all new marriages are expected to end in divorce, a radical change in the rules for ending marriage inevitably affects the rules for marriage itself and the intentions and expectations of those who enter it (Weitzman, 1985, p. xv; see also Davis, 1986). The no-fault reforms have done just that: They have created new expectations for the behavior of husbands and wives in marriage and redefined the scope of their responsibilities as spouses and as parents.

Before 1970, every state required fault-based grounds such as adultery or mental cruelty for divorce. Rooted in the English common law, these laws reinforced the traditional marriage contract in which the husband, as the family breadwinner, and the wife, as the homemaker and mother, were committed to sexual fidelity in a lifelong partnership. In order to obtain a

Portions of this chapter are excerpted from *The Divorce Revolution: The Unexpected Social and Economic Consequences for Women and Children in America* (Lenore J. Weitzman, New York: The Free Press, 1985) and from Weitzman and Dixon (1979, 1980), Dixon and Weitzman (1980, 1982), and Weitzman (1981b, 1984).

I am indebted to my colleague Professor Ruth Dixon for her collaboration in planning this research and for her continued wisdom throughout its execution.

Lenore J. Weitzman, Ph.D. Department of Sociology, Harvard University, Cambridge, Massachusetts.

divorce one party had to prove that the other had violated that contract—that he had failed to support her, or that she had not performed her wifely duties, or that one of them had been cruel or sexually unfaithful.

A couple could not simply decide to end their marriage by mutual consent. The legal system of divorce required an "innocent" party and a "guilty" party. The innocent spouse had to produce evidence of the other's adultery or cruelty to justify the court's granting the divorce. The court would then provide redress for that innocent victim by compensating her (or him) with alimony (if the wife was the innocent party, as she typically was) and a larger share of the marital property.

By the late 1960s there was widespread dissatisfaction with this fault-based system of divorce: It forced spouses to become adversaries, and it encouraged and exacerbated marital mudslinging. After all, since the "innocent" party was rewarded financially, it "paid" to charge one's spouse with all the horrible deeds one could remember (or imagine). Often the parties had to distort the truth and lie in order to satisfy the legal requirements for fault. For example, if there had been no adulterous behavior, the evidence might be "manufactured" by staging an adulterous scene with private detectives and photographers waiting conveniently in the wings.

In some cases the legal process was merely a charade: But in others it was ugly, demeaning, and humiliating, especially when friends and relatives were brought into court as witnesses and were asked to corroborate the charges. Finally, the acrimonious legal process increased the antagonism between divorcing spouses and made it more difficult for them to cooperate in postdivorce parenting.

In this climate, California's no-fault law was welcomed as a major step forward. It sought to remove acrimony and hostility from the legal process by eliminating the need for any fault-based grounds for divorce. Instead, one party's claim that "irreconcilable differences" had caused the breakdown of the marriage was sufficient to justify a divorce. The new law required no grounds, no fault, and no consent. Since financial awards could no longer be based on who did what to whom, new standards for dividing property and awarding support were created to treat men and women fairly and equally. Property would be divided equally, and support for wives and children would be based on "need."

With this seemingly simple move, California pioneered sweeping reforms that quickly spread to other states. While not all states adopted the California model and completely abolished fault, by 1985—just 15 years later—every state but South Dakota had adopted some form of no-fault divorce law.

Although these laws were designed to create more equity, they have had unintended and unfortunate consequences: They have created substantial inequalities between divorced men and women and have led to the impoverishment of many divorced women and their children.

THE UNINTENDED CONSEQUENCES

When I began my research, I shared the reformers' optimism and assumed that only good could come from an end to the vilification and sham testimony of the old fault-based system of divorce. How much better, I thought, to end a marriage in a nonadversarial fashion that sought to reduce acrimony and hostility and to encourage parents to fashion fair and equitable financial arrangements for themselves and their children.

Equally important was the fact that the new law promised equality between men and women. Here, finally, was a law that recognized wives as equals in the marital partnership. California was the first state to guarantee wives an equal share—a mandatory 50%—of the property accumulated during the marriage.

When, in the early days of my research, I began to confront cases of upper-middle-class women who had been married for 20 to 30 years and were being cut off with only a few years of alimony and hardly any property, who were being forced to move so that their homes could be sold, who, with little or no job experience and minimal court-ordered support, were headed for near-poverty, I assumed that they were the exceptions—the women who had incompetent lawyers or the wrong judge.

Similarly, when I first confronted cases of young mothers who were awarded so little child support that there was not enough to cover the cost of day care, and who then told me that the child support order "wasn't worth the piece of paper it was written on" because they couldn't collect the support the court had ordered, I again thought that these women were the exceptions. Perhaps they hadn't fought hard enough to press for their legal entitlement to adequate support for their children.

But as the systematic data from the court dockets became computer printouts with statistically significant results, it became clear that these women were not the exceptions. The data revealed a disquieting pattern, a pattern that pointed to substantial hardship for women and children. Somehow the elimination of grounds, fault, and consent, and the institution of gender-neutral standards for financial awards were having unanticipated and unfortunate consequences.

The major unintended result of the no-fault reforms has been widespread economic disruption for divorced women and their children. The new rules for alimony, property, and child support end up shaping radically different economic futures for divorced men on the one hand and for divorced women and their children on the other. My research reveals that women and the minor children in their households (90% of the children of divorced parents live with their mothers after divorce) experience a sharp decline in their standard of living after divorce: Their standard of living drops an average of 73% in the first year after divorce. In contrast, their ex-husbands experience a rise in their standard of living—an average 42% increase in the first year after divorce (Weitzman, 1985).

Why have these supposedly "enlightened" legal reforms had such devastating effects? How could laws that were designed to create more equitable settlements end up impoverishing divorced women and their children?

One reason is that the court's interpretation of "equality" in divorce settlements often produces unequal results by ignoring the very real inequalities that marriage creates for men and women. It also ignores the economic inequalities between men and women in the larger society. Thus, a woman who has been a homemaker and mother during marriage may not be "equal" to her husband at the point of divorce. Rules that treat her as if she is equal (in the mistaken belief that she can quickly enter the labor force and become the economic equal of her husband) simple serve to deprive her—and her children—of the support all of them need.

A second reason is that an ostensibly equal division of property is not in fact equal when women have the responsibility for child care in nine out of ten divorces that involve children (Weitzman, 1985). To divide the property equally between husband and wife typically means that one half of the family assets are awarded to one person, the husband, while the other half are left to an average of three people: the wife and two children. In addition, judges often interpret the equal division rule as requiring the forced sale of the family home. This increases the disruption, dislocation, and distress in the lives of many women and children. In fact, the children's interest in marital property is simply ignored in the present legal system of divorce.

A third factor is that the elimination of grounds, fault, and consent have reduced women's bargaining leverage to secure adequate financial awards. Since the wife was usually the "innocent" party under the old law, she was in a stronger position to negotiate support for herself and her children (in return for her agreement to file for and obtain the divorce her husband wanted).

A final cause of the economic disparity between divorced men and women lies in the courts' failure to understand the changing nature of property in our society. In many cases, the major assets of the marriage are not divided equally. In fact, new forms of marital property are often not divided at all. This is because courts often ignore the husband's career assets—his enhanced earning capacity, his pension, professional license, and health insurance—and fail to award the wife a share of these valuable assets that were built and acquired during the marriage.

OVERVIEW AND RESEARCH

The unintended economic consequences of the legal changes in divorce provide one major theme of this chapter. The second major theme traces the effects of no-fault divorce on the institution of marriage. The final theme concerns the public policy implications of the findings and the congruence between womens' and childrens' interests in legal reforms.

The main section of this chapter summarizes the findings of a large-scale study of the social and economic effects of California's no-fault divorce reforms. Its research methods are briefly described below (for more detail see Weitzman, 1985).

I first examine the impact of the changing legal rules for dividing property, awarding alimony, and obtaining child support. I then examine the societal consequences of these rules, noting that the growth in female poverty and child poverty are a direct result of the current legal system of divorce.

The third section of this chapter considers the policy implications of the findings and recommends policies that would better protect those who are most disadvantaged: minor children, older homemakers, and the mothers of preschool children. The concluding section explores the ways in which the present system of divorce is transforming the nature of marriage and parent-hood in our society.

Throughout this discussion, it will be evident that the interests of women and children are usually congruent in divorce, since, as has been mentioned, 90% of the children live with their mothers after divorce. Thus, any policies that enlarge the mother's share of marital property or family income will usually benefit her children as well. Similarly, any policies that provide better economic protection for children—policies that improve child support or recognize the child's interest in the family home—will usually benefit their mother as well.

The perception of conflict between women's and children's interests in divorce is based on an inaccurate and simplistic assessment of the best interests of children. For example, it is only when a judge assumes that the child's best interests are purely economic and therefore believes that a child is better off living in his or her father's household, if he has a higher standard of living (and if, in addition, the judge is unwilling to award more adequate child support to the mother as a way of equalizing the standards of living in the two households) that a potential "conflict" emerges between the mother's interest in remaining the child's primary caretaker and the child's interest in maximizing his or her standard of living. Similarly, it is only when a woman's interest is defined as purely economic—as maximizing the amount of money she has to spend on herself after divorce—that one perceives a conflict between her improving her standard of living and her children's interest in living with her.

In other words, most of the situations in which a conflict between women's and children's interest are perceived are the result of myopic perceptions of the interests of women and children.

The Research

To provide a comprehensive portrait of the social and economic effects of the divorce law reforms, Professor Ruth Dixon and I collected and analyzed five types of data: systematic random samples of about 2,500 court dockets over a 10-year period; in-depth face-to-face interviews with 169 family law attorneys; in-depth face-to-face interviews with 44 family law judges; similar interviews with a sample of English legal experts; and comprehensive personal interviews with 228 divorced men and women about 1 year after their legal divorce.

This research design is unusual in that it uses a variety of sources. It does not rely solely on judges (as legal scholars tend to do) or solely on divorced men and women (as sociologists and psychologists tend to do). It also has the advantage of a systematic data base in the random samples of divorce decrees drawn from court records. Although most of the data were collected in California, the findings are relevant to the entire United States because many of the major features of the California law have been adopted by other states.

THE TRANSFORMATION OF MARRIAGE

No-fault divorce has not only redefined the rules for divorce, it has also transformed the legal rules for marriage. No-fault divorce has recast the legal rights and responsibilities of husbands and wives and the legal relationship between parent and children. As a result, it is creating new norms and new expectations for marriage and family commitments in our society.

A divorce provides an important opportunity for a society to enforce marital norms, rewarding the marital behavior it approves and punishing transgression. It does this by handing out legal rewards and punishments and by ordering people to pay for their transgressions in dollars and cents.

Consider, for example, the issue of alimony. If a divorce court awards alimony to a 50-year-old woman who has spent 25 years as a homemaker and mother, it is reinforcing the value of her domestic activities by rewarding the woman's devotion to her family. It may also be punishing the husband for abandoning his wife in middle age. But if, in contrast, the divorce court denies the wife alimony, and tells her that she must instead get a job and support herself, it is undermining the value of her domestic activities and penalizing her for investing in her family, home, and children at the expense of her own career. The court is also releasing the husband from his traditional responsibility for his wife's support. When divorce courts make these decisions, they are revealing and enforcing new expectations for husbands and wives. Although these expectations are being applied retroactively in divorce decrees, they necessarily suggest new expectations for marriage as well.

These expectations are not confined to those who experience divorce themselves. As Kingsley Davis also notes (see Chapter 4), awareness of the consequences of divorce affects the aspirations and intentions of those who are about to enter marriage, as well as the behavior of men and women who are already married. A law that penalizes a woman for the years that she spends as a homemaker and mother sends a chilling message to married women who want to give priority to their families and children. It warns them that they had better not forgo their own career advancement because they will suffer greatly if their marriage dissolves. This is a powerful threat in a society with a high divorce rate, especially when the no-fault, no-consent laws of many states give a woman no choice about whether her marriage will dissolve.

Of course, the new norms provide an equally sobering message to the man who gives priorities to his wife and children, a message evident to the men and women we interviewed. For example, one Los Angeles surgeon complained that all the sacrifices he made "to work like a dog . . . and earn the money so my kids and wife could have everything they wanted" were ignored in the present legal system of divorce. As he put it,

> "Now, she walked out on me and what do I get? Nothing. Nothing. And what does she get? She gets half of my house, half of my pension. . . . For what, I ask you? For running off with a jerk psychologist. That's my reward?"

MARITAL PROPERTY

Historically, there have been two distinct legal systems governing the property of married couples in the United States: Forty-two states have the separate property system,* based on the English common law, which segregates the assets of the husband and wife into two categories: "his" and "hers." Each spouse retains all the property he or she earns or inherits during the course of the marriage.

In contrast, in California and the small minority of other community property states, all property acquired during marriage is "theirs." The community property system assumes that all property acquired during marriage is "earned" by the joint efforts of the two spouses and it therefore belongs to both of them.

The two systems have different approaches to the division of property upon divorce. In most separate property states, the starting point for dividing marital property is typically one third of the property to the wife and two thirds to the husband (if he was the one who "earned" it). In a community property system, the starting point is a fifty–fifty division of the property, one half to the wife and one half to the husband.

*Wisconsin, one of the separate property states, instituted a community property type system in 1986.

How Property Is Divided

Before 1970, when every state had a fault-based system of divorce, property awards were often linked to findings of fault in both types of legal regimes. The innocent party typically received a greater share of the property than the guilty party.

One of the major innovations of California's 1970 legal reform was the institution of a fixed no-fault standard for dividing property: It *required* judges to divide the property acquired during marriage *equally* upon divorce—half to the husband, half to the wife. The equal division standard was seen as fair—and "protective" of wives—because it guaranteed each spouse one half of the jointly accumulated property.

Surprisingly, the equal division rule has reduced the wife's share of the property in California because California wives were typically awarded more than half of the marital property before 1970, under the old fault-based divorce law, since they were usually the innocent plaintiffs. In 1968, wives were awarded more than half (60% or more) of the property both in San Francisco and in Los Angeles divorce cases. Most of the awards allowed the wife to keep the family home, which was often the family's most valuable asset. Without the old lever of fault, the wife's share of the property dropped to exactly 50%.

The Problem of the Family Home

The major impact of the equal division rule has been on the disposition of the family home. Today more homes are being sold so that the proceeds can be divided equally: The number of cases in which there was an explicit court order to sell the home rose from about one in ten in 1968 to about one in three in 1977 (Weitzman, 1985). Those wives who do manage to keep the family home typically have other property they can trade for their husband's share of the home—such as an interest in their husband's pension.

Surprisingly, the presence of minor children in the home has not deterred judges from ordering it sold. Our data reveals that 66% of the couples who were forced to sell their homes had minor children. These sales mean residential moves that disrupt children's school, neighborhood, and friendship ties, and create additional dislocations for children (and mothers) at the very point at which they most need continuity and stability. The emotional upheaval is underscored by a quote from a typical respondent who was ordered to vacate her home in 3 months so that it could be sold:

> "I begged the judge. . . . All I wanted was enough time for Brian [her son] to adjust to the divorce . . . . I broke down and cried on the stand . . . but the judge refused. He gave me 3 months to move—3 months to move 15 years— right in the middle of the school semester. . . . My husband's attorney threatened me with contempt if I wasn't out on time . . . he also warned me not to

interfere with the real estate people—in my house—he said if I wasn't coopera-
tive in letting them show the house when they wanted to, he'd 'haul me into
court for contempt.' It was a nightmare . . . . The most degrading and unjust
experience of my life."

When we asked judges about their decisions to force the sale of the
family home they offered three explanations: It permitted a "clean break"
between parties, it did not unduly hamper the husband by tying up his
equity in the house, and it relieved the burden on the wife.

Most California judges stressed the husband's "right" to "his half" of
the family property. Since the home is the only substantial family property
in many divorce cases, its sale was seen as necessary to give the husband the
money he would need to start a new life. As one California respondent
explained:

"You have to be fair to the husband. If you award a house to a woman when it
is the only asset, you are then faced with the man who asks, 'Why am I not
entitled to the present enjoyment of the community asset that we have? Why
should I stand still for deferred enjoyment?' He wants to start a new life. He
doesn't want to hang around waiting for his equity. And, by law, he has a right
to that equity."

The second justification judges offered for the sale of the family home
was that it would make life "easier" for the wife. Many of them said that the
wife was "better off" without a home that tied her down to old neighborhoods and children's schools and children's friends, that locked her into the
suburbs and restricted her personal, social, and economic options. But our
interviews with divorced women revealed that the new solution often caused
many more hardships as mothers and children were evicted from their
neighborhoods and their system of social support. The forced sale of the
family home intensifies the disruption, dislocation, and distress in the postdivorce lives of mothers and children.

The disposition of the family home in California is quite different from
what is seen as the "equitable" solution in England. Among the English
experts I interviewed, the first priority was given to preserving the family
home for the children (Weitzman, 1984). For example, in responding to a
typical case in which the home was the only family asset, one barrister
explained the way the English courts would approach this case:

"First, let's make sure the children are looked after . . . the children have always
lived in that house . . . you want to finish a child's schooling."

Similarly, a solicitor predicted:

"The wife would get the house because she has to make a home for the children,
and the children come first—you don't want their home to be disrupted. You
want to stabilize the situation for them."

The underlying principle in the English approach is that "children come first" because they are the most vulnerable members of the divorcing family and they most need societal protection. As one English judge said: "It's my job to protect the children."

In contrast to the English emphasis on the children's welfare as the court's first priority, the "interests" of children were rarely mentioned by the California experts. Marital property was defined solely in terms of the relative rights of the husband and wife, and it was divided between the two of them.

It is not only children and their mothers who suffer from the forced sale of the family home. Some of the most tragic victims are older homemakers who not only lose their residence of 25 or 35 years, but also lose their whole social structure in a forced move to the other side of town. As one woman described her reaction:

> "I had lived in that home for 26 years and my three children still considered it their home. But the judge ordered it sold. . . . He said he had to follow the letter of the law. . . . I married at a time when a woman who spent 30 years of her life raising a family was worth something . . . but in the eyes of the court I was merely "unemployed." No one would rent me an apartment because my only income was $700 a month spousal support and landlords said that was "unstable" and "inadequate." Two months later my husband's attorney took me into court for contempt because I hadn't moved. . . . He said I was interfering with the sale of the house. . . . The judge gave me ten days to get out. . . . I am still outraged. It is a total perversion of justice. I was thrown out of my own house."

Significantly, the California legislature did *not intend* that the family home be sold in order to meet equal division requirement. Indeed, a 1970 Assembly Committee report specifically states that a temporary award of the home to the spouse who has custody of minor children should be seen as a valid reason to delay the division of property:

> Where an interest in a residence which serves as the home of the family is a major community asset, an order for the immediate sale of the residence in order to comply with the equal division mandate of the law would, certainly, be unnecessarily destructive of the economic and social circumstances of the parties and their children. (California Assembly, 1970, p. 787)

The California appellate courts have upheld the rationale for maintaining the family home for minor children when a sale would have an adverse economic, emotional, or social impact on them. Fran Leonard, attorney for The Older Women's League, echoes these thoughts in asserting the importance of a similar delay to allow older homemakers to retain their homes:

> For the older woman, especially a homemaker [the sale of the family home] is a major cruelty. Upon divorce, she loses her husband and her occupation—then

all too often, her home. This nearly comprises her universe. Unlike her spouse, she may have no credit history, no income aside from alimony, and almost no prospects of recovering her lost earning capacity. The chances of her ever buying another home are almost nil. Yet all too commonly the court orders the home sold, in order to divide its value. Attorneys frequently favor this, because their fees can be paid out of escrow . . . . Instead older women should try to keep the family home. (Leonard, 1980, p. 9)

But despite the legislative and judicial authority for exempting the home from the immediate equal division of community property, the judges we interviewed in 1974, 1975, 1981, and 1983 attested to the prevailing pattern of ordering the home sold and the proceeds divided upon divorce. While some judges were willing to leave the home in joint ownership for "a few years," very few were willing to let it remain unsold until small children attained majority. Even fewer were willing to make an exception for an older woman, who, they asserted, didn't "need" the home anymore (even if her college-age children considered it their home as well).

Once again, the responses of the English judges reveal a very different approach. Their first priority is to provide the older housewife with the home or a comparable home so that she can maintain her life without grave hardship. The English assume that after a long marriage, a husband has a responsibility to provide for his exwife for the rest of her life. To ensure that his obligations are fulfilled, the English courts often require an older (and well-to-do) husband to provide more than housing and support during his life: He may also be required to purchase an insurance policy or annuity to compensate his exwife for the widow's benefits she forfeits by getting divorced.

Changes in the Nature of Property: The Importance of Career Assets

Despite the equal division rule in California, we found that the courts were not, in fact, dividing property equally. This is partially a result of major changes in the nature of property in our society. Today husbands and wives are increasingly likely to invest in careers and human capital—most particularly in the husband's human capital and career. The new property resulting from this kind of investment is often the family's major asset. Yet this property is not being divided equally upon divorce. In fact, it is often not divided at all. It is simply presumed to belong to the husband. But if the law allows men to retain their career assets—their professional education, degrees, licenses, health insurance, and earning capacities—then their wives are not in fact being awarded an equal share of the joint property, despite the equal division rule.

"Career assets" is the term I coined to refer to the tangible and intangible assets that are acquired as a part of either spouse's career or career potential (see Weitzman 1981 and 1985 for more detail). "Career assets" encompass a large array of specific assets, such as pension and retirement benefits, a license to practice a profession or trade, medical and hospital insurance, the goodwill of a business, and entitlements to company goods and services. If these assets have been acquired in the course of a marriage, they should be included in the pool of marital or community property to be divided upon divorce.

Consider these facts: We found that the average divorcing couple has less than $20,000 in fixed assets when they divorce (Weitzman, 1985, p. 56 and Table 2). Yet the average couple can earn more than the value of their assets in less than 1 year (Weitzman 1985, p. 59 and Table 4). This means that the value of the couple's career assets—indeed the value of their earning capacity alone—is much greater than the value of their physical property (Weitzman, 1985, p. 60).

These data have important implications. If one partner builds his or her earning capacity during the marriage while the other is a homemaker and parent, the partner with the earning capacity has acquired the major asset of the marriage. If the earning power—or the income it produces—is not divided upon divorce, the two spouses are left with very unequal shares of their joint assets.

An awareness of this inequity was echoed over and over again in our interviews. As one veteran of a 30-year marriage to a college professor explained:

> "We married at 21, with no money. . . . When he was a graduate student, I worked as a secretary and then typed papers at night to make extra money. When he became an assistant professor I 'retired' to raise our children but I never stopped working for him—typing, editing, working on his books. . . . My college English degree was very useful for translating his brilliant ideas into comprehensible sentences. . . . My name never appeared on the title page as his co-author, where it belonged, only in the dedication or thank you's. . . . There's more, lots more—the hours mothering his graduate students, hosting department parties, finding homes for visiting professors. . . . I was always available to help. . . . I got $700 a month for 3 years. The judge said, I was 'smart and healthy enough to get a job.' I am to 'report back like a school girl' in 3 years. Never mind that I am 51. . . . Never mind that I had a job and did it well and am old enough to be entitled to a pension. . . . It's not that I regret my life or didn't enjoy what I did. But it was supposed to be a partnership—a fifty–fifty split. It isn't fair that he gets to keep it. It isn't fair for the court to treat it as his. . . . I earned it just as much as he did."

Career assets are also of great importance for younger couples. In many cases one spouse's professional education or license is the only asset acquired during marriage. The issue arises when one spouse, usually the wife, supports the other's professional education and training with the expectation that she will share the fruits of her investment through her husband's enhanced earning power. If they divorce soon after the student spouse completes training, the young couple typically has few tangible assets because most of their capital has been used to finance the student's education.

In a landmark 1985 case in New York, O'Brien v. O'Brien, the Court of Appeals took this position and ruled that a medical license obtained during marriage is marital property (whose value must be divided at the time of a divorce). The O'Brien case involved a 9½ year marriage in which Loretta O'Brien worked as a school teacher in Guadalajara, Mexico to support her husband in medical school. Mrs. O'Brien, who knew no Spanish when the young couple moved from New York to Mexico, learned the language and found work teaching kindergarten and tutoring English. Three months after Michael O'Brien received his medical license, he sued for divorce.

What then are our conclusions about the extent to which property is being divided equally or equitably upon divorce? Since career assets are typically acquired during marriage in the same manner that other marital property is acquired, and since these assets are, along with the family home, often the most valuable assets a couple own at the time of the divorce, if the courts do not recognize some or all of these assets as marital property, they can not divide marital property equally or equitably because they are excluding a major portion of a couple's property from the pool of property to be divided upon divorce. In addition, if the courts treat these assets as the property of the major wage earner, in most cases they allow the husband to keep the family's most valuable assets for himself. It is like promising to divide the family jewels equally, while setting aside all the diamonds for the husband.

The husband's career assets are "the diamonds" of marital property. Without them, the property cannot be divided equally or fairly.

ALIMONY: THE NEW TRENDS

The second area in which the new divorce laws attempt to treat men and women "equally" is in maintenance awards, or what is typically referred to as alimony or spousal support. The old divorce laws assumed that husbands were responsible for the financial support of their former wives. The reformers thought that that was inappropriate: They pointed to women's increased participation in the labor force, and assumed that women were now equally capable of supporting themselves and their children after divorce.

Our California data reveals several changes in the patterns of alimony awards that reflect these new standards (Weitzman, 1985, pp. 143–183). First, in accord with the new law's goal of making the wife self-sufficient after divorce, there has been a shift from permanent alimony awards, awards based on the premise of the wife's continued dependency, to time-limited awards. Between 1968 and 1972, permanent alimony—awards labelled permanent, until death or remarriage—dropped from 62% to 32% of the alimony awards in Los Angeles County (Dixon & Weitzman, 1980). By 1972 (and in subsequent years) two thirds of the alimony awards were transitional awards for a limited and specified duration. The median duration of these fixed-time awards was 25 months, or about 2 years. Thus, the average award carries an expectation of a short transition from marriage to self-sufficiency.

Second, the standards of the new law have dictated a greater reliance on the wife's ability to support herself. Economic criteria, such as the wife's occupation and predivorce income, are therefore more important than the old standards of fault and innocence.

Although it is reasonable for courts to consider a wife's ability to support herself, it is shocking to see how little "earning capacity" is necessary to convince a judge that a woman is capable of self-sufficiency (see Weitzman, 1985, pp. 178–180, 187–194). We found countless wives with low earning capacities and limited and marginal employment histories who were denied spousal support altogether because judges presumed they were capable of supporting themselves.

These irregular work histories of many divorced women leave a lot of room for judicial discretion in deciding whether any individual woman is "capable of engaging in gainful employment at the time of the divorce." A judge may conclude that a woman who was employed during the first 3 years of her marriage but has not worked in the last 16 years is immediately capable of self-sufficiency. Similarly, a judge may decide that because a woman has done volunteer work at a hospital she can now obtain a paid job there, or that because a woman has spent 3 months a year in an accounting office during the tax season, she is now capable of earning an equivalent salary 12 months a year.

Since few women in longer marriages have held full-time long-term jobs, their "employment histories" tend to be ambiguous. As an example of how judges tend to gloss over the ambiguities in assessing a woman's ability to get a job and be self-sufficient, consider the following two statements from judges we interviewed:

[Referring to a case just presented in court] The best thing for her is to get right out and get a job—earn her own money—and make her own life.

[Q: What kind of job do you think she can get?] Oh, anything. She can get a job in a store selling . . . clothes . . . or whatever. . . . There are lots of jobs out there, just read the want ads.

[Q: What about that woman? What kind of a job do you think she might find?] She said she used to work as . . . a . . . oh, what did she say? In an office or something—a bookkeeper or something like that. Well, that's a good job. She could probably get good hours, too . . . and be able to pick up her kids after school, as she was worried about that."

[Referring to a woman who testified that she had not taught for 20 years and did not have California teaching credentials.] Just because she's been married

20 years doesn't mean she can be a sponge for the rest of her life. If she was once a teacher, she can always get a job teaching. Maybe she'll have to work as a substitute for a while, or at a not so fancy school, but just because she hasn't taught in 20 years doesn't mean she can't teach. She is a teacher.

Both cases suggest how easily judges can read evidence of employability in a diversity of situations and conclude that a woman does not need support. Yet both of these women had not been employed since the early years of marriage, and both of them had spent most of their married years raising children. They still had children at home (both of them were now in their late 40s). The first woman had no formal training as a bookkeeper, but had worked as one many years earlier. The second woman had not held a paid teaching job for 20 years of a 22-year marriage (which the judge apparently misheard as 20 years) but had taught on a volunteer basis in the adult education program at her church.

How realistic is it to assume that these women can easily find well-paid full-time jobs and become self-supporting? If they are like most divorced women we interviewed—especially those in their late 40s who had been career homemakers and mothers—it is totally unrealistic (see also Shields, 1981).

Many employers do not recognize homemaking skills as having a market value. They only recognize "recent paid work experience" and even with such experience, older women are unwanted in today's labor market. Consider the difficulties two of the older women we interviewed faced:

"There is no way I can make up for 25 years out of the labor force. . . . No one wants to make me president of the company just because I was the president of the PTA."

"The judge told me to go for job training—but no training can recapture 27 years of my life. I'm too old to start from the beginning and I shouldn't have to. I deserve better."

Professor Herma Kay suggests that judges were affected by the feminist movement in the early 1970s and thus were using women's demands for equality as a justification for denying and terminating alimony (Kay, 1978, personal communication). Along the same lines, attorney Riane Eisler quotes a California judge who described his colleague's attitudes as, "What they (divorcing women) need is to go to work, so they can get themselves liberated" (Eisler, 1977, p. 46).

The results of these standards is that more than 85% of the divorced women in the United States are presumed capable of self-sufficiency and denied any alimony whatsoever (U.S. Bureau of the Census, 1987, p. 6).

Although alimony has always been rare (because it has been, for the most part, confined to the wives of middle-class and upper-middle-class men, and these couples always comprised a small minority of the divorcing population), the awards and the length of the awards have been drastically cut under the new divorce laws. (In California these awards average $370 a month in 1984 dollars [Weitzman, 1985, p. 171]; nationally they averaged $331 a month in 1985 [U.S. Bureau of the Census, 1987, p. 7]).

Instead of the old law's assumption that these women need permanent alimony to enable them to continue to share their husband's standard of living (which they, of course, helped to build), the new laws create an expectation that they will become independent and self-sufficient soon after the divorce.

The Gap Between Theory and Reality: Mothers and Older Homemakers

In theory, alimony is still supposed to be available for women with custody of young children and older homemakers incapable of self-sufficiency. However, we found that alimony awards to mothers of children under 6 dropped, since 1970, more than for any other group of women. Today, only 13% of the California mothers of preschool children are awarded spousal support (Weitzman, 1985, p. 186 and Table 17).

Why does the need to care for young children appear to have so little effect on alimony awards? Two thirds of the Superior Court judges we interviewed see the goal of making the wife self-sufficient as more important than supporting the custodial parent. As they said, it is "good for a divorced woman to earn money instead of being dependent on her former husband," "work is a healthy form of rehabilitation that will help her build a new life," and "combining work and motherhood is now normal in our society." Although many of the young mothers we interviewed shared these sentiments and *wanted* to be self-sufficient, the *economic reality* of their low earnings and the need to support their children compelled support from their former husbands.

The judges are always balancing the interests of children against their concern for the father and his need for his income. When they can justify the mother's work as "healthy and good for her," and when they can overestimate her earning capacity, they can justify allowing the husband to keep most of his income for himself. As one of our respondents described the result of this attitude:

> "It's an insult . . . but I can't live and feed my son on my pride, so I take it. . . . Why am I and my son worth so much less than he is? . . . It's because the judge looks at him and thinks he needs it—but I can get by. . . . He gets a company car and the privilege of eating out whenever he wants to—I have the privilege of food stamps. . . . I've never lived like this before in my life . . . it's degrading and it's not fair."

Our empirical analysis of the awards judges make reveals that the husband is rarely ordered to part with more than one third of his income to support his wife and children. His is therefore allowed to retain two thirds for himself while his former wife and children, typically three people, are expected to survive on the remaining one third.

One reason for the disparity is that the judges we interviewed gave first priority to the husband's needs. They expressed great sympathy for the plight of divorced men and regarded the income of most divorced men as too low to support two households adequately, too low to provide even half of the support for the husband's children who are in the custody of their former wives. They therefore decide that it is often "better" to leave most of the family's postdivorce income with the husband, viewing it as his rather than theirs. Most judges appear to view the law's goal of equality as a mandate to place an equal burden of support on men and women without regard to the fact that the parties' capacities to support that burden are clearly unequal.

Self-Sufficiency Standards and the Older Homemaker

A second group of women who are hurt by the new law's standard of self-sufficiency are the older homemakers who have been housewives and mothers throughout marriages of long duration. Although many more women in this category are awarded spousal support, one out of three is not.

It is not surprising to find that the women who feel most betrayed by the legal system of divorce are those older homemakers who are denied alimony. As one woman said:

> "You can't tell me there's justice if someone uses you for 25 years and then just dumps you and walks out scot-free. . . . It's not fair. It's not justice. It's a scandal . . . and those judges should be ashamed of themselves sitting up there in their black robes like God and hurting poor people like me."

When we compare the postdivorce incomes of long-married husbands and wives, we find that wives are expected to live on much smaller amounts of money, and are economically much worse off, than their former husbands. For example, wives married 18 years or more with predivorce family incomes of $20,000 to $30,000 a year have, on the average, a median annual income of $6,300 after the divorce. Their husbands, in contrast, have a median annual income of $20,000—even if we assume that they actually paid the support awards. The result is that the postdivorce income of these wives is 24% of the previous family income, whereas the average postdivorce income for their husbands is 87% of that standard (Weitzman, 1985, p. 190).

Once again, the judges approach these cases mindful of the husband's need for "his income" and his limited capacity to support two families. And once again, it is clear that the judges simply misunderstand the economic reality of the wives' job prospects. In our interviews the judges assured us that most of these women would "be able to find jobs." But they did not interview the women a year later, as we did, and did not hear about the women who applied for 50 jobs without success, or those who could only find jobs at the minimum wage after long marriages to professional men. As one woman said:

"It's so hard to start at the bottom when you've been a respected member of the community for years. . . . I just never realized that the respect and admiration and civic work doesn't count for anything in the job market . . . and it certainly doesn't help pay my rent."

As these examples suggest, the woman who has few marketable skills cannot make up for 20 or 25 years out of the job market. Most end up in low-paying jobs, living in greatly reduced circumstances, often on the edge of poverty (Leonard, 1980).

Obviously, the problem is not limited to California. Consider the case of Edith Curtis, a 55-year-old Idaho woman who applied for state unemployment compensation after her divorce from a college professor. Edith Curtis' 2-year job search and 75 applications proved "fruitless to a shopworn and obsolete housewife . . . with a 30-year-old B. A. in English and a lack of salable skills" (Chase, 1985, p. 1). She was finally offered and accepted a job as a fast-food cashier, part time, at the minimum wage (Chase, 1985, p. 12).

No wonder the older homemaker typically feels betrayed by the new laws. She was promised, by both her husband and our society—her contract, if you prefer, both implied and expressed—that their marriage was a partnership and that he would share his income with her. Instead, the courts have changed the rules in the middle of the game, after she has fulfilled her share of the bargain and passed the point where she can choose another life course.

CHILD SUPPORT AWARDS

Our research uncovered two major problems with child support: low awards and inadequate enforcement. The U.S. Census shows that the average award for two children in the United States is about $200 a month—much less than half of the cost of raising two children (U.S. Bureau of the Census, 1987, p. 3 and Table C). In California, the average child support award was less than the average cost of day care alone.

Ironically, young mothers have a greater need for support from their exhusbands after divorce—just at the point where judges are telling them to make do with less. Most custodial mothers have to take over many of their husband's family responsibilities and face greater burdens and greater expenses as single parents.

Yet, it is very rare for any court to order more than 25% of a man's income in child support or more than 32% of a man's income in combined child support and alimony (Weitzman, 1985, p. 267; see also Cassetty, 1978, and Chambers, 1979). Even though judges say that their typical award is closer to one half of the husband's income, the data from our analysis of court dockets and our interviews with divorced persons shows that the real proportion is quite different. Instead of a 50–50 division of the husband's income, the typical award is one third for the wife and two children to two thirds for the husband. Among upper-income men it is one-fifth to four-fifths: men who earn $50,000 or more a year retain an average of 81% of their net incomes for themselves (Weitzman, 1985, pp. 266–267 and Table 24).

What do the current child support awards mean in terms of standards of living? If California men paid the child support the courts ordered them to pay, 73% of them would have enough money left for themselves to live comfortably (i.e., above the lower standard budget established by the U.S. government). However, if women and children had to live on the child support the courts ordered, only 7% of them would have enough money to live comfortably. Most of them—fully 93% of the women and children— would have to live *below* the poverty level (Weitzman, 1985, p. 275, Figure 2). These shocking differences would result from current child support awards even if men complied fully with court orders. (See also Chambers, 1979 for similar results in Michigan.) But if the court orders for child support are not paid, or are not paid fully—as we shall see below, an all-too-common occurrence—the differences in the standards of living between fathers and mothers and children would be even greater.

Some people have questioned whether men can afford to pay the amounts of child support ordered by the courts. The answer is an unequivocal "yes." Whether one considers the percentage of the supporter's income, or the standard of living he has after paying, the vast majority of divorced fathers can pay child support and still maintain a relatively comfortable standard of living.

Significantly, both divorced men and divorced women agree with this conclusion. When asked, "Can you (or your exhusband) afford to pay the child support the court ordered," fully 80% of the women and 90% of the men say yes (Weitzman, 1985, p. 276). Thus, both men and women see the award as reasonable in terms of the husband's ability to pay. Only a small minority think the awards are excessive.

Along the same lines, when asked about their satisfaction with the amount of child support awarded in their case, the vast majority (91%) of divorced men see the awards as reasonable in terms of their income. Only 9% of the men say they were dissatisfied. (As might be expected, a larger percentage of the women, 36%, are dissatisfied with the amount of child support awarded and see it as inadequate.)

In summary, the data point to three conclusions. First, the amount of child support ordered is typically quite modest in terms of the father's ability to pay. Second, the amount of child support ordered is typically not enough to cover even half the cost of actually raising the children. Third, the major burden of child support is typically placed on the mother even though she normally has fewer resources and much less "ability to pay."

Support Enforcement: The High Rate of Noncompliance

Even though child support awards are modest to begin with, they are often unpaid because many divorced fathers have simply ignored court orders. U.S. Census data show that fewer than half of the fathers fully comply with court orders to pay child support (U.S. Bureau of the Census, 1987, pp. 1–2).

Surprisingly, this is not because the father cannot "afford" to pay. In California, we found that men who earn between $30,000 and $50,000 a year were just as likely to fail to pay child support as those who earn less than $10,000 a year (Weitzman, 1985, p. 296, Table 25). The result is that the mother, who is the primary custodial parent in 90% of the divorce cases, is left with the major burden of supporting her children after divorce.

The typical child support order calls for the father to send the mother a check every month or every pay period. It is up to the mother to keep track of the checks and to try to obtain the money when the checks are late or are for less than the full amount ordered. This puts the burden of collection on the mother who typically has few resources to begin with. As one mother explained:

> "Each time I went to court I lost a day's pay, and I had to pay my lawyer for his court rate. We had to wait two hours for the case to be called, and [my exhusband] got a postponement to get his papers together. . . . The next time he was sick. . . . Then he changed attorneys. . . . Each time the judge said he had a right to have his side represented . . . but I couldn't afford it anymore. They let him get away with murder."

Wage assignments have proven most effective in securing compliance. Yet the vast majority of the California judges are reluctant to order them. In our 1977 random sample of court records, only 5% of the cases with a child support award had a wage attachment (Weitzman, 1985, p. 293). What is surprising about these data is that California law requires judges to order a wage assignment if the man has not paid support for 2 months.

Even more telling are the judges' responses to the question, "How many wage assignments have you ordered in the past 6 months?" The average was only one or two wage assignments per judge over the 6-month period, and more than a quarter of the judges said they had *never* ordered a wage assignment (Weitzman, 1985, p. 302). When one considers that there were about 36,000 divorce cases heard in Los Angeles County each year, and that the Los Angeles County judges (and commissioners) are a "specialized bench" assigned to hear only family law cases, it is evident that these judges heard thousands of noncompliance complaints during this 6-month period. Yet they ordered wage assignments in only a tiny fraction of the cases—less than one in a hundred.

Noncompliance and lax enforcement are not unique to California; they are common throughout the United States (see Bernstein, 1982; Chambers, 1979; Hawkins, 1984; House Hearings, 1984). If, as Dean Pound said, "The life of the law is in its enforcement" (Matter of Farmer, 1984), it is clear why the child support laws make a mockery of the legal system. Precisely these sentiments were echoed over and over again by the women we interviewed:

"It literally makes me sick. . . . It is so contrary to everything I was taught about the law, the courts, and justice. I feel totally betrayed. . . . He totally disregards the whole legal system."

Another judicial practice undermines the legal obligation to pay child support: Many judges simply "excuse" arrearages (i.e., money owed for past-due child support). As one mother who spent 5 years tracking down her nonsupporting husband complained:

"The judge said he could pay off the arrearage (of $12,000) at the rate of $20.00 per month . . . with no interest or anything. . . . It's outrageous—he gave him 50 years to pay me back! . . . But I'm stuck paying interest on the money I borrowed to keep the kids alive."

The judges explained this practice by saying they did not want to make payments too difficult ("It would be a financial hardship for a man to make back payments in full"); or that they wanted to give the father a break so that he can get on the right track; or that they were trying to look to the future rather than the past. "After all," some judges reasoned, "the children have managed to survive." The implicit message in the judges' treatment of arrearages is that fathers are rewarded for noncompliance by having their debt reduced or forgiven.

In summary, "the present legal system provides virtually every incentive for fathers not to pay child support" (Hunter, 1983). And in the end, the children are the tragic victims of the present system of inadequate and unpaid child support. Even though the typical child support award provides less than half the cost of raising a child, chances are that the noncustodial father will not pay it, and the legal system will do nothing about it.

In the end, the current legal system places the economic responsibility for children on their mothers and allows fathers the "freedom" to choose not to support their children. The result is that children almost always experience a decline in their standard of living after divorce. The dislocation from friends, neighborhoods, and family that many of these children endure, and the bitterness and anger they may harbor against one parent or the other, often translate into a pervasively unhappy, distrustful, and pessimistic view of life (Wallerstein & Kelly, 1980). This has profound implications for the future of a society that expects more than half of its children to experience the dissolution of their parents' marital relationship before they reach the age of 18.

THE ECONOMIC AND SOCIAL CONSEQUENCES

The net effect of the present rules for property, alimony, and child support is severe financial hardship for most divorced women and their children. They experience sharp downward mobility—dramatic drops in income and drastic cuts in their standards of living. Even women who shared comfortable middle- and upper-class standards of living during marriage are impoverished by divorce. In fact, the major economic result of the divorce law revolution is the systematic impoverishment of divorced women and their children. They have become the new poor.

Our data show that just 1 year after the legal divorce, women and children experience a 73% drop in their standard of living (while men experience a 42% improvement). Simply put, divorce is a financial catastrophe for most women. Every single expenditure that one takes for granted— clothing, food, housing, heat—must be cut to one half or one third of what one is accustomed to.

It is difficult to absorb the full implications of these statistics. What does it mean to have a 73% decline in one's standard of living? How does one deal with such severe deprivation? When asked how they coped, many of the divorced women said that they themselves were not sure. It meant "living on the edge" and "living without." As some of them described it:

> "We ate macaroni and cheese 5 nights a week. There was a Safeway special for $.39 a box. We could eat seven dinners for $3.00 a week. . . . I think that's all we ate for months.

> I applied for welfare. . . . It was the worst experience of my life. . . . I never dreamed that I, a middle-class housewife, would ever be in a position like that. It was humiliating . . . they make you feel it. . . . But we were desperate, and I *had* to feed my kids."

Even those who had relatively affluent life-styles before the divorce faced hardships they had not anticipated. For example, the wife of a dentist sold her car "because I had no cash at all, and we lived on that money— barely—for close to a year." The wife of a policeman told an especially poignant story about "not being able to buy my 12-year-old son Adidas sneakers." The boy's father had been ordered to pay $100 a month child support but had not been paying. To make up that gap in her already bare-bones budget, she had been using credit cards to buy food and other household necessities. She had exceeded all her credit limits and felt the family just couldn't afford to pay $25 for a new pair of Adidas sneakers.

But, as she said a year later, "You forget what it's like to be 12 years old and to think you can't live without Adidas sneakers . . . and to feel the whole world has deserted you along with your father."

Explaining the Disparity Between Husbands' and Wives' Standards of Living

How can we explain the strikingly different economic consequences of divorce for men and women? How could a law that aimed at fairness create such disparities between divorced men and their former wives and children?

The explanation lies first, in the inadequacies of the court's awards that we have discussed; second, in the expanded demands on the wife's resources after divorce; and third, in the husband's greater earning capacity and ability to supplement his income (See Strober's Chapter 8).

Since the wife typically assumes the responsibility for raising the couple's children, her need for help and services increases as a direct result of her becoming a single parent. Yet at the very time that her need for more income and more financial support is greatest, the courts have drastically reduced her income. Thus the gap between her income and her needs is wider after divorce.

In contrast, the gap between the husband's income and needs narrows. Although he now has fewer absolute dollars, the demands on his income have diminished. While he loses the benefits of economies of scale, and while he may have to purchase some services (such as laundry and cooking) that he did not have to buy during marriage, he is much better off because he is no longer financially responsible for the needs of his exwife and children. Since he has been allowed to retain most of his income, he can afford these extra expenses and still have more surplus income than he enjoyed during marriage.

The final explanation for the large income discrepancy between former husbands and wives lies in the different earning capacities of the two adults at the time of the divorce. Women are doubly disadvantaged at the point of divorce. Not only do they face the male–female income gap that affects all working women; they also suffer from the toll the marital years have taken on their earning capacity. In the United States at the present time, one third of the working mothers who are employed *full-time* cannot earn enough money to support themselves and their children above the poverty line (Feminization of Poverty, 1983).

In addition, the responsibility for children inevitably restricts the mother's job opportunities by limiting her work schedule and location, her availability for overtime and her freedom to take advantage of special training, travel assignments, and other opportunities for career advancement.

The discrepancy between divorced men and women has been corroborated by other research. Sociologist Robert Weiss and economist Thomas Espenshade found parallel disparities in the standards of living of former husbands and wives after divorce, and Weiss corroborates the finding that the greatest reduction in postdivorce income is experienced by women who shared higher family incomes before the divorce (Espenshade, 1979; Weiss, 1984). Census Bureau data also document the disparities in both income and standards of living of men and women after divorce. In 1979, the median per capita income of divorced women who had not remarried was $4,152, just over half of the $7,886 income of divorced men who had not remarried (U.S. Bureau of the Census, 1981b, p. 23).

The situation of divorced women with young children is even more grim. The median income in families headed by women with children under 6 years of age was only 30% of the median income for all families whose children were under 6 (U.S. Bureau of the Census, 1980). Thus, for the United States as a whole, "the income of families headed by women is at best half that of other families; the income of families headed by women with young children is even less, one-third of that of other families" (National Center on Women and Family Law, 1983).

Societal Consequences

The rise in divorce has been the major cause of the increase in female-headed families, and that increase has been the major cause of the feminization of poverty. Sociologist Diana Pearce, who coined the phrase "feminization of poverty," was one of the first to point to the critical link between poverty and divorce for women. It was, she said, the mother's economic and emotional responsibility for childrearing that often impoverished her family (Pearce, 1978).

Contrary to popular perception, most female-headed single-parent families in the United States are *not* the result of unwed parenthood: They are the result of marital dissolution. Only 18% of the nearly 10 million female-headed families in the United States are headed by an unwed mother, over 50% are headed by divorced mothers, and the remaining 31% by separated mothers (House Hearing, 1984: 13).

When a couple with children divorces, it is probable that the man will become single but the woman will become a single parent. And poverty, for many women, begins with single parenthood. More than half of the poor families in the United States are headed by a single mother.

The Rise in Female Poverty

The well-known growth in the number of single-parent female-headed households has been amply documented elsewhere. The 8% of all children who live in mother–child families in 1960 rose to 12% by 1970, and to 20% by 1981. Also well-documented is the fact that these mother-headed families are the fastest growing segment of the American poor.

In recent years there have been many suggestions for combatting the feminization of poverty. Most of these proposals have envisioned two routes to change: alterations in the structure of jobs and occupations and expanding social welfare programs. The first set of proposals has focused on altering the sex segregation in jobs and professions, eliminating the dual labor market and the disparity between jobs in the primary and secondary sectors, eradicating the discriminatory structure of wages, and providing additional services, such as child care, for working mothers (Pearce & McAdoo, 1981). The second set of proposals has focused on expanding social welfare programs by increasing AFDC benefits to levels above the poverty line, augmenting Medicaid, food stamp, and school lunch programs, and making housewives eligible for Social Security and unemployment compensation (Ehrenreich & Piven, 1984).

I believe there is a third route to reducing the feminization of poverty, a route that has been almost totally ignored. It is to change the way that courts allocate property and income at divorce. If, for example, custodial mothers and their children were allowed to remain in the family home, and if the financial responsibility for children were apportioned according to the means of the two parents, and if court orders for support were enforced, a significant segment of the population of divorced women and their children would not be impoverished by divorce.

The Rise in Child Poverty and Economic Hardships for Middle-Class Children of Divorce

Not surprisingly, the children of divorce often express anger and resentment when their standard of living is significantly less than that in their father's household. They realize that their lives have been profoundly altered by the loss of "their home" and school and neighborhood and friends, and by the new expectations their mother's reduced income creates for them. It is not difficult to understand their resentment when fathers fly off for a weekend in Hawaii while they are told to forgo summer camp, to get a job, and to earn their allowance. Their resentment is "a festering source of anger":

> When the downward change in the family standard of living followed the divorce and the discrepancy between the father's standard of living and that of the mother and children was striking, this discrepancy was often central to the life of the family and remained as a festering source of anger and bitter preoccupation. (Wallerstein & Kelly, 1980, p. 231)

The middle-class children of divorce may also feel betrayed by their disenfranchisement in their parents' property settlement. Since the law divides family property between the husband and wife and makes no provisions for a child's share of the marital assets, many children feel they have been unfairly deprived of "their" home, "their" piano, "their" stereo set, and "their" college education. The last item is indicative, for children's taken-for-granted expectations about the future are often altered by divorce. For example, one mother reported that the most upsetting thing about the divorce was her son's loss of the college education he'd been promised. His father, who had always pressed him to follow in his footsteps at Dartmouth, told him that a private college was now out of the question: He would have to stay home and take advantage of the low tuition at the state college. While his father could still afford to send his son to Dartmouth, the divorce had changed his priorities.

Inasmuch as about 1.2 million children's parents divorce each year, the 30% who receive no support from their fathers adds up to 360,000 new children each year. Over a 10-year period, this amounts to 4 million children. If we add to these the approximately 3 million over the years who receive only part of their child support (or receive it only some of the time), we find a 10-year total of 7 million children deprived of the support to which they are entitled. Remembering that fewer than 4 million children are born each year helps put all these figures in perspective.

The failure of absent parents to provide child support has taken an especially severe toll in recent years because of sharp cutbacks in public programs benefiting children since 1979. The Children's Defense Fund shows that children's share of Medicaid payments dropped from 14.9% in 1979, to 11.9% in 1982, despite a rise in the child proportion among the eligible. The Aid to Families with Dependent Children (AFDC) program has also been sharply cut back. In 1979, there were 72 children in AFDC for every 100 children in poverty, but only 52 per 100 in 1982.

It is not surprising to find a strong relationship between the economic and psychological effects of divorce on children. Economic deprivation following divorce has been linked to increased anxiety and stress among American children. Mounting evidence also shows that children of divorce who experience the most psychological stress are those whose postdivorce lives have been impaired by inadequate income. For example, Hodges, Tierney, and Buchsbaum (1984) find "income inadequacy" the most important factor in accounting for anxiety and depression among preschool children in divorced families. When family income is adequate, there are no differences in anxiety-depression levels between children in divorced families and those in intact families. However, "Children of divorced families with inadequate income had substantially higher levels of anxiety-depression (Hodges et al., 1984, p. 614). In an earlier study these researchers found significant correlations between income and adjustment for preschool children of divorce (but not, interestingly, for preschool children of intact families) (Hodges et al., 1984).

HOW CAN WE EQUALIZE DIVORCE?

We do not have to return to a fault-based system of divorce to alter the economic results of the present system, for the hardships of the present system are not inevitable. What is required to alleviate them is a commitment to fairness, an awareness of the greater burdens that the system imposes on women and children, and a willingness to require fathers to shoulder their economic responsibility for their children.

What are the most serious cases of injustice in the present system? Where should we direct our efforts? There are four groups that deserve our special attention. First, there are *the children of divorce* who need more financial support and more effective means of securing the support they are awarded. The goal of child support awards should be to equalize the standards of living in the custodial and noncustodial households; children are entitled to share the standard of living of their higher-earning parent.

College-age children of divorce also need "child" support past age 18 if they are full-time students and financially dependent. In addition, all support awards should include automatic adjustments for cost of living increases and more effective and automatic methods of assuring payment. The 1984 federal law, which provides for wage assignments, income tax refund intercepts, national location efforts, and property liens and bonds that will reach self-employed fathers, is an important step in the right direction.

Most children of divorce would also benefit from rules that allow them to remain in the family home. When these rules are optional, as they are in California, their use depends on judicial discretion, and they are often ignored. What works best are laws that *require* judges to maintain the family home for children after divorce.

The children of divorce would also benefit from a primary caretaker presumption for sole custody awards, and laws that allow joint custody only upon agreement of both parents (Weitzman, 1985, pp. 394–395). Such clear standards for custody awards would make it more difficult for parents (and their lawyers) to use children as "pawns" in divorce negotiations, and would reduce both the threat and use of custody litigation in order to gain financial advantages in property or support awards. Since custody litigation and the prolonged hostility it typically generates are likely to have an adverse psychological and financial impact on the welfare of children, custody laws that designate clear priorities and minimize litigation are clearly preferable.

The second type of clear injustice involves *the long-married older housewife* with little or no experience in the paid labor force because she has devoted herself to her husband, home, and children in the expectation that she would share the family assets that she helped to build. Justice and fairness for these women necessitates rules that require, rather than allow, judges to redistribute the husband's postdivorce income in order to equalize the standards of living in the two households.

This recommendation rests on the same principle that underlies community property rules: It is the assumption that marriage is an equal partnership in which all the assets should be shared. This principle, as we have seen, is strongly supported by the divorced men and women we interviewed (Weitzman, 1985, pp. 152–159). They view the sharing of income through alimony—or whatever name we choose for income transfers after divorce—as the means for providing the wife with her share of the fruits of their joint endeavours. These sharing principles are fundamental elements in the "marital contract" that most married couples agreed to and lived by during marriage.

Older women should not be measured by the new standards of equality and self-sufficiency after divorce. It is both impractical and unfair to expect women who married and lived most of their lives under a different set of social and legal rules to be forced to find employment and to support themselves. They have earned an interest in their husband's income for the rest of their lives and require a legislative presumption of permanent (i.e., continuing, open-ended) support.

Women who divorce after long marriages should also be entitled to remain as members in their husband's health insurance plans, to share his pension and retirement benefits, and to maintain their home. If the family home and the husband's pension are the only major assets of the marriage, the older wife should be allowed to retain her home without forfeiting her share of the pension.

In summary, we need "grandmother clauses" for the long-married older women who married and lived their lives under the traditional rules. It is unfair to change the rules on them in the middle of the game.

The third group that merits a new approach is *the mothers who retain major responsibility for the care of minor children after divorce*. Whether the custody award is labelled "sole custody," or "joint custody," or even "joint physical custody," if this woman assumes most of the day-to-day caretaking, she requires a greater share of the family's resources. This includes the continued use of the family home (which should be viewed as part of the child support award rather than as an unequal division of property) and a significant portion of her exhusband's income so that the two households maintain, insofar as is practical, equal standards of living after divorce.

Since employment will play a critical role in the postdivorce lives of younger divorced mothers, and thus in their ability to contribute to their children's and their own support, they should be awarded full support in the early years after divorce to enable them to maximize their long-range employment prospects. This means generous support awards and balloon payments immediately after divorce to finance their education, training, and career counselling. Every effort should be made to provide younger divorced mothers and their children with full support in the transitional years so that forced employment does not interfere with their training and child care.

The fourth group that requires special attention are those of *the transitional generation*—women who divorce in their 40s. Many of these women have been employed, often part-time, during marriage while raising children who are now approaching maturity. Yet, even though these women have experience in the labor market, they have typically given priority to their families and their husband's careers. Since these women usually have passed the point where they can recapture their lost career opportunities, it is manifestly unfair to hold them to the new standards of self-sufficiency at the point of divorce, as the courts do now. On the other hand, the means of bringing them to parity are less clear. But we can go a long way toward achieving a greater equality of results by assuring them an equal share of the fruits of the marital partnership (with an equal share of their husband's career assets, including his enhanced earning capacity); support to maximize their employment potential with additional training, counseling, and education; and where appropriate, compensation for the detriment to their own careers.

THE DIVORCE REVOLUTION AND
THE TRANSFORMATION OF MARRIAGE

If we step back from our analysis of the empirical results and policy alternatives, we can look at some of the broader implications of these legal changes and assess their impact on the institution of marriage. How has the new legal system of divorce influenced and altered our understanding of the nature of marriage?

From State Protection of Marriage to Facilitation of Divorce

The divorce law reforms reflect an underlying shift in the role of the state from a position of protecting marriage (by restricting marital dissolution) to one of facilitating divorce. The new divorce laws adopt a laissez-faire attitude toward both marriage and divorce, leaving both the terms of the marriage contract and the option to terminate it squarely in the hands of the individual parties. States with pure no-fault divorce laws also eliminate the traditional moral dimension from divorce: guilt and innocence, fidelity and faithlessness no longer affect the granting of the decree or its financial consequences (Weitzman, 1985, pp. 22–26, 28–31).

The individual's freedom to end his or her marriage is further bolstered in some states by no-consent rules that give either party the right to obtain a divorce without the other's agreement. Since no-fault and no-consent states allow one spouse to make a unilateral decision to terminate the marriage, they transfer the economic leverage from the spouse who wants to remain married to the spouse who wants to get divorced. This is an important difference. Under the traditional law the party who wanted a divorce might well have had to make economic concessions, or "buy" a spouse's agreement. But under the no-consent rule, it is the one who hopes to preserve the marriage who must do the bargaining. Apart from the economic implications, which are considerable, these laws strengthen the hand of the party who seeks the divorce, and thereby increase the likelihood that divorce will in fact occur.

From a Lifetime Contract to an Optional, Time-Limited Commitment

The new divorce laws no longer view marriage as a lifelong partnership. Instead it is a union that is contingent upon the happiness and satisfaction of both partners. In addition, the traditional obligations of marriage, like the institution itself, are increasingly being redefined by the new divorce laws as optional, time-limited, contingent, open to individual definition, and most important, terminable upon divorce.

In contrast to the traditional marriage contract, whereby a husband undertook lifelong responsibility for his wife's financial support (Weitzman, 1981a), the new divorce laws suggest that this and other family responsibilities can be terminated soon after divorce. This is evident in the new rules for alimony, which emphasize short-term transitional support and press women to become immediately self-sufficient to relieve their exhusband's "burden" of support (Freed & Walker, 1985).

Similar in its effects is the emphasis on a speedy resolution of the spouses' property claims. There are many more forced sales of family homes than in the past, to hasten the day when each spouse can "take his (or her) money and leave." Arrangements that delay the sale of the home, so that minor children do not have to move, are viewed with disfavor by the courts because they "tie up the father's money." (Recall that the judges we interviewed asserted that each spouse is entitled to his or her share of the property and should not have to wait for it.) There is also a tendency to "cash out" other shared investments, such as pension and retirement benefits, to provide a "clean break" between the parties at the time of the divorce.

Even parenting is becoming increasingly optional and terminable upon divorce. Indeed, the *de facto* effect of the current laws is to deprive children of the care, companionship, and support of their fathers. This is evident in the courts' treatment of postdivorce visitation and child support. Furstenberg *et al.* (1983) found that 52% of the children of divorce in a nationally representative sample had not seen their fathers at all in the past year, and only 17% of the children had seen their fathers at least once a week. These data indicate that a majority of divorced fathers are abandoning their parental roles after divorce and are being allowed to do so without legal punishment. In fact, there is no legal course of action to compel a parent to see his or her children. The implicit message is that parenting has become an "optional" responsibility for fathers after divorce.

While child support awards have always been inadequate and poorly enforced, what appears to be unique about the current situation is the willful disregard of court orders among middle-class and upper-middle-class fathers. For example, as noted above, our California data reveal that fathers with incomes of $30,000 to $50,000 a year are just as likely to avoid child support payments as fathers with incomes of under $10,000 a year (Weitzman, 1985, p. 296). Although the 1984 federal child support enforcement law suggests a possible improvement in this area, it is important to recall that the wage assignments mandated by the federal law were already required in California at the time of this research, but the judges chose to ignore them.

Preston (1984) contends that the financial and social "disappearing act of fathers" after divorce is part of a larger trend: "The conjugal family is gradually divesting itself of care for children in much the same way that it did earlier for the elderly. To date, indications of parental abandonment have focused on fathers. Thus far, most analysts have seen mothers as firmly committed to their children. But as the norms of the new divorce laws permeate popular awareness, this picture also may change.

This is because the import of the new custody laws, especially those that eliminate a maternal preference and institute a joint custody preference, undermine women's incentives to invest in their children. As women increasingly recognize that they will be treated "equally" in child custody decisions, that caretaking and nurturance of children find no protection in the law and are punished by the job market, and that joint custody awards may push them into difficult, restrictive, and unrewarding postdivorce custodial arrangements, they may increasingly take to heart the new laws' implied warning that they not become so invested in their children.

The optional and time-limited marital commitments embodied in the new divorce laws have a different effect on men and women. While they free men from the responsibilities they retained under the old system, they "free" women from the security that system provided. Since women's investments in home, family, and children have typically meant lost opportunities in the paid labor force, they are more dependent on the long-term protection and security that the traditional law promised them. It is not surprising that our research finds women "suffering" more under the new laws, for these laws remove the financial safeguards of the old law—with a decline in alimony awards and a decrease in women's share of the community property—at the same time that they increase the financial burdens imposed on women after divorce.

For men, by contrast, the new legal assumption of time-limited commitments means a new freedom from family financial obligations. In fact, the new laws actually give men an incentive to divorce by offering them a release from the financial burdens of marriage. And the wealthier a man is and the longer he has been married, the more he has to gain financially from divorce (Weitzman, 1985, pp. 326, 328, 333, 338).

From Protection for Housewives and Mothers to Gender Neutrality

If the new legal assumptions were accompanied by provisions that in fact enable both spouses to choose the extent to which they would assume breadwinning and homemaking roles, and if they then gave each spouse "credit" for the roles they in fact assumed during marriage, then the law would accurately reflect the complexity and variety of marital roles in these years of "transition." But the present legal system seems to leave no room for such flexibility.

Rather it suggests that a woman (or a man) who chooses homemaking and parenting risks a great penalty because she (or he) will pay heavily for that choice in the event of a divorce. Even if two parties agree to form an equal partnership in which they give priority to his career while she assumes the larger share of the housework and child care, and even if they agree that he will share his earnings and career assets with her, their agreement may have no legal standing. The woman will still be expected to be self-sufficient after divorce, and the man's promise of continued support and a share of his earnings—the promise that is implied in most marriages with a traditional division of labor—will be ignored in most courts. The penalty can be equally severe for the woman who works during marriage, or who works part-time but nevertheless gives priority to her family over her work. Her claims to share her husband's income fall on deaf ears in courts that base support awards solely on her "earning capacity."

Thus one implication of the present allocation of family resources at divorce is that women had better not forgo any of their own education, training, and career development to devote themselves fully or even partially to domesticity. The law assures that they will not be much rewarded for their devotion, and they will suffer greatly if their marriage dissolves.

The concept of marital roles embodied in the new divorce laws carries an equally sobering message about motherhood. Divorcing mothers of preschool children have experienced a greater decline in alimony awards than any other group of women since the no-fault laws were instituted and the vast majority of these mothers (87%) are awarded no alimony at all. They are expected to find jobs immediately, to support themselves completely, and for the most part to support their children as well.

Finally, the woman who has raised her children to maturity and who, as a result of the priority she has given to motherhood, finds herself with no marketable skills when she is divorced at 45 or 55 typically faces the harshest deprivations after divorce. The courts rarely reward her for the job she has done. Rather, the new assumptions imply that her motherhood years were wasted and worthless, for she too is measured against the all-important new criterion of earning capacity.

Thus, the new divorce laws are institutionalizing a set of norms that may be as inappropriate in one direction as the old norms were in another. The old law assumed that all married women were first and foremost housewives and mothers. The new law assumes that all married women are employable and equally capable of self-sufficiency after divorce. Both viewed are overly simplistic, impede women's options, and exert a rigidifying influence on future possibilities.

From Partnership to Individualism

The new divorce laws alter the traditional legal view of marriage as a partnership by rewarding individual achievement rather than investment in the family partnership. (See also Chapter 7 by Meyer and colleagues.) Instead of the traditional vision of a common financial future within marriage, the new laws confer economic advantages on spouses who invest in themselves at the expense of the marital partnership.

The traditional law embodied the partnership concept of marriage by rewarding sharing and mutual investments in the marital community. Implicit in the new laws, in contrast, are incentives for investing in oneself, maintaining one's separate identity, and being self-sufficient. The new stress is on individual responsibility for one's future, rather than on joint or reciprocal responsibilities.

Once again, it is easy to see how these new assumptions reflect larger cultural themes: the rise of individualism, the emphasis on personal fulfillment, the belief in personal responsibility, and the importance we attach to individual "rights." These trends have at once been applauded for the freedom they offer and criticized as selfish, narcissistic, and amoral (Lasch, 1979). Whether this change represents a decline or an advance depends on one's personal values: Do we long for the security and stability that the old order provided or do we applaud the new opportunities for spouses, to escape from the misery of unhappy, lifelong marriages?

Our evaluation will also depend on how we see the past. The belief that the rise of individualism has fostered a decline in the family rests on the assumption that the family was stable and harmonious in the past. But historians have not yet identified an era in which families were stable and harmonious or one in which all family members behaved unselfishly and devoted their efforts to the collective good (Skolnick, 1983, p. 22). That "classical family of western nostalgia," to use William J. Goode's term for the stereotype (Goode, 1968, pp. 6–7), has been one of the major casualties of recent research in family history (Skolnick, 1983, p. 22).

But historical research does suggest a change in the psychological quality of family life and a rise in what Lawrence Stone calls "affective individualism," a growing focus on individuals as unique personalities and a political emphasis on individual rights (Stone, 1977). The rise of affective individualism has brought emotional closeness between nuclear family members and a greater appreciation for the individuality of each person in the family. Historically, this trend strengthened the husband–wife unit at the expense of the larger family and the kinship network in which it was embedded. More recently, as rising divorce rates demonstrate, the strength of the husband–wife unit has declined and the values of "pure" individualism are emerging. The new divorce laws reflect this evolution in that they encourage notions of personal primacy for both husband and wife. They imply that neither spouse should invest too much in marriage or place marriage above self-interest.

One implication of these changes is that marriage is likely to become increasingly less central to the lives of individual men and women. The privileged status of marriage in traditional family law, as well as the protections and restrictions placed on its inception and dissolution, reinforced its importance and encouraged husbands and wives to make it the center of their lives. The new laws, in contrast, discourage spouses from investing in the marital partnership. As more men and women follow the apparent mandate of the new laws, it seems reasonable to predict that marriage itself will lose further ground.

Indeed, William J. Goode (1984) persuasively argues that the trend is already well in progress. He observes that for both men and women marriage is simply less important today than it was in the past, and he foresees the further "decline of individual investments in family relationships over the coming decade" because investments in one's individual life and career pay off better in modern society. As more women seek to follow men in the path of acquiring status, self-esteem, and a sense of individual accomplishment from their jobs, the importance of marriage will rest increasingly on its ability to provide individuals with psychic and emotional sustenance. This, Goode observes, is a difficult and fragile bond. In these trends, he sees profound implications for the future of intimate relationships and the bearing and rearing of children in Western nations.

The Clouded Status of Children

A final feature of the new divorce laws is their ambiguous message about parental responsibility for children. In the past, the sustained well-being of the children of divorce was assumed to be the state's primary concern in any legal proceedings involving children. Indeed, it was this concern that dictated most of the traditional legal protections for women: Women were recognized as the primary custodian of children, and in that capacity were to be accorded preferences and support to ensure the fulfillment of their responsibilities. Similarly, women who had devoted the productive years of their lives to childrearing were to be rewarded for that honorable effort.

Under the new laws, the state's concern for the welfare of children—and their custodians—is far less evident. Rather, in many ways, children have been ignored in the courts' preoccupation with equality for their parents.

The same rules that facilitate divorce facilitate the disruption of children's lives. The gender-neutral rules that encourage or force mothers to work also deprive children of the care and attention they might otherwise have. Equally important, the *de facto* effects of the current laws deprive many children of the care and the support of their fathers.

In sum, under the present laws divorced fathers *may* participate more in the lives of their children if they choose to do so, but they need not so choose; and mothers *must* work outside the home whether they wish it or not, and thus *must* divide their energies between jobs and children. Few legal protections remain to insure parenting for children after divorce.

These themes emphasize the complex interaction between law and social reality. Even as the law evolves to reflect social reality, it also serves as a powerful force in creating social reality. Although the divorce law reformers knew that equality between the sexes was not yet a reality when they codified assumptions about equality in the law, they had seen trends in that direction and believed that the new law would accelerate those trends. But the new law had the opposite effect: it increased economic inequality. It worsened women's condition, improved men's condition, and widened the income gap between the sexes.

So long as the laws remain in force in their present form and their present application, postdivorce equality between men and women will remain an impossibility. Without equality in economic resources, all other "equality" is illusory.

EPILOGUE

In 1986, in response to my book *The Divorce Revolution*, the California State Senate established a blue ribbon "Task Force on Family Equity." Sponsored by California State Senators Gary Hart and David Roberti, the President pro Tempore of the Senate, the enabling legislation directed the Task Force to study the findings of my research and to develop legislative proposals to "equalize the effects of divorce."

The Task Force Report, issued in June 1987, included 23 legislative proposals and "model" bills. Most of these, condensed into 14 bills, were introduced in the California legislature in 1987 and 1988. By the end of 1987, five of these bills had become law—requiring judicial education and training, automatic wage assignments for every child support award, security deposits for delinquent child support (for the self-employed and those who change jobs frequently), and permanent jurisdiction over spousal support in marriages of long duration.

As of July 1988 another eight bills passed the Senate and are awating action in the Assembly. Among these are provisions for a delayed sale of the family home in the interests of minor children, improved standards for spousal support awards (based on the standard of living during marriage), wage assignments for spousal support awards, and extending child support to age 21 (to include most college-age children).

In January 1988 a coalition of women's groups, representing 50,000 California women, organized a "Coalition for Family Equity" to lobby for the passage of these bills. They mounted an extremely well-organized and energetic grass roots lobbying effort and were successful in getting the bills out of critical Assembly committees. They are continuing their campaign to make these bills become law.

For further information contact Mimi Modisett in California Senator Gary Hart's office or Sara McCarthy in the Senate Office of Research, Sacramento, California.

REFERENCES

Bernstein, B. (1982). Shouldn't low income fathers support their children? *Public Interest, 66.*

California Assembly. (1970). California Assembly Committee on the Judiciary Report on Assembly Bill No. 530 and Senate Bill No. 252 (The Family Act), Assembly J. 785, 787 (Reg. Sess. 1970).

Cassetty, J. (1978). *Child support and public policy.* Lexington, MA: D. C. Heath. pp. 64–65, Table 4-1.

Chambers, D. (1979). *Making fathers pay.* Chicago: University of Chicago Press.

Chase, M. (1985, January 21). The no-fault divorce has a fault of its own, many women learn. *The Wall Street Journal, 1,* 12.

Davis, K. (1986). The future of marriage. In K. Davis & A. Grossbard-Shechtman (Eds.), *Essays on contemporary marriage.* New York: Russell Sage Foundation.

Dixon, R., & Weitzman, L. J. (1980). Evaluating the impact of no-fault divorce in California. *Family Relations, 29,* 297–307.

Dixon, R., & Weitzman, L. J. (1982). When husbands file for divorce. *Journal of Marriage and the Family, 44,* 103–114.

Ehrenreich, B., & Piven, F. F. (1984). The feminization of poverty: When the family wage system breaks down. *Dissent., 31*(2), 162–170.

Eisler, R. T. (1977). *Dissolution: No-fault divorce, marriage and the future of women.* New York: McGraw Hill.

Espenshade, T. (1979). The economic consequences of divorce. *Journal of Marriage and the Family, 41,* 615–625.

Feminization of Poverty, The. (1983, April 8). Briefing paper prepared for California Assemblyman Thomas H. Bates, San Francisco, CA.

Freed, D. J., & Walker, T. (1985). Family law in the fifty states: An overview. *Family Law Quarterly, 18,* 369–471.

Furstenberg, F. F., Nord, C. W., Peterson, J. L., & Zil, N. (1983). The life course of children of divorce: Marital disruption and parental contact. *American Sociological Review, 48,* 656–668.

Goode, W. J. (1968). *World revolution in family patterns.* New York: Free Press.

Goode, W. J. (1984). Individual investments in family relationships over the coming decades. *The Tocqueville Review, 6,* 51–84.

Hawkins, P. (1984). *Statement of Senator Paula Hawkins in hearings before the Committee on Finance, United States Senate, Ninety-eighth Congress, Second Session.* Washington DC: U.S. Government Printing Office.

Hodges, W. F., Tierney, C. W., & Bushbaum, H. K. (1984). The cumulative effect of stress on preschool children of divorced and intact families. *Journal of Marriage and the Family, 46*(3), 611–629.

House Hearings. (1983, July 14). *Statement in hearing before the Subcommittee on Public Assistance and Unemployment Compensation of the Committee Note and Means.* U.S. House of Representatives, Ninety-eighth Congress, First Session *Serial 98–41.* Washington, DC: U.S. Government Printing Office.

Hunter, N. (1983). Women and child support. In I. Diamond (Ed.), *Families, politics, and the state*. New York: Longman.

Lasch, C. (1979). *The culture of narcissism*. New York: Norton.

Leonard, F. (1980). The disillusionment of divorce of older women. *Gray Paper*(6). (Washington DC: Older Women's League).

Matter of Farmer. (1984, January 16). *New York Law Journal*, p. 13, col. 2. New York: New York City Family Court, 1984.

National Center on Women and Family Law. (1983). Sex and economic discrimination in child custody awards. *Clearinghouse Review*, *16*, 1132.

O'Brien v. O'Brien (1985), 66 N.Y. 2d 576, 498 N.Y.S. 2d 743.

Pearce, D. (1978). The feminization of poverty: Women, work and welfare. *Urban and Social Change Review*, *11*, 28–36.

Pearce, D., & McAdoo, H. (1981). *Women and children in poverty*. Washington, DC: National Advisory Council on Economic Opportunity.

Preston, S. (1984). Children and the elderly: Divergent paths for America's dependents. *Demography*, *21*, 435–457.

Shields, L. (1981). *Displaced homemakers—Organizing for a new life*. New York: McGraw-Hill.

Skolnick, A. (1983). *The intimate environment*. Boston: Little Brown.

Stone, L. (1977). *The family, sex and marriage in England 1500–1800*. New York: Harper & Row.

U.S. Bureau of the Census. (1979). Divorce, child custody and child support. *Current Population Reports*, Series P-23(84),7. Table 1.

U.S. Bureau of the Census. (1980). *Families maintained by female housholders 1970–1979*. (Current Population Reports, Series P-23(107), 36). Washington, DC: U.S. Government Printing Office.

U.S. Bureau of the Census. (1981a). *Child support and alimony: 1978* (Current Population Reports, Series P-23(112)). Washington, DC: U.S. Government Printing Office.

U.S. Bureau of the Census. (1981b). *Money income of families and persons in the United States: 1979* (Current Population Reports, Series P-60(129)). Washington, DC: U.S. Government Printing Office.

U.S. Bureau of the Census. (1983). *Child support and alimony: 1981* (Current Population Reports, Series P-23(124 and 127)). Washington, DC: U.S. Government Printing Office.

U.S. Bureau of the Census. (1987). *Child support and alimony: 1985* (Current Population Reports, Series P-23(152)). Washington, DC: U.S. Government Printing Office.

Wallerstein, J., & Kelly, J. (1980). *Surviving the breakup: How children and parents cope with divorce*. New York: Basic Books.

Weiss, R. S. (1984). The impact of marital dissolution on income and consumption in single-parent households. *Journal of Marriage and the Family*, *28*, 615.

Weitzman, L. J. (1981a). *The marriage contract: Spouses, lovers, and the law*. New York: Free Press.

Weitzman, L. J. (1981b). The economics of divorce: Social and economic consequences of property, alimony and child support awards. *University of California Los Angeles Law Review*, *28*, 1181–1268.

Weitzman, L. J. (1984). Equity and equality: A comparative analysis of property and maintenance awards in the U.S. and England. In J. M. Eckelaar & S. Katz (Eds.), *The resolution of family conflict*. Toronto: Butterworth.

Weitzman, L. J. (1985). *The divorce revolution: The unexpected social and economic consequences for women and children in America*. New York: Free Press.

Weitzman, L. J., & Dixon, R. B. (1979). Child custody awards: Legal standards and empirical patterns for child custody, support and visitation rights after divorce. *University of California Davis Law Review*, *12*, 473–521.

Weitzman, L. J., & Dixon, R. B. (1980). The alimony myth: Does no-fault divorce make a difference. *Family Law Quarterly*, *14*, 141–185.

11

Divorce and Children

SUSAN E. KRANTZ

Each year, 2 million children are newly introduced to their parents' divorce (Monthly Vital Statistic Report, 1985). It is estimated that by 1990, more than half of all American children under 18 will have experienced a divorce or separation of their natural parents (Hofferth, 1983; Weitzman, 1985).

Divorce changes the lives of children. During a confusing period of high emotional intensity, the child must attempt to understand a complex series of events and to restructure numerous assumptions and expectations about the self, the family, and the future. He or she may be required to leave a familiar school, residence, neighborhood, and the social ties established in these places (see Chapter 10 by Weitzman). The child must often assume new household tasks; temporarily receive less support, nurturance, and supervision from one or both parents; and witness the distress of the parents individually and as a couple (Wallerstein & Kelly, 1980).

These events in the child's life raise several questions: First, what are the effects of divorce on the child? Second, how do we explain any undesirable postdivorce reactions of children? The "parental absence" perspective assumes that negative effects of divorce are related to the breakup of the nuclear family per se. The "marital distress" and "economic hardship" perspectives, on the other hand, argue that the effects of divorce on children are not the result of the divorce per se but rather stem from other factors, such as the discord between the parents or the low financial status of the custodial parent. The "multiple factor" perspective stresses the multiple and interacting factors that contribute to the effects of divorce on children.

The purposes of this chapter are to : (1) examine critically the different perspectives on the effects of divorce on children, (2) evaluate the validity of the research procedures in studies of children's postdivorce functioning, (3) review the research findings, and (4) discuss their policy implications.

Susan E. Krantz, Ph.D. Bay Area Center for Cognitive Therapy, Palo Alto, California.

DIFFERING PERSPECTIVES ON DIVORCE AND CHILDREN

Parental Absence

The "parental absence" view asserts that two parents are necessary for the well-being of a child. The father, who is the absent parent in approximately 90% of divorces (Glick, 1979), is thought to be necessary for sex-role socialization, supervision, and discipline. This approach assumes that divorce is harmful because the departure of the father means the loss of a main agent of socialization.

The role of the father, however, may be overemphasized in the parent absence approach. Some fathers in two-parent families are relatively unavailable to their children and so do not perform the functions traditionally attributed to them. According to Szalai, Converse, Feldheim, Schench, & Stone (1972), employed fathers living with their children share activities with their children for only 2 hours per week compared to the 5½ hours of the employed mother and the 11 hours of the homemaker. Blanchard and Biller (1971) found that sons of relatively uninvolved fathers in intact families and boys with absent fathers showed similar academic deficits in comparison to boys with involved fathers in intact families. Thus, the physical absence of the father appears to be no more harmful than his emotional absence, at least with respect to academic performance.

Similarly, the role of other adults may be underemphasized. It is obvious that the mother plays a crucial role in the socialization of the child. Friends, relatives, teachers, and even heroes of the mass media may also serve as models for the child. Indeed, Aldous (1972) found no differences in the perceptions of young children with absent or present fathers regarding which sex performs conventional sex-typed tasks.

The position that the absence of a parent is harmful to children was dominant in an era when the nuclear family unit was almost unquestioningly valued. More recently, western culture began to move toward a philosophy of individualism and self-fulfillment (Conger, 1981). In this new climate, it is expected that satisfied, fulfilled parents living apart will provide a healthier emotional atmosphere for their children than will dissatisfied, unhappy parents living together. Any negative concommitants of divorce observed in children are attributed not to the divorce itself, but rather to the marital distress or to the economic hardships of divorce.

Marital Distress

Several observers have suggested that the personal or intellectual difficulties among children of divorced parents are due to the disturbed marital relationship, rather than to the divorce, and that, in fact, divorce can enhance the well-being of children by reducing or eliminating the tension between their parents. Indeed, marital distress has been linked to difficulties in the child's psychosocial functioning, as will be discussed below.

Several assumptions of the "marital distress" view, however, have yet to be examined. The typical assumption that distressed marriages are characterized by open conflict and antagonism overlooks other forms of marital dissatisfaction, such as the gradual and quiet loss of intimacy (Kressel, Jaffee, Tuchman, Watson, & Deutsch, 1980). It is not known whether these other types of distress are as detrimental to children.

Nor should it be assumed that the termination of even a conflict-ridden marriage will be beneficial to the child if the child has not been exposed to the conflict. Wallerstein and Kelly (1980) and Landis (1960) discovered that youngsters who perceived family life as happy and had little awareness of their parents' problems initially reacted to the divorce more intensely than did those who had been exposed to their parents' conflict. While the separation of openly hostile parents results in at least some new tranquility in the child's environment, the separation of outwardly compatible parents may produce unexpected difficulties for the child.

The notion that the termination of a distressed marriage will be beneficial to the children is more reasonable, of course, when the divorce serves to remove overt conflict and to foster more satisfactory conditions. However, acrimony between the divorced parents may continue or even intensify after the separation and divorce. Wallerstein and Kelly (1980), for instance, reported continuing conflict between approximately two thirds of divorced parents at a 5-year follow-up; conflict over child support is apparent in many families at a 10-year follow-up (Wallerstein, 1984). A substantial proportion of continuing conflicts are so severe that they must be settled by the courts: Cline and Westman (1971) found that 52% of divorces in families with children that were granted in a Wisconsin county required court intervention within 2 years after the divorce.

To the extent that theorizing about the effects of marital distress on children reflects the recent belief that happier parents raise happier children, it is useful to determine the typical level of custodial parent satisfaction following the divorce. Does divorce produce happier parents? Although divorced persons do not report that they are less satisfied with their lives in comparison to married persons (Haring-Hidore, Stock, Okun, & Witter, 1985; Weingarten, 1985), and although divorce may minimize several sources of stress, it often creates new stresses or fails to solve existing problems for the parents. Colletta (1983), Hetherington, Cox, & Cox (1977), McLanahan (1983), Spivey and Shermann (1980), and Weinraub and Wolfe (1983) reported that female-headed families experience more chronic life strains, more major stressful life events, and lower levels of social and psychosocial support. Stress decreased with time, but women divorced for over 6 years continued to report somewhat more stress than married women (Spivey & Shermann, 1980). As might be expected, divorced mothers in this stressful situation have negative self-images and negative views about the future (McLanahan, 1983). All too often, these problems are associated with serious emotional disorder: a review by Bloom, Asher, & White (1978) found consistent evidence that divorced or separated persons are overrepresented among psychiatric inpatients and among victims of suicide, homicide, disease, and even car accidents. Of course, these serious physical and mental health problems among the divorced are not necessarily caused by divorce; rather, the problem may have precipitated the divorce. Nonetheless, it is clear that divorce does not necessarily produce more satisfied parents.

Just as predivorce conflict and parental dissatisfaction may lead to disruptions in the child's life, so too do these postdivorce stressors and stress reactions. Although Weinraub and Wolf (1983) found no overall differences between divorced and married mothers in their interactions with their preschoolers, stress is associated with impaired mother–child interactions among both groups of mothers (Weinraub & Wolf, 1983), a lesser quality of life for the children (Morrison, 1983), and difficulties in their social and emotional adjustment (Kurdek & Blisk, 1983; Pett, 1982). Hence, it cannot be assumed that the termination of a distressed marriage will be beneficial to children.

Economic Disadvantage

The "economic disadvantage" explanation of difficulties in children's postdivorce functioning suggests that the substantial differences in the finances of one- or two-parent families, rather than divorce itself, is responsible for any problems suffered by the child. The median 1979 income of divorced women was $8,391 compared to $20,601 for married couples (U.S. Bureau of the Census, 1981a). Whereas 16% of all children were living under the poverty line in 1979; a staggering 48.6% of children in households headed by women were living in poverty (U.S. Bureau of the Census, 1981b). This economic disparity is related to both the higher likelihood of divorce among the poor (Goode, 1956; Norton & Glick, 1979; Ross & Sawhill, 1975) and the drop in the income of mother-headed families following the divorce (Burman & Turk, 1981; Day & Bahr, 1986; Duncan & Morgan, 1976; Hoffman & Holmes, 1976; Jacobs, Guidubaldi, & Nastasi, 1986; Kurdek, 1986; Maclean & Eekelaar, 1983; Weitzman, 1985). The "economic disadvantage" view suggests that the overwhelming practical and psychological stresses imposed by poverty can account for any differences in behavior between children in one- or two-parent families.

Although financial hardship appears to be one aspect of divorce that affects children, it is unlikely that financial status can fully account for any increased risks for children following divorce. The children of widows, unlike the children of divorce, do not evidence significantly more aggression and delinquency than do children of intact families (Felner, Stolberg, & Cowen, 1981; Rutter, 1971; Zill, 1978) even though the widowed suffer economic hardships almost as severe as the divorced. Shinn (1978) reviewed research showing that children whose fathers were temporarily absent or worked night shifts—yet continued to provide income—scored lower than others on cognitive tests, thereby indicating that children's academic performance may suffer from the father's absence even when his absence does not involve a loss of income. Indeed, Dornbusch *et al.* (1985) found that parental absence had a greater influence on adolescent deviance than did family income. Both factors have been found to be independently and strongly related to delinquency (Guidubaldi, Cleminshaw, Perry, & McLoughlin, 1983; Willie, 1967).

The financial hardship of custodial parents and their children following divorce plays an important role in the child's well-being, but it is not the only important factor. Efforts of the legislature and the judicial system to reverse their impoverishment and to increase support services (e.g., low-cost, high quality day care and equal pay for women) are likely to reduce significantly, but not eliminate, the difficulties of these families.

The Multiple Factor Perspective

Most contemporary observers believe that children's adjustment following divorce is influenced by numerous interacting factors (Guidubaldi & Cleminshaw, 1985; Jacobs, Guidubaldi, & Nastisi, 1986). These factors include characteristics of the child (e.g., age, sex, predivorce level of adjustment), the family (e.g., financial status, degree of conflict between the parents, parent–child relationships), and the social environment (e.g., social services, a social support network) (Hetherington, 1979; Longfellow, 1979; Wallerstein & Kelly, 1980, 1984). Cultural values and social policies may also be important for adjustment (Kurdek, 1981). In addition, children influence their own adjustment as they form their own perspective on the divorce. Their perspective on the divorce may then influence their emotional and behavioral reactions (Krantz, Clark, Pruyn, & Usher, 1985; Kurdek, 1981; Longfellow, 1979).

While children are affected by the events and people around them, they in turn affect these events and people (Bell & Harper, 1977; Hetherington *et al.*, 1977) as their anger, cheerfulness, sullenness, cooperativeness, or other emotions and behaviors elicit reactions from others. The nature of the reciprocal influences between the child and other people are constantly changing as the child matures and the others change.

The complexity of this perspective is both a strength and a limitation. It is intuitively compelling that the numerous components of any system—in this case, the family—will affect and be affected by the other components of the system and the culture in which it is imbedded. The difficulties with the study of complex systems include: (1) the limitations in our ability to chart the multiple and reciprocal influences of one factor upon another and (2) the large differences between families in the types of events determining their child's behavior. Because of these complexities, a detailed and clear-cut picture of the effect of divorce on children does not exist and would be difficult to verify if it did.

RESEARCH PROCEDURES

Accurate, reliable, and relevant information on children's postdivorce adjustment and the conditions affecting adjustment is essential to the formation of policies that best serve the interests of children and their parents. How much confidence can be placed in the validity of the currently available information?

There are serious limitations to the current information, but contrary to Blechman's position (1982), the information need not be rejected if conclusions are made cautiously and with full recognition of their limitations. As Emery (1982) noted, the overall trends that emerge from repeated replications are unlikely to be seriously distorted because the different methodological deficiencies are likely to bias the results in different directions. This speculation was supported by Shinn's (1978) report that the overall findings of the more methodologically adequate studies of intellectual performance did not differ substantially from the findings of the seriously flawed research. This section will thus detail the major threats to the validity of divorce research, but the review in the next section will include studies that vary in their methodological sophistication. This combination of a discussion of the limitations of the data with a comprehensive review of the findings is intended to encourage the cautious use of the available information.

The following section will describe two of the major challenges to research on divorce and children. First, it is imperative that measurements of children's behavior accurately reflect their actual behavior. Second, we must isolate the conditions presumed to influence behavior from the myriad of other related conditions that may be more important influences on behavior than those targeted in a given study. The current strategies for accomplishing these goals and the threats to the effectiveness of these strategies will be examined.

Validity of the Measurements

Interpretation of the results on divorce and children's adjustment should be interpreted cautiously because a number of biases influence our attempts to assess the child's behavior. First, the information provided by adults about children with divorced parents may reflect the stereotypes of the adults more than the actual behavior of the child. For example, Santrock and Tracy (1978) showed a videotape of an 8-year-old boy to 30 teachers. Some teachers were told that the boy came from a divorced home; others were told that he came from an intact home. The boy was rated happier and better adjusted by the teachers who were told that he came from an intact home in comparison to the teachers who were told that he came from a divorced home.

The high personal involvement of parents and children may also bias their reports. Furey and Forehand (1986) found that the mother's perception of her child's adjustment is related to her relationship with the child's father, and to their personal adjustment. A parent opposed to the divorce or the custody arrangement may be aware only of the difficulties in their child's postdivorce adjustment; the parent who is satisfied with the divorce or custody arrangement may do just the opposite. Fulton (1979) found that the fathers' assessment of the impact of the divorce on their children was more strongly related to the custodial arrangement than it was to any other factor: Forty-five percent of noncustodial fathers believed that the divorce harmed their children compared to only 29% of the custodial fathers. While it is quite possible that children with custodial fathers were, indeed, functioning better than those with custodial mothers,[1] it was implied that the difference was in part due to a bias of the custodial fathers toward self-approval and the bias of noncustodial fathers toward showing disappointment in the performance of their exwives.

Even presumably objective records may be biased. Herzog and Sudia (1971), for example, reviewed research suggesting that when compared to adolescents in two-parent homes, those in one-parent homes are arrested for less serious offenses and are more likely to be put on probation or committed to correctional institutions. If arrested at all, adolescents living with two parents are more likely to be released to their parents. Thus, the different delinquency rates of adolescents in one- or two-parent families reported below may reflect the biases of the legal system rather than the behaviors of the youths. It would be a mistake to conclude that divorce is or is not harmful to children if the various measurement procedures were biased in the same direction.

Second, it should be recognized that assessment instruments that purportedly tap some objectively defined behavior are often biased by prevailing cultural norms and values. These values and norms change over time and at any point in time may be disputed. For example, Herzog and Sudia (1971) have criticized the conceptualization of masculinity and femininity used in self-report inventories as outdated and class-related. One such inventory counts the reported desire to race cars or start a fist fight as indicators of masculinity. Boys who do not report a desire to race cars or fight score low on this masculinity scale. Similarly, Hetherington (1972) interpreted girls' physical proximity to boys at a dance and their initiation of dances, touching or other encounters with boys as evidence of the girls' "inappropriate" assertion. These measures tap cultural values as well as child behavior.

Isolating the Determinants of Postdivorce Functioning

The hypothesized influences on adjustment (e.g., the absence of a parent) are entangled with other related variables. Marital status, for example, is related to the parents' age, socioeconomic status, and incidence of alcoholism, criminality, and promiscuity (McCord, McCord, & Thurber, 1962; Zill, 1978). Unless the effects of all of these other variables are controlled, the conclusion that divorce causes psychosocial difficulties is not warranted: These other variables may be the key determinants of both the child's behavior and also of the parents' marital status. For instance, a father's criminality may influence his son toward delinquency and lead his wife to initiate a divorce; the divorce itself may have little or no effect on the son's delinquency.

Because many studies of the effects of divorce on children do nothing to control for the factors other than marital status that may in part explain the child's behavior, their findings should be interpreted with extreme caution. Other studies use one of three basic methods to examine the effects of marital status apart from the other influences. One method is to form groups of children in one- or two-parent families that are similar in terms of important characteristics such as socioeconomic status (SES). Unfortunately, the divorced tend to cluster at the lower end of any given SES group (Herzog & Sudia, 1971).

A second method matches each divorced person to a nondivorced person with a similar social class level to control for divorced–nondivorced differences within a single social class. Well-matched samples, however, are not representative of the general population (Blechman, 1982): They necessarily contain proportionately more lower-class married individuals and upper-class divorced individuals than are in the general population.

Third, the influence of extraneous factors such as socioeconomic status can be controlled statistically. These computations adjust the data so that the participants in the study are equalized on the factors other than marital status. Once these factors are statistically equalized, the investigator can assess the relationship between marital status and child behavior independently of these other factors. With a few exceptions (Dornbusch et al., 1985; Guidubaldi et al., 1983; Nelson, 1981; Svanum, Bringle, & McLaughlin, 1982; Willie, 1967; Zill, 1978), relatively few studies have used this stringent procedure to isolate divorce from other influences on children's functioning.

The discussion thus far has focused on controls for social class because the "economic hardship" perspective convincingly argues that many childhood difficulties may be explained by the economic troubles of divorced mothers rather than by divorce itself. However, social class is but one of many factors related to marital status. The ideal study would isolate the effects of marital status from all other related variables.

As noted earlier, biases in the available information are unlikely to distort the conclusions to the extent that the data are (1) repeatedly replicated and (2) biased in different directions. Therefore, the following review will describe the findings that have been repeatedly replicated, regardless of the methodological sophistication of the study. The review will also identify areas where conclusions can not yet be drawn because of the mixed results thus far available.

CHILDREN'S POSTDIVORCE FUNCTIONING

Each child is unique, and so the short- and long-term functioning of children after a divorce varies widely. Wallerstein and Kelly (1980), from their observations and interviews with parents and children at three points in time over a 5-year period, estimated that approximately one third of the children emerge from the divorce unscathed and may be even more mature than expected for their age. Another one third function adequately although they experience some enduring difficulties, and the remaining one third suffer severe disruptions in their developmental progress. These results must be regarded with caution because the parents may have been drawn to the study in part by the counseling offered and so may overrepresent those who are in need of counseling. Caution is also necessary because counseling may (and was certainly intended to) alter the course of adjustment to the divorce. Perhaps most importantly, the conclusions about the children from divorced families were made without the benefit of comparisons with children from two-parent families; hence, it is not known whether the development of children of divorce differs in any significant way from that of other children.

Are there, nonetheless, overall trends in the functioning of children after divorce in comparison to the functioning of children in intact families or in other family arrangements? What particular areas of functioning are most vulnerable to the stresses of divorce? The areas most frequently discussed are intellectual performance, juvenile delinquency and aggression, social and emotional well-being, and cognition and perception.

Intellectual Performance

The majority of studies on intellectual performance report that children in one-parent families (usually the product of divorce) are at a disadvantage, but this finding is far from consistent. Shinn (1978) reviewed 28 methodologically adequate studies of children with an absent parent. Parental absence was associated with disruptions in academic achievement in 16 of these studies: Children with absent fathers were up to 1.6 years behind their peers who lived with both parents. Of the remaining 12 studies, 9 found no differences between children with or without a father in the household and 3 found either positive effects of an absent father or mixed positive and negative effects. Interestingly, the proportion of studies showing a link between father absence and intellectual deficits were very similar in 19 additional studies that failed to control for SES.

Several large scale studies (with 700 to 18,000 subjects sampled from multiple states) completed since Shinn's review also tended to find academic deficits among children of divorce. Four (Brown, 1980; Guidubaldi et al., 1983; Lazarus, 1980, Zakariya, 1982) of five studies found that the academic achievement of children in one-parent families lagged behind those in two-parent families. All but one of these four studies found impairments in academic progress even after controlling for social class. There is thus some reason to suspect that the intellectual performance of children in one-parent families is weaker than that of their peers, but definitive conclusions would be premature at this time (see Dornbusch & Gray, Chapter 12).

Antisocial Behavior

Based upon parents' and children's reports and upon court and school records, antisocial actions occur more frequently among children of divorce than among a variety of other groups including children in intact families in the general population (e.g., Brown, 1980; Dornbusch et al., 1985; Hess & Camara, 1979; Hetherington et al., 1978; Lazarus, 1980; McDermott, 1970; Saucier & Ambert, 1982; Zill, 1978), children in intact families in an outpatient mental health facility (Kalter, 1977) and children who experienced the death of a parent (Felner, 1977; Felner et al., 1975). Researchers have defined antisocial behavior in many ways: parents' and teachers' reports of fighting and bullying other children, cheating, lying, and stealing (e.g., Zill, 1978); running away from home, truancy, suspension or expulsion from school, smoking, drinking, drug use, and inappropriate sexual behavior (e.g., Brown, 1980; Dornbusch et al., 1985; Kalter, 1977; Lazarus, 1980; Saucir & Ambert, 1982) and contact with the law (e.g., Dornbusch et al., 1985; Glueck & Glueck, 1950; Willie, 1967).

Many of these aspects of antisocial behavior pertain mostly to middle childhood and adolescence, but similar conclusions have been reached about the aggressive behavior of younger children (e.g., Hodges & Bloom, 1984; McDermott, 1968). These findings concerning the antisocial behavior of children of divorce are relatively strong. The strength of the conclusions derives from: (1) the repeated replications of the results; (2) the multiple sites across the nation used in several studies (Dornbusch et al., 1985; Lazarus, 1980; Zill, 1978) that ensured that the results are maximally representative and are not limited to a single school, neighborhood, or city; and (3) the controls for social class in several studies (e.g., Dornbusch *et al.*, 1985; Felner, 1977; Glueck & Glueck, 1950; McDermott, 1970; Willie, 1967; Zill, 1978).

Sex-Role Socialization

Sex-role socialization can be defined as the acquisition of the goals, values, and behaviors deemed masculine or feminine by a given culture. Sex roles are thought to develop as the child becomes aware of the different physical characteristics of the sexes, adopts the stereotypes linked to those character-istics (Kohlberg, 1966), and imitates the behavior of same-sex models (Mi-schel, 1970). Will children learn the behaviors considered to be appropriate to their sex in the absence of the same-sex parent?

Reviews by Kohlberg (1966) and Biller (1976) revealed some associa-tion between father absence and feminine play preference, feminine self-concepts, lowered aggression, and increased dependency among boys. This association, however, was found only among preschool children. Thus, the absence of the father may slow the development of masculine sex roles but does not appear to be associated with long-term development.

Social and Emotional Functioning

Social and emotional well-being is a broad-band construct that encom-passes numerous components of functioning, including interaction with peers; emotional states such as fear, anxiety, and depression; and the capac-ity to cope with stress or frustration.

The assessment of psychosocial adjustment largely consists of inter-views and questionnaires administered to parents, teachers, and children. A few exceptions are the observations by researchers of peer contact and play in preschoolers (e.g., Deutsch, 1983; Hetherington *et al.*, 1978). The subjec-tive review and questionnaire responses are valuable because the respon-dents are integral parts of the situation, but biases in their reports are unavoidable. Therefore, the results in this area can be examined, but their limits must be recognized.

The majority of studies of the social–emotional functioning of children of divorce conclude that they function less smoothly than their peers in intact families. Children in one-parent families show difficulties in their play (Hetherington *et al.*, 1979); interactions with peers (Felner, Ginter, Boike, & Cowen, 1981; Guidubaldi *et al.*, 1983); coping with stress and frustration (Felner *et al.*, 1981; Hess & Camara, 1979; Stolberg & Anker, 1983), and emotional comfort (Hodges *et al.*, 1983). Adolescents of divorced parents also act out sexually (Booth, Brinkerhoff, & White, 1984; Kalter, 1977; Kalter & Rembar, 1981). These difficulties are sometimes sufficiently serious to warrant intervention: Guttentag *et al.* (1980) and Kalter (1977) found that there is a disproportionate number of children of divorced parents in outpatient mental health facilities.

These findings, however, are not uniformly supported: Several studies have found no differences between youngsters in one- or two-parent families (Ellison, 1983; Enos & Handal, 1986; Hodges *et al.*, 1979; Raschke & Raschke, 1979; Santrock & Warshak, 1979); mixed results (Hess & Camara, 1979; Slater, Stewart, & Linn, 1983) or evidence of better functioning among children of divorce (Deutsch, 1983). In addition, the emotional injuries tend to heal at least to some degree with the passage of time (Wallerstein, 1983b). The typical conclusion is that children of divorce are at risk for social and emotional difficulties. This conclusion holds even if consideration is limited to the disappointingly few studies that have controlled for family relationships (Hess & Camara, 1979), IQ, or SES (Guidubaldi *et al.*, 1983; Kalter, 1977).

Cognition and Perception

On the average, children of divorce have a somewhat more negative outlook on their world as compared to children in intact families. They are more likely to evaluate their parents unfavorably (Nunn *et al.*, 1983; Warshak & Santrock, 1983) and are more pessimistic about their future in general (Saucier & Ambert, 1982) and their own future marriages in particular (Warshak & Santrock, 1983). As reported by the parent or child, approximately 10 to 30% of youngsters in divorced families perceive rejection from the father, devalue the noncustodial parent, believe that divorce is stigmatized, or predict that they will not marry (Reinhard, 1977).

Cognitive appraisals of one's world, one's future, and the available coping resources are important because they consistently have been found to be related to coping in children and adults following stressful events (Peterson, Leigh, & Day, 1984). As expected, this relationship has also been found among children of divorce. Krantz, Clark, Pruyn, & Usher (1985) found that boys of divorced parents who maintained a positive or balanced evaluation of various divorce situations and were optimistic about their future were more well-adjusted than their negative and pessimistic peers. Their personal adjustment was also related to the number of coping strategies they generated to handle problematic divorce situations.

In summary, children's cognitive appraisal of their family situation are more negative among children of divorce than among children in families that have not experienced divorce. The extent to which children of divorce perceive the divorce situation in a positive or balanced manner is related to their behavioral and emotional adjustment.

FACTORS ASSOCIATED WITH POSTDIVORCE ADJUSTMENT

What aspects of the child, the family, and the divorce situation influence the adjustment of the child in the wake of divorce? The following section describes those aspects that have received the most research attention: age, gender, parental relationship, parent–child relationship, and socioeconomic status. Additional factors (e.g., parental functioning, the predivorce adjustment of the child, the family's social support network) may also be important influences on the child's postdivorce adjustment, but the paucity of research on these other factors precludes a review.

Although the various influences on adjustment are discussed separately, they do not act separately. Hodges, Weschler, & Ballantine (1979), Rutter (1979), and Stolberg and Anker (1983) reported that a single stressor did not place the child at risk for disorder, but that problems tended to mount when multiple stressors were present.

Age

Does the child's age influence his or her adjustment to divorce? Investigators agree that children of different ages show qualitatively different types of responses after their parent's separation, but disagree on whether the responses are quantitatively different in terms of their severity.

The qualitative differences between children of different ages are apparent from descriptive accounts of the preschool, middle childhood, and adolescent periods. Preschool children, with their unsophisticated and egocentric forms of reasoning, may blame themselves for the departure of a parent and may interpret this departure as a personal rejection. Associated adjustment problems are usually manifested in disturbed eating, sleeping, play, and toileting (Hetherington *et al.*, 1979; McDermott, 1968; Wallerstein & Kelly, 1975, 1980).

School-age children, by contrast, are sometimes buffeted by loyalty conflicts and may fantasize or actually attempt to reconcile the parents. Adjustment problems at this age are manifested by declines in academic performance or psychosomatic symptoms. Finally, adolescents may be prone to anger and may break the conventions that usually govern aggressive and sexual behavior (Booth, Brinkerhoff, & White, 1984; Kalter, 1977; Kalter & Rembar, 1981; Sorosky, 1977; Wallerstein & Kelly, 1974, 1980). Alternatively, growing exposure to the world outside the family and increasing ability to reason sometimes permits enhanced interpersonal sensitivity, maturity, and moral growth (Wallerstein & Kelly, 1980; Weiss, 1979).

The qualitatively different patterns of responses of children of different ages are related to their stage of cognitive and social development at the time of the divorce (Kalter & Rembar, 1981) and at the time of the follow-up assessment. The older child has the opportunity to obtain support outside the home if it is not forthcoming from his or her parents, or to find distractions from the tensions in the home by participating in pleasurable activities. The older child's more complex, abstract reasoning permits him or her to perceive the divorce in ways that differ from those of the younger child (Hetherington, 1979; Kurdek, 1981; Kurdek, Blisk, & Siesky, 1981; Longfellow, 1979).

There is mixed evidence on whether these qualitative differences between the different age groups accompanied by differences in the intensity of the symptoms. In Longfellow's (1979) review of 10 studies examining the relationship between age at separation and adjustment, one half found that preschool children are more adversely affected by their parents' divorce; the remainder found either that middle childhood or adolescence is the most vulnerable period or that adjustment is unrelated to age at the time of separation.

Because these data on the severity of problems at different ages are mixed, it would be premature to conclude that no age group is particularly vulnerable or protected. It may be a mistake to lump together different aspects of children's functioning because the different aspects may become vulnerable or invulnerable at different ages. Three of the five studies that failed to find that preschool children were at greatest risk were studies of intellectual performance. Hence, early separations may be associated with deficits in social and emotional functioning, but not with intellectual functioning. Consistent with this possibility, Hetherington et al. (1979) reviewed research showing that intellectual deficits in the children of divorce are not observed in the preschool years but become increasingly evident with increasing age. Hetherington et al. speculated that the greater abstraction and complexity of test items for older children is more susceptible to interference from the stresses of divorce in comparison to the rote memory, simple vocabulary, and sensorimotor tasks given to preschoolers. Further research is needed to determine whether different areas of children's functioning becomes vulnerable at different ages.

Gender

Most research shows that boys are more vulnerable than girls to divorce-related stresses, and recover from any difficulties more slowly (Guidubaldi et al., 1983; Hess & Camara, 1979; Hetherington et al., 1979; Hodges et al., 1983; Hodges & Bloom, 1984; Krantz et al., 1985; Kurdek & Berg, 1983; McDermott, 1968; Rutter, 1970; Wallerstein & Kelly, 1980; Zakariya, 1982). Wallerstein and Kelly (1980) found that the immediate postdivorce disadvantage of boys was still evident at a 5-year follow-up, but had dissipated at least somewhat. The disadvantage of boys, however, is not always found (Deutsch, 1983; Hodges et al., 1979; Pett, 1982; Slater, Stewart, & Linn, 1983).

Why are boys more likely than girls to exhibit behavior problems after their parents' divorce? There are several possibilities but no definitive answers. One possibility is that living with the opposite-sex parent is more difficult than living with the same-sex parent (Santrock & Warshak, 1979; Warshak & Santrock, 1983; Hodges & Bloom, 1984). Because the mother is most often the custodial parent, boys are exposed to this relatively difficult situation more often than girls. Alternatively, it has been suggested that boys are more often exposed to parental conflict (Wallerstein & Kelly, 1980). This possibility, however, is inconsistent with the findings that parents report an equivalent degree of fighting in the presence of sons and daughters (Porter & O'Leary, 1980) and that boys did not report a greater awareness of parental fighting than did girls (Emery & O'Leary, 1982). Other speculations are that parents are less supportive of their sons (Hetherington, 1979) and that boys are simply more vulnerable to stress (Rutter, 1970). These possibilities are only speculative; we are not aware of research that substantiates any of them.

Parental Relationship

The relationship between the parents is thought to be an important determinant of children's reactions to divorce. Parents in a distressed marriage may serve as models for verbal or physical violence and poor communication. Moreover, marital distress may disrupt the parents' ability to provide adequate supervision, discipline, nurturance, and warmth. The parents' conflict may create conflicting loyalties for the child who rightly or wrongly believes that bonds with one parent will provoke anger, hurt, or rejection from the other. When the worth, sanity, intentions, or competence of one parent is attacked by the other in the presence of the child, the maligned parent's ability to function as a parent is undermined.

A number of studies have found that parental conflict is associated with poor child adjustment (Booth et al., 1984; Ellison, 1983; Enos & Handal, 1986; Guidubaldi & Cleminshaw, 1983; Hess & Camara, 1979; Hetherington et al., 1978; Jacobson, 1979; Kurdek & Blisk, 1983; Leupnitz, 1979; Long et al., 1987; Nelson, 1981; Raschke & Raschke, 1979; Rutter, 1971). The association between parental conflict and child functioning is not unique to divorced families: Children in distressed two-parent families exhibit problems similar to, or worse than, children in one-parent families (Berg & Kelly, 1979; Nye, 1957; Zill, 1978). These findings that parental conflict is harmful to children are especially important in the context of divorce, however, because of the relatively high likelihood of conflict.

Parent–Child Relationship

Parent–child relationships often deteriorate in the aftermath of divorce. Parents become less available, more demanding, less responsive, and less able to maintain household routines when they must struggle with new

emotional and practical burdens (Colletta, 1983; Morrison, 1983; Wallerstein, 1983a; Wallerstein & Kelly, 1980). According to Hetherington *et al.*
(1977), mothers become more coercive and fathers become more lax and
indulgent; both become less consistent in their discipline. Divorced parents
also make less demands for mature behaviors, communicate less effectively,
or provide less affection than married parents. Their children are relatively
less compliant. Hetherington *et al.* found that these differences are most
pronounced a year following the divorce; they are still apparent, although to
a lesser degree, after 2 years. Dornbusch *et al.* (1985) observed that single
parents permit earlier autonomy in decision making by their adolescents
within most income and racial groups.

Not surprisingly, less adequate parent–child relationships have consistently been found to be associated with behavior problems in children
(Dornbusch *et al.*, 1985; Guidubaldi *et al.*, 1983; Hodges *et al.*, 1983; Hess
& Camara, 1979; Pett, 1982; Rutter, 1971; Santrock & Warshak, 1979;
Wallerstein & Kelly, 1980). Thus, there is abundant and consistent evidence
that (1) parenting among the divorced, especially the newly divorced, is
impaired relative to that of married parents, and (2) parenting styles are
strongly related to the child's adjustment.

Socioeconomic Status

As in the general population (e.g., Coleman, 1966; Fleisher, 1966; Willie,
1967), the social status of the children of divorce is related to their intellectual performance and other aspects of personal functioning (Desimone-Luis, O'Mahoney, & Hunt, 1979; Guidubaldi *et al.*, 1983; Hodges
et al., 1979; Pett, 1982; Svanum *et al.*, 1982). Although a few studies did
not replicate the greater difficulties of low-SES children (Fulton, 1979;
Hetherington, Cox, & Cox, 1977; Nelson, 1981), these studies are marred
by (1) small samples and/or (2) a range in social class too narrow to permit
the detection of an association with children's adjustment. Therefore, it
may be concluded that it is very likely—albeit not certain—that children
belonging to the lower socioeconomic classes after the divorce experience
greater personal hardships compared to those in the higher socioeconomic
classes.

POLICY IMPLICATIONS OF RESEARCH
ON DIVORCE AND CHILDREN

The current review indicates that the psychosocial adjustment of children
who have experienced the divorce of their parents is at risk. The evidence on
the school performance of children of divorce is equivocal, but it, too, is
suggestive of difficulties. Problems are most pronounced in the first 2 years
of divorce, but still can be observed years later. The extent of the youngster's

difficulties depends on many factors including sex, parental harmony, parent–child relationships, and socioeconomic class.

These research findings have implications for policy in at least three domains. First, they have important implications for the judicial process. Second, policy makers must wrestle with questions of providing services to divorcing families to prevent or ameliorate the hardships for children. Finally, the implications for political and organizational issues will be discussed.

Implications for the Judicial Process

Several of the factors shown to be related to child adjustment are strongly influenced by both the process and the outcome of courtroom decisions. Perhaps the most clear-cut outcomes of judicial decisions that influence the child's well-being are the financial consequences of (1) the court's order concerning the division of property, spousal support, and child support and (2) the enforcement of the support order (see Chapter 10 by Weitzman).

Current norms in support awards typically leave custodial mothers with serious economic hardships. The large discrepancy between the postdivorce financial state of men and women is likely to provoke resentment in women, and, consequently, increased conflict between the former spouses. Indeed, preliminary findings reported by Krantz *et al.* (1985) indicate that the size of the disparity between men's and women's incomes is associated with the number of postsettlement returns to court reported at least 2 years following the separation. The conflict is likely to be associated with the child's behavior.

In summary, whether the mother's low income is viewed relative to the general population or relative to the father's income, the child suffers. When the mother's income is low relative to the general population, she undergoes numerous stresses that impair her parenting capacities. When the mother's income is low relative to the father's income, conflict often results that is also disruptive for the child. Providing better financial resources for mothers is not a panacea, but this policy change will reduce the mother's level of stress and parental conflict. As a result, the child's well-being is likely to be bolstered.

The custody decision is another important outcome of the judicial process. Because children's adjustment in alternative custody arrangements is beyond the scope of this chapter, the policy implications of research on this topic will not be discussed. The interested reader is referred to Clingempeel & Reppucci (1982).

In addition to re-evaluating the outcomes ordered by the court, it is also important to re-evaluate the processes by which these outcomes are achieved. Although it is becoming increasingly common for states to require mediation of disputes and for attorneys to recommend mediation to their clients as a preferable alternative to a court battle, the adversarial nature of the legal system continues in many domains and can be harmful to children. For example, a custody dispute can entail attempts by each parent to degrade the other. The parent who can most effectively argue that the other parent is an unfit parent wins the court battle and "wins" the child. To construct a strong argument, the parent often selectively attends to, articulates, and exaggerates the other parent's flaws. This process erodes a more balanced perspective in the parent looking for flaws, antagonizes the maligned parent, elicits countercharges, and inflames the battle. The child is often aware that a parent is labelled as unfit, uncaring, crazy, or abusive. When the court decides against one parent, its decision may be taken by one or more family members as validation for the argument that the losing parent is, indeed, unfit (Johnston et al., 1985). The heightened parental conflict and associated parent–child tensions emerging from such a battle are harmful to the child and difficult to repair (Buehler, Hogan, Robinson, & Levy, 1985/1986).

Future policy decisions would serve children best if they supported the development and testing of alternatives to the adversarial system. One trend in this direction is the move of many states toward increasing use of mediation in disputes. Mediation works best when the legitimacy of both parents' interests and the interests of the child are taken into account. Training mediators to be psychologically as well as legally sophisticated may enhance the acceptability of mediation to the divorcing parties and improve the process of dispute settlement.

Implications for Prevention and Remediation

There are numerous ways in which educational, psychological, and social services might reduce the harmful influences of divorce on children. High quality day and evening care would reduce some of the pressure on single working parents. Subgroups at high risk should be identified, and educational and psychological services should be provided to prevent difficulties or hasten recovery. For example, parents might be helped to maintain or reestablish consistent supervision and nurturing relationships with their children. Research is needed on the efficacy of various interventions.

SUMMARY

This chapter has examined several perspectives on children's postdivorce functioning, reviewed the literature on children's adjustment, and discussed the policy implications of this review. After examining four perspectives on divorce, the discussion concludes that the complexity of families and of divorce demand the recognition of multiple and interacting factors. The "parent absence," "marital distress," and "economic hardship" formulations each account for some but not all of the findings on children's postdivorce functioning.

The review of research shows that children with divorced parents develop difficulties in some areas of functioning. Disturbances in the ability to cope with stress and in cognitive appraisals of one's world are frequently found. Relationships with peers, teachers, parents, and the community are sometimes aggressive and antisocial in nature. The development of appropriate sex-role behaviors may be delayed but resumes its usual course by the early school years. Deficiencies in intellectual functioning are suspected but are not demonstrated.

The likelihood that a child will have difficulties depends on a number of factors. Most research shows that girls are more resistant to the stresses of divorce than are boys. There is some tentative evidence that preschool children are more vulnerable than older children to social and emotional difficulties, but less vulnerable to intellectual deficits. The relationship of the parents with each other and with the child is almost uniformly found to be linked to the child's functioning. The data on the socioeconomic status of the divorced parent generally show that low social class handicaps children's postdivorce well-being.

The factors associated with children's postdivorce functioning discussed in this chapter are limited to those that have been repeatedly investigated. However, other factors are also likely to be important, including psychological problems of the custodial parent, predivorce adjustment of the child, availability of support from friends and relatives, frequent changes in residence or household composition, and insufficient community or social support.

The findings presented in this review have important implications for social policy. If financial awards can be made more equitably and enforced more consistently, the improved standard of living would be expected to lead to better parenting and, consequently, better adjusted children. Improved social services would be another means of improving the living conditions of divorced families. Finally, educational, counseling, and mediation services might help prevent or shorten the period of conflict and emotional trauma experienced by parents and children. The high frequency of divorce makes the need for these changes compelling.

ACKNOWLEDGMENT

The author is grateful to Jeffrey Clark, Ann Hallum, and Eileen Menteer for their assistance in the review of the literature and for the comments of Jeffrey Clark, Janet R. Johnston, David L. Rosenhan, and Lenore J. Weitzman on an earlier draft of this chapter.

NOTE

1. If, indeed, children in the custody of their fathers are better adjusted than those in the custody of their mothers, the representatives of those in this atypical arrangement must be questioned before concluding that fathers are usually the better parent. Custodial fathers may be unusually involved with their children compared to other divorced fathers; noncustodial mothers may be less interested in or able to have custody compared to other divorced mothers.

REFERENCES

Aldous, J. (1972). Children's perceptions of adult role assignment: Father-absence, class, race, and sex influences. *Journal of Marriage and the Family, 34,* 55–65.

Bell, R. Q., & Harper, L. V. (1977). *Child effects on adults.* Hillsdale, NJ: Erlbaum.

Berg, B., & Kelly, R. (1979). The measured self-esteem of children from broken, rejected and accepted families. *Journal of Divorce, 2,* 363–369.

Biller, H. B. (1976). The father and personality development: Paternal deprivation and sex-role development. In M. E. Lamb (Ed.), *The role of the father in child development.* New York: Wiley.

Blanchard, R. W., & Biller, H. B. (1971). Father availability and academic performance among third-grade boys. *Developmental Psychology, 4,* 301–305.

Blechman, E. A. (1982). Are children with one parent at psychological risk? A methodological review. *Journal of Marriage and the Family, 44,* 179–191.

Bloom, B. L., Asher, S. J., & White, S. W. (1978). Marital disruption as a stressor: A review and analysis. *Psychological Bulletin, 85,* 867–894.

Booth, A., Brinkerhoff, D. B., & White, L. K. (1984). The impact of parental divorce on courtship. *Journal of Marriage and the Family, 46,* 85–94.

Brown, B. F. (1980). A study of the school needs of children from one-parent families. *Phi Delta Kappan, 61,* 537–540.

Buehler, C. A., Hogan, M. J., Robinson, B. E., & Levy, R. J. (1985/86). The parental divorce transition: Divorce-related stressors and well-being. *Journal of Divorce, 9,* 61–81.

Bureau of Labor Statistics. (1968). U.S. Department of Labor, Bulletin No. 1570-2.

Burman, W. H., & Turk, D. C. (1981). Adaptation to divorce problems and coping strategies. *Journal of Marriage and the Family, 43,* 179–189.

Cline, D. W., & Westman, J. C. (1971). The impact of divorce on the family. *Child Psychiatry and Human Development, 2,* 78–83.

Clingempeel, W. G., & Reppucci, N. D. (1982). Joint custody after divorce: Major issues and goals for research. *Psychological Bulletin, 91,* 102–107.

Coleman, J. S. (1966). *Supplemental appendix to the survey on equality of educational opportunity.* Washington, DC: U.S. Government Printing Office.

Colletta, N. D. (1979). The impact of divorce: Father absence or poverty. *Journal of Divorce, 3,* 27–35.

Colletta, N. D. (1983). Stressful lives: The situation of divorced mothers and their children. *Journal of Divorce, 6,* 19–31.

Conger, J. J. (1981). Freedom and commitment: Families, youth and social change. *American Psychologist, 36,* 1475–1486.

Day, R. D., & Bahr, S. J. (1986). Income changes following divorce and remarriage. *Journal of Divorce, 9,* 75–88.

Desimone-Luis, J., O'Mahoney, K., & Hunt, D. (1979). Children of separation and divorce: Factors influencing adjustment. *Journal of Divorce, 3,* 37–42.

Deutsch, F. (1983). Classroom social participation of preschoolers in single-parent families. *Journal of Social Psychology, 119,* 77–84.

Dornbusch, S. M., Carlsmith, J. M., Bushwall, S. J., Ritter, R. L., Leiderman, H., Hastorf, A. H., & Gross, R. T. (1985). Single parents, extended households, and the control of adolescents. *Child Development, 56*, 326–341.

Duncan, G. J., & Morgan, J. N. (1976). Introduction, overview, summary and conclusions. In G. J. Duncan & J. N. Morgan (Eds.), *Five thousand American families: Patterns of economic progress.* Ann Arbor, MI: University of Michigan, Institute of Social Research.

Ellison, E. (1983). Issues concerning parental harmony and children's psychosocial development. *American Journal of Orthopsychiatry, 53*(1), 73–80.

Emery, R. E. (1982). Interparental conflict and the children of discord and divorce. *Psychological Bulletin, 92*, 310–330.

Emery, R. E., & O'Leary, K. D. (1982). Children's perceptions of marital discord and behavior problems of boys and girls. *Journal of Abnormal Child Psychology, 10*, 11–24.

Enos, D. M., & Handal, P. J. (1986). The relation of parental marital status and perceived family conflict to adjustment in white adolescents. *Journal of Consulting and Clinical Psychology, 54*, 820–824.

Felner, R. D. (1977). *An investigation of crisis in childhood: Effects and outcomes in children experiencing parental death or divorce.* Unpublished doctoral dissertation, University of Rochester.

Felner, R. D., Ginter, M. A., Boike, M. F., & Cowen, E. L. (1981). Parental death or divorce and the school adjustment of young children. *American Journal of Community Psychology, 9*, 181–191.

Felner, R. D., Stolberg, A., & Cowen, E. L. (1975). Crisis events and school mental health referral patterns of young children. *Journal of Consulting and Clinical Psychology, 43*, 305–310.

Fleisher, B. M. (1966). The effect of income on delinquency. *American Economic Review, 56*, 118–137.

Fulton, J. A. (1979). Parental reports of children's post-divorce adjustment. *Journal of Social Issues, 35*, 126–139.

Furey, W. M., & Forehand, R. (1986). What factors are associated with mother's evaluations of their clinic-referred children? *Child and Family Behavior Therapy, 8*, 21–42.

Glick, P. O. (1979). Children of divorced parents in demographic perspective. *Journal of Social Issues, 35*, 170–182.

Glueck, S., & Glueck, E. (1950). *Unraveling juvenile delinquency.* Cambridge, MA: Harvard University Press.

Goode, W. J. (1956). *After divorce.* New York: McMillan.

Guidubaldi, J., & Cleminshaw, H. K. (1983, August). *Impact of family support systems on children's academic and social functioning after divorce.* Paper presented at the Annual Convention of the American Psychological Association, Anaheim, CA.

Guidubaldi, J., Cleminshaw, H. K., Perry, J. D., & McLoughlin, C. S. (1983). The impact of parental divorce on children: Report of the nationwide NASP study. *Study Psychology Review, 12*(3), 300–323.

Guidubaldi, J., & Cleminshaw, H. K. (1985). Divorced family health and child adjustment. *Family Relations, 34*, 35–41.

Guttentag, M., Salasin, S., & Belle, D. (1980). *The mental health of women.* New York: Academic Press.

Haring-Hidore, M., Stock, W. A., Okun, M. A., & Witter, R. A. (1985). Marital status and subjective well-being: A research synthesis. *Journal of Marriage and the Family, 47*, 947–953.

Herzog, E., & Sudia, E. (1971). *Boys in fatherless families.* Washington, DC: U.S. Government Printing Office.

Hess, R. D., & Camara, K. A. (1979). Post-divorce family relationships as mediating factors in the consequences of divorce for children. *Journal of Social Issues, 35*, 79–96.

Hetherington, E. M. (1972). Effects of father absence on personality development in adolescent daughters. *Developmental Psychology, 7*, 313–326.

Hetherington, E. M. (1979). Divorce: A child's perspective. *American Psychologist, 34*, 851–858.

Hetherington, E. M., Cox, M., & Cox, R. (1977). Beyond father absence: Conceptualization of the effects of divorce. In E. M. Hetherington & R. D. Parke (Eds.), *Contemporary readings in child psychology*. New York: McGraw-Hill.

Hetherington, E. M., Cox, M., & Cox, R. (1978). The aftermath of divorce. In J. H. Stevens & M. Matthews (Eds.), *Mother–child; father–child relations*. Washington, DC: National Association for the Education of Young Children.

Hetherington, E. M., Cox, M., & Cox, R. (1979). Play and social interactions in children following divorce. *Journal of Social Issues, 35*, 26–49.

Hodges, W. F., & Bloom, B. L. (1984). Parent's report of children's adjustment to marital separation: A longitudinal study. *Journal of Divorce, 8*, 33–50.

Hodges, W. F., Buchsbaum, H. H., & Tierney, C. W. (1983). Parent–child relationships and adjustment in preschool children in divorced and intact families. *Journal of Divorce, 7*, 43–58.

Hodges, W. F., Weschler, R. C., & Ballantine, C. (1979). Divorce and the preschool child: Cumulative stress. *Journal of Divorce, 3*, 55–68.

Hofferth, S. (1983). *Updating children's life course*. Washington, DC: National Institute of Child Health and Human Development, Center for Population Research.

Hoffman, S., & Holmes, J. (1976). Husbands, wives, and divorce. In G. J. Duncan & J. N. Morgan (Eds.), *Five thousand American families: Patterns of economic progress*. Ann Arbor, MI: University of Michigan, Institute for Social Research.

Jacobs, N. L., Guidubaldi, J., & Nastasi, B. (1986). Adjustment of divorced family day care children. *Early Childhood Research Quarterly, 1*, 361–378.

Jacobson, D. S. (1979). The impact of marital separation/divorce on children: Interpersonal hostility and child adjustment. *Journal of Divorce, 2*, 3–19.

Johnston, J. R., Campbell, L. E. G., & Tall, M. C. (1985). Impasses to the resolution of custody and visitation. *American Journal of Orthopsychiatry, 55*, 112–119.

Kalter, N. (1977). Children of divorce in an outpatient psychiatric population. *American Journal of Orthopsychiatry, 47*, 40–51.

Kalter, N., & Rembar, J. (1981). The significance of a child's age at the time of parental divorce. *American Journal of Orthopsychiatry, 51*, 85–100.

Kohlberg, L. (1966). A cognitive-development analysis of children's sex-role concepts and attitudes. In E. Maccoby (Ed.), *The development of sex differences*. Berkeley, CA: Stanford University Press.

Krantz, S. E., Clark, J., Pruyn, J., & Usher, M. (1985). Cognition and adjustment among children of separation and divorce. *Cognitive Therapy and Research, 9*, 61–77.

Krantz, S. E., Johnston, J. R., Gonzalez, R., & Clark, J. (1985). *Predictors of long-term post-divorce conflict*. Unpublished manuscript.

Kressel, K., Jaffee, N., Tuchman, B., Watson, C., & Deutsch, M. (1980). A typology of divorcing couples: Implications for mediation and the divorce process. *Family Process, 19*, 101–116.

Kurdek, L. A. (1981). An integrative perspective on children's divorce adjustment. *American Psychologist, 36*, 856–866.

Kurdek, L. A., Blisk, D., & Siesky, A. E. (1981). Effects of divorce on children. *Journal of Divorce, 4*, 85–99.

Kurdek, L. A., & Berg, B. (1983). Correlates of children's adjustment to their parents' divorces. In L. A. Kurdek (Ed.), *Children and divorce*. San Francisco: Jossey-Bass.

Kurdek, L. A., & Blisk, D. (1983). Dimensions and correlates of mother's divorce experiences. *Journal of Divorce, 6*, 1–24.

Kurdek, L. A. (1986). Custodial mothers' perceptions of visitation and payment of child support by non-custodial fathers in families with low and high levels of preseparation interpersonal conflict. *Journal of Applied Developmental Psychology, 7*, 301–323.

Landis, J. (1960). The trauma of children when parents divorce. *Marriage and Family Living, 22*, 7–13.

Lazarus, M. (1980). One-parent families and their children. *Principal, 60*, 31–37.

Leupnitz, D. A. (1979). Which aspects of divorce affect children? *Family Coordinator, 28*, 79–85.

Long, N., Forehand, R., Fauber, R., & Brody, G. (1987). Self-perceived and independently observed competence of young adolescents as a function of parental conflict and recent divorce. *Journal of Abnormal Child Psychology, 15*, 15–27.

Longfellow, C. (1979). Divorce in context: Its impact on children. In G. Levinger & O. C. Moles (Eds.), *Divorce and separation: Context, causes and consequences.* New York: Basic Books.

Maclean, M., & Eekelaar, J. (1983). *Children and divorce: Economic factors.* Oxford, England: Centre for Socio-legal Studies.

McCord, J., McCord, W., & Thurber, E. (1962). Some effects of paternal absence on male children. *Journal of Abnormal and Social Psychology, 64*, 361–369.

McDermott, J. F. (1968). Parental divorce in early childhood. *American Journal of Psychiatry, 124*, 1424–1432.

McDermott, J. F. (1970). Divorce and its psychiatric sequelae in children. *Archives of General Psychiatry, 23*, 421–427.

McLanahan, S. S. (1983). Family structure and stress: A longitudinal comparison of two-parent and female-headed families. *Journal of Marriage and the Family, 45*, 347–357.

Mischel, W. (1970). Sex-typing and socialization. In P. H. Mussen (Ed.), *Carmichael's manual of child psychology.* New York: Wiley.

Monthly Vital Statistics Report. (1985). *National Center for Health Statistics, 3*(11), Supplement 1. Washington, DC: U.S. Government Printing Office.

Nelson, G. (1981). Moderators of women's and children's adjustment following parental divorce. *Journal of Divorce, 4*, 71–83.

Norton, A. J., & Glick, P. C. (1979). Marital instability in America: Past, present and future. In G. Levinger & O. C. Moles (Eds.), *Divorce and separation: Context, causes and consequences.* New York: Basic Books.

Nunn, G. D., Parish, T. S., & Worthing, R. J. (1983). Perceptions of personal and familial adjustment by children from intact, single parent, and reconstituted families. *Psychology in the Schools, 20*(2), 166–174.

Nye, F. I. (1957). Child adjustment in broken and unhappy unbroken homes. *Marriage and Family Living, 19*, 356–361.

Peterson, G. W., Leigh, G. K., & Day, R. D. (1984). Family stress theory and the impact of divorce on children. *Journal of Divorce, 7*, 1–20.

Pett, M. G. (1982). Correlates of children's social adjustment following divorce. *Journal of Divorce, 5*(4), 25–39.

Porter, B., & O'Leary, K. D. (1980). Types of marital discord and childhood behavior problems. *Journal of Abnormal Child Psychology, 80*, 287–295.

Raschke, H. J., & Raschke, V. J. (1979). Family conflict and children's self-concepts: A comparison of intact and single-parent families. *Journal of Marriage and the Family, 41*, 367–373.

Reinhard, D. W. (1977). The reaction of adolescent boys and girls to the divorce of their parents. *Journal of Clinical Child Psychology, 6*, 21–23.

Ross, H. L., & Sawhill, I. V. (1975). *Time of transition: The growth of families headed by women.* Washington, DC: Urban Institute.

Rutter, M. (1970). Sex differences in children's response to family stress. In E. J. Anthony & C. Koupernik (Eds.), *The child in his family*. New York: Wiley.

Rutter, M. (1971). Parent–child separation: Psychological effects on the children. *Journal of Child Psychology and Psychiatry, 12*, 233–260.

Rutter, M. (1979). Maternal deprivation, 1972–1978: New findings, new concepts, new approaches. *Child Development, 50*, 283–305.

Santrock, J. W., & Tracy, R. L. (1978). Effects of children's family structure status on the development of stereotypes by children. *Journal of Educational Psychology, 70*, 754–757.

Santrock, J. W., & Warshak, R. A. (1979). Father custody and social development in boys and girls. *Journal of Social Issues, 35*, 112–125.

Saucier, J. F., & Ambert, A. M. (1982). Parental marital status and adolescents' optimism about their future. *Journal of Youth and Adolescence, 11*(5), 345–354.

Shinn, M. (1978). Father absence and children's cognitive development. *Psychological Bulletin, 85*, 295–324.

Slater, E. J., Stewart, K. J., & Linn, M. W. (1983). The effects of family disruption on adolescent males and females. *Adolescence, 18*, 931–942.

Sorosky, A. D. (1977). The psychological effects of divorce on adolescents. *Adolescence, 45*, 123–136.

Spivey, P. B., & Sherman, A. (1980). The effects of time lapse on personality characteristics and stress of divorced women. *Journal of Divorce, 4*, 49–59.

Stolberg, A. L., & Anker, J. M. (1983). Cognitive-behavioral changes in children resulting from parental divorce and consequent environmental changes. *Journal of Divorce, 7*(2), 231–241.

Svanum, S., Bringle, R. G., & McLaughlin, J. E. (1982). Father absence and cognitive performance in a large sample of six- to eleven-year-old children. *Child Development, 53*, 136–143.

Szalai, A., Converse, P. E., Feldheim, P., Scheuch, E. K., & Stone, P. J. (Eds.). (1972). *The use of time: Daily activities of urban and suburban populations in twelve countries*. The Hague; The Netherlands: Mouton.

U.S. Bureau of the Census. (1981a). Money income of families and persons in the United States: 1979. *Current Population Reports*, Series P-60, no. 129, 152, 197.

U.S. Bureau of the Census. (1981b). *Statistical Abstract of the United States: 1981*. (102nd ed.). Washington, DC: U.S. Government Printing Office.

Wallerstein, J. S. (1983a). Children of divorce: Stress and developmental tasks. In N. Garmezy & M. Rutter (Eds.), *Stress, coping and development in children*. New York: McGraw-Hill.

Wallerstein, J. S. (1983b). The psychological tasks of the child. *American Journal of Orthopsychiatry, 53*, 230–243.

Wallerstein, J. S. (1984). Children of divorce: Preliminary report of a ten-year follow up of young children. *American Journal of Orthopsychiatry, 54*(3), 444–498.

Wallerstein, J. S., & Kelly, J. B. (1974). The effects of parental divorce: The adolescent experience. In E. J. Anthony & C. Koupernik (Eds.), *The child in his family: Children at psychiatric risk*. New York: Wiley.

Wallerstein, J. S., & Kelly, J. B. (1975). The effects of parental divorce: Experiences of the preschool child. *Journal of the American Academy of Child Psychiatry, 14*, 600–616.

Wallerstein, J. S., & Kelly, J. B. (1980). *Surviving the break-up: How children and parents cope with divorce*. New York: Basic Books.

Warshak, R. A., & Santrock, J. W. (1983). The impact of divorce in father-custody and mother-custody homes: The children's perspective. In L. A. Kurdek (Ed.), *Children and divorce: New directions for child development*. San Francisco: Jossey-Bass.

Weingarten, H. R. (1985). Marital status and well-being: A national study comparing firstmarried, currently divorced and remarried adults. *Journal of Marriage and the Family, 47*, 653–661.

Weinraub, M., & Wolf, B. M. (1983). Effects of stress and social supports on mother–child interaction in single- and two-parent families. *Child Development, 54,* 1297–1311.

Weiss, R. S. (1979). Growing up a little faster: The experience of growing up in a single-parent household. *Journal of Social Issues, 35,* 97–111.

Weitzman, L. J. (1985). *The divorce revolution: The unexpected social and economic consequences for women and children in America.* New York: The Free Press.

Willie, C. N. (1967). The relative contribution of family status and economic status to juvenile delinquency. *Social Problems, 14,* 326–334.

Zakariya, S. B. (1982). Another look at the children of divorce: Summary report of the study of school needs of one-parent children. *Principal, 62,* 34–37.

Zill, N. (1978, February). *Divorce, marital unhappiness, and the mental health of children: Findings from the FCD survey of children.* Presented to the NIMH workshop on Divorce and Children, Bethesda, MD.

12

Single-Parent Families

SANFORD M. DORNBUSCH AND KATHRYN D. GRAY

INTRODUCTION

Typically, discussions of single-parent families in the United States start with an alarmist perspective, considering them an anomaly whose prevalence represents a threat to the American family system. Since our perspective on the new families considers single-parent families as one of the major forms of family structure—one that policy makers must take into consideration—we will try to go beyond the usual presentation of negative outcomes associated with single parents and their offspring. Our concern is to understand the processes that lead to various outcomes, not just to report on the conditions associated with single-parenthood. We attempt to understand the processes that lead to certain results of single parenting and to suggest possible alternatives that might improve the well-being of single-parent families.

Accordingly, we will first discuss the increasing prevalence of single-parent families, and the poverty that is associated with them. This poverty is a major factor leading to many of the problems associated with single-parent families. Most single-parent families are headed by women, and their impoverishment is a product of divorce and its negative economic consequences for women and their children (see Weitzman, Chapter 10). The feminization of poverty is a major social trend in the United States whose impact adds to the common outcomes for single mothers and their children.

Although most single-parent families are headed by women, the minority of single-parent families headed by fathers must not be overlooked. Single-father families have different problems from those found in families headed by a woman, but they do have problems nonetheless. Although only 10% of single-parent families are headed by a man, this still amounts to a substantial number of families. The special needs of single-father families are therefore discussed next.

Teenage parents are another special form of single-parenthood. A dramatic increase in never-married mothers has resulted in the growing

Sanford M. Dornbusch, Ph.D. Department of Sociology, Stanford University, Stanford, California; Stanford Center for the Study of Families, Children, and Youth, Stanford, California. Kathryn D. Gray, M.A. Department of Sociology, Drew University, Madison, New Jersey.

proportion of single-parent families headed by teenage mothers. These young women who become teenage parents are, in numerous ways that we will describe, deviating from the normative expectations of our society.

Children from single-parent families are more likely to exhibit deviance from societal standards than are children from two-natural-parent households. We attempt to look at the underlying processes that lead to this set of negative outcomes, processes such as family decision making as it relates to adolescent deviance. These children also have repeatedly been shown to do somewhat less well in school than one would expect on the basis of their intellectual ability. Part of the explanation for somewhat lower grades is probably related to difficulties in self-control, an aspect of social deviance. Additional difficulties arise from the lack of appropriate perceptions by teachers of the role that single parents can play in cooperation with the school. We discuss familial and school processes that influence the level of school performance of children from single-parent families.

Before turning to the discussion of processes, we describe how single-parent families now fit into the structure of American society. This approach enables us to point to some key problems associated with single-parenthood, as well as to emphasize the pervasiveness of those problems. Only after putting single-parent families and their problems into perspective do we turn to the delineation of family processes and their impact.

CHARACTERISTICS OF SINGLE-PARENT FAMILIES

The Increasing Number of Single-Parent Families

The growth in the number of single-parent families has been dramatic and is continuing. From 1970 to 1984 the number of single-parent families more than doubled, from 3.2 million to 6.7 million (Norton & Glick, 1986). Today, almost 23% of all children under 18 are living in a single-parent family. This rise in the proportion of single-parent families can be largely attributed to an increasing divorce rate and to a startling increase of 500% in never-married mothers (Norton & Glick, 1986).

Although single-parent families now contain more than one fifth of all children, that does not express the full importance of this family form. Most divorced persons remarry, and they tend to do so within 3 or 4 years after their divorce. Thus, numerous children are temporarily living in single-parent families and later are counted as members of two-parent households or stepfamilies. In discussing single-parent families, we are dealing with a phenomenon of great magnitude. Half of all American children can be expected to live in a single-parent household before they reach the age of 18 (Glick, 1979).

Although there is an erroneous image that the single-parent family is a recent phenomenon, there have always been numerous single parents, usually a product of the death of the other parent. Indeed, it is only since World War II that divorce has created more single-parent families in the United States than were created by widowhood. As American mortality rates have declined, there continues to be a substantial decrease in widowhood. The decline in the production of single-parent families through death has been more than offset by the increasing numbers of never-married mothers and by the increased number of divorces (Stannard, 1979).

Ethnic differences in the incidence of single parenthood are dramatic. For example, among non-Hispanic whites in 1985, 18% of all children live in single-parent families, compared to 28.8% among Hispanics and 53.9% among blacks (U.S. Bureau of the Census, 1986). Henry Walker in Chapter 5 discussed the historical background of this current low proportion of two-natural-parent families within the black community.

As has been mentioned, most single parents continue to be women. About 88% of single-parent families in 1984 were headed by a mother, not different from the 1970 figure of 89% (Norton & Glick, 1986). When a divorce involves children in America, it typically produces a bachelor and a single mother. The economic disadvantages faced by women produce special difficulties for families in which there is no father present.

The Poverty of Single Mothers and Their Children

The rise in single-parent families, primarily headed by women, has contributed greatly to the feminization of poverty. If we look at single-mother families, 60% of the children were living below the poverty level in 1983 (Norton & Glick, 1986). The poverty of single-parent families is thus having a negative impact upon over 8 million American children, and disproportionately affects minority children—about 70% of black children and Hispanic children living in single-mother families are poor (Ford Foundation, 1984). Fuchs (1986), while arguing that the relative poverty of women compared to men hit its peak in the 1960s and has not increased since then, shows that the increased number of women in households without men is the principal source of the feminization of poverty. Indeed, he concluded that the increase in female-headed households is also the reason why the trends in female poverty are more adverse for blacks than whites.

A recent report by the Bureau of the Census ("Wealth in Black and White," 1986) has shown that the poverty associated with single-parenthood is also clear when one looks at wealth rather than income. When a white family is headed by a married couple, the median wealth (assets minus liabilities) is $54,184. For white female-headed households, the median is only $22,500. Finally, and most sadly, the median wealth of black households headed by women is a mere $700.

Younger children are the most impoverished. The poverty rate among school-age children in female-headed households was 50% in 1983, compared to a startling 68% for preschool children. These figures are much higher than the rate of poverty for children in male-present households, which is 12% and 15% respectively (Congressional Budget Office, 1984).

The situation of single-parent families is not getting any better. Although the poverty rates for non-Hispanic White two-parent families have declined since 1960, poverty in one-parent families headed by minority women has become even more prevalent. The number of blacks and Hispanics in poor female-headed families has more than doubled during this period (U.S. Commission on Civil Rights, 1983).

Women in the Labor Market

The traditional male/breadwinner–female/homemaker family so well analyzed in Chapter 4 by Davis is now a steadily declining minority of all families. In 1982 only 37% of all children in the United States lived in such families, and among low-income black children, the proportion in such traditional households was only 18% (Hayes & Kamerman, 1983).

Labor-force participation by single-parent mothers is higher than for mothers in general. Two of every three single mothers with children under 18 years of age in 1984 (66%) were members of the labor force, compared to 59% of married mothers (Norton & Glick, 1986). The rates are considerably higher for single mothers with school-age children (77%) than for those with preschool children (53%). Yet, compared to rates a few decades ago, the rates are high even for parents of preschoolers. Indeed, today 45% of single mothers with children under 3 are in the labor force (Norton & Glick, 1986).

Ethnic differences in labor-force participation of single mothers are striking. While 71% of white single-parent mothers with children under 18 years of age are in the labor force, only 58% of black and 48% of Hispanic single mothers are in the labor force. Proposals in Congress in 1987 are designed to move towards the participation of single mothers in the labor force. Single mothers with children over 3 years of age would be eligible for state initiatives designed to provide job training or jobs for mothers on welfare.

It is worthy of note that, while black single mothers were less likely to be in the labor force, black married mothers were more likely than non-Hispanic white married mothers to be in the labor force. These ethnic differences are likely to be associated with ethnic differences in the unemployment of husbands, cultural differences in approval of mothers working outside of the home, and the operation of the welfare system (Norton & Glick, 1986).

The poverty of female-headed families derives in part from inequalities in the labor market that are associated with gender. Women who have been forced by divorce to seek employment when they have children at home face multiple handicaps in pursuing jobs. As noted by Strober in Chapter 8, their interrupted employment and part-time employment, often a product of the family responsibilities they assume, interfere with the attainment of higher level positions. The occupational distribution of women compared to men emphasizes white-collar work, but women are concentrated in the lower paid and less skilled portions of the white-collar occupational structure. Finally, a gender gap persists even after allowing for the effects of education, work experience, occupation, and industry—women usually get paid less than men for the same work.

The burden of labor-force participation falls more heavily upon a parent who does not have a partner with whom to share family responsibilities. Since single-parent households are predominantly headed by women, they have the burden of parenthood as well as the problems of women in the labor market. This produces additional problems for the mothers, and negative consequences for their children.

Welfare

The economic disadvantages of the female-headed family mean that the low level of financial support from the absent husband (and the frequent lack of any substantial contribution from him) puts both mother and children at risk and often dependent on state aid. Only a minority of single-parent families received child support from the husband in 1983 (21% of the children in single-parent families), and the level of support, even when received, is usually inadequate (Norton & Glick, 1986). Chapter 10 by Weitzman has discussed the economic problems of families with children after a divorce. Congressional initiatives in 1986 and 1987 have sought to increase the proportion of fathers who contribute to the support of their children.

Faced with these economic problems, single-parent mothers are often forced to go on welfare. Indeed, one third (34%) of the children in single-mother families received Aid to Families with Dependent Children (AFDC) in 1983 (Norton & Glick, 1986). Critics of the welfare system often believe that the welfare system creates single-parent families. Senator Moynihan has introduced legislation in 1987 that would remove any prohibitions against aid to two-parent families below the poverty level.

> Many people have concluded that the availability of welfare encourages husbands to leave home, knowing that public stipends will provide for their wives. Others go further, suggesting that women deliberately have more children to get larger checks. While there evidently are such cases, it is not clear they play a significant role in the growth of welfare rolls. At the same time, however, it does seem true that some pregnant women decide to have and keep their babies because they know support will be forthcoming. Between 1970 and 1980 the proportion of women-headed households in which the mother had never been married almost doubled, from 8.6 percent to 16.4 percent. (Hacker, 1982)

A common image of single-parent families is that they form a perpetual class of welfare recipients. Although single-parent families do indeed make up the bulk of such recipients (80%), under AFDC, most single-parent families are only temporarily in need of aid. In a longitudinal study that followed families over a 10-year period and recorded their welfare status, the typical single-parent household received aid for about 2 years, left the welfare rolls, and returned later in the period during another period of deprivation. Only 700,000 female-headed families in the United States were continuously on welfare for the entire period.

The Panel Study of Income Dynamics Project reported in 1984, based on a 15-year study, that only about 1 child in 20 was poor for 10 or more of his first 15 years of life. Single-parent families, black families, and families in rural and southern areas show heavier concentrations of persistent childhood poverty (Duncan, 1984).

Being on welfare, despite a few widely publicized cheaters, is not the route to Easy Street. Ninety-four percent of families headed by women that had only public assistance as a source of income were living below the poverty level (Johnson, 1979). Many of these mothers were staying home with young children, about 7% were physically handicapped (Johnson, 1979), and those participating in the labor force were often not able to earn a living for their family. Mothers in single-parent households are lower in educational level, labor-force participation, and pay, and higher only in the likelihood of unemployment (Johnson, 1979). Thus, even those who participate in the labor force in single-parent families are usually in need of governmental aid because of their low earning power.

Governmental policies in the Reagan administration have attempted to deny support to many poor women who were working. Short-sighted policies oriented to immediate budgetary savings often have long-term negative consequences. Reducing aid to the working poor produces more nonworking poor families, for an increasing number of women have been forced to stop working and rely completely on AFDC, since if they continue to work they become ineligible for aid under such policies. It is ironic that those who have vilified welfare recipients as preferring to be on the dole have forced many to give up jobs and live as if they agreed with this negative stereotype. Kaus (1986) has noted the flaws in the current "workfare" programs and their failure to take into account their potential impact on family formation and out-of-wedlock births.

Health

One arena in which the disadvantages of poverty are clear is the health of mothers and children. The U.S. Commission on Civil Rights (1983) notes that data are seldom available concerning the health status of mothers and children in female-headed households. Nevertheless, it is clear that while health care is a problem for women generally, it is even more troublesome for female heads of households. For example, single-parent households are forced to cut back on health-related expenditures more than other groups in our society. To cope with inflation, for example, 72% of single-parent families reported reducing their health-related expenses, compared to 60% of minority families, and 56% of families with low family income and low parental education. (Yankelovich, Skelly, & White, 1979)

Although it is difficult to find data on the direct impact of single-parenthood on the health of family members, McAdoo (1978) found that black single mothers, even when middle-class in status, experience more stress than mothers who have a husband present. In a continuing series of research reports on the American family, Yankelovich *et al.* (1979) found that 55% of single parents were finding it increasingly difficult to cope with the problems of everyday life. Ferri (1976), using a British sample and school absences as an indirect measure of health status, reported little difference in the health of children in one-parent or two-parent homes. On the other hand, the mothers themselves were more prone to chronic or serious illness in single-parent households.

We are left with little guidance on the relation of family structure per se to health, but the link of single-parenthood to poverty implies increased health problems, both mental and physical, in single-parent families. According to the Children's Defense Fund, providing medical care and nutritional services to needy pregnant women could save at least 2,700 lives over the next 5 years; and a study by Shelia Kamerman of Columbia University found that the United States was the only one of 75 countries surveyed without a law ensuring basic health and social supports for pregnant working women ("Milk for Babies," 1985). Given the poverty of most single-parent households, the lack of a safety net is injuring the health of single parents and their children.

Single Fathers

The number of single-parent families headed by fathers has nearly doubled since 1970, though this increase is largely due to the rapid rise in single-parent families as a whole. The proportion of single-parent families that are headed by a father has in fact remained relatively unchanged at about 10%. Orthner, Brown, & Ferguson (1976) link custody by the father upon separation or divorce to parental decisions rather than to decisions by a court. Paternal custody is usually based on the former wife not wanting or being unable to care for the children. The proportion of single-parent families headed by a father varies by ethnic and racial background. For whites, 13.2% of all single-parent families were headed by fathers compared to 5.4% for blacks and 7.7% for Hispanics (U.S. Bureau of the Census, 1986).

Although the proportion of single-parent families headed by fathers has increased only slightly during the past decade, the labor force participation rate among men in this group has declined somewhat. In 1970, more than 91 percent of single-parent fathers with children under 18 years of age were in the labor force; in 1979 only 86 percent of them were. . . . This decline has followed the general pattern of male labor force participation during the past decade. The decrease is largely attributable to longer education, earlier retirement, and longer life spans. (Kamerman & Hayes, 1982)

Male single parents experience a decline in living standards after the wife's departure, although the decline in income is not nearly so great as that found by Weitzman for single mothers (Chapter 10). A British study (George & Wilding, 1972) found that the economic status of these mother-less families declined 44% of the time, although the decrease was based on a direct loss of the wife's earnings only 12% of the time. The economic impact was largely a product of the mother's hidden contribution to the family budget through her time and effort on household tasks. Fathers were unable to continue to work overtime and about a third did not work some period of time. It was difficult to combine work and the day care needs of the children, a finding repeated over and over in studies of fatherless families.

Yet, not surprisingly, one of the most striking differences between single-father and single-mother families is in family income. In 1985, the mean income for single-parent families headed by fathers was $22,164, compared to $10,694 for single-parent families headed by mothers. In 1985, 60.2% of single-mother families had incomes under $10,000 compared to only 25.8% of single-father families. At the same time, only 1.7% of single mothers earn $40,000 or more per year, compared to 11.6% of single fathers. In addition, single fathers, compared to single mothers, are older, better educated, and less likely to be living with a relative (U.S. Bureau of the Census, 1986).

The typical separation of the genders in American society more often assigns household tasks and childrearing to women, and it also trains females for the tasks of emotional nurturance. Single-parent fathers report—in addition to economic problems and the difficulty of combining work and family responsibilities—that they originally felt most inadequate with respect to their emotional relationship with their children (Schlesinger, 1978). Single fathers tended to rely more on relatives, female friends, and hired help for assistance in household tasks and child care than do single mothers (Brandwein, Brown, & Fox, 1974; Hetherington, Cox, & Cox, 1982). For these fathers, the demands of single-parenthood eventually required a major shift in life-style, restructured the bond between father and children, and led to a closer relationship with their children (Keshet & Rosenthal, 1978).

Teenage Parents

Teenage mothers are deviating from the norms of our society. The problems that result from early pregnancy are almost always problems of the female, for less often does teenage fatherhood result in major shifts in the life chances of the male. This form of adolescent deviance, for which females are more penalized, affects not only the teenagers but the children whom they bring into the world with a lower level of resources.

In Chapter 5, Walker examines the bases for the recent historical increase in out-of-wedlock births among black teenagers. The black community faces special problems in addressing these issues. In our brief discussion of teenage pregnancy, we seek to place it within the context of single-parenthood.

The program for AFDC has been described as "Aid to Children with Dependent Children." The majority of women participating in this program were at one time teenage mothers. A substantial and increasing proportion of welfare households arise from a relatively recent increase in teenage pregnancy. Wendy Baldwin (1983–1984) has characterized the so-called epidemic of adolescent pregnancy in a fashion that puts it into demographic perspective. During the 1970s, there were about 35% more teenagers than in the earlier period. Even though the birth rate for teenage mothers was declining, this meant that the number of children born to teenagers stayed the same. Since the fertility of those mothers past their teens was declining even faster, this led teenage births to form an increased proportion of total births.

The category "teenage births" includes heterogeneous age groups. The data are often reported for mothers under 15, and then lumped together for mothers 15 to 19. As Baldwin (1983–1984) notes, the latter category combines junior high school students with high school graduates. The older teens are not in the group at high risk. It is important to realize that the decline in fertility was greatest for the older teenagers, who usually have good pregnancy outcomes, and that birth rates actually rose for the younger teenagers. Those who are most at risk are forming an increasing proportion of teenage mothers.

The increased public awareness of teenage fertility is accentuated by a parallel increase in out-of-wedlock births. Today, teenage mothers account for more than half of the children born out-of-wedlock in the United States each year. Unlike the pattern for total births, both the number and the proportion of births to unwed teenagers have been increasing rapidly. From 1940 to 1960 the number of out-of-wedlock births doubled, from 1960 to 1980 it almost tripled, and the increase in births outside of marriage has not yet slowed (Levitan & Belous, 1981): "Between 1970 and 1981, families headed by never-married women increased by almost 356 percent" (U.S. Commission on Civil Rights, 1983). Even among white families, the proportion of children "who lived with a parent who had never been married increased from 7% to 13% during the last 5 years (from 1980 to 1985)" (U.S. Bureau of the Census, 1986).

The increase in out-of-wedlock teenage births has occurred for both whites and blacks, but the magnitude of the problem is far greater for blacks. For unmarried women 15 to 19 years of age in 1984, the number of births per 1,000 women is 87.1 among black teenagers and 19.0 among white teenagers (U.S. Department of Health and Human Services, 1986). Since 1975, the majority of all births outside of marriage occur among women 19 or younger. Rates of out-of-wedlock births may increase while childbearing rates are decreasing. The number of teenage out-of-wedlock births depends on more than teenage fertility; it is also a function of teenage inability or unwillingness to marry.

Hardy *et al.* (1978) were surprised by the impact of marriage and education on the successful socialization of the children of teenagers. In a small pilot study, the more successful 12-year-olds had mothers who, though teenagers at the time of birth, had almost all married and finished high school. Teenagers can be successful parents, but being both a teenage mother and not marrying is a difficult combination—yet only 15% of teenage mothers marry (Zelnik & Kantner, 1980).

Contraceptive information and the availability of abortion are reducing the number of births to teenagers, just as the decline in the number of adolescents reduces the number of such births (Furstenberg, 1976). Yet, the teenage mothers are typically unwilling to use various methods to reduce their fertility, partly because it is difficult for young women to face their own sexuality, while teenage fathers typically view the avoidance of pregnancy as predominantly the responsibility of the young woman (Baldwin, 1983–1984).

Not using contraceptive methods to prevent pregnancy is associated with an unwillingness on the part of the young woman to define herself as sexually active. Most contraceptive methods require planning in advance that assumes some probability of having sexual intercourse, and many young women, including many who have already been pregnant and had abortions, are unwilling to accept and act on the likelihood of their own sexual activity.

But unwillingness to have an abortion or unwillingness to get married cannot be explained by a self-concept of sexual inactivity. Why do these young women choose to have and keep a child out-of-wedlock? That choice, often made in a situation of multiple pressures and emotional turmoil, can often be best understood by comparing it with other options or alternatives available to the teenage mother.

Becoming a teenage mother may appear to the outsider to be undesirable, but undesirable compared to what? The young mother has to assess her current potential income as a participant in the labor force; her academic standing if she is in school; the stigma, if any, associated with early and out-of-wedlock pregnancy; and the impact of early motherhood upon her future life chances and those of her child. Similarly, marriage as an option is viewed comparatively. As Walker noted in Chapter 5, the characteristics of the available husbands-to-be in the marriage market influence the extent to which marriage is preferable to out-of-wedlock birth.

In dealing with a social problem like teenage pregnancy, it is important to assess its impact by data that are as objective as possible. Card and Wise (1978) have done a careful comparison of the long-term impact of teenage pregnancy to both mother and child, arguing that the assessment of impact must compare mothers and children involved in teenage pregnancy with mothers and children of the same general social strata. When those comparisons are made, there remains a negative impact upon the life chances of the child of a teenage mother. But what is powerful and sad is that the life chances of the teenage mother are even more affected: The mother's social, economic, and physical well-being are all negatively affected over the long term (Card & Wise, 1978).

One reason for the severe negative impact of teenage pregnancy upon the unwed mother is that it disturbs the usual life cycle for women. Typically, a young woman finishes her education, enters the labor force, marries, and then has a child. By having the child while still in school, there is an abrupt disruption of this usual pattern (Hogan, 1982). The discontinuity of teenage pregnancy often leads to the abrupt cessation of the education of the unwed mother, a decline in her employment prospects, and a set of long-term problems associated with low income, welfare dependency, lack of skills, and low expectations for the future. Even 12 years after the birth of their child, only 35% of adolescent mothers had completed high school (Hardy, 1982).

With this perspective, Joy G. Dryfoos (1983–1984) has argued that teenage pregnancy as a social problem cannot be handled merely via sex education, family planning, and abortion services. Such interventions are important and useful, but the most central priority of public policy should be the broadening of the life options of these disadvantaged children (who are also potential mothers). These children should be assisted educationally in order that they stay in school, develop literacy, and increase their vocational aspirations and expectations. Though indirect, policies that enhance the alternatives available for female teenagers and their male companions will make the option of childbearing less acceptable.

PROCESSES AND THEIR RESULTS

At this point we shift our approach to examine the processes that are leading to difficulties within single-parent families. Instead of focusing on results or symptoms, we hope to illuminate the behaviors of families and institutions that lead to or mitigate the problems of single-parent families. Much of the research on single-parent households adds to the burden of single parents. While a single parent is told that her child is more at risk for delinquency, for poor grades in school, or for emotional upset, there is usually no set of behaviors that the single parent is encouraged to utilize to overcome these disadvantages. In this chapter we seek, to the extent possible, to discuss behaviors to be recommended to the single parent, to the school, and to various agencies in order to reduce the problems of children in single-parent families, as well as to indicate behaviors that should be avoided. We begin with family decision-making, looking at its relation to adolescent deviance and to academic performance in the high school.

Family Decision Making and Adolescent Deviance in Single-Parent Families

To help develop preliminary answers concerning the differences between single-parent families and two-parent families in family decision making, we have turned to Cycle III of the National Health Examination Survey, a national sample of noninstitutionalized youth in the years 1966–1970. That remarkable survey included information from parents, school, physician, and adolescent about family decision making, youthful deviance, school performance, and other measures of the activities of American adolescents. Although the data are increasingly out of date, we must turn to them because of the lack of any other large-scale and representative sample of American youth that contains information from such diverse sources.

The analysis of family decision making is complicated because there are differences between middle-class and lower-class families in the pattern of childrearing. Few studies have had a sufficient number of families so that the relative impact of family structure upon family functioning can be examined within each social class. This representative national sample of adolescents is large enough so that we can do analyses within each social class and determine the association of family decision making with various adolescent behaviors.

Our research (Dornbusch et al., 1983; Dornbusch et al., 1985) indicates a powerful tendency for single-parent families to permit adolescent youths earlier control over their own behavior (youth-alone decision making) in such areas as choice of friends, choice of clothes, spending money, and time they must come home. The middle-class pattern emphasizes joint decision making, shared among parents and child, while parents alone are more likely to decide these issues in lower-class families. But across all class levels, giving the adolescent sole control over his or her own behavior in these areas of decision making occurs earlier in adolescence for families led by a single-parent.

Of course, the American system of socialization of adolescents and young adults is oriented towards the autonomy of American youth: The children must "leave the nest and learn to fly," "go their own ways." What our data reveal is a tendency for the single-parent to give such autonomy to the child at an age earlier than is typical in the American family system. Such early decision making by the youth alone may be a reasonable response by single parents to the difficulties encountered by one parent attempting to monitor the behavior of an adolescent and inculcate socially approved values in the child. But it has an unfortunate consequence, an increased probability to engage in deviant acts on the part of the youth.

Too early autonomy for adolescent children is an apparent response to the overload of responsibility for the single parent. This national sample of American youth is large enough so that we can divide single-parent families into those that have an additional adult present and those in which the single parent is the only adult in the household. We do not know who those additional adults are, for the data are unavailable. The additional adult might be a grandparent, a lover, an aunt, or a friend. In any case, when there is an additional adult present, there is a tendency for single-parent families to be more like two-parent families in youth-alone decision making. The presence of an additional adult may function to increase the possibility of surveillance, add another voice for the postponement of youthful autonomy, or may simply be social support for the single parent. Whatever the mechanism, the presence of an additional adult makes the decision-making pattern in single-parent households more similar to that found in two-parent households.

Each form of adolescent deviance in the National Health Examination Survey provides similar results. Whether the measure is running away from home, truancy, needing more discipline in the classroom, contact with the juvenile justice system, or arrests, children of single parents are more likely to commit deviant acts than are children in two-parent households. Within each social class, whether using parental income or parental education as the measure of social status, adolescents in single-parent households are somewhat more likely to violate societal norms. This pattern of differences according to family structure holds for both males and females, although, just as was true for social class, the absolute level of deviance differs from group to group.

Numerous investigators have reported on the relative impact of social class and family structure upon adolescent deviance. This long tradition of research has made it clear that for most forms of deviation, social class affects deviance more than does the presence or absence of a father. Johnstone (1978) argues in his summary of the literature that variation in family patterns affects less serious norm violations more than it does more serious norm violations. For serious acts of delinquency, the research suggests that the economic circumstances of the family are more influential than family structure or functioning. Our finding that family structure does have an impact on adolescent deviance should not be viewed as contradicting views of the relatively greater importance of social class. We have controlled for the social class level of the family and found that family structure makes an additional contribution to adolescent deviance.

Since the presence of additional adults in single-parent households changes the pattern of family decision making, and the pattern of family decision making was related to adolescent deviance, one would expect that the presence of additional adults would reduce the probability of deviant acts. That expectation has been confirmed; additional adults in single-parent households do indeed reduce adolescent deviance.

Our emphasis is on family structure, and that may cause the reader to get a distorted image of the relative impact of family structure and social class. In general, for most social phenomena, the differences among the social classes—whether measured by income or education—are more powerful than differences in family structure. Thus, our reports on the impact of family structure should be viewed as an incremental effect after social class has been taken into account.

But it is also possible that we are underestimating the impact of family structure. As Weitzman has shown in Chapter 10, divorce impoverishes a large proportion of households that are headed by mothers. This family-structure-induced poverty changes life conditions for the mother and for her children. Thus, controlling for income of the family is in fact underestimating to some extent the impact of family structure. We therefore urge the reader to view family income and family structure as jointly contributing to many of the problems of households dependent upon a mother alone. Her lack of income and her lack of help in supervising her children, compared to two-parent households, both produce problems for her and for her children.

Our emphasis on family structure and the quality of monitoring or supervision of the children by the single parent fits into a series of findings in the literature on child development. The Gluecks (1962) emphasize the importance of the mother's supervisory role as compared to the sheer absence of the second parent. Pulkkinen (1982) has shown in Finland that the quality of parental monitoring is the single best predictor of children's conformity or deviance. Our emphasis on the problems of monitoring within single-parent families is consistent with the trend of recent research on parental control of children.

We would like to add that the findings of this section on the impact of single-parent households upon adolescent deviance are not a reflection of the mother's participation in the labor force. Whether or not the mother works outside the home, or whether her labor-force participation is full-time or part-time, has almost no impact on adolescent deviance. This finding is no different than is reported for two-parent households: Maternal employment does not have a major negative or positive impact on the children in the household, despite general beliefs to the contrary (Hayes & Kamerman, 1983).

The size of our representative sample of adolescents in Cycle III of the National Health Examination Survey permitted us to see whether family decision making was the single process that produced the higher rates of adolescent deviance within single-parent families. Controlling for sex, race, family income, and parental education, we found that the too-early autonomy and being in a mother-only household made independent contributions to adolescent deviance. Single parents do tend to give their children autonomy at an early age, but that is not the sole basis for differences in rates of deviance associated with family structure.

Single-Parent Families and the Schools

We will shortly examine the relation of family decision making and other processes upon the educational performance of adolescents. Before turning to analyses of processes, let us examine the relation of family structure to various educational outcomes.

The research on the impact of single-parent households on the cognitive or educational performance of their children is crystal clear on one point: Social class differences are far more important than differences in family structure when the dependent variable is intelligence, school grades, or performance on achievement tests. Those studies that do a poor job of controlling for the influence of social class are the ones that are most likely to see cognitive losses for children of single-parent families (Milne, Meyers, Ellman, & Ginsburg, 1982).

Our own data from the National Health Examination Survey permit comparison of children from single-parent and two-parent households at each social class level for four different cognitive outcomes: an intelligence test, a wide-ranging achievement test, and teacher judgments of both the intellectual ability and achievement level of cach child. As would be expected, on all four measures there are substantial differences among the social classes. Sadly, such differences are expected.

Our results for this national sample were somewhat surprising. After controlling for social class, children in single-parent households were not doing worse on IQ tests or achievement tests; yet they showed a tendency to be rated lower by their teachers on intellectual ability and performance. Further analysis of this surprising difference produced a result consonant with that of the preceding section: The apparent lower ratings from their teachers received by adolescents from single-parent homes were more associated with the level of deviance that we have already discussed than with family structure per se.

Let us restate the argument to this point. Social class is a powerful determinant of school performance. After controlling for social class, family structure has a small additional impact. But it appears that this impact occurs not directly through cognitive difficulties, but rather through the increased deviance associated with single-parent households. It is those students who are less controlled by social norms, and probably show their lack of discipline in the classroom, who are doing less well in school than one would expect. Schools demand conformity, and those students who cannot deliver it are negatively evaluated.

Family Decision Making and High School Grades

We have data on family decision making, using exactly the same measures that were used in the National Health Examination Survey, Cycle III. Our analyses show that, just as for adolescent deviance, giving an adolescent autonomy too early has negative consequences with respect to school work. After controlling for sex, parental education, income, and ethnicity, we found that a high score on the youth alone making decisions, without parental influence, was associated with low high school grades. This finding was repeated within each type of family structure.

As we discussed earlier, single parents are more likely to give early autonomy to their adolescent offspring than are two-parent households. Therefore, since "youth-alone" decision making is associated with low grades (as it was with adolescent deviance), single parents are more frequently employing a style of family decision making that has negative educational consequences. Thus, the lower grades among high school students from single-parent families are partially explained by differences in the style of decision making.

It is probably the lack of social support systems and accompanying time pressures that cause single parents to give too early autonomy to their children. Once again, the results of the economic and social difficulties faced by the single parent suggest that the investment of public resources to assist single parents would prove wise.

Permissive Parenting

Just as we studied too-early autonomy among adolescents, Baumrind & Black (1967) studied a consonant form of parenting, permissive parenting. We found in our sample of high school students and their parents that permissive parenting is more frequent among single parents, and that permissive parenting is associated with low grades. In permissive parenting, parents are tolerant and accepting towards the child's impulses, use as little punishment as possible, make few demands for mature behavior, and allow considerable self-regulation by the child.

The authoritarian style of parenting, on the other hand, had the following characteristics: attempts to shape, control, and evaluate the behavior and attitudes of children in accordance with an absolute set of standards; emphasis on obedience, respect for authority, work, tradition, and the preservation of order; discouragement of verbal give-and-take between parent and child. Baumrind later described the authoritarian pattern, somewhat more formally, as being high in demandingness on the part of the parents and low in parental responsiveness to the child.

Authoritative parenting is the third type described by Baumrind. This pattern contains the following elements: an expectation of mature behavior from the child and clear setting of standards by the parents; firm enforcement of rules and standards, using commands and sanctions when necessary; encouragement of the child's independence and individuality; open communication between parents and children, with encouragement of verbal give-and-take; and recognition of the rights of both parents and children.

The studies of Baumrind and others have focused on preschool children and children in elementary school. Studies of family processes and school achievement beyond childhood are rare. We have extended Baumrind's typology of authoritative, authoritarian, and permissive parenting to a very large and diverse sample of adolescents, using the typology to predict high school grades. In our large-scale questionnaire study of adolescents in high schools, we derived indirect measures of the style of parenting (Dornbusch, Ritter, Leiderman, Roberts, & Fraleigh, 1987).

We found that, for their sons only, single mothers show lower levels of both authoritarian and authoritative parenting when compared to households containing both natural parents, and higher levels of permissive parenting. For their daughters, single mothers do not differ as much from two natural parents in parenting style. Single fathers also show differences in their parenting of the two sexes. They are more permissive and less authoritative for males, and more permissive and less authoritarian for females, when compared to families containing both natural parents. Thus, the general tendency is for single parents, compared to two natural parents, to be higher on permissive parenting and lower on both authoritarian and authoritative parenting.

Within every type of family structure, we found that both authoritarian and permissive parenting styles were negatively associated with grades, and authoritative parenting was positively associated with grades, for both sexes at every age. Single parent families were less often using a style of parenting (authoritarian) that had negative associations with grades and were also less often using a parenting style (authoritative) that had positive associations with grades. These tendencies appear to balance out.

Since permissive parenting is a style associated with lower grades and is more frequent among single parents, the prevalence of this relatively unsuccessful style of parenting among single parents may partially explain the lower grades of children from single-parent households. Such permissiveness as a parenting style is consonant with our findings with respect to family decision making, both permissiveness and early adolescent autonomy in decision making being common among single parents.

Family–School Relations

A series of studies by Joyce Epstein (1984) and her collaborators at Johns Hopkins University has illuminated one aspect of the problems faced by children from single-parent families. She showed that, in the first year of elementary education, children from single-parent households averaged lower grades than children from two-parent households. What makes her work so interesting is that she did not merely report this difference as being due to family structure, but sought ways to reduce the difference by family structure and to show the efficacy of certain teacher initiatives.

Teachers of first-grade children tended to believe that children from single-parent households would do less well in school. One reason, they believed, was the lower probability that single parents would work with their children at home in ways that would improve their school performance. Epstein showed that single parents were just as willing to assist their children in ways that would improve their learning in first grade. More important, teachers who tried to involve parents in helping their children at home found that cooperation was just as great in single-parent households as in two-parent households. Finally, those teachers who sought increased parental assistance, compared to teachers who did not try to develop a partnership with parents, gave grades that reduced markedly the usual discrepancy between children with one parent and children with two parents.

Epstein's work helps us to understand another aspect of single-parent-hood that might be associated with lower grades in school. If single parents are less active in interactions with school personnel, or if they are perceived to be less interested or active, that can have an effect on both the child and the teacher.

We had congruent findings at the high school level (Dornbusch, 1986; Dornbusch et al., 1987). Our first finding is that parental participation in school functions, such as Open School Night, has a substantial positive association with the grades of high school students, even after controlling for the influence of parental education and ethnicity. The meaning of this result is not clear, for one could argue that this is just a good indicator of underlying values. Parents to whom we have reported these results suggest that their participation may help them to understand better the world that their children face in school or, more cynically, that contact with the school and with teachers affects the treatment of the child in such areas as curricular assignment. Schools may feel less free to assign the children of more active parents to unpopular teachers or to nonacademic tracks.

Single parents, subject to numerous pressures on their time, are less likely to engage in school-related activities. Attendance at Open School Night, advisory sessions on college admission requirements, and other school functions are all less frequent activities of single parents compared to families containing both natural parents. Within single-parent families, the association between parental participation in school functions and high school grades is found, a result for the high school that is reminiscent of Epstein's finding for first-grade children. Thus, the lower involvement of single parents in school functions indicates a serious problem for them. It is noteworthy that single parents have less total contact with the school than do two biological parents, with the difference found in every measure of involvement in school.

We do know that most parents care very much about the education of their children, and that includes most parents who don't attend school functions or school activities. The school should be considering ways to enhance the likelihood that single parents would attend school functions. Schools should stress the importance of coming to various school events and activities, urging a little extra effort to attend school occasions that seemingly are unimportant. Special sessions for single parents to deal with their specific problems may be appropriate. Various forms of child care may be needed so that over-burdened single parents can be brought into more active partnership with the school.

Some Helpful Family Processes in Single-Parent Families

We close this discussion of family processes by noting some ways in which the average single parent appears to be more frequently engaged in activities that prove to be positively associated with high school grades, and less frequently engaged in activities associated with low grades.

First, high school students do not see their single parents as uninvolved in their school performance. Although we have noted the lack of active participation of single parents in school activities, their children do not perceive them as uncaring. The perception by children that their parents are uninvolved in their schooling is correlated with low grades, and it is a good sign that single parents are even less likely to be so perceived than are two natural parents. It is, however, less good that single parents are more likely to get upset and upset their children when poor grades are received. Such expressions of negative emotions are associated with lower grades and with a decline in grades.

Second, an emphasis on social conformity by parents is associated with lower grades. Among children from single-parent households, compared to children from two-natural-parent households, such pressure towards conformity is less frequent. Such is the bright side of the general picture we have noted of less monitoring and more autonomy for children in single-parent households.

Finally, we found that encouragement, praise, and offers to help by the parents were the one group of parental reactions to grades that were associated with high grades. Indeed, these positive responses were also associated with an improvement in grades over a two-year span. Single parents, compared with two-natural-parents, were more likely to engage in these helpful responses. The only failure of this low-key approach comes when student grades are low to begin with. For really poor performance, no parental response seems to be effective. Here is a place where school efforts should be joined with parental efforts.

We can conclude by noting that school–parent cooperation is typically lower for single-parent families. It seems appropriate, though difficult, for schools to urge a higher level of school-related activity for parents of students who are doing poorly in the first years of high school. A single teacher, counselor, or administrator, working with the caring single parent, may help to stop or reverse the pattern of low grades. Here, as in other arenas, single parents care and are trying. They need guidance as to where to invest their limited resources of time and energy, and they need social support and a sense of partnership.

RECOMMENDATIONS

Our first recommendation to policy makers is that they not consider the employment of single mothers as a social problem. Female employment is not going to recede, and the economic needs of single mothers dictate their entrance into the labor force. Policymakers therefore should be considering alternative forms of assistance to working single mothers. Day care, for example, is a necessity if single mothers are not to be forced on welfare and then condemned for being on the dole. The poverty of female-headed families may represent a symptom of gender inequality in the labor market, but that inequality is hard to address directly. Financial assistance to single mothers and to the children who are dependent upon them must not force the working poor to stay at home. Rather, supplemental payments should be designed to make labor-force participation a feasible choice for mother and child.

Single fathers typically have a different set of problems. First, they need social support in childrearing as well as in household duties. Despite an increasingly egalitarian ideology in America, most men are inexperienced in household and childrearing tasks. For the long term, special homemaking courses for men within high school and junior colleges might address this gender difference in household skills. Second, single fathers do experience a decline in income because of the loss of the mother's hidden contribution. Their economic needs, though not as serious as those of single mothers, could be markedly assisted through the provision of day care and cash grants for working fathers.

Both single mothers and single fathers are, according to our empirical data on adolescent deviance and school performance in high school, typically engaging in behaviors that are not helpful for their children. Although it is easy to understand why an overburdened single parent would allow early autonomy for a child, our data indicate that single parents are injuring the child through permissive parenting and the too-early granting of sole responsibility for decision making. It will not be easy to inform single parents of these problems or of appropriate ways of dealing with them. It does seem reasonable to expect that schools, faced with a relatively low rate of single-parent participation in school activities, might undertake special programs to attract their attendance. Such programs might well focus on the problems that single parents have in common, and thus might improve family–school relations for this less involved set of parents.

The plight of teenage parents is increasingly recognized by public and private agencies. Young mothers, in particular, should be encouraged to continue their education and to enter into the labor force. In addition to the restructuring of AFDC so as not to penalize women who work outside the home, there is a need for job-oriented training. Finally, the health risks for the children of teenage parents can be reduced through not only making prenatal care available, but financially rewarding teenage mothers who take advantage of it. Such a reward system would be cost-effective (Bernfield, Personal Communications, 1986).

For single parents in particular, as well as for many parents in two-parent households, greater flexibility in the occupational world would reduce some of the burden of parenthood. Working outside the home increases the happiness of most women over the long term. A greater number of part-time positions may be an appropriate response to the smaller cohorts of working-age adults, attracting single-parents into the labor force at an earlier age. Such occupational flexibility must be matched by improved provision of support services for single parents, from day care to provisions for family emergencies. These and other recommendations will be discussed in greater detail in Chapter 14.

REFERENCES

Baldwin, W. (1983–1984). Adolescent fertility—facts, fads and fallacies. *Impact* '83–84. Syracuse University Institute for Family Research and Education. Syracuse, N.Y.

Baumrind, D., & Black, A. E. (1967) Socialization practices associated with dimensions of competence in preschool boys and girls. *Child Development, 38*, 291–327.

Bernfield, M. (1986, July). Personal communication.

Brandwein, R. A., Brown, C. A., & Fox, C. M. (1974). Women and children last: The social situation of divorced mothers and their families. *Journal of Marriage and the Family, 36*(3), 498–514.

Card, J. J., & Wise, L. L. (1978). Teenage mothers and teenage fathers: The impact of early childbearing on the parents' personal and professional lives. *Family Planning Perspectives, 10*(4), 199–205.

Congressional Budget Office. (1984). *Poverty Among Children* (Tech. Rep.). Senate Subcommittee on Education, Arts, and Humanities.

Corcoran, M., Duncan, G. J., & Hill, M. S. (1984). The economic fortunes of women and children: Lessons from the panel study of income dynamics. *Signs: Journal of Women in Culture and Society, 10*(2), 232–248.

Dornbusch, S. M. (1986, Summer). Helping your kid make the grade. *The Stanford Magazine,* 47–51.

Dornbusch, S. M., Carlsmith, J. M., Bushwall, S. J., Gross, R. T., Ritter, P. L., & Fraleigh, M. J. (1983, April). *Social class, race and sex differences in family influence upon adolescent decision making.* Paper presented at the meeting of the Pacific Sociological Association, San Jose, CA.

Dornbusch, S. M., Carlsmith, J. M., Bushwall, S. J., Ritter, P. L., Leiderman, H., Hastorf, A. H., & Gross, Ruth T. (1985, April). Single parents, extended households, and the control of adolescents. *Child Development, 56*, 326–341.

Dornbusch, S. M., Ritter, P. L., Leiderman, P. H., Roberts, D. F., & Fraleigh, M. J. (1987). The relation of parenting style to adolescent school performance. *Child Development*, *58*, 1244–1257.

Dryfoos, J. G. (1984). A new strategy for preventing unintended teenage childbearing, *Family Planning Perspectives*, *16*(4), 193–195.

Duncan, G. J. (1984). *Years of poverty years of plenty: The changing economic fortunes of American workers and families.* Ann Arbor, MI: Institute for Social Research, The University of Michigan.

Epstein, J. L. (1984). *Single parents and the schools: The effect of marital status on parent and teacher evaluations* (Report #353). The Center for Social Organizations of Schools, The John Hopkins University.

Ferri, E. (1976). *Growing up in a one-parent family: A long-term study of child development.* London: NFER Publishing Company Ltd.

Ford Foundation. (1984, October). *Ford Foundation Letter*, *15*(5), 1–2.

Fuchs, V. R. (1986). *The Feminization of Poverty Working Paper Series* (No. 1934). Cambridge, MA: National Bureau of Economic Research, Inc.

Furstenberg, F. F., Jr. (1976). *Unplanned parenthood: The social consequences of teenage childbearing.* New York: The Free Press.

George, V., & Wilding, P. (1872). *Motherless families.* London: Routledge & Kegan Paul.

Glick, P. C. (1979). Children of divorced parents in demographic perspective. *Journal of Social Issues*, *35*, 170–181.

Glueck, S., & Glueck, E. (1962). *Family environment and delinquency.* Boston, MA: Houghton Mifflin Company.

Hacker, A. (1982, August 12). The lower depths. *New York Review of Books*, 15–19.

Hardy, J., Welcher, D., Stanley, J., Wessel, K., Dallas, J., & Blaustein, R. (1978). *Socialization of the urban child.* Final Report to the Office of Child Development.

Hardy, J. B. (1982). Adolescents as parents: Possible long-range implications. In T. J. Coates, A. C. Petersen, & C. Perry (Eds.), *Promoting adolescent health: A dialog on research and practice.* New York: Academic Press, Inc.

Hayes, C. D., & Kamerman, S. B. (Eds.). (1983). *Children of working parents: Experiences and outcomes.* Washington, DC: National Academy Press.

Hetherington, E. M., Cox, M., & Cox, R. (1982). Effects of divorce on parents and children. In M. E. Lamb (Eds.), *Nontraditional families.* Hillsdale, NJ: Lawrence Erlbaum Associates. 233–288.

Hogan, D. P. (1982). *Teenage fertility among American Blacks: A life course perspective.* Paper delivered to the Department of Sociology, Stanford University.

Johnson, B. L. (1979). *Single-parent families: Outlook 80.* Bureau of Labor Statistics. Paper Presented at the National Agricultural Outlook Conference, Session #18, November 7, Office of Current Employment Analysis Bureau of Labor Statistics.

Johnstone, J. W. C. (1978). Juvenile delinquency and the family: A contextual interpretation. *Youth and Society*, *9*(3), 299–313.

Kamerman, S. D., & Hayes, C. D. (Eds.). (1982). *Families that work: Children in a changing world.* Washington, D.C.: National Academy Press.

Kamerman, S. B. (1984). Women, children, and poverty: Public policies and female-headed families in industrialized countries. *Signs: Journal of Women in Culture and Society*, *10*(2), 249–271.

Kaus, M. (1986, July 7). The work ethic state. *The New Republic*, 22–33.

Keshet, H. F., & Rosenthal, K. M. (1978). Single parent fathers: A new study. *Children Today*, *7*(3), 13–17.

Levitan, S. A., & Belous, R. S. (1981). *What's happening to the American family?.* Baltimore, MD: Johns Hopkins University Press.

McAdoo, H. P. (1978). Factors related to stability in upwardly mobile black families. *Journal of Marriage and the Family*, *40*(4), 761–776.

Milk for babies. *The New Republic* (1985, September 2, pp. 5–6).

Milne, A., Meyers, D. E., Ellman, F., & Ginsburg, A. (1982). *Single parents, working mothers, and the educational achievement of school age children.* Unpublished paper.

Norton, A. J., & Glick, P. C. (1986). One parent families: A social and economic profile. In *The single parent family: Special issue of Family Relations.* The National Council on Family Relations.

Orthner, D. K., Brown, T., & Ferguson, D. (1976). Single-parent fatherhood: An emerging family life style. *The Family Coordinator*, *25*(4), 429–437.

Pulkkinen, L. (1982). Self-control and continuity from childhood to adolescence. In P. B. Baltes and O. G. Brim (Eds.), *Life-span development and behavior.* New York: Academic Press.

Schlesinger, B. (1978, May–June). Single parent fathers; A research review. *Children Today*, 12, 18–39.

Stannard, D. (1979). Changes in the American family: Fiction and reality. In V. Tufte & B. Myerhoff (Eds.), *Changing images of the family.* New Haven: Yale University Press.

U.S. Bureau of the Census. (1985, March). *Marital status and living arrangements* (Current Population Reports, Series P-20, No. 399). Washington, DC: U.S. Government Printing Office.

U.S. Commission on Civil Rights. (1983). *A growing crisis: Disadvantaged women and their children.* Washington, DC: U.S. Government Printing Office.

U.S. Department of Health and Human Services. (1986, July 18). Advance report of final natality statistics, 1984. *Monthly Vital Statistics Report*, *35*(4). Supplement.

Wealth in black and white. (1986, July 24). *New York Times*

Yankelovich, Skelly, & White, Inc. (1979). *Family health in an era of stress.* The General Mills American Family Report: 1978–1979.

Zelnik, M., & Kantner, J. (1980). Sexual activity, contraceptive use and pregnancy among metropolitan teenagers 1971–1979. *Family Planning Perspectives*, *12*, 230.

13

Exploring Stepfamilies from a Feminist Perspective

MARGARET CROSBIE-BURNETT, ADA SKYLES,
AND JANE BECKER-HAVEN

INTRODUCTION

When a single parent remarries, Americans feel reassured because we perceive the new couple to have "reconstituted" a traditional nuclear family. Use of the word "reconstitution" assumes that the single-parent family is a deficient family form, and that the remarriage has recreated the "true" family. This terminology reflects the lack of recognition that single-parent families are viable families, not just temporary, stop-gap arrangements, and that stepfamilies are different from two-biological-parent families, which are also referred to as intact or nuclear families. Our society is particularly uninformed about the structural and psychological differences between the two forms of two-parent families.

This chapter is organized as follows: The first section reports statistics on the prevalence of stepfamilies, delineates psychological and social issues that are unique to stepfamilies, compares children in stepfamilies to children in other family structures, and discusses whether remarrige and the formation of stepfamilies serve feminist interests and/or children's interests. The second section explains why existing family policy is not appropriate for stepfamilies, since it is based on our society's nuclear family ideology. Finally, suggestions for reforms in educational, social, and legal policy are made.

Definitions are in order. In this chapter a "nuclear" or "intact" family denotes a household consisting of a mother, a father, and their biological children. A "stepfamily" denotes a household in which there is a stepparent–stepchild relationship. Although stepfamilies are formed when never-married parents marry for the first time, when a widow or widower remarries, and when homosexual or heterosexual parents cohabit, at present most

Margaret Crosbie-Burnett, Ph.D. Department of Counseling Psychology and Counselor Education, University of Wisconsin, Madison, Wisconsin.

Ada Skyles, Ph.D. Office of Child Support, Wisconsin Department of Health and Social Services, Madison, Wisconsin.

Jane Becker-Haven, Ph.D. Palo Alto, California.

stepfamilies are formed by remarriage after divorce. This paper mainly addresses the latter group, but many of the issues are relevant for the less common forms of stepfamilies. "Full-time stepfamily" designates the custodial household, in which the children reside and the biological parent has remarried. "Part-time stepfamily" designates the noncustodial household, in which the children "visit" and the biological parent has remarried. "Single-parent family" denotes the custodial household, in which the children reside and the biological parent has not remarried. In this paper the terms "custodial" and "noncustodial" refer to physical custody—the place of children's residence for the majority of the time. Although increasing numbers of parents share major decision-making power through joint legal custody, most children still reside primarily with one biological parent and visit the other. The few situations where children truly split their time between the two households of their biological parents are referred to as "half-time stepfamilies".

Our notion of extended family should be revised to reflect more accurately the new patterns of family relationships that result from contemporary changes in marriage patterns. The term "extended stepfamily network" is used to denote a group of households that are connected to one another through biology or marriage; it is a combination of the traditional extended family of grandparents, aunts, uncles, cousins, and so on, and the modern extended family that is formed by the divorce of individuals who share biological children and the remarriage of divorced parents. For example, one's exspouse is part of one's modern extended family if there are children that the exspouses continue to coparent. Further, one's ex-in-laws are part of one's modern extended family, because they will always remain the children's biological grandparents regardless of the legal marital status of the children's parents.

THE PSYCHOLOGY AND SOCIOLOGY OF STEPFAMILIES

Prevalence of Stepfamilies

A better understanding of stepfamily functioning is vital, since stepfamilies are not the small esoteric population many people believe them to be. The stepfamily is an emerging family form in America and its prevalence is increasing. Three fourths of all previously married women and five sixths of all previously married men remarry; half do so within the first 3 years of divorce or widowhood (Cherlin, 1981). In 1970 30% of marriages were remarriages for at least one of the partners; in 1980 this figure was 42% (Furstenburg, 1980). Nearly 90% of the remarrying brides and grooms have been divorced or had their marriage annulled; the rest are widowed (Glick, 1980). In one fifth of the households maintained by a married couple in 1980, one or both of the spouses had been divorced. This means that 2.3 million households contain at least one stepparent–stepchild relationship at any one point in time (Cherlin & McCarthy, 1985).

There are complex relationships between rate of remarriage and sex, income, age, and presence or absence of children. Men with higher incomes are *more* likely to remarry than men with lower incomes, and remarrying men are choosing women who are, on average, 6 years younger than themselves (Glick, 1980). The picture is very different for women. Women remarry less quickly than men and factors that suggest economic independence (higher education and income) are associated with lower rates of remarriage (Ambert, 1983; Glick & Lin, 1986). Even among low-income divorced women, the remarriage rate is reported to be three times greater for non-AFDC recipients, who are presumably less independent economically, than for AFDC recipients (Bahr, 1979). A variety of other studies have identified some consistent factors that are associated with high rates of remarriage for women: youth, low levels of education, unemployment or low paying employment, few children, young children, rurality, and good health (Bumpass & Rindfuss, 1979; Glick, 1980; Glick & Lin, 1986; Gurak & Dean, 1979; Mott & Moore, 1983; Teachman & Heckert, 1985). One exception to the relationship between presence of children and rate of remarriage has been found by Koo & Suchindran (1980): Among women who divorce at 35 and older, the presence of children is associated with a higher rate of remarriage.

As discussed by Weitzman (Chapter 9), Dornbusch & Gray (Chapter 12) and Bachrach (1983), mother-only families are associated with poverty to a much greater degree than father-only or two-parent families. This poverty may propel the single mother to escape her plight via remarriage, since economic well-being improves with remarriage, especially for white women (Buehler, Hogan, Robinson, & Levy, 1986). This does appear to be the case, especially for economically dependent women with young children. Therefore, many women are entering remarriage from an impoverished one-down position (Goldner, 1985). This may account for the higher rates of spouse abuse in remarried families than in nuclear families (Kalmuss & Seltzer, 1986) and for the lower levels of marital happiness and satisfaction reported by remarried women when compared with remarried men (Glenn, 1981; Glenn & Weaver, 1977; Ishii-Kuntz, 1986; Renne, 1971; White, 1979) and first-married women (Glenn, 1981).

A substantial portion of our nation's children are affected by remarriage. Sixty percent of all remarrying partners have custody of one or more minor children, thereby creating full-time stepfamilies; another 20% are noncustodial parents, forming part-time stepfamilies (Glick, 1980). To indicate the magnitude of these numbers, 900,000 minor children became members of full-time stepfamilies and another 300,000 minor children became visiting members of part-time stepfamilies in 1980 alone. Each year more than half a million new full-time stepfamilies are formed. Ten million children, or 13% of all minor children, are stepchildren (Glick, 1985; Weingarten, 1980). If we include children born into stepfamilies, there are 15 million minor children living in stepfamilies. Another 3.4 million, 18- to 22-year-olds, are transient inhabitants of stepfamilies (Roosevelt & Lofas, 1976).

If the present divorce and remarriage rates continue through the 1980s and 1990s, 25% of all American children will become stepchildren; similary, 25% of all American adults will become stepparents (Cherlin, 1981). Some researchers have gone so far as to claim that Americans have a probability of one in two that they will participate in a stepfamily either in their childhood families or in their adult families (Furstenberg, 1980). These figures do not include individuals who will have experience with stepfamilies by indirect participation through extended family or by direct participation in de facto stepfamilies formed by the rising number of previously married individuals who live with a partner to whom they are not legally married (Furstenburg, 1979).

The prevalence of stepfamilies, as reflected in the above statistics, justifies public and expert attention to this poorly understood family form. The need to understand stepfamilies is even more compelling because remarrying parents and their new partners report that being unprepared for stepfamily issues is their foremost problem (Schlesinger, 1978). What are these potential issues that are inherent in the stepfamily structure? The issues discussed below are organized into issues stemming from membership in a previous intact family, issues stemming from the single-parent period, and issues related to the formation and functioning of the new stepfamily.

Psychological and Social Issues Unique to Stepfamilies

Issues Related to the Previous Family

Unresolved mourning of the loss of the previous family frequently results in children's withdrawing from or being hostile to a new stepparent. Children often hold onto hopes of reuniting their biological parents, even after one or both have remarried. Further complicating this situation is the children's dilemma over loyalty to both biological parents (Lutz, 1983; Wallerstein & Kelly, 1980). Many children fear that acceptance of a stepparent means disloyalty to the same sex biological parent, probably because our culture's model of family, the nuclear family, has only one parent of each sex. Clinicians and researchers commonly report that jealousies among the adults exacerbate this problem (Turnbull & Turnbull, 1983), making it difficult for children to enjoy relationships with all the parents (Crosbie-Burnett, 1984a) and negatively affecting children's well-being (Crosbie-Burnett, 1984b; Wallerstein & Kelly, 1980). This jealousy impeded coparenting by the divorced biological parents (Ahrons, 1981).

Links to the previous marriage may create problems for the adults as well, especially with respect to coparenting and financial issues (Messinger, 1976). There is growing evidence that continuing coparenting relationships with exspouses can stress the remarried couple's relationship. Marital quality was found to be lower in mother–stepfather families where the stepfather coparented children from a prior marriage with an exspouse than in stepfamilies where the stepfather had no children from a prior marriage (Clingempeel, 1981; Clingempeel & Brand, 1985). Giles-Sims (1984) found that the quality of contact with exspouses may be more important than the number of exspouses, positive contact being associated with cohesion, expressiveness, and lack of conflict in the stepfamily, and negative contact having the opposite characteristics. Unresolved emotions from first marriages, especially jealousy or hostility toward one's own or spouse's first mate, inhibits successful remarriage. Accepting children's loyalties to noncustodial parents, accepting a spouse's continued coparenting relationship with an exspouse, and resolving other problems raised by previous marriages appears to facilitate a happy remarriage (Schlesinger, 1978).

Other problems revolving around previous families are imposed on the stepfamily household by prior spouses. Clinicians report that the remarriage is often experienced as threatening to exspouses, who frequently attempt to cope with this perceived threat by creating new conflict and/or new court battles with respect to child support, family support, custody, or visitation.

Issues Related to the Transition from Single-Parent Family to Stepfamily

While a single parent may welcome a new partner who may help with the financial burden and the parenting, there is some evidence that children may not share this enthusiasm. Children of previously single parents may fear that their parent's attachment to a new spouse means the loss of time, attention, and nurturance from the custodial parent (Wallerstein & Kelly, 1980). This fear is often based on reality, especially during the courting period. Consequently, rather than welcoming the stepparent, children often resent his or her presence in the previously single-parent family.

The oldest child in a single-parent family is often the most resistant because he or she has the most power, status, and authority to lose in a remarriage, being demoted to "child" status again after being second in command in many cases the single parent's confidant. While this can be a relief for some children and adolescents, many resent the change. The previously single parent (most often a woman) may also resist sharing the unilateral control she had over her family; at the other extreme, she may expect her new spouse to take total control over a chaotic family situation. This reallocation of leadership from the oldest child–single parent liaison to the couple is reported by clinicians and researchers alike to be one of the most stressful transitions for new stepfamilies (Ihinger-Tallman & Pasley, 1981; Keshet, 1980; Ransom, Schlesinger, & Derdeyn, 1979; Visher & Visher, 1979).

Issues Related to the Integration of the Stepfamily

New stepfamilies frequently have unrealistic expectations. Very often they expect to instantly *recreate* a loving and cohesive nuclear family (Mead, 1970; Visher & Visher, 1979), instead of expecting a 2-year or more adjustment period, with the goal of creating a healthy stepfamily. Stepfamilies are quite different from intact families *structurally*, due to the coparenting connection between households of exspouses, and *psychologically*, due to relationships between stepfamily members being quite different from those in a nuclear family:

1. The stepparent and stepchild begin their relationship when the child is partly grown.

2. The stepparent is a newcomer to an ongoing family group.

3. Stepparents and stepchildren often have primary bonds to children and parents, respectively, outside of the household.

4. There is no role definition for the relationship between a stepparent and stepchild when both of the child's biological parents are coparenting (Giles-Sims, 1984).

5. There are less clear incest taboos for relationships between stepparents and stepchildren and between stepsiblings.

For all of these reasons, unrealistic and unfulfilled expectations (based on the desire to recreate a nuclear family) about one's own and others' behavior in the family often create disappointment, guilt, and hostility.

The newly married couple faces other problems as well. In addition to intermittent conflict with exspouses over money, the everyday financial arrangements in stepfamilies are not only complex, but fraught with emotional connotations. Finances are consistently reported by remarrieds to be a major problem (Albrecht, 1979; Ihinger-Tallman & Pasley, 1981; Schlesinger, 1978). Child support and alimony payments may flow in and out of the household; differences in affluence are blatantly visible. Because certain monies are earmarked for individuals inside and/or outside the stepfamily, jealousies are compounded. There is always the question of how much stepparents should support their stepchildren, for whom they are not legally responsible (Kargman, 1983). Preliminary evidence suggests that about 50% of the financial support of adolescent stepchildren comes from the stepfather in upper-middle-class homes (Crosbie-Burnett, 1984a).

Remarried adults report that stepchildren (especially the disciplining of them), money, and prior families are the major sources of stress and conflict in stepfamilies (Albrecht, 1979; Duberman, 1975; Messinger & Walker, 1981; Visher & Visher, 1979). Adolescents share adults' perceptions; they also report that divided loyalties between prior and present families and discipline are the major sources of stress for adolescents in stepfamilies (Lutz, 1983). The impact of stepchildren in the remarried household can be potent enough to outweigh the remarried spousal bond in predicting stepfamily happiness (White & Booth, 1985). Among middle and upper-middle-class families with adolescents, the quality of the stepfather–stepchild relationship was shown to be more closely related to family happiness than was the quality of the marital relationship (Crosbie-Burnett, 1984b). Furthermore, multiple sources of evidence suggest that friendship between stepparent and stepchild is a prerequisite to the child's acceptance of discipline from that stepparent (Schlesinger, 1978; Stern, 1978; Wallerstein & Kelly, 1980). Yet, even when stepfathers are apparently integrated into the stepfamily, they and their stepchildren still perceive themselves and each other more negatively than children and their biological fathers. However, stepchildren report "getting along with" stepfathers as frequently as children report "getting along with" biological fathers (Perkins & Kahan, 1979). To complicate the situation further, many stepparents feel guilt for not fully parenting their noncustodial biological children, and this can affect the quality of stepparenting.

There do appear to be age and gender (perhaps gender-role) differences in stepparent–stepchild relationships. Demographic predictors of the quality of intrafamilial step relationships in "stable" stepfamilies suggest that stepfathers generally enjoy better relations with their stepchildren than do stepmothers. Younger stepmothers fare better, as do younger stepchildren (Duberman, 1975); analogous date for stepfathers show mixed results (Crosbie-Burnet, 1984a; Duberman, 1975; Wallerstein & Kelly, 1980).

Stepmothering appears to be substantially more difficult than mothering. Both full-time and part-time stepmothers have been found to be more anxious, depressed, and angry than biological mothers (Nadler, 1976) and to have more feelings of ambivalence and jealousy toward stepchildren than biological mothers have toward children (Sardanis-Zimmerman, 1977). Societal factors provide other clues to understanding these findings. Until recently, most biological fathers who had custody of children were divorced from mothers who were "unfit." Perhaps stepmothers are entering families that have experienced a more traumatic history than have stepfather families. Recent studies suggest that involvement in the parenting role may be a factor. Stepmothers who report high participation in parenting report better marital adjustment than stepmothers with low participation in parenting (Skyles, 1983) and residential stepmothers report a more positive stepparenting experience than do nonresidential stepmothers (Ambert, 1986).

Gender differences are emerging for stepchildren also. Parenthetically, it is important to remember that most stepfamilies are stepfather families. Parental remarriage is more problematic for girls than for boys (Hetherington, Cox, & Cox, 1985). Remarried mothers of adolescents reported more psychosocial problems for their daughters than their sons (Crosbie-Burnett, in press-a). Stepdaughters report having more stress than stepsons (Lutz, 1983) and stepdaughters have more difficult relationships with stepparents, and especially stepmothers, than stepsons (Clingempeel, Ievoli, & Brand,

1984; Clingempeel & Segal, 1986; Peterson & Zill, 1986). More research is needed to explore stepdaughters' experiences in stepfamilies, but clinicians frequently report stepmother–stepdaughter difficulties based on the step-daughter's displacement as woman of the house and "Daddy's girl." Expla-nation for difficulties in the stepfather–stepdaughter relationship is more inferential, but sexuality issues accompanied with the lack of the incest taboo have been suggested.

Many stepchildren also have to cope with the sudden introduction of stepsiblings into their lives. This may create stresses like sudden changes in ordinal position, abrupt changes in family size, additional loyalty issues, sexual issues, and competition for time, space, and relationships (Rosenberg & Hajal, 1985). Relationships between stepsiblings are reportedly better when the stepsiblings live in the same house, when they share a half sibling, and when they are younger (Ambert, 1986; Duberman, 1975).

Numerous other factors that relate to successful stepfamily integration have been identified. In a pioneering study by Bernard (1971), many of these factors were reported. Being older at first marriage and waiting 6 or more years before remarrying after divorce were associated with successful remar-riage. Shared custody for women and no custody for men were related to less marital success. Positive attitudes toward the remarriage by children, exspouses, grandparents, and community members were associated with success. More recently, Ihinger-Tallman and Pasley (1983) reported results consistent with the Bernard study; frequent contact with friends, relatives, and organizations (indicators of social support) were found to be more common in successful remarriages. Intrafamilial factors include similar perceptions of family life by family members (Crosbie-Burnett, 1984a; Ihin-ger-Tallman & Pasley, 1981; Pasley & Ihinger-Tallman, 1984; Perkins & Kahan, 1979), role clarity for the stepparent (Crosbie-Burnett, in press-b), and a respect for emotional ties between children and non-custodial parents (Crosbie-Burnett, 1984a).

Stepfamilies in Distress

When stepfamilies seek counsel from sources outside their family, they encounter some of their most basic problems—no cultural norms for step-family functioning, few visible successful role models, and counselors and therapists who are not only unaware of the unique issues and problems of stepfamilies, but share the culture's negative biases toward members of stepfamilies (Bryan, Ganong, Coleman, & Bryan, 1985). Moreover, those families in states where joint custody is presumed in the divorce proceedings discover that they are participants in a social experiment, the outcome of which is unknown. To quote Visher and Visher (1979), stepfamilies feel that "the rules of the game are not available, but the game is already underway."

This lack of institutionalization of the stepfamily is evident when one examines the law, the language, and the lack of norms (Cherlin, 1978). For

example, there is no word in English for the relationship between a biological mother and a stepmother (or between a biological father and a stepfather), even though they may be cooperatively parenting common children.
A culture that has no word to denote a relationship certainly has no norms
for that relationship (Goetting, 1980). Lack of institutionalization and the
many situational stresses common to stepfamily life are believed to be
responsible for the greater risk of separation and divorce for remarrieds,
despite their older age and higher motivation to make the marriage work
(Bernard, 1971; Duberman, 1975). Others argue that people who have
experienced divorce once may be less committed to an unhappy remarriage
than first marrieds (Furstenberg & Spanier, 1984) or that some people are
simply more "divorce-prone" (Duberman, 1975).

Although the reasons are unclear at present, the redivorce rates are
higher than the divorce rates for first marriages. Compared to a divorce rate
for first marriages of 49%, the redivorce rate is 54% for women and 61% for
men (Glick, 1983). This difference between divorce and redivorce rates is
independent of various socioeconomic variables: husband's educational
level (Bumpass & Sweet, 1972), husband's earnings (Becker, Landes, &
Michael, 1977), and husband's and wife's total earnings, employment status,
and savings (Cherlin, 1977).

When we examine the influence of children on the divorce rate for
remarrieds, we find some clues for locating the causes of this higher divorce
rate. Remarriages involving children from either or both previous marriages
are at the highest risk for divorce (Cherlin, 1977; White & Booth, 1985).
However, even when children from previous marriages exist, the remarriages with the lowest risk of divorce are those that have produced at
least one "ours" child—that is, one or more children born into the second
marriage (Becker, Landes, & Michael, 1976; Bernard, 1971). Those remarrieds with no children from any previous marriages have an inter-
mediate divorce rate. These data suggest that we probably should not
dismiss the higher divorce rate for remarrieds by simply postulating a
psychological attribute of "divorce proneness." Divorce rates suggest that
the divisive stresses associated with the existence of children from previous marriages contribute to marital distress; it also appears that the
birth of a child in the remarriage functions to hold the family together.
However, these additional children do not appear to contribute to the
couples' satisfaction (Pasley & Ihinger-Tallman, 1982). Furthermore, evidence suggests that stepfamilies with one adolescent from a previous
marriage and one or more "ours" children may be the least happy stepfamilies (Crosbie-Burnett, 1984a). It appears that remarrieds with "ours"
children may be staying together because of the *presence* of the children
born into the remarriage, not because they are happier than other remarrieds.

Outcomes for Children from Various Family Structures

Despite the problems discussed above, many remarriages endure. How do children in stepfamilies fare in comparison with children from other types of families? Earlier studies have reported that children from stepfather families have achieved academically about as well as those from intact families and better than those from single-parent families (Bohannan & Erikson, 1978; Chapman, 1977). However, children from stepmother families have been reported to have more school behavior problems than children from intact families (Touliotos & Lindholm, 1980). Using a representative national sample, a recent study by Dornbusch, Ritter, & Fraleigh (1987) has revealed that adolescents in stepfamilies earned lower grades than adolescents in nuclear families, but higher grades than those in single-parent households. These results may be explained by additional findings that stepparents were less active than biological parents in school affairs and in decision making related to the adolescents. Interestingly, there was no disposition on the part of the adolescents to want the stepparents to participate more in school activities.

With respect to psychosocial adjustment, research results are mixed. While nearly all studies report that the best adjusted children tend to reside in intact families (Garbarino, Sebes, & Schellenbach, 1984; Halperin & Smith, 1983; Parish, 1982), some studies have reported children from stepfather families to be better adjusted than children from single-parent families (Oshman & Manosevitz, 1976; Parish & Taylor, 1979; Parish & Dostal, 1980), and other studies report no difference between children from stepfather and single-parent families (Kellam, Ensminger, & Turner, 1977; Nunn, Parish, & Worthing, 1983; Wilson, Zurcher, McAdams, & Curtis, 1975). When comparisons are made between intact families and stepfather families, it is generally agreed that stepfathers tend to mitigate the negative effects of loss of the biological father in the home (Bachrach, 1983; Bohannan & Yahreas, 1979; Chapman, 1977; Parish & Taylor, 1979). Recent research has suggested that the quality of family life may be as important as family structure in predicting children's adjustment (Dornbusch, Carlsmith, Bushwall, Ritter, Leiderman, Hastorf, & Gross, 1985; Parish & Parish, 1983; Santrock, Warshak, Lindbergh, & Meadows, 1982). There is growing evidence that the presence of a second adult in single-parent families is the crucial factor in children's adjustment, and that the child's (particularly a male adolescent) adjustment may be better if that second adult is an extended family member rather than a stepparent (Dornbusch & Gray, Chapter 12; Dornbursh et al., 1985; Kellam, Ensminger, & Turner, 1977). It is important to note that income is confounded with family structure in most of the above studies; that is, single-parent households have much lower incomes than intact and stepparent households. The above findings of poor adjustment of children in single-parent homes could be accounted for by lower socioeconomic status, and the mitigating effect of stepfathers could be mainly a rise in family income and the concommitant benefits. However, Dornbusch *et al.*'s (1985) findings, controlling for socioeconomic status, suggest that adult supervision may also be a key factor.

With respect to gender differences, girls have been observed to be more anxious in stepfather families than in intact families and less warm than boys toward stepfathers (Santrock *et al.*, 1982). The emotional distance and anxiety that girls express toward stepfathers could stem from discomfort related to sexuality.

Both social scientists and practitioners have long been concerned about stepfamilies' vulnerability to physical and sexual abuse of children, because both the bonding which usually occurs between biological parents and children, and the incest taboos, are lacking between the stepparents and stepchildren (Mead, 1970; Wilson, Daly, and Weghorst, 1980). While accurate statistics are unavailable, the evidence suggests that children in stepfamilies experience a disproportionately high occurrence of abuse and neglect when compared with children in intact families (Husain & Chapel, 1983; Lightcap, Kurland, & Burgess, 1982; Russell, 1984; Wilson, Daly, & Weghorst, 1980). Other researchers warn that available data are not controlled for social class and other demographic factors, which are related to child abuse and neglect, and that therefore conclusions about the relationship of family structure to abuse and neglect cannot be made (Giles-Sims & Finkelhor, 1984).

Feminist Interests and Children's Interests

Does remarriage serve feminist interests? Does it serve children's interests? It depends.

For remarrying women and men, it depends upon whether the marriage is egalitarian or traditional. If the marriage is egalitarian, the custodial parent gains a helpmate with whom to share housework, child care, and financial responsibility; the stepparent gains the responsibilities and joys of family life. If the marriage is traditional, the wife may gain financial security (particularly if she is white) and, if she is a custodial mother, some help with children, especially the disciplining of them. However, she will lose the power she had as head of the single-parent household, and will have more household labor to do in caring for her new spouse and any of his biological children who visit or live with him. The traditional husband increases his financial responsibility and gains a homemaker; if he has children from a prior marriage, remarriage may decrease his emotional responsibility to his children and the labor associated with child care. Alternatively, he may feel more stress if he is functioning as "the father" for two sets of children, his noncustodial biological children and his stepchildren. Many remarriages produce additional children born to the new couple, adding to the shared financial and household burden of men and women in egalitarian marriages and to the financial burden of men and the household burden of women in traditional marriages. For women, the larger one's household responsibilities, the harder it is to compete in the labor force. Traditional relationships in remarriages as well as first marriages thwart the feminist goal of equality between men and women in the home and in the labor force. However, remarriage nearly always means a rise in standard of living for traditional women and their children and for egalitarian women and men and their children.

Of course, most remarriages fall somewhere between strictly traditional and completely egalitarian. Most remarriages are also dual-earner marriages. This means that most wives in stepfamilies have the stress of maintaining employment outside the home and being the person in their families mainly responsible for the complicated and emotionally difficult home life of stepfamily living. Does this situation serve women's interests? The results suggest it does not. While some studies report no difference between the happiness of men and women in remarriages (Albrecht, 1979; DeMaris, 1984), other studies have found women to be less happy than men in remarriages (Bernard, 1980; Glenn & Weaver, 1977; Skyles, 1983; White, 1979). In addition, women in second marriages have reported being less happy than women in first marriages (White, 1979). These findings are even more understandable in light of the poor marriage market for remarrying women. As noted above, remarrying men are choosing younger women. Due to this factor and the fact that men's life expectancy is less than women's, women who wish to remarry must choose from a dwindling population of men.

Men are not immune to the stresses of remarriage. Both men and women in remarriages have reported more stress than men and women in first marriages (Weingarten, 1985). In a longitudinal study, remarriage after divorce was not associated with enhanced well-being for either women or men (Spanier & Furstenberg, 1982).

What are the consequences of the remarriage of one's exspouse? To custodial parents it means a threat to the financial and emotional support in coparenting between the exspouses (Ahrons & Wallisch, 1987). To noncustodial parents, it often means less pressure to make child support payments and a higher probability that one's children will be geographically moved further away, resulting in less time spent with one's children, especially for noncustodial fathers with female children.

Does remarriage serve children's interests? A generalization seems impossible. On the positive side, remarriage of one's custodial parent usually means a rise in standard of living, the gaining of additional extended family and adult role models, and the possibility for more adult nurturance and supervision from an adult of the same sex as the noncustodial parent. The latter result can be especially beneficial if the child has little or no contact with the noncustodial parent. In a well-functioning stepfamily a stepparent can add another dimension to childrearing. Because a stepparent probably has a more objective view of a child than a biological parent, the stepparent is more easily able to identify problematic behaviors in the child. By changing these behaviors before the child has to experience the consequences of them outside of the family, the child may be saved from some painful experiences later in life.

On the negative side, remarriage of one's custodial parent means a higher probability of moving and changing schools, sharing the biological parent's time and energy with more people, and possibly, physical and/or sexual abuse. As has been mentioned, there may also be a loss in status within the family and adjustment to stepsiblings and/or half-siblings.

While remarriage of a noncustodial parent means that the child need worry less about the welfare of that parent, it also means a higher probability of less visitation and less financial support from that parent (Ahrons & Wallisch, 1987). Visitation time may now have to be shared with the new spouse and possibly stepsiblings and/or half-siblings. Depending upon the situation, this could be enriching for the child or it could diminish the child's relationship with the noncustodial parent.

At the societal level, remarriage for many custodial mothers is a stopgap measure in response to economic desperation; it serves women's and children's interests only in that it raises their standard of living and puts a second adult into their household. Forcing women to choose between remarriage and a lower standard of living for their family certainly does not serve feminist interests. Bringing a new stepparent into the household merely on the basis of economic need does not appear to be in the best interest of children's emotional needs, especially for stepdaughters, although, bringing a loving stepparent into the home for any reason would appear to support children's interests.

At the societal level, remarriage of the noncustodial father appears not to serve children's interests because they tend to lose financial and emotional support from that parent, whose resources are demanded elsewhere. Of course, there are many exceptions; in some situations the remarried noncustodial household becomes a better environment for children than it had been previous to the remarriage.

One thing seems certain. If the remarried households are egalitarian, supportive environments, in which neither husbands nor wives are being exploited for money or services and children receive nurturance from both adults, both feminist interests and children's interests are served.

POLICY IMPLICATIONS

Cultural Ideology and Existing Policy

Existing family policies are based on our cultural ideology that the basic family unit consists of mother, father, and their biological children, living together in one household. In reality we have many viable family structures. Our policies must be responsive to the needs and realities of various types of families, rather than inappropriately treating them as deviant, as not being "true" families. For example, although stepparents have no legal rights and responsibilities to stepchildren and often are not socially accepted as "real" parents of stepchildren, they are expected to behave like responsible parental surrogates. Our ideology encourages people to make stepfamilies respectable by perceiving them as "reconstituted," "normal" two-parent families, and therefore much existing family policy is applied to stepfamilies. These reactions reflect our ambivalence toward stepfamilies and our lack of knowledge about their situations.

Much of our family policy is still based on the tenets of traditional sex roles (see Chapter 3) and the "breadwinner" economic system, in which the husband is employed outside the home and the wife is homemaker (see Chapters 2 and 4). The premises of this traditional family model often do not apply to stepfamily households. The differences are as follows:

1. The traditional model assumes that the wife does not work outside the home and that the husband earns and controls the family's income. Most stepfamilies are dual-earner households; in addition to working outside the home, some women receive child support monies in addition to their earned income. The more money the wife brings into the household, the more control she tends to have over how family income is spent. In addition, the wife's exspouse's child support payment is helping to support some members of the household; having another man in this breadwinner role diminishes the sole-male-provider image of the traditional model.

2. The traditional model assumes that all of the husband's income comes into his household. Many stepfathers are also noncustodial biological fathers and part of their income is diverted to support children and perhaps an exspouse in another household.

3. The traditional model assumes that the husband uses his money to support his own biological children, not another man's children. In most cases, stepfathers contribute to the financial support of their stepchildren in varying degrees. In even greater contradiction to traditional norms, stepmothers' incomes frequently contribute to the support of stepchildren.

4. The traditional model assumes that the husband supports the wife because her sole responsibility is homemaking for him and their biological children. Wives overwhelmingly continue to have the responsibility for housework even when they work outside the home. Furthermore, in step-

father households the wife may be rearing only her biological children, or any combination of her, his, and their children. In stepmother households, the wife may be partly or completely rearing children that her husband had with another woman, or any combination of his, her, and their children.

5. The traditional model assumes that the husband will support his wife in her old age. Remarried women have learned not to count on a husband for permanent financial support, because alimony is usually temporary, inadequate, or nonexistent (see Weitzman, Chapter 10). The vast majority of divorced women are in the labor force (see Cohen & Katzenstein, Chapter 2) and they tend to stay there even after they remarry. Although they may derive psychological benefit from working outside the home, remarried women are employed because the financial needs of stepfamilies dictate that the women be in the labor force.

6. The traditional model assumes that the husband is the head of the household. This is particularly inappropriate for many stepfather households. Generally, remarrying mothers were heads of single-parent households and earning incomes to support their families. For healthy stepfamily adjustment, stepparents should not initially be the primary authority figure over stepchildren, since they are outsiders to the family norms. Furthermore, stepparents who have no biological children have no experience with the role of parent figure. For these reasons the biological parent initially has much more psychological power in the household than does a new stepparent. Therefore, it is quite appropriate for remarrying women to function as the heads of their households. For many of the above reasons, it appears that there may be a better chance for egalitarian marriages to emerge (as Davis predicts in Chapter 4) in stepfamilies than in first families. Fleming's findings (see Chapter 3) add an interesting twist to this issue. If single and divorced women are more feminist than married women, and single men are more feminist than married and divorced men, what kinds of relationships are negotiated in remarriages, and what does the process of the negotiation look like? Lest we become too optimistic about the chances for egalitarian marriages in stepfamilies, we must remember that this remarriage is usually taking place between economic unequals. Remarrying custodial mothers often trade their autonomy (see Cohen and Katzenstein, Chapter 2) for a better life for their children. This economic inequality of spouses entering remarriages relates to our final point on the contrast between the myth of the American family and the reality of stepfamily life.

7. The traditional model assumes that the marrying individuals have made the decision to marry unencumbered by concerns for existing children's needs. On the contrary, children's needs are often a prime consideration in a decision to remarry. The poverty of single-mother households is well-documented (see Chapters 10 and 12). The poverty and the stress of rearing children alone makes the decision to remarry less than free. Many women are grateful to be rescued, and consequently, tolerate physically

and/or sexually abusive treatment toward themselves and/or their children rather than return to poverty. Fathers also may rush into a remarriage out of concern for their children. Some divorced fathers feel overwhelmed by part-time or full-time child-care responsibilities and remarry with the expectation that the new wife will nurture the children and do child-related household chores. If the feminist ideals of equality at work and in the home were a reality, mothers and children would not be so financially dependent and, therefore, so vulnerable in a remarriage, and fathers would learn to nurture, much to the benefit of their children. Here again, feminist interests and children's interests are one and the same.

It is clear that policies based on the traditional nuclear family are inappropriate for stepfamilies. Perhaps more important, the *lack* of public policy about intrafamilial matters is based on the traditional concept of father in the role of protector of family members. Society assumes that the more vulnerable family members (women and particularly children) will be well cared for as a result of the marital commitment between the adults and the biological bond between the adults and their children. We know now that this trust is not warranted, even for nuclear families, and consequently, intrafamilial issues are being brought into the public domain for the protection of these vulnerable family members (see Meyer, Ramirez, Walker, Langton, & O'Connor, Chapter 5). This trust is even less warranted for stepfamilies since the inculturated bases for protecting women's and children's welfare are weakened. For example, not all stepfamily members are related biologically; there are emotional loyalties and financial obligations to others outside the household; bonding and the building of trust take time to be created and developed.

Meyer *et al.* argue that while the conflicts between family members are not new, bringing them into the public domain *is* new. However, for stepfamilies, many of the conflicts *are* new. Given the dramatic increase in the number of stepfamilies and the current redivorce rates, focusing attention on the needs of stepfamilies comes none too soon. Formal supports and appropriate responses in societal institutions are sorely needed for these families. Not to respond will only increase the dysfunction and disruption of many stepfamilies.

Pro-Stepfamily Policy

There is a dearth of policy addressing the needs of individuals living in extended stepfamily networks for the purpose of supporting healthy stepfamily functioning. Suggestions for supportive policy follow.

Parental Rights for Stepparents

At present stepparents have no legal parental rights. There are two major areas in which stepparents need parental rights: (1) some version of legal guardianship that would enable them to perform parenting duties in lieu of, or in addition to, the biological parents, and (2) visitation rights if the marriage ends. The lack of parental rights means that they cannot sign medical forms, school permission slips, and other legal forms for their stepchildren. In situations when the biological parent is unavailable (e.g., out of town), this is not simply an inconvenience; it could mean exacerbating a medical or legal incident into a life-threatening situation.

Less obvious to the public, but equally important to families, are the psychological consequences of this lack of rights. The message that society gives to the stepparent is, "Your willingness, ability, and years of actual functioning as a parent to your stepchild are worth nothing in the eyes of the state." The following examples show how this message impedes healthy stepfamily adjustment:

1. A full-time stepmother may have been the one who applied bandaids to cuts and kissed bruises for years, but if a trip to the emergency room is necessary, she cannot give permission for the child to be properly treated. A young child cannot understand why she is powerless to help her or him then. The child learns not to trust that she will help her or him, especially when she or he is most vulnerable, perhaps even in pain. In addition, from the child's perspective, important people do not respect and value the stepmother's relationship to her or him, thus throwing into question the child's own valuing of the relationship.

2. Not being able to sign a school permission slip may mean that a child is denied the right to go on a school trip with her or his class, and has to be left behind, feeling angry with the stepparent for not being a "real" parent.

3. After spending months teaching a stepchild to drive a car, not being able to sign for her or his new driver's license denies the stepparent and stepchild the chance to share a milestone in an adolescent's life, the kind of precious times that strengthen fragile relationships.

These are examples of how our policy actually hinders the development of positive stepparent–stepchild relationships by not giving stepparents any legal rights with respect to stepchildren. When the law says "You are nothing to this child," there is little motivation to try to be something. In contrast, public policy that would promote healthy stepfamily functioning, in our opinion, would be based on the premise that the stepparent who has carried out parental responsibilities should be accorded parental rights.

In most states, when remarriages end in divorce or death, stepparents are entitled to neither custody nor visitation rights. Here again, the state denies the importance of the stepparent–stepchild relationship. Even when the stepparent may have been the major child caretaker and the "psychological" parent, upon divorce the stepparent and stepchild must rely on the benevolence of the custodial parent in order to be allowed to continue their relationship. In most states, when the custodial parent dies, custody reverts to the remaining biological parent, even if that person had abandoned or had limited contact with the children. In these cases the loss for the children is unnecessarily tragic—not only must they endure the death of their custodial parent, they must suffer the loss of their second psychological parent and be placed with a psychological stranger. The law narrowly assumes that the other biological parent is the rightful caretaker and neglects to weigh sufficiently the child's place within the stepfamily context when determining the child's best interest.

The lack of stepparent visitation rights also undermines the development of a nurturing stepparent–stepchild relationship from the beginning of the remarriage. Stepparents may be unwilling to become emotionally close to a child who may be taken away, especially if they have already experienced physical or psychological loss of biological or stepchildren.

Adoption. Adoption, in its traditional form, involves the termination of parental rights and is rarely the answer. Adoption is replacement of one or both parents; it is part of the "no more than two real parents" and "one parent must be a failure" mentality that is based on our nuclear family ideology. This thinking is not supportive of healthy extended stepfamily functioning for many reasons:

1. Noncustodial parents would have to surrender legal parental rights and responsibilities, which, needless to say, most noncustodial parents do not want to do.

2. When the noncustodial parents ceased paying child support, the stepfamily would be more financially stressed.

3. The stepparent may not want to legally adopt stepchildren, especially if he or she already has biological children for whom he or she is legally responsible.

4. Legal adoption means loss of social security benefits for children of a deceased biological parent.

5. Many older children do not want to be adopted by a stepparent, wanting to be able to benefit from having relationships with all of their parents, not to be forced to choose between them.

6. The change of family surname that accompanies adoption signifies a loss of identification with the paternal branch of the stepfamily network, a name change that results in emotional hardship for many paternal grandparents.

In most stepfamilies, *replacing* the noncustodial parent with the stepparent is certainly not in the best interests of the children, and may not be in the interest of anyone in the extended stepfamily network.

If we can let go of our "only two real parents" thinking and conceptualize stepparents as additional parents, we could grant them some type of legal guardianship. It is time for us to move beyond our evil stepparent mythology. Legally validating the positive contribution that most stepparents make to the rearing of children would go a long way in supporting the development of healthy stepfamilies.

Acknowledgment of Stepparents' Financial Contribution

While stepparents receive no formal recognition for the time and energy that they contribute to their stepchildren's upbringing, they also receive no rewards for their economic contribution. In fact, in some instances legal and economic structures penalize the stepfamily household for the stepparents' financial contribution (Ramsey, 1986) and yet threaten child neglect if they do not contribute.

For example, Aid to Families with Dependent Children (AFDC) is based on household income. Thus, if a stepparent enters the household and has an income, he or she is forced to contribute to the support of the stepchildren, because eligibility for AFDC funds is based on the income of both adults. If the stepparent refuses to support the needy stepchildren who live in the household (perhaps because he is supporting family members elsewhere or because his work is temporary), the stepparent can be charged with child neglect. This is an example of the way in which the welfare system limits financial options for family members who try to live together.

A second example of the unrewarded financial contribution of stepparents is found in the setting of child support payments required of the noncustodial parent. In some states the income of a new spouse is considered part of a parent's household income in child support considerations. Consequently, full-time and part-time stepparents indirectly support stepchildren, and yet they are not acknowledged as doing so in the tax structure by allowing tax-reducing credit for the contributor. Even in states where child support payments are supposed to be based only on biological parents' income, stepparent income is considered informally. For example, if a custodial mother returns to court for enforcement of child support payments, the judge is likely to be more forgiving of the noncustodial father not meeting his full financial responsibilities if the mother has remarried a man who has substantial income. This encourages the biological father to be irresponsible to his children and penalizes the stepfather for marrying a custodial mother.

A third example of not validating the stepparents' economic contribution is college financial aid, which is based on biological parents' *and* stepparents' incomes. In principle this is unfair to stepparents who have no legal rights or responsibilities to their stepchildren. In practice this is quite inappropriate for many stepfamilies, as in the cases of stepparents who had never lived with their college-age stepchildren and may be saving for their own biological children's education. The present financial aid policy promotes resentment of stepchildren and jealousy between stepsiblings.

Supporting a child through college has another twist in extended stepfamily networks. Because noncustodial parents are required to pay child support only until the child becomes 18, the support of the college-age child and the tuition costs (less any financial aid) often falls on the stepfamily household. Given the accepted necessity for higher education, extending the biological parents' child support responsibilities through college seems like a more appropriate solution (Crosbie-Burnett & Skyles, in press).

It is obvious that the amount of money that a stepparent contributes to the rearing of stepchildren is related to the amount of child support that the noncustodial parent pays. In other words, the stepfamily household "picks up the slack" when child support payments are small, irregular or nonexistent. The lax enforcement of child support payments and the resultant poverty for single mother families is well documented (see Weitzman, Chapter 10). This lax enforcement is also detrimental to extended stepfamily networks. When a stepfamily household is receiving little or no child support payments from a noncustodial parent, there is less money that can be paid out as child support to a household that is supporting a stepparent's own noncustodial biological children—note the interdependence of these households. The situation forces the stepparent to make a cruel choice between his biological children and his stepchildren. No matter what choice is made, the situation promotes feelings of frustration, anger, guilt, and/or resentment between spouses, stepsiblings, biological parents and children, and stepparents and stepchildren.

What about parents who faithfully support noncustodial children? They and their new spouses (part-time stepparents) may pay the price of a childless marriage, because they cannot afford to support more children. Alternatively, they can manipulate the child support system by giving birth to more children and applying for a reduction in the child support payments to the noncustodial children. The issues are similar to those in the above example: Whatever money one household gets, the other goes without, creating an adversarial situation and all of the concommitant feelings. This is especially detrimental for the children, because the adults in these households need to cooperatively share the financial and emotional rearing of the children.

Laws both reflect and create society's values. Laws regarding the care of children after divorce should both encourage financial and emotional responsibility for one's biological children *and* reflect the reality that stepparents tend to substantially support the children living in their households. Such laws ought to reflect as well that the financial burden of this new family may lessen their ability to financially and emotionally (through visitation) support biological children living elsewhere. If biological mothers and fathers were held accountable for the financial support of their children, stepfathers and stepmothers would not be financially penalized for remarrying and, therefore, would be better able to continue the financial support of their own biological children. In addition, single-parent households might experience less poverty via such changes. Alternatively, if laws encouraged adults to support financially and emotionally the children living in their present households, emotional ties with noncustodial parents might dwindle and nonremarrying single-parent households would suffer financially and emotionally.

It is clear that financial stress is inherent in the extended stepfamily network. Supporting children in two households is more expensive than supporting them in one; there is duplication of shelter, services, some clothing, and extra travel and telephone expenses. Changing the tax structure could help compensate stepfamilies for this added financial stress and validate stepparents for their financial contribution. In the present tax structure a dependent child can be claimed as one deduction for one household, because the tax laws are still based on the nuclear family form. We suggest a revision: Part-time and full-time stepfamilies could share 1½ or 2 deductions for each child who moves between the two households. There are also many adults, usually men, who are supporting two households almost single-handedly. This may occur when his divorced exspouse and children are in one household, his present spouse and stepchildren are in his household, and there is no child support coming into his household for the stepchildren. Clearly, these people deserve financial benefits of some kind for the responsibilities they are shouldering.

Critics might assert that society cannot afford to give tax benefits and other financial assistance to these families. We respond that it need not amount to large sums of money. The validation of the contribution of stepparents is equally as important as the small amount of financial aid to the households. No matter what it costs society, it is less than redivorce would cost in terms of lowered job performance, use of human services, and the present and future consequences of impoverished children and women.

One final point in the argument for validation of stepparents' nurturant and financial contribution to the rearing of their stepchildren: While full validation is desirable, consistency of treatment of stepparents is a must. At present, our society takes from the stepparent and gives nothing back, as in the case of a stepfather who cannot sign a school permission slip but is expected to pay thousands of dollars of college tuition, or the stepmother who spends years of her life rearing stepchildren who can be suddenly and permanently taken from her. This treatment of stepparents leaves them feeling used, but not respected or appreciated, inhibiting commitment in the marital relationship and bonding between stepparent and stepchild. The inconsistency and the lack of validation for stepparents in our present policy actually erodes stability in stepfamilies and promotes redivorce.

Remarriage Mediation

The remarriage of one's exspouse can be emotionally threatening. This threat is often acted out by taking the remarrying exspouse back to court. In most states the law allows the court to modify the parenting agreement in response to any "change in circumstances." A remarriage is one such change. There is preliminary evidence that about 10% of upper-middle-class remarrying men and women return to court over custody, visitation, or money battles (Crosbie-Burnett, 1983). Although the percentages are small, the growing numbers that they represent as more remarriages occur will put added strain on the courts.

In addition, returning to court around the time of remarriage puts additional financial and emotional stress on an already stressed extended stepfamily network. Counselors could be helpful in deescalating these situations by mediating changes in the coparenting relationship between exspouses (Ahrons & Perlmutter, 1982) and their new partners, guiding all those involved through the feelings that accompany changes brought about by a remarriage. If returning to court is unavoidable, remarriage mediation (similar in concept to divorce mediation) using a lawyer–counselor team might be successful in saving court time, lowering costs, and supporting successful adjustment in the extended stepfamily network (Bernstein & Haberman, 1981).

Socializing Institutions

Schools. Policy mandating the development of curriculum, policies, and procedures that reflect the changing reality of American families (Crosbie-Burnett & Skyles, in press) would accomplish two major goals: (1) Children living in nonnuclear family homes would not be made to feel deviant, and (2) children and adolescents would be better prepared for living in the variety of family structures that about half of them will encounter, either as children or as adults. While textbooks now portray a variety of family structures, other components of curricula lag behind. Class discussions about family life could include issues from many types of families. This could decrease unrealistic expectations (that all families should resemble nuclear families) and increase understanding and successful decision making. For example, a discussion of stepfamilies might help young people to understand that if, in the future, they consider marrying someone who has children, they must be prepared to "marry" the parent–child group and accept the financial and emotional responsibility that the parent has to the children, even if the parent is noncustodial.

Manifestations of this oversight, school policies and procedures that are still based on nuclear families, range from excluding stepparents' names from school mailings to not including all appropriate parents at teacher–parent conferences. Much of the invalidation of stepparents in the school setting is based on our legal invalidation, as has been discussed above. But school policies could embrace stepparents as another source of adult support for their students without formal legal changes. Making the effort to examine forms, policies, and procedures, and modifying them to include stepparents would probably pay off in the human energy that validated stepparents would give back to the school and the students.

School teachers should be required to have training in stepfamily issues. Recently teachers have been sensitized to the experience of children in single-parent households, but they may not understand the distress that a child of a remarrying parent may be enduring.

Leaders in all similar institutions that have a socializing function, such as churches, athletic teams, and scouting, should receive information about diverse family forms.

Corporations. Corporations often place company needs before family needs. Managers have been expected to work long hours, travel, and relocate at the whim of the company; the family was expected to endure the stress that these policies have placed upon it. Because these policies were based on the traditional family, they cause even more stress in today's two-earner family (see Strober, Chapter 6). The impact of these policies is extremely detrimental to the extended stepfamily network. For example, relocating a stepfamily is more disruptive for family members than relocating the relatively self-contained nuclear family, because the stepfamily may be an integral part of a complex extended stepfamily network. Since moving provides the type of change of circumstances necessary for the modification of a custody or visitation order, relocation can often provoke disputes that result in financially and emotionally costly returns to court. Due to the rising number of executives who are or will be members of extended stepfamily networks, companies would do well to explore policies that are supportive of these individuals' family needs.

Media. The media could use its power to modify our cultural ideology about families by presenting the stepfamily as one of many normal family forms. Television, books, and magazines could sensitize the public to the stepfamily experience and also help stepfamilies by presenting realistic examples of stepfamilies enjoying happy times and working through typical problems. Even greeting card companies could model appreciation for stepparents by making cards that express positive thoughts about stepparents.

Perhaps most important, the media could show models of healthy nonsexual male–female relationships. This might teach all couples how to be better friends, but it may particularly give nonresidential fathers suggestions for activities they could share with their daughters and help stepfathers relate to their stepdaughters.

Training of Professionals

Those in the helping professions must be trained to perceive the stepfamily as a normal two-parent family that is different from nuclear two-parent families, and has unique stresses that are inherent in the stepfamily structure. They need to expand their notion of appropriate family behaviors.

Stepfamily members sometimes adopt behaviors that would appear bizarre or maladaptive in a nuclear family context, but may be quite adaptive in an extended stepfamily network. For example, professionals must stop viewing a good relationship between exspouses with suspicion and see it as a healthy basis for the continuing coparenting relationship. They must be open to unusual solutions to stepfamily issues, solutions like having children live in one household and the parents taking turns "visiting" their children.

Therapeutic and preventive models of intervention at the family and community level need to be created and integrated into the training of professionals who serve families. For example, premarital counseling for remarried couples and their children could teach family members skills to cope with the stresses they may face and also give them a forum in which to safely discuss sensitive issues like jealousy and sexuality as they are manifested in stepfamilies. Community support groups could provide ongoing dissemination of information and emotional support to stepfamilies.

Research and Theory Development
Researchers have little understanding of stepfamilies. We particularly need longitudinal studies, studies that include children's perceptions, and studies with populations that are not white and middle-class. An examination of the communication patterns and family dynamics of well-adjusted stepfamilies would generate healthy models from which to guide others.

Family theorists are being challenged by the new phenomena that the extended stepfamily network creates. For example, the process of divorce and remarriage forces the definition of "immediate family" to expand across household boundaries. Life-cycle models of human development will have to integrate divorce and remarriage stages (Messinger & Walker, 1981). In addition, family theorists must rethink heretofore unquestioned definitions of concepts like family cohesion in light of the apparent paradox observed in some stepfamilies, such as subjective feelings of family closeness that have been reported even when the children spend large amounts of time out of the family's household.

Most modern remarriages that include children are mergers of families, not replacements of absent family members. Theorists need to let go of our normative notion that the "real" or "correct" family is the nuclear family and welcome models of healthy single-parent and extended stepfamily networks, in which children can enjoy relationships with multiple parents.

Redefining Incest
There is a final recommendation for change that cuts across the above sections on socializing institutions, media, training of professionals, and research and theory. In an attempt to protect millions of stepchildren, incest must be redefined. Webster defines incest as "sexual relations between persons so closely related that they are forbidden by law to marry." Consid-

ering the social phenomenon of rapidly increasing numbers of stepfamilies, this definition is inadequate. In the public mind the incest taboo must be expanded to include stepparent–stepchild relationships.

Reconceptualization of Family as a Prerequisite for New Policy

Present policy is based on the narrow conceptualization of the nuclear family, a conceptualization that is limiting and outdated in modern America. It is the basis of the widely held belief that the only people who are and should be financially and emotionally rearing children are the biological parents, even after divorce and remarriage. Anyone else who is financially and/or emotionally supporting children is not acknowledged for his or her contribution. While we must continue to hold biological parents responsible for rearing their children, we must also take a less myopic view of families and parenting. We must see divorce and remarriage as creating a complex network of households that form a modern extended family kinship system, with biological children forming the links betwen single or remarried parents' households, which are linked with the more traditional extended family kinship networks of grandparents, aunts, uncles, cousins, and in-laws. We must validate and utilize all adults who are available and may already be helping to rear children.

There already exist models of this expanded view of family. Black families have learned to cope with factors that are now being experienced by the growing number of divorced and remarried white families: limited finances, single-mother households with men in a more peripheral role, and working parent(s). These families have coped by using social support and a broad definition of family, both of which include an expansion of family boundaries to encompass all significant adults who might contribute to the rearing of children.

It is in the best interests of children that we accept and work with this broader definition of who can meet their needs. If we place the whole burden on divorced or remarried biological parents, who are often more stressed than parents in nuclear families, children's needs will remain unmet.

SUMMARY

Stepfamilies are an emerging family form. They are structurally and psychologically different from nuclear families. The unique issues with which stepfamilies cope are a function of both living in a culture whose institutions and ideology are based on nuclear families, and relating to a variety of different people playing various and often undefined roles in family life. At present, the scant research on stepfamilies precludes making statements about whether or not stepfamily formation supports feminist interests or children's interests, but studies suggest that the quality of family life is probably more important than the family structure in reaching goals of equality for the sexes and well-being for the children. Suggested changes in educational, social, corporate, and legal policy are based on a delineation of the reasons why present policies are inappropriate and detrimental to healthy stepfamily functioning.

REFERENCES

Ahrons, C. R. (1981). The continuing coparental relationship between divorced spouses. *American Journal of Psychiatry, 5*, 415–428

Ahrons, C. R., & Perlmutter, M. S. (1982). The relationship between former spouses: A fundamental subsystem in the remarriage family. In L. Messinger (Ed.), *Therapy with remarried families*. Rockville, MD: Aspen Systems Corp.

Ahrons, C. R., & Wallisch, K. (1987). Parenting in the binuclear family: Relationships between biological and step parents. In N. K. Pasley & M. Ihinger-Tallman (Eds.), *Remarriage and stepparenting: Current research and theory*. New York: Guilford Press.

Albrecht, S. L. (1979). Correlates of marital happiness among the remarried. *Journal of Marriage and the Family, 41*, 857–867.

Ambert, A. M. (1983). Separated women and remarriage behavior: A comparison of financially secure women and financially insecure women. *Journal of Divorce. 6*(3), 43–54.

Ambert, A. (1986). Being a stepparent: live-in and visiting children. *Journal of Marriage and the Family, 48*, 795–804.

Bachrach, C. A. (1983, February). Children in families: Characteristics of biological step- and adopted children. *Journal of Marriage and the Family, 45*(1), 171–179.

Bahr, S. J. (1979). The effects of welfare on marital stability and remarriage. *Journal of Marriage and the Family, 41*, 553–560.

Becker, G. S., Landes, E. M. & Michael, R. P. (1977). An economic analysis of marital instability. *Journal of Political Economy, 85*, 1141–1187.

Bernard, J. (1971). *Remarriage: A study of marriage* (2nd ed.). New York: Russell & Russell.

Bernard, J. (1980). Afterword. *Journal of Family Issues, 1*(4), 561–571.

Berstein, B. E., & Haberman, B. G. (1981). Lawyer and counselor as an interdisciplinary team: Problem awareness in the blended family. *Child Welfare, 60*, 211–219.

Bohannan, P., & Erickson, R. (1978). Stepping-in. *Psychology Today, 11*(8), 53–54, 159.

Bohannan, P., & Yahraes, H. (1979). Stepfathers as parents. In E. Corfamn (Ed.), *Families today: A research sampler on families and children*. Washington, DC: U.S. Government Printing Office. NIMH Science Monograph.

Bryan, S. H., Ganong, L. H., Coleman, M., & Bryan, L. R. (1985, April). Counselors' perceptions of stepparents and stepchildren. *Journal of Counseling Psychology, 32*(2), 279–282.

Buehler, C., Hogan, M., Robinson, B., & Levy, R. (1986). Remarriage following divorce, stressors and well-being of custodial and non-custodial parents. *Journal of Family Issues, 7*, 405–420.

Bumpass. L. L., & Rindfuss, R. R. (1979). Children's experience of marital disruption. *American Journal of Sociology, 85*(1), 49–65.

Bumpass, L. L., & Sweet, A. (1972). Differentials in marital instability. *American Sociological Review, 37*, 754–766.

Chapman, M. (1977). Father absence, stepfathers, and the cognitive performance of college students. *Child Development, 48*, 1155–1158.

Cherlin, A. (1977). The effects of children on marital dissolution. *Demography, 14*, 265–272.

Cherlin, A. (1978, November). Remarriage as an incomplete institution. *American Journal of Sociology, 84*, 634–650.

Cherlin, A. (1981). *Marriage, divorce, and remarriage.* Cambridge, MA: Harvard University Press.

Cherlin, A., & McCarthy, J. (1985). Remarried couple households: Data from the June 1980 current population survey. *Journal of Marriage and the Family, 47*(1), 23–30.

Clingempeel, W. G. (1981). Quasi-kin relationships and marital quality in stepfather families. *Journal of Personality and Social Psychology, 41*(5), 890–901.

Clingempeel, W. G., & Brand, E. (1985). Quasi-kin relationships, structural complexity, and marital quality in stepfamilies: A replication, extension, and clinical implications. *Family Relations, 34*, 401–409.

Clingempeel, W. G., Ievoli, R., & Brand, E. (1984, December). Structural complexity and the quality of stepfather–stepchild relationships. *Family Process, 23*(4), 547–560.

Clingempeel, W. G. and Segal, S. (1986). Stepparent–stepchild relationships and the psychological adjustment of children in stepmother and stepfather families. *Child Development, 57*, 474–484.

Crosbie-Burnett, M. (1983). *Impact of remarriage on labor force participation, divorce decree modification, exspousal relationship, and extended family reorganization.* Paper presented at the annual meeting of the National Council on Family Relations, St. Paul, MN.

Crosbie-Burnett, M. (1984a). *Assessment of stepfamily adjustment.* (Doctoral dissertation, Stanford University, 1983). *Dissertation Abstracts International, 44*(9), 2890B.

Crosbie-Burnett, M. (1984). The centrality of the step relationship: A challenge to family theory and practice. *Family Relations, 33*, 459–464.

Crosbie-Burnett, M. (in press-a). Effects of custody arrangements and family structure complexity on adolescents in remarried families. *Conciliation Courts Review.*

Crosbie-Burnett, M. (in press-b). Impact of custody arrangement and family structure on remarriage. *Journal of Divorce.*

Crosbie-Burnett, M., & Ahrons, C. (1985). From divorce to remarriage: Implications for therapy with families in transition. *Journal of Psychotherapy and the Family, 1*(3), 121–137.

Crosbie-Burnett, M. & Skyles, A. (in press). Stepchildren in schools and colleges. Recommendations for educational policy changes. *Family Relations.*

Daly, M., & Wilson, M. (1980). Discriminative parental solicitude: A biological perspective. *Journal of Marriage and the Family, 42*, 277–288.

DeMaris, A. (1984). A comparison of remarriages with first marriages on satisfaction in marriage and its relationship to prior cohabitation. *Family Relations, 33*, 443–450.

Dornbusch, S. M., Carlsmith, J. M., Bushwall, S. J., Ritter, P. L., Leiderman, H., Hastorf, A. H., & Gross, R. T. (1985). Single parents, extended households, and the control of adolescents. *Child Development, 56*, 326–341.

Dornbusch, S., Ritter, P. L., & Fraleigh, M. (1987). Family processes and the schools. *Final Report to Stanford and the Schools for the Hewlett Foundation.*

Duberman, L. (1975). *The reconstituted family: A study of remarried couples and their children.* Chicago: Nelson-Hall Publishers.

Furstenberg, F. F., Jr. (1979). Recycling the family: Perspectives for a neglected family form. *Marriage and Family Review, 2*(3), 12–22.

Furstenberg, F. F., Jr. (1980) Reflections of remarriage. *Journal of Family Issues, 1*, 443–453.

Furstenberg, F. F., Jr., & Spanier, G. (1984). The risk of dissolution in remarriage: An examination of Cherlin's hypothesis of incomplete institutionalization. *Family Relations, 33*, 433–442.

Garbarino, J., Sebes, J., & Schellenbach, C. (1984, February). Families at risk for destructive parent–child relations in adolescence. *Child Development, 55*(1), 174–183.

Giles-Sims, J. (1984). The stepparent role: Expectations, behavior, and sanctions. *Journal of Family Issues, 5*(1), 116–130.

Giles-Sims, J., & Finkelhor, D. (1984). Child abuse in stepfamilies. *Family Relations, 33*, 407–414.

Glenn, N. D., & Weaver, C. N. (1977). The marital happiness of remarried divorced persons. *Journal of Marriage and the Family, 39*, 331–337.

Glenn, N. (1981). The well-being of persons remarried after divorce. *Journal of Family Issues, 2*, 61–75.

Glick, P. C. (1980). Remarriage: Some recent changes and variations. *Journal of Family Issues, 1*(4), 455–478.

Glick, P. C. (1983). U.S. divorces. First decline in 20 years, but is it permanent? *Marriage and Divorce Today, 8*(34), 1.

Glick, P. (1985). *An update on the demographics of single-parent and step families.* Paper presented at the Annual Meeting of the National Council on Family Relations, Dallas.

Glick, P., and Lin, S. (1986). Recent changes in divorce and remarriage. *Journal of Marriage and the Family, 48*, 737–747.

Goetting, A. (1980). Former spouse-current spouse relationships. *Journal of Family Issues, 1*(1), 58–80.

Goldner, V. (1985). Feminism and family therapy. *Family Process, 24*, 31–47.

Gurak, D. T., & Dean, G. (1979). The remarriage market: Factors influencing the selection of second husbands. *Journal of Divorce, 3*(2), 161–173.

Halperin, S. M., & Smith, T. A. (1983, Fall). Differences in stepchildren's perceptions of their stepfathers and natural fathers: Implications for family therapy. *Journal of Divorce, 7*(1), 19–30.

Hetherington, E. M., Cox, M., & Cox, R. (1985). Long-term effects of divorce and remarriage on the adjustment of children. *Journal of the American Academy of Child Psychiatry, 24*, 518–530.

Husain, A., & Chapel, J. (1983). History of incest in girls admitted to a psychiatric hospital. *American Journal of Psychiatry, 140*, 591–593.

Ihinger-Tallman, M., & Pasley, K. (1981, August). *Factors influencing stability in remarriage.* Paper presented at the XIXth International Sociological Association, Committee on Family Research Seminar on Divorce and Remarriage, Leuven, Belgium.

Ihinger-Tallman, M., & Pasley, K. (1983, October). *Remarriage and "community" embeddedness.* Paper presented at the Annual Meeting of the National Council on Family Relations, St. Paul, MN.

Ishii-Kuntz, M. (1986). *Sex and race differences in marital happiness in first-married and remarried persons: Update and refinement.* Washington State University.

Kalmuss, D., & Seltzer, J. (1986, February). Continuity of marital behavior in remarriage: The case of spouse abuse. *Journal of Marriage and the Family, 48*(1), 113–120.

Kargman, M. W. (1983). Stepchild support obligations of stepparents. *Family Relations, 32*(2), 231–238.

Kellam, S. G., Ensminger, M. E., & Turner, R. J. (1977, September). Family structure and the mental health of children. *Archives of General Psychology, 34*, 1012–1022.

Keshet, J. K. (1980). From separation to stepfamily: A subsystem analysis. *Journal of Family Issues, 4*, 517–532.

Koo, H. P., & Suchindran, C. M. (1980). Effects of children on women's remarriage prospects. *Journal of Family Issues, 1*(4), 497–515.

Lightcap, J., Kurland, J., & Burgess, R. (1982). Child abuse: A test of some predictions from evolutionary theory. *Ethology & Sociobiology, 3*, 61–67.

Lutz, P. (1983, July). The stepfamily: An adolescent perspective. *Family Relations, 32*, 367–375.

Mead, M. (1970). Anomalies in American post divorce relationships. In P. Bohannon (Ed.), *Divorce and after.* New York: Doubleday & Co.

Messinger, L. (1976). Remarriage between divorced people with children from previous marriages: A proposal for preparation for remarriage. *Journal of Marriage and Family Counseling, 2*, 193–200.

Messinger, L., & Walker, K. (1981). From marriage breakdown to remarriage: Parental tasks and therapeutic guidelines. *American Journal of Orthopsychiatry, 51*, 429–438.

Mott, F. L., & Moore, S. F. (1983). The tempo of remarriage among young American women. *Journal of Marriage and the Family, 45*(2), 427–435.

Nadler, J. (1976). The psychological stress of the stepmother. *Dissertation Abstracts International, 37*, 5367B.

Nunn, G. D., Parish, T. S., & Worthing, R. J. (1983). Perceptions of personal and familial adjustments by children from intact, single-parent, and reconstituted families. *Psychology in the Schools, 20*(2), 166–174.

Oshman, H. P., & Manosevitz, M. (1976). Father absence: Effects of stepfathers upon psychosocial development in males. *Child Development, 12*, 479–480.

Parish, T. S. (1982). Locus of control as a function of father loss and the presence of stepfathers. *Journal of Genetic Psychology, 140*, 321–322.

Parish, T. S., & Dostal, J. W. (1980). Relationships between evaluations of self and parents by children from intact and divorced families. *Journal of Psychology, 104*, 35–38.

Parish, T. S., & Parish, J. G. (1983). Relationship between evaluations of one's self and one's family by children from intact, reconstituted, and single-parent families. *Journal of Genetic Psychology, 143*(2), 293.

Parish, T. S., & Taylor, J. C. (1979). The impact of divorce and subsequent father absence on children's and adolescent's self-concept. *Journal of Youth and Adolescence, 8*, 427–432.

Pasley, K., & Ihinger-Tallman, M. (1982). Remarried family life: Supports and constraints. In G. Rowe (Ed.), *Building family strengths*. Lincoln, NE: University of Nebraska Press.

Pasley, K., Ihinger-Tallman, M., & Coleman, C. (1984). Consensus styles among happy and unhappy remarried couples. *Family Relations, 33*(3), 451–457.

Perkins, T. F., & Kahan, J. P. (1979). An empirical comparison of natural-father and stepfather family systems. *Family Process, 18*, 175–183.

Peterson, J., & Zill, N. (1986). Marital disruption, parent–child relationships and behavior problems in children. *Journal of Marriage and the Family, 48*, 295–307.

Ransom, J. W., Schlesinger, S., & Derdeyn, A. P. (1979). A stepfamily in formation. *American Journal of Orthopsychiatry, 49*, 39–43.

Roosevelt, R., & Lotas, J. (1976). *Living in Step*. New York: Stein & Day.

Sardanis-Zimmerman, I. (1977). The stepmother: Mythology and self-perception. *Dissertation Abstracts International, 38*(6-B), 2884.

Schlesinger, B. (1978). *Remarriage in Canada*. Toronto: Guidance Center, University of Toronto.

Skyles, A. (1983). *Selected variably affecting stepparent perception of dyadic adjustment in remarriage*. Doctoral dissertation, University of Wisconsin-Madison.

Spanier, G. B., & Furstenberg, F. F., Jr. (1982). Remarriage after divorce: A longitudinal analysis of well-being. *Journal of Marriage and the Family, 44*, 709–720.

Stern, P. N. (1978). Stepfather families: Integration around child discipline. *Issues in Mental Health Nursing, 1*, 49–56.

Teachman, J. D., & Heckert, A. (1985). The impact of age and children of remarriage. *Journal of Family Issues, 6*(2), 185–203.

Touliatos, J., & Lindholm, B. W. (1980). Teachers' perceptions of behavior problems in children from intact, single-parent, and stepparent families. *Psychology in the Schools, 17*, 264–269.

Turnbull, S. K., & Turnbull, J. M. (1983). To dream the impossible dream: An agenda for discussion with stepparents. *Family Relations, 32*, 227–230.

Visher, E. B., & Visher, J. S. (1979). *Stepfamilies: A guide to working with stepparents and stepchildren*. New York: Brunner/Mazel.

Wallerstein, J. S., & Kelly, J. B. (1980). *Surviving the breakup*. New York: Basic Books.

Weingarten, H. R. (1980). Remarriage and well-being: National survey evidence of social and psychological effects. *Journal of Family Issues, 1,* 533–559.

Weingarten, H. R. (1985). Marital status and well-being: A national study comparing first-married, currently divorced, and remarried adults. *Journal of Marriage and the Family, 47,* 653–662.

White, L. K. (1979). Sex differentials in the effects of remarriage on global happiness. *Journal of Marriage and the Family, 41,* 869–876.

White, L. K., & Booth, A. (1985). The quality and stability of remarriages: The role of stepchildren. *American Sociological Review, 50,* 689–698.

Wilson, K. L., Zurcher, L. A., McAdams, D. C., & Curtis, R. L. (1975). Stepfathers and stepchildren: An exploratory analysis from two national surveys. *Journal of Marriage and the Family, 37,* 526–536.

Wilson, M., Daly, M., & Weghorst, S. J. (1980). Household composition and the risk of child abuse and neglect. *Journal of Biosociological Science, 12,* 333–340.

14

Public Policy Alternatives

MYRA H. STROBER AND SANFORD M. DORNBUSCH

In recent years, massive social and economic changes have produced large numbers of families that do not conform to the traditional conception of *the* American family. The two-parent, male/breadwinner–female/homemaker family, the reigning family form of yesteryear, has been replaced in its dominance by two-earner families, single-parent families, and stepfamilies. In 1984, the traditional male/breadwinner–female/homemaker family with children represented only 13% of all families.[1]

How should public policy react to these changes in family forms? One answer has been to clamor for a return to the past; to exhort mothers to return to full-time homemaking and childrearing, and to seek to make divorce and single-parenthood morally reprehensible (see, e.g., Bauer, 1986.)

In today's economic and social reality, such exhortations are doomed to failure. Mothers are in the workforce for a combination of reasons, including pleasure in their work and their families need for income. Moreover, the economy needs their labor. Mothers with children under 18 represent about 17% of the workforce.[2] To call for all mothers to "return" to full-time homemaking is to call for economic chaos. Similarly, as the analyses in several of our chapters indicate, the rise in divorce and single-parenthood stem from complex economic and psychological developments that have emerged over decades; these developments are unlikely to be reversed merely as a result of public pronouncements or handwringing. The new families are here to stay.

The role of public policy in this realm, as in any other, is to serve its citizens. Rather than exhorting men and women to form only "real" families—"real" being defined as the male/breadwinner–female/homemaker family—public policy needs to assist all citizens in meeting their needs, regardless of the type of family to which they belong. It is inadmissible for policy makers to denigrate the new family forms. People in single-parent

Myra H. Strober, Ph.D. Stanford School of Education, Stanford University, Stanford, California.

Sanford M. Dornbusch, Ph.D. Department of Sociology, Stanford University, Stanford, California; Stanford Center for the Study of Families, Children, and Youth, Stanford, California.

families, stepfamilies or two-earner families perceive themselves as members of "real" families. Their family ties seem to them as strong and significant (or as weak and painful) as those in other families. We need to move toward a public policy that recognizes diversity in family types.

In recent years, some policy analysts and policy makers have called for the United States to develop a national policy toward families (Kamerman & Kahn, 1978; Moynihan, 1986). Others have argued that family policy is an elusive concept, hardly a pillar on which to base public policy; that not only do we have numerous types of families, and individuals moving back and forth among them, but that within families the interests of individuals are often divergent (Boles, 1983; Scanzoni, 1983; Steiner, 1981).

The fact that we have numerous types of families suggests, rather than abandon policies to aid families, that we develop policies that take diversity of family forms into account. Similarly, although the fact that individuals move between families and indeed are often part of more than one family (as in stepfamilies) suggests that designing policies to aid families will be complex, it doesn't imply that such efforts should be foresaken.

With respect to possible divergence of interest among family members, the chapters in this book indicate that most policies designed to aid families benefit all family members. Instances of divergence of interest between mothers and children are rare; and, in general, policies designed to aid families also benefit fathers, although there are some important exceptions.

The concept of family policy connotes a comprehensive, well-coordinated, and largely legislative effort to deal with family issues. Since our federal system reserves for the states many of the key legislative initiatives concerning families, it is unlikely that the United States will soon develop a comprehensive, coordinated family policy. Even more significantly, as we shall see, federal and state legislation is not enough. Policies are needed as well in such decentralized settings as schools, local courts, local communities, businesses, unions, and private foundations. Urging a comprehensive national family policy is likely to be not only frustrating, but also unsatisfactory. We suggest that multiple policies to aid the new families be developed by multiple institutions.

We group our policy recommendations around three major problems, disequilibria if you will, that have grown out of the development of new families:

1. Men and women are performing tasks at work and in the family that are at odds with the traditional male–female division of labor and with the traditional roles of mother and father. New public policies are needed to enable adults to perform nontraditional tasks more effectively and to assist them in reconciling work and home responsibilities.

2. Traditional arrangements for the care of children have broken down. Public policies are needed to develop new arrangements for child care.

3. Divorce constitutes an acutely painful transition between two family forms. New public policies are needed to ease this transition.

Focusing on these three disequilibria, we suggest broad policy recommendations for schools, employers, governmental institutions and agencies, unions, and private foundations. Because of space limitations, we have not tried to include in our discussion every useful recommendation that has been offered for the new families.

In some cases the broad policy recommendations we offer for governmental and private institutions complement one another; in other instances, they may be viewed as alternatives. Given the diversity of family types, preferences, and resources across communities, we expect that states and localities will vary considerably in the mix of policies they choose to adopt.

FACILITATING THE SEX-ROLE REVOLUTION

Among the most important policies for the sex-role revolution are those that educate women for employment and assure equity of earnings and employment opportunity in the labor market. Equally vital are policies that encourage men to learn and perform domestic tasks and parenting. In this section we present policy recommendations related to education, housing, and employment that are designed to enhance the ability of women and men, together and independently, to function effectively in the new families. We also examine policies related to housing and to stepfamilies.

Education

Curricular Changes
Increasingly, as women have moved into more permanent participation in the labor market, textbooks have begun to show mothers as workers, and teachers have begun to encourage girls to plan for their work lives. Textbooks and teachers have been much slower, however, in preparing boys for the nurturing roles they are likely to play in two-earner families or as single parents. Preparing and teaching a "curriculum for caring," in Urie Bronfenbrenner's words (1979), must become a top priority for boys and girls at all grade levels.

In high schools, students need course work that introduces them to the realities of the new families and the new expectations and roles for men and women. Both boys and girls need to learn basic domestic skills, such as sewing, cooking, and making simple household repairs.

Schools, particularly community colleges and adult education programs, should offer courses for adults who are taking on tasks they never expected to perform. Single fathers often need training in childrearing and domestic skills. Single mothers sometimes need assistance in disciplining children, managing finances, or making minor home repairs. As Dornbusch *et al.*'s (1985) results show clearly, single parents need to be informed about the detrimental effects of giving adolescents too much decision-making authority too soon. Stepparents of both sexes often wish to know more about child development and successful means of fulfilling their often difficult roles. Providing such courses will help adults to be better parents. In the end, it will be children who benefit most from the training of adults.

Teenage Parents

Schools have a particularly critical part to play with regard to families headed by teenage girls. As discussed in Chapter 12, families headed by teenage girls face severe economic and psychological difficulties. What should be the role of schools with regard to these families?

Most observers agree that public policy toward these families ought to be aimed at preventing teenage pregnancy in the first place (see National Research Council, 1986). Schools may not be the most effective agency to develop programs aimed at preventing teenage pregnancy. Sex education courses, at least as they are usually taught, do not seem to have reduced teenage pregnancy. We agree with Cuban (1986) that it is probably better to allow nonschool agencies to deal directly with the prevention of teenage pregnancy—through state-funded family planning clinics, television advertisements, and multiethnic coalitions—than to give the public the illusion that sex education courses are likely to solve the problem.

But if schools do not have much of a part to play in the prevention of teenage pregnancy, they do have an important role with respect to families headed by a teenage girl. One of the most severe consequences of early motherhood is failure to complete a high school education. Girls who drop out of school when they become mothers are in a poor position to obtain employment that pays even enough to cover their child-care costs, so that they often must apply for AFDC benefits. Schools could help break this cycle by helping teenage mothers to complete their education.

High school programs for teenage parents should begin with prenatal education—information about the importance of prenatal physical examinations, nutrition during pregnancy, and the effects of drugs and alcohol on a fetus. In communities with large populations of pregnant teenagers, prenatal physical care might be provided at the high school itself.

After birth, teenage mothers should be encouraged to continue their education. High schools should educate teenage mothers (and fathers when possible) about how to care for an infant and should permit teenage parents to form a support group with a teacher to discuss the difficulties and frustrations of young parenthood. Such support groups could improve the overall quality of physical and psychological care for the children of teenage parents.

School-Parent Communication

How far should schools go in changing their policies in order to facilitate communication with parents in the new families? The answer to this question depends in part upon how broadly or narrowly schools view their mission. To the extent that schools construe education narrowly, ignoring what takes place outside the boundaries of school and playground, schools will make relatively few adjustments to the new families. But those schools that recognize childrens' home lives as important determinants of their success in mastering cognitive material and in preparing for future work and family roles will wish to make rather sweeping changes in their policies.

In a world populated largely by families of the male/breadwinner-female/homemaker variety, schools could count on most mothers being available to meet with teachers during the day, and on many mothers being willing to chaperone field trips and assist as classroom aides. All of these activities furthered parent-school communication. In addition, schools could schedule short days and long holidays and refuse to make any provision for the care of even mildly sick children, because most mothers were available to care for their children before and after school, during school holidays and vacations, and during periods of illness. Today, however, the presence of new families in large numbers has made it impossible for schools to continue making their old assumptions about the availability of mothers. Moreover, many fathers, including noncustodial fathers and stepfathers, wish to play a greater role in communicating with the school about their children.

At a minimum, schools need to introduce more flexibility in scheduling parent-teacher conferences about student progress and problems. Conferences may need to be scheduled in the evening. For parents who cannot easily afford a babysitter, schools may need to provide for child care at the school during parent-teacher conferences. In some cases, where divorced or separated parents or parents and stepparents do not get along with one another, it may be necessary for teachers to schedule separate conferences to discuss a particular child.

Schools need to recognize the importance of teacher communication with noncustodial parents and with stepparents who play a role in the child's life. Sometimes dealing with these parents is complicated by the specific provisions of divorce settlements or by laws regulating which adults may be permitted to receive privileged communications from schools. School officials need to act as advocates for the child, educating both parents and legislators about the importance of good home-school communication with all adults who are involved in raising children.

Schools interested in furthering parent-school communication and also wishing to continue to schedule field trips, despite the absence of mothers to serve as chaperones during the week, should consider weekend trips. Such trips could continue to provide educational benefits for children and also assist parents in the new families, who are often short on leisure time, to pursue interesting activities with their children. In effect, the school would be assisting parents in the selection and planning of their outings. At the same time, such outings could help to foster better communication between parents and their children's teachers.

It would be necessary to compensate teachers for evening conferences, for additional meetings with more than one parent or set of parents, and for weekend field trips. In general, school districts have been reluctant to provide such additional compensation. Perhaps the research findings on the importance of parent–school communication will persuade school districts to incur these relatively modest additional expenditures.

Employment

Nondiscrimination, Affirmative Action, and Comparable Worth

Women's earnings have now become crucial to both single-parent and two-earner families. In families maintained by women, their earnings are the single most important source of family income. In two-earner families, in 1984, family earnings were 23% higher than if wives had not worked (and all other sources of income had remained the same). In addition, poverty was 35% lower and the income share of the bottom quintile of family earnings 15% higher than if wives had not worked (Danziger & Gottschalk, 1986, p. 38).

Yet, as we have seen in Strober's Chatper 8, women who work continue to face outmoded assumptions about their need for earnings. Because of wage discrimination and occupational segregation, women do not earn income commensurate with their abilities, education, and motivation. In a continuing adjustment to the sex-role revolution, we must move to redress this inequality of reward.

The Equal Pay Act requires that employers provide equal compensation to men and women doing the same job. Title VII of the 1964 Civil Rights Act is broader, requiring nondiscrimination in hiring and promotion and in the determination of earnings and fringe benefits. Affirmative action has been required in some instances by a judge, when an employer has been found in violation of Title VII. But most affirmative action plans have resulted from executive orders mandating that organizations doing business with the federal government develop and follow a plan to bring minorities and women into positions from which they have been excluded.

Although the concept of affirmative action has been highly controversial, recent Supreme Court cases have confirmed its legality in some circumstances. Even strong supporters see it as only a way-station on the road to the ultimate goal of race and gender blindness in hiring and promotion (Bergmann, 1986).

Increasingly, employers have viewed certain aspects of affirmative action in hiring and promotion as excellent additions to their personnel practices (Fisher, 1985). Posting all job vacancies, advertising widely to increase the pool of minority and female applicants, and encouraging minority and female candidates to apply have led to improved use of organizations' scarcest resource, employee talent. In fact, because they find these policies beneficial, many employers have continued to practice certain aspects of affirmative action in hiring and promotion even though federal pressure to do so has been reduced in recent years.

Nonetheless, research suggests that antidiscrimination legislation and the executive orders have had only very modest effects on reducing occupational segregation or the gender gap in pay (Beller, 1979; Beller, 1982; Brown, 1982; Eberts & Stone, 1985; Heckman & Wolpin, 1976; Leonard, 1985; U.S. General Accounting Office, 1975). The enforcement mechanisms for both Title VII and the executive orders need strengthening. The Equal Employment Opportunities Commission (EEOC), the agency charged with enforcing Title VII, needs increased funding and the right to investigate without waiting for a complaint. The Office of Federal Contract Compliance (OFCC), the agency administering the executive orders requiring affirmative action plans, needs a wider variety of remedies for noncompliance. The current remedy, disbarment from the ability to enter into contracts with government agencies, is draconian and hence almost never employed. The OFCC needs the power to implement lesser remedies as well.

Using affirmative action to break down the system of occupational segregation is an exceedingly important strategy for reducing the gender gap in pay and accommodating the new families. But because of the highly skewed distribution of men and women across occupations, and because of the tenacity of occupational segregation, most women will remain in female-dominated jobs for the forseeable future. To achieve pay equity will require broadening the concept of nondiscrimination to include the concept of equal pay for work of comparable worth. Skills required in female-dominated jobs will have to be financially rewarded according to the same criteria used to reward the skills required in male-dominated jobs.

Some have argued that redefining nondiscrimination to include comparable worth is incompatible with a capitalist labor market and will prove economically disruptive. The experiences of numerous public employers in the United States and the experience of Australia, whose labor courts increased female pay by 30% without any discernible negative results for the economy (Gregory & Duncan, 1981; Gregory & Ho, 1984), suggest that setting wages according to criteria that include comparable worth is often economically possible.

In the United States, where judicial involvement in wage setting is looked upon unfavorably, it is likely that movement toward pay equity will take place in a slower and more decentralized fashion than it has in Australia. We suggest several steps be taken in the movement toward pay equity. We agree with Bergmann (1986) that, to assist employers in realigning men's and women's wage rates, it would be useful to have a document that illustrates for key occupations the relative wages that emerge when taking a set of comparable worth principles into account. Such a document could be prepared by a panel of labor-market researchers with input from employers, unions, and job-evaluation experts. The initiative for convening such a panel could come from the Labor Department, the National Academy of Sciences, the National Science Foundation, or from a private foundation.

At the same time, pay equity should continue to be on the agenda for union–management negotiations. Several unions have learned that issues of pay equity are useful in organization drives and in maintaining the interest and support of members. We urge additional unions to place pay equity on their lists of issues for collective bargaining.

The concept of pay equity has moved forward most noticeably among public employees. More than 20 states have initiated job evaluation studies and 13 have begun to make up the difference between male and female jobs requiring similar skill ("Comparable Pay," 1986). We urge state legislatures and city and county governments to continue to push for pay equity among their public employees. And, finally, we suggest that private employers also consider the benefits of moving, even if slowly, toward equitably rewarding job skill and responsibility, regardless of the gender-type of the job. We do not expect a speedy acceptance of comparable worth, but based on current trends we do expect continued movement toward gender equality in pay.

Hours of Work and Career Ladders

One of the most difficult tasks faced by parents in the new families is balancing their work and home responsibilities. Flexibility in hours of work and in career ladders are important aids in this balancing.

In May 1985, the Current Population Survey (CPS) conducted a special survey about hours of work and hours of work preference. The responses are instructive. Despite much discussion about flexible scheduling of the workday (flextime), very few full-time wage and salary workers are able to vary the time they begin and end work. In May 1985, only about 12% of workers had that privilege; interestingly, the percentage was slightly higher for men (13.2%) than for women (11.1%) (Mellor, 1986). There is clearly a good deal of room for employers to assist parents by offering them the opportunity for flexibility in the beginning and ending times of their work days.

The survey indicates that there is also not much flexibility in hours worked per week. In May 1985, about 19% of all employed men worked part-time, that is less than 35 hours per week. The percentage for women was about the same, 20%. About 64% of men and 70% of women in full-time nonagricultural jobs worked a 40-hour week (Smith, 1986). And, although almost 9 million persons worked at least 8 hours a week at home in May 1985, only about 2 million worked entirely at home (Horvath, 1986).

About two thirds of American workers are satisfied with the number of hours they work. When asked if they would like to trade hours for income (keeping their hourly pay rate the same), about one fourth of respondents to the survey said they would like to work more hours and earn more income; only about 9% of women and 6% of men were willing to trade income for time that they can use for other purposes. Even in the 25 to 54 age group, where childrearing responsibilities are greatest, the percentage who said they would be willing to decrease their income if they could work fewer hours is small, about 10% of women and 6% of men (Shank, 1986).

The questions on the CPS that elicited preferences about hours of work had a much higher than usual nonresponse rate (20%) and so should be interpreted cautiously. Still, it would appear that the demand for part-time work among parents is rather modest. One can draw two conclusions: if employers offered part-time hours to parents of young children, they could probably satisfy a small percentage of their workforce without fearing a major exodus to part-time employment. At the same time, given present preferences (or necessity) for income, it appears that part-time employment for parents, with concomitant declines in income, is unlikely to prove a popular means of balancing work and family demands. For the most part the child-care problem will be solved not by having parents work a reduced schedule, but rather by developing a child-care system.

If we were to adopt a major change in work hours for parents with young children—for example, the so-called full-cyclic plan, where "education, work, and leisure would be much more evenly distributed over the life span, instead of being concentrated in youth, the middle years and old age respectively" (Stoper, 1982, p. 99)—we would need to find a mechanism to replace parents' foregone income (Strober, 1981). It may be that we could adopt an intergenerational transfer system that would transfer funds from older workers to workers in their childrearing years. Or, we might develop a capital market so that young parents could get publicly guaranteed loans and pay back interest and principal from incomes earned in the years after childrearing.

For those in professional and managerial careers, we think it sensible for employers to develop new models of career development. Most current career patterns call for very long work weeks and extraordinary work effort in the early stages of a career (at precisely the ages when one rears children). This pattern was designed for men whose wives took full responsibility for all domestic and parenting tasks. It is an unsatisfactory pattern for single parents or for men and women who wish to share parenting.

It is in employers' interests to develop alternative models as a means of retaining talented young men and women who cannot (or will not) sacrifice

parenting to extremely high-stress work weeks of 50 to 60 hours. Lotte
Bailyn (1982) has suggested one such model, the apprenticeship model,
where the early years of a career are devoted to activities promoting a broad
exposure to a company or field and can accommodate the bearing and
rearing of a young child. Later, when the child is grown, the required career
commitment increases and progress up the ladder is more rapid. Employers
should be encouraged to experiment with Bailyn's model as well as with
other modifications of the usual career path.

Changes in Income Taxation and Social Security Benefits

In Chapter 8, Strober argues that the federal income tax schedules and the
social security benefit packages as they now operate discriminate against
families with two earners. Because the income tax is progressive and because
it treats married couples as a single tax unit (even if they file separately), it
discourages some married women from working. We favor an income tax
system where all persons are taxed as individuals, regardless of their marital
status. Such a policy will not only eliminate the negative work incentive for
some married women, but will also reflect the notion that adult women and
men are independent economic entities.

With regard to social security benefits, as detailed in Strober's chapter,
the current system also discriminates against employed married women. We
favor changing the benefit structure so that earnings of both members of a
married couple are considered as community property. Under such a
system, half of the husband's earnings would be credited toward his social
security account and half toward his wife's, and vice versa if the wife earned
income. Although we recognize that the old system of benefits would have
to be phased out slowly so that those who planned their work behavior and
retirement strategy under that system will not be harmed, we suggest that,
with more than half of married women now employed, it is time to move to
the new system.

Employment and Welfare Reform

In 1984, according to the official measures of poverty, of families with
children that were maintained by a woman, almost half (47%) were poor; of
black families with children that were maintained by a woman, 58% were
poor. These figures contrast sharply with the percentage of all households in
poverty in that year, 13%, and the percentage of two-parent families in
poverty, 11% (Fuchs, 1986). As Walker argues in Chapter 5, what is clearly
tragic about female-headed single-parent families is their high incidence of
poverty.

The antidiscrimination, affirmative action, and comparable worth policies described in the previous section are important tools for all women,
those in poverty as well as those above the poverty line. But women in
poverty also need additional policy instruments.

Aid to Families with Dependent Children (AFDC), as currently conceived and administered, hurts poor women and their children by increasing their risk of long-term dependency. In an era in which the majority of mothers with preschool children are employed, it is unacceptable to have a welfare program that calls for full-time motherhood for AFDC recipients. The AFDC system must be revised so that poor women who maintain families can in time achieve economic self-sufficiency through the combination of their own earnings and child support payments. In practice, this means providing training programs and subsidized child care for mothers of preschool children, ameliorating the current high tax on earnings and the loss of health benefits faced by AFDC recipients who work, and improving the system of awarding and collecting child support payments.

Since 1968, the Work Incentive Program (WIN) has been on the books to provide training programs and other employment-related assistance to AFDC recipients. However, in practice, shortages of staff and funds have led to a situation where more than two thirds of those who register for WIN receive no services (Wiseman, 1986). Moreover, women with preschool children have not been encouraged to register for WIN.

In 1981, Congress gave states the right to develop voluntary work opportunities and mandatory community work experience programs for AFDC recipients. As a result, several states have instituted so-called workfare programs. These programs provide a mix of child care (mostly through voucher systems), career counseling, education and training programs, job placement services, on-the-job training, and assistance in providing for transportation and for health care. Although mothers with preschool children have sometimes participated in these programs, in the future their participation must be greatly expanded.

Welfare reforms currently proposed will probably increase the federal funding available to states that institute more extensive job training programs for AFDC recipients. We applaud such efforts. Although popular wisdom has it that training programs are ineffective, new studies indicate that intensive training for the disadvantaged does improve employment and earnings and is often particularly successful for women (Bassi & Ashenfelter, 1986).

Housing

The nation's housing arrangements also need to be reviewed in light of drastic shifts in the place that domestic work now occupies in the lives of men and women. Housing needs are changing for both genders as fertility patterns, employment opportunities, cohabitation arrangements and the timing of marriage and divorce affect the use of housing. Our stock of housing, both for ownership and for rental, was built primarily for families that fit the male/breadwinner–female/homemaker model.

As Friedan (1981) points out, changes in domestic tasks and the labor-force participation of women have created a need for more flexible housing.

Spatial designs that permit or encourage the sharing of space and tasks across family units will do much to relieve the burdens of men and women as they try to cope with diverse demands and the loneliness often felt by adults raising children by themselves. Such shared space can be placed near space that fulfills American standards for privacy and individual control.

Architects and planners have an opportunity to create physical structures that reduce the burdens of family life and increase the opportunities for pleasure. Our typical single-family detached house is already out of the economic reach of most Americans. Its heyday reflected the era of the suburban housewife; now there are new demands for housing, a new market waiting to be served. The needed housing for tomorrow will require the building of new dwellings as well as the remodeling of existing houses and apartments.

Yet there are barriers to the development of new forms of housing, many of them political, including zoning and building codes. We urge foundations to encourage architects and planners to work on new housing designs. This will increase the pressure on governmental agencies to rethink the regulation of housing arrangements. The market is waiting; what is needed is a broader vision within the building industry, its regulators and the public.

Stepparents

While the sex-role revolution has certainly not created the stepparent role, it has made that role both more salient and more demanding. As Crosbie-Burnett, Skyles, and Becker-Haven argue in their chapter, the increase in the number of stepfamilies and the marked increase in the number of children who move between households on a regular basis have created a need for new thinking and new action, especially on the part of government.

Generally, we are accustomed to thinking that a child has only two real parents. In fact, however, children in stepfamilies often have three or even four adults with whom they have a parent–child relationship. In many families, stepparents paly a critical role in children's upbringing. Yet, as Crosbie-Burnett *et al.* point out, stepparents are not recognized by the state as having any rights or responsibilities with respect to their stepchildren. They highlight three changes that need to be made.

States need to provide some version of legal guardianship to stepparents so that they can sign permission slips for school, sign medical forms in case of emergencies, sign to authorize driving permits, and so on. In addition, states need to recognize that stepparents and their stepchildren may wish to have visitation rights in case a second (or third) marriage fails. These wishes should be considered valid by courts issuing divorce decrees. Finally, on the grimmer side of stepparenting, the increased number of stepfamilies makes it necessary to revise incest laws. In particular, sexual relations between stepparents and their stepchildren should be legally defined as incest.

Recent studies by Dornbusch, discussed in Chapter 12, indicate that most stepparents, especially stepfathers, react to the lack of norms for stepparenting by being essentially inactive as parents. Alternatively, faced with resistance from the child, stepfathers who are more active often tend to be authoritarian. Schools, media, and support groups should inform children and adults of the need for authoritative (but not authoritarian) participation by stepparents. Increased parenting by stepparents can reduce the high rates of adolescent deviance (smoking, early dating, truancy, contacts with the police, and arrests) and improve the low school grades that are often associated with children from stepfamilies.

PROVIDING NEW ARRANGEMENTS FOR THE CARE OF CHILDREN

In a society where families are of the male/breadwinner–female/homemaker type, physical and psychological care of children are provided largely by the child's own mother and economic care largely by the child's own father. Such arrangements have both negative and positive attributes.

If the mother is incompetent, or resentful, full-time care by the mother can be detrimental for both the child and the mother. Similarly, if the father is unable to provide an adequate income, the child's well-being may be seriously threatened. When the mother is caring and competent and the father economically successful, the child is usually well-cared for. Even under these circumstances, however, there may be undesirable outcomes. If the father is straining to provide all of the required economic support, he may experience considerable stress, with concomitant difficulties for other family members. At the same time, the mother may frequently feel frustrated. Under such circumstances, there may be little positive parent–child or husband–wife interaction. At the same time, if the mother feels undervalued, her talents underutilized, she may feel frequently frustrated.

But only in extreme cases of malfunction, such as physical violence or unemployment, has public policy become involved in childrearing in the "intact" breadwinner–homemaker family. Despite some instances of considerable unhappiness, that family type is traditionally viewed as structurally capable of providing its own childrearing.

Among single-parent and two-earner families, providing adequate child care within the family is much more problematic. According to a Census survey in Winter 1984–1985, only 3.5% of employed single mothers cared for their preschool child "while working," and another 2.2% obtained child care from the child's father. Among married mothers, 9.2% cared for their youngest preschool child while working and 18.8% obtained child care from the child's own father (U.S. Bureau of the Census, 1987). Members of extended families also provide child care to single-parent and two-earner families; in Winter 1984–1985, 24% of the youngest preschool children of employed women were cared for by a relative, either in the child's home or in the relative's home (U.S. Bureau of the Census, 1987). Still, as Skold's Chapter 6 explains, there remain considerable problems in the provision of child care.

What are the public policy alternatives with respect to child care? Some argue that there is no role for public policy at all, that if people wish to have children, they must figure out how to care for them, physically, psychologically, and economically. Yet such public policy pronouncements seem largely irrelevant when one considers the fact that some people who already have children find it difficult to provide for them. The future economic well-being of our society, as well as our concerns for equity, demand that we assist these children. In addition, we note that many people who could provide offspring with economic and psychological sustenance are not having children because of an inability to provide for their full-time physical care without a change in life-style.

In our view, the rise of the new families requires a fundamental shift in our perceptions about children. Children are not simply a private asset requiring investments by families and returning to parents psychic and economic goods and services. Children are also a public good, requiring public investment and returning public goods and services to society.

All children require full-time care at the time of birth and for the next several years. But if single-parent families or two-earner families require the parent or parents of young children to work in order to provide for their economic care, who will provide for their physical and psychological care? A system for child care is a necessity.

Toward a Child-Care System

The provision of child care is not simply an issue of money. It is also an issue of organization, as Skold has made clear in Chapter 6. The sources of funding for child care are likely to come from a combination of parental, employer, and public funds. Regardless of the sources of funds, foundations, employers, unions, and government will have to take the lead in organizing child-care systems.

It is virtually impossible for individual parents to organize child-care systems even if they can pay the full costs of their children's care. And because most parents *cannot* pay the full cost of their children's care and in addition provide a profit for an entrepreneur, private for-profit providers are unlikely to be major players in creating a child-care system.

What do we mean by a child-care *system*? In the U.S. today extrafamily child care is a nonsystem, a collection of ad hoc, uncoordinated arrangements. A child-care system would differ from our current arrangements primarily in its degree of organization and coordination; it would emerge from a conscious process of decision making about what types of services we wish to provide, and the desired relationships among services, organization, ownership, control, financing, and management.

Why do we need a child-care system? Why not continue with our current ad hoc arrangements? From the point of view of parents, we need a system because the current nonsystem has too many "care gaps," times in childrens' lives when it is exceedingly difficult, if not impossible, to find care. The gaps occur for new-born infants, and virtually every time a child is sick.

In addition, the current nonsystem is unreliable. It has an inadequate supply of places for children as evidenced by long waiting lists for good day-care centers in most communities. And there is very high turnover among caregivers (in part because of the low wages they earn), so that parents frequently find themselves needing to make new temporary or permanent child-care arrangements. Finally, the current situation, because it relies so heavily on nonlicensed family day care and private babysitting, is inadequate in providing information to parents about safety and quality of care. There is nothing so frightening to parents as facing an information vacuum when trying to find care for a young child who cannot provide feedback about what happens during the parents' absence.

From a public policy point of view, the current nonsystem is inefficient. Despite the low wages of child-care workers, the labor intensity of the service makes it very expensive. Because there has never been any systematic thinking about how to design a child-care system, or indeed even what our goals for such a system might be, we have not taken the opportunity to search for innovative solutions.

Need for Research

The creation of a child-care system requires research to determine exactly what type of system best combines the dual goals of quality and cost-effectiveness. Surprisingly little research on child-care systems now exists. (See Kahn and Kamerman, 1987, for a review.) Such research should be developed as soon as possible and be sponsored by a variety of organizations, both governmental and private. It should include work by scholars in diverse fields, including child psychology, pediatrics, education, economics, and the sociology of organizations.

We are at a very exciting point for obtaining fruitful information from research on child care. The federal government has restricted its interest in child care to the child-care tax credit and to the subsidization of child care for limited groups of disadvantaged children and families. But a number of states and localities have recently begun to experiment with various types of child-care services (see Pipho, 1985). Many of these programs are now ready to be evaluated. At the same time, several countries with considerable experience in providing extensive child-care services are now evaluating the cost-effectiveness of their systems (Jansson & Stromquist, 1988).

Research should do more than simply evaluate existing arrangements and systems. It should also design and initiate innovative new systems and evaluate their performance. Beginning with a recognition of the ubiquity of the new families, we need a careful, systematic look at the costs and benefits of alternative arrangements for providing care at different age levels for different types of families. We need to examine alternative arrangements for the provision of infant care, preschool care for toddlers, before- and after-school care, care during school vacations, and care for sick children.

The issues to be addressed include: the educational, psychological, and medical advantages and disadvantages of alternatives types of services; the cost implications of each alternative; the trade-offs between cost and quality; the appropriate roles of the federal, state, and local governments, business, community groups, and parents in the ownership, control, management, and financing of a child-care system; the recruitment, training, licensing, and payment of child-care workers; and the coordination of the child-care system with our educational system.

By initiating a child-care system we would develop incentives for thinking creatively about efficiency while continuing to maintain or enhance the quality of care. For example, suppose that within a given community we combined family day-care homes and child-care centers into an integrated satellite network (see Strober, 1975).

Acting on the Results of the Research

We have suggested that both governmental and private organizations sponsor research on child care. Who will act on the results of the research we propose? In the current political climate, it is likely that state and local governments will be the ones to review the research findings and make the major decisions about organization, management, control, coordination, and financing. However, in the future the federal government may also play a role in the design and operation of child-care systems, as is the case in other countries.

Suppose, for example, that research findings suggest considerable educational and cost advantages to child-care services run by school districts. State legislatures may then wish to provide financial incentives for school districts, especially those with excess space, to play the major coordinating role in developing and managing child-care systems. The federal government, for its part, may wish to provide financial incentives to states to provide such incentives to school districts. Alternatively, research may point to the wisdom of strengthening county-wide child-care coordinating councils, such as those in California.

Although governments will set up the child-care system, we expect that the private sector will continue to play major roles in the management, financing, and provision of services. Exactly what these roles will be in different states and communities will depend not only upon research findings but also upon existing institutions, local preferences, and local political pressures.

Some people avoid discussion of a system of child care because it connotes to them a monolithic bureaucracy, unresponsive to childrens' needs for flexibility and parents' desires for participatory decision making. But calling for a child-care system that is more organized and better coordinated hardly prejudges the particular configurations of the system or precludes care in the child's own home or in the home of relatives. A child-care system could, of course, be highly centralized with few options for alternative types of care; but it could also be decentralized at the community level, providing multiple types of service with joint participation by parents, corporations, religious groups, school districts, and colleges and universities. Some care could be provided in the community where the child lives, some at or near a parent's workplace, some at the child's school, and some at the child's own home.

Care of School-Age Children

Care of school-age children also needs to be part of a child-care system. With most mothers no longer available to care for children before and after the usual school day, during school holidays that are not also work holidays and during extended winter, spring, and summer vacations, we need to examine alternatives for the care of children during these periods.

We are not suggesting that children should fill these periods with more schooling or that schools should take responsibility for planning and directing alternative activities. But school districts, as advocates for the well-being of children, should ensure that if schools do not themselves take on the charge, they actively prod local governments to assume responsibility.

Some school districts are already providing care for children before and after school, either with their own resources or through contracting with others for the use of school buildings. In addition, some school districts are discussing running schools for an extended school year and significantly attenuating the traditional 2 to 3 month summer vacation. In effect, we have, and are about to have more, natural experiments. These should be carefully studied so that we learn about their costs, their effects on educational attainment, and the satisfaction of parents, children, and school personnel.

Care of Sick Children

When a child becomes ill at school and winds up at the office of the school secretary, school policy generally requires that the child must leave school, no matter how mild the illness. In the absence of a resident school nurse, there is no one at school to determine the seriousness or potential seriousness of the child's illness and no one to supervise an ill child.

Numerous difficulties arise when the school secretary calls a working mother (or father) to pick up a sick child at school. The parent has no notion of how sick the child may be and has little choice but to drop all activity and head for the school. The child and the school secretary may need to wait for quite a while until the parent is located, arranges to leave work, and travels to the school.

Other types of difficulties arise when children become ill at home and are unable to go to school at all. Generally one of the child's parents (most often the mother) takes off several days from work to care for a sick child. A few communities provide trained caregivers for sick children to parents who pay on a fee-for-service basis.

Because situations vary so much across communities, school districts will need to work out new policies in collaboration with organizations of parents, local physicians, nurses, Health Maintenance Organizations (HMOs), and employers. The first step in dealing with the problem might be to devise a system of on-call nurses who would be called to schools when required to make judgments about the relative seriousness of illnesses. In some communities the services of these nurses could be covered by parents' medical insurance policies or HMO services. In others, the nurses might be employed by the school district. Children who are deemed to be only mildly ill might be able to stay at school, either returning to their classroom or resting in a quiet room supervised by an aide. Children who are more seriously ill could be taken to a particular physician or emergency room, designated in advance, with their parent being asked to join the child at the physician's office or emergency facility.

Community-wide meetings called by school districts to discuss alternative modes of caring for children who become ill at school should also discuss the generic question of care for sick children. Some physicians and parents believe firmly that all sick children should be isolated from other sick children and from well children. Others believe that, except for highly contagious diseases, it is permissible for sick children to mingle with one another and with well children because sick children may have been infectious long before they exhibited recognizable symptoms of illness.

Parents, physicians, nurses, school personnel, and representatives of employers may decide that they wish to provide for a community infirmary to which parents would bring sick children, or for a system of trained personnel available for home care. Alternatively, communities might opt for a system whereby parents are given a certain number of days of paid leave each year by their employer in order to care for their sick children. It is also possible that communities will wish to have a mixture of care alternatives.

Paid Parental Leave

Given the extraordinary cost of extrafamily child care for new-born infants and the importance of good care for them, one vital piece of any child-care system will include a paid parental leave program, with job protection, for the first several months of a child's life. The United States is the only major industrial country that does not have publicly mandated maternity leave; and there is virtually no provision in this country for paid paternity leave (see Pleck, 1985).

Under the Pregnancy Discrimination Act of 1978, employers are required to treat pregnancy and childbirth as they do other disabilities. Nine states have laws that require employers to provide benefits not necessarily granted to other disabled employees—an unpaid leave of up to 4 months and rights to job reinstatement. In 1987, the Supreme Court upheld the constitutionality of the California law, ruling that it was not inconsistent with Federal law prohibiting sex discrimination.

We agree with Kamerman et al. (1983) that the issue of paid leave for pregnancy and childbirth is better conceptualized as a care benefit for infants than as a sick benefit for women. It is important that either parent be permitted to take paid leave to care for a young child. From an economic point of view, if only women are eligible for such leave, employers will find that hiring women is more expensive than hiring men; thus they will have an incentive not to hire women or to compensate themselves for the cost of the women's leaves by paying women less than they pay men. For purposes of achieving equity, such an outcome is undesirable.

From a psychological point of view, child development specialists have noted the importance of father care during early infancy for creating strong father–child bonds (Lamb, 1986; Leiderman, 1983). Such research suggests that policies making it financially possible and socially desirable for fathers to care for their infants could have important benefits for fathers and children. For example, if strong father–child bonds were more widespread, the number of instances in which fathers desert or refuse to support their children might be reduced.

As noted in Chapter 8, in 1986 Congresswoman Patricia Schroeder introduced a bill that, if passed, would require all firms with more than 15 employees to provide up to 18 weeks of unpaid, job-guaranteed leave for the care of a new-born, newly adopted, or seriously ill child or dependent parent. While the bill treats men and women equally (either may take leave), it falls far short of the paid benefits provided to mothers in other industrialized countries (Kammerman et al., 1983). Even so, the United States Chamber of Commerce has opposed the bill, arguing that it would present severe difficulties for small companies and that government rules mandating paid leaves would soon follow ("When the Stork," 1986).

Sweden's experience with parental leave indicates that merely making it possible for fathers to take a paid leave to care for their infants will not, by itself, usually induce fathers to do so. Some men continue to feel uncomfortable or inept at caring for infants; others fear that despite the availability of paid leave, taking leave to care for a child may negatively affect their career prospects. In still other cases, men would be willing to take leave, but accede to their wives' preference to take parental leave themselves (see Pleck, 1985).

Even in Sweden, where the female/male earnings differential is smaller than it is in the United States, husbands generally earn more than wives. So mothers' taking leave becomes the economically rational choice for a family unless the worker is paid full salary while on leave. At a time when gender roles are in transition, we should not expect a large number of fathers to move immediately toward requesting paid leaves for childrearing. Yet national policy should recognize and encourage the development of new norms for fathering.

Infant care leaves should be paid for, in some combination, by the three parties that benefit from them: the employee, the employer, and the general public. The employee's share could be paid through a form of insurance; the employers' share might be a fringe benefit chosen by the employee from a menu of possible benefits; and the taxpayer's share could be collected and disbursed in a variety of forms, though the last should be a relatively small proportion of the total amount. Although the public benefit is large, public funds should be reserved to care for children whose parents have inadequate resources to contribute to insurance premiums and who have no employer to provide fringe benefits.

Economic Support for Children in New Families

In addition to developing a child-care system to provide for children's psychological and physical needs, the expansion of new families requires new policies for the economic support of children.

The first part of any program to provide economic support for children in the new families must center on their mothers' wages and employment opportunities. Unlike children in male/breadwinner–female/homemaker families, who rely solely on their fathers for economic support, children in new families rely either on both parents or solely on their mothers. The employment policies discussed earlier in this chapter are thus essential not only to women's economic well-being, but also to the well-being of children.

A second important part of a program to provide for the economic care of children in new families is to ensure that noncustodial parents contribute to the support of their children if they are able. Noncustodial parents who are able to contribute to their children's support but do not do so should feel the moral opprobrium of society.

In addition to moral suasion, however, new legislation is required. Wisconsin has passed interesting legislation to revamp its system of child support. The key features of the Wisconsin Child Assurance Support Program are collection through witholding and benefits based on a percentage of the absent parent's gross earnings (17% for one child, 25% for two children, 29% for three children, 31% for four children and 34% for five or more children) (Corbett, 1986). The Act will be fully implemented in 1987 and appears so far to be successful (Corbett, 1986). We think other states would do well to follow carefully the results of the Wisconsin legislation.

One of the key questions in the debates about child support is whether to base payments on the cost of rearing a child or on the absent parent's income (see Hunter, 1983). Critics of cost sharing argue that it is impossible to determine the cost of rearing a child except in terms of the income level of the parents. Critics of income sharing, often noncustodial fathers, argue that income sharing is unfair, that it is the child's mother, rather than (or in addition to) the child, who benefits from payments beyond a fixed minimum. Moreover, critics argue that if the child support payment benefit is dependent upon income, fathers are at a financial disadvantage if they wish to have additional children in a second or third family.

We have support payments based on a percentage of the noncustodial parent's income, in large part because we are persuaded that public policy should ensure that fathers care for the children they already have. We also agree with the Poverty Institute researchers (Corbett, 1986) that the AFDC system should be carefully coordinated with child support payments. When a woman's own earnings plus child support from the child's father remains below some specified level, AFDC payments can make up the difference.

Because problems of child support enforcement so often cross state lines, they require federal action. The Department of Health and Human Services (HHS) estimates that 30% of all child support enforcement cases involve situations where the custodial parent seeks to collect child support from a noncustodial parent who now resides in a different state ("U.S. Offers," 1986). A good first step is the 1984 Child Support Enforcement Amendments, legislation based on Weitzman's research (see Chapter 10), which requires states to enforce out-of-state orders for child support.

Ultimately, a national system for collecting child support payments is required. Like Garfinkle and McLanahan (1986), we think that universal witholding of child support payments, with the cooperation of the employer and the Internal Revenue Service is needed. In Sweden, once the amount of child support is set by a court or through private agreement of the parties, the government assumes the responsibility of collecting monthly child support payments from the noncustodial parent and sending them to the custodial parent. If for some reason it is not possible to collect from the noncustodial parent (e.g., in case of a loss of employment), the government nonetheless sends the full payment to the custodial parent.

In return for responsible behavior with respect to child support, we think it important that government agencies also guarantee the noncustodial parent, generally the father, visitation rights with the chldren, unless such rights would be harmful to the child. One of the tragic effects of divorce is often the estrangement between fathers and their children. Guaranteeing both support payments and visitation rights may increase mutually beneficial contacts between divorced fathers and their children.

One additional support issue concerns children attending college. About one half of all 18- and 19-year-olds and one third of all 20- and 21-year-olds are enrolled in school, yet state laws and judicial practice generally terminate child support requirements when a child reaches 18. There are a number of thorny questions concerning child support for those attending college. Should both parents be required to make college support payments? Should the size of the payments be lower, equal to, or higher than those mandated for younger children? Should low-income parents be exempt from making these payments? Is it fair to provide a support guarantee to children of divorced parents that is more than children have when they are in an intact family? More consideration of these issues is clearly warranted.

DEALING WITH THE DISLOCATIONS OF DIVORCE

As the chapters of Weitzman, Krantz, and Crosbie-Burnett *et al.* (Chapters 10, 11, and 13, respectively) all make clear, divorce is often a painful transition for both adults and children. Moreover, the problems of divorce are no longer confined to a minority of the population. It is estimated that, by the time they are 18, about half of all children will experience their parents' divorce (Norton & Glick, 1986).

Both governments and schools can assist in easing the economic and psychological burdens of divorce. Weitzman suggests that legislatures and courts revise their notions of property so that, in addition to real property, divorce settlements divide "career assets." She argues persuasively that for many couples dividing property without dividing career assets is tantamount to dividing the jewels after the husband has kept all of the diamonds.

Weitzman also finds fault with the current American legislative and judicial concept of community property as applied to the family home. The home, she argues, should not be considered only the property of husband and wife; because the home determines the child's neighborhood, school and friends, the child has a profound interest in what happens to the family home. Weitzman suggests that American practice emulate the British law on the subject of the family home. In England, children's rights are considered foremost in judicial decisions concerning the disposition of the family home. Krantz and Weitzman are both eloquent on the serious dislocation suffered by children who, at what may be the most painful time of their childhood, are robbed of neighborhood and friends. We agree that divorce settlements should not assume that equity is served if the family's major asset, the home, is divided and sold at the time of divorce.

Children also suffer from particularly acrimonious divorce proceedings, and Krantz suggests that states do whatever possible to reduce long, drawn-out, and venomous cases and in particular that they more fully investigate the potential for mediation in divorce cases. We agree on the need for a reduction in the level of animosity often found in divorce cases, but we are wary about recommending mediation as a pat solution. Most mediators (unless they are legally trained) are not substitutes for legal counsel; and often the parties to a divorce need legal counsel in order to understand fully their rights and options. We suggest that states continue to experiment with methods of reducing painful divorce proceedings, including giving mediators more legal training and giving lawyers more training in methods of conflict resolution.

Schools can also help to ease the difficulties of divorce for children and their parents. Annual in-service workshops for school personnel to discuss problems of separation and loss in families (Damon, 1979) could help make teachers more sensitive to the problems and challenges of students and parents in new families.

Schools could organize support groups for children whose parents are involved in separation and divorce. Recent evidence indicates that such support groups can be useful. One study evaluated a 10-week group program that permitted fourth- through sixth-grade children to share feelings and learn some interpersonal skills. Children in the experimental group scored significantly better on parent and teacher ratings of behavior and self ratings of well-being (Pedro-Carroll & Cowen, 1985). A second study found that, among children aged 9 to 11, depression was more likely to be reduced, and behavior more likely to improve, within a group focused on social role playing and assertive communication skills than in a group that merely discussed feelings (Roseby & Deutsch, 1985).

The efficacy of school intervention seems clear. Yet many schools do not see such expenditures of time and money as directly related to their educational mission or as sufficiently cost-efficient. We hope that evidence such as that presented in Chapter 12 by Dornbusch and Gray will convince them.

CONCLUSION

In the preceding pages we have made numerous policy recommendations for the new families. We have also examined policies for facilitating the sex-role revolution and policies for dealing with the dislocations of divorce. We have spent a considerable amount of our space on new arrangements for the care of children; although issues of child care are central in the life of families, some aspects rarely receive attention from researchers, policy makers, or the media. In this conclusion we briefly summarize our recommendations and then analyze their likely effects on the three parties to the new families: men, women, and children.

Summary

In order to assist adults in performing nontraditional tasks we recommend changes in education, in employment, in housing, and in our treatment of stepfamilies.

With respect to education, we suggest curricular changes that introduce children and adolescents to the new roles they are likely to play as adult men and women, and the institution of special courses for adults who find themselves in unfamiliar gender roles. We also urge that in cases of teenage pregnancy schools offer prenatal education, encourage teenage mothers to continue their education, and provide classes for teenage mothers and fathers on the physical and psychological care of young children. Finally, we suggest means for facilitating school communication with parents in new families.

Our suggestions for employment include strict enforcement of antidiscrimination laws, continued use of affirmative action, and movement toward pay equity. With regard to hours of work, we think that more flexibility should be encouraged. But, because of parents' need for income, we doubt that offering parents a reduction of hours at work will reduce appreciably the need for child care. Flexibility of career patterns for professional and managerial workers is also on our agenda, and we urge employers to think creatively about establishing new career patterns.

To end the negative incentives to work and the current discrimination against married women who work, we suggest changing the federal income tax system so that each person is taxed as an individual regardless of marital status. We also suggest slowly phasing out the current system of determining social security benefits and, for purposes of determining benefits, treating as community property the earnings of both members of a married couple.

With respect to AFDC benefits, we suggest that mothers with preschool children be encouraged to seek employment. Fostering employment will require training programs, job-placement assistance, subsidized child care, and assurance of continuity of medical benefits. We recommend that states study the experience of those states that have started experiments in this area. We also applaud efforts to increase federal funding for states that institute more extensive training programs for AFDC recipients.

Our suggestions for housing call for imaginative designs by architects and planners to facilitate the building of housing that combines flexibility, sharing, and privacy. The new housing should be compatible with new arrangements for domestic tasks and for adult companionship.

So far as stepparents are concerned, we endorse the suggestion of Crosbie-Burnett et al. that we change our thinking so as to recognize that in stepfamilies children often have more than two "real" parents. To this end, we suggest several legal changes that would give stepparents official recognition for their role in childrearing, making their signatures valid on official forms and providing them with visitation rights in case of divorce. We also suggest that incest laws be extended to the stepparent–stepchild relationship.

On the child care front, we argue for the development and implementation of a child care system, although we are careful to point out that such a system need not be monolithic. We endorse the view that parental leave be considered a way of caring for children rather than as a disability benefit for women. Although we commend proposed legislation on parental leave, particularly its applicability to both men and women, we note that it does not provide for financial benefits, a minimal venture in comparison to the financial benefits provided in Western European countries.

So far as economic support for children is concerned, we point out that improving women's education and employment opportunities and their earnings is beneficial not only to women, but also to their children. We also argue for reform in the system of determining the amount of child support and enforcing the orders. We favor child support based on a percentage of the income of the noncustodial parent and using a witholding system at the workplace in order to collect payments. We suggest that the Wisconsin laws on child support merit careful review and possible emulation. Because problems of child support so often cross state lines, the federal government needs to be involved in the process; we commend current efforts by the administration to implement the 1984 Child Suport Enforcement Amendments. We also advocate the extension of child support requirements beyond the age of 18 for parents whose children are attending institutions of higher education.

In return for responsible behavior with respect to child support, we advocate state guarantees of visitation rights by the noncustodial parent, unless granting such rights would be harmful to the child.

We endorse Weitzman's suggestion that legislatures and courts include career assets in their definition of property to be divided at the time of divorce. We also endorse her recommendation that childrens' interests be considered paramount when decisions are made about the disposition of the family home. With respect to reducing the acrimony in divorce proceedings, we cautiously endorse further exploration of the use of mediation in divorce.

Schools can be useful in reducing the effects of divorce upon children. We recommend in-service workshops on divorce for school personnel, and support groups at school for children whose parents are in the process of separation or divorce.

The Impact of A Feminist Agenda on Men, Women, and Children

How do our policy recommendations affect men, women, and children? All of the policies we have recommended are beneficial to women and children. The vast majority are also beneficial to men, although it is true that, because many of our recommendations require public funds, they may be financially costly to both men and women in their roles as taxpayers. On the other hand, in their role as citizens, taxpayers also benefit from our suggestions.

In some cases, our proposals could benefit mothers and children at the expense of fathers. Improving the mechanisms for collecting child support will be financially costly to those fathers not now making regular payments or making only small payments. And calculating child support as a percentage of income rather than as a fixed cost could be harmful to fathers with relatively high incomes. Fathers who would otherwise have received half of the proceeds from the sale of a family home will also be worse off in a situation where the sale of the house is postponed in order to allow the children (and their mother) to continue to live there during the children's years of schooling. Similarly, assuming that husbands' career assets are greater than wives', husbands lose to the extent that wives and children gain when career assets are included in the division of property at the time of divorce.

Of course, in situations where children live with their father and their mother has the major share of career assets and income-earning capacity, it would be women who would be called upon to make child support payments and, if women would otherwise be reluctant to pay, our proposals would benefit fathers and children at the expense of mothers. In all cases, however, the financial cost to the noncustodial parent might well be made up for, at least in part, by improved relationships with children.

The analysis of the costs and benefits of these policies on men and women is further complicated by the existence of stepparents. The costs to natural parents may be precisely matched by the financial benefits to stepparents.

Our agenda for improving women's work opportunities may not be beneficial for men in their capacity as workers. To the extent that women obtain desirable jobs that would otherwise have gone to men, women gain what men lose.

But even with respect to the labor market, men's potential losses are likely to be at least partially offset. For every man who loses a job or a promotion because a woman received it, another man is likely to have his financial burden eased by the new job or promotion just received by his wife, mother, or daughter. Because men and women so often live together in families, the mutuality of their relationships remains ever-present; and analyzing that mutuality remains ever-challenging, especially for social scientists and policy makers tracking the new families.

ACKNOWLEDGMENT

We wish to thank Michael Abkin, Carolyn Arnold, and Marianne Ferber for comments on an earlier draft of this chapter.

NOTES

1. In 1984, half of all families had no children under 18 (Norton & Glick, 1986, p. 9). About 75% of all families with children were two-parent families; and 35% of all two-parent families had a mother not in the work force (Danziger & Gottschalk, 1986, pp. 10a, 33).

2. In March 1985, in the civilian labor force, there were 19,068,000 mothers with children under 18, (14,766,000 wives and 4,302,000 women maintaining families) (See Hayghe, 1986, p. 44). In that same month, the total civilian labor force was 115,335,000. See *Monthly Labor Review*, February 1986, p. 70.

REFERENCES

Bailyn, L. (1982). The apprenticeship model of organizational careers: A response to changes in the relation between work and family. In P. Wallace (Ed.), *Women in the Workplace*. Boston: Auburn House.

Bassi, L. J., & Ashenfelter, O. (1986). The effect of direct job creation and training programs on low-skilled workers. In S. H. Danziger & D. H. Weinberg (Eds.), *Fighting poverty: What works and what doesn't*. Cambridge, MA: Harvard University Press.

Bauer, G. (1986). *The family: Preserving America's future*. Washington, DC: U.S. Government Printing Office.

Beller, A. H. (1979). The impact of equal employment laws on the male/female earnings differential. In C. B. Lloyd, E. Andrews & C. L. Gilroy (Eds.), *Women in the labor market*. New York: Columbia University Press.

Beller, A. H. (1982). Occupational segregation by sex: Determinants and changes. *Journal of Human Resources, 17*(3), 371–392.

Bergmann, B. R. (1986). *The economic emergence of women*. New York: Basic Books.

Boles, J. K. (1983). The family impact statement: Ideology and feasibility. In I. Diamond (Ed.). *Families, politics, and public policy: A feminist dialogue on women and the state*. New York: Longman.

Bronfenbrenner, U. (1979). Our schools need a curriculum for caring. *Instructor Magazine, 7*, 34–36.

Brown, C. (1982). The federal attack on labor market discrimination: The mouse that roared. In R. Ehrenberg (Ed.), *Research in labor economics*. Greenwich, CN: JAI Press.

Comparable pay for comparable work gains acceptance, if slowly. (1986, July 15). *Wall Street Journal*, p. 1.

Corbett, T. (1986). Child support assurance: Wisconsin demonstration. *Focus, 9*(1), 1–5.

Cuban, L. (1986). Sex and school reform. *Phi Delta Kappan, 68*(4), 319–321.

Damon, P. (1979, October). When the family comes apart: What schools can do. *The National Elementary Principal, 59*(1), 66–75.

Danziger, S., & Gottschalk, P. (1986, January). *How have families with children been faring?* University of Wisconsin, Madison: Institute for Poverty Research, Discussion Paper, #801-86.

Dornbusch, S. M., Carlsmith, J. M., Bushwall, S. J., Ritter, P. L., Leiderman, H., Hastorf, A. H., & Gross, Ruth T. (1985, April), Single parents, extended households, and the control of adolescents. *Child Development, 56* 326–341.

Eberts, R. W., & Stone, J. A. (1985). Male–female differences in promotions: EEO in public education. *Journal of Human Resources, 20*(4), 504–21.

Fisher, A. B. (1985, September). Businessmen like to hire by the numbers. *Fortune, 112*(6), 26–30.

Friedan, B. (1981). *The second stage*. New York: Summit Books.

Fuchs, V. (1986, May). *The feminization of poverty*. Working Paper No. 1934, National Bureau of Economic Research.

Garfinkel, I., & McLanahan, S. (1986). *Single mothers and their children: A new American dilemma*. Baltimore, MD: Urban Institute Press.

Gregory R. S., & Duncan, R. C. (1981). The relevance of segmented labor market theories: The Australian experience of the achievement of equal pay for women. *Journal of Post Keynesian Economics, 3*, 404–428.

Gregory, R. G., & Ho, V. (1984). *Equal pay and comparable worth: What can the U.S. learn from the Australian experience?* Unpublished manuscript.

Hayghe, H. (1986). Rise in mothers' labor force activity includes those with infants. *Monthly Labor Review, 109*(2), 43–45.

Heckman, J. J., & Wolpin, K. I. (1976). Does the contract compliance program work? An analysis of Chicago data. *Industrial and Labor Relations Review, 29*(4), 544–564.

Horvath, F. W. (1986). Work at home: New findings from the current population survey. *Monthly Labor Review, 109*(11), 31–35.

Hunter, N. D. (1983). Women and child support. In I. Diamond (Ed.), *Families, politics and public policy.* New York: Longman.

Jansson, T., & Stromquist, S. (1988). *Child care in the Nordic countries: Costs, quality, management.* Stockholm: Swedish Agency for Administrative Development (SAFAD).

Kahn, A. I., & Kamerman, S. B. (1987). *Child care: Facing the hard choices.* Dover, MA: Auburn House.

Kamerman, S. B., & Kahn, A. J. (Eds.). (1978). *Family policy: Government and families in fourteen countries.* New York: Columbia University Press.

Kamerman, S. B., Kahn, A. J., & Kingston, P. (1983). *Maternity policies and working women.* New York: Columbia University Press.

Lamb, M. E. (Ed.). (1986). *The father's role: Applied perspectives.* New York: Wiley.

Leiderman, P. H. (1983). Social ecology and childbirth. In N. Carmezy and M. Rutler (Eds.), *The newborn nursery as environmental stressor.* New York: McGraw Hill.

Leonard, J. S. (1985). What promises are worth: The impact of affirmative action goals. *Journal of Human Resources, 20*(1), 3–20.

Mellor, E. F. (1986). Shift work and flexitime: How prevalent are they? *Monthly Labor Review, 109*(11), 14–21.

Monthly Labor Review. (1986). Vol. 109(2), Table 4, p. 70.

Moynihan, D. P. (1985, September–October). We can't avoid family policy much longer. (Interview.) *Challenge,* 9–17.

Moynihan, D. P. (1986). *Family and nation: The Godkin lectures, Harvard University.* San Diego: Harcourt, Brace, Jovanovich.

National Research Council. (1986). *Risking the Future.* Washington, DC: National Academy of Sciences Press.

Norton, A. J., & Glick, P. C. (1986, January). One parent families: A social and economic profile. *Family Relations, 35,* 9–17.

Pedro-Carroll, J. L., & Cowen, E. L. (1985). The children of divorce intervention program: An investigation of the efficacy of a school-based prevention program. *Journal of Consulting and Clinical Psychology, 53,* 603–611.

Pipho, C. (1985, February). Will the states take charge of child care? *Phi Delta Kappan,* 389–390.

Pleck, J. (1985). *Paternity leave: Current status and future prospects.* Wellesley College Center for Research on Women: Working Paper #157.

Roseby, V., & Deutsch, R. (1985). Children of separation and divorce: Effects of a social role-taking group intervention on fourth and fifth graders. *Journal of Clinical Child Psychology, 14*(1), 55–60.

Scanzoni, J. (1983). *Shaping tomorrow's family.* Beverly Hills: Sage.

Shank, S. E. (1986). Preferred hours of work and corresponding earnings. *Monthly Labor Review, 109*(11)a, 40–44.

Smith, S. J. (1986). The growing diversity of work schedules. *Monthly Labor Review, 109*(11), 7–13.

Steiner, G. Y. (1981). *The futility of family policy.* Washington, DC: The Brookings Institution.

Stoper, E. (1982). Alternative work patterns and the double life. In E. Boneparth (Ed.), *Women, power and policy.* New York: Pergammon Press.

Strober, M. H. (1975). Formal extrafamily child care—Some economic observations. In C. B.

Lloyd (Ed.), *Sex, discrimination, and the division of labor*. New York: Columbia University Press.

Strober, M. H. (1981). Market work, housework and child care: Burying archaic tenets, building new arrangements. In National Institute of Mental Health, *Women, a developmental perspective: A conference on research*. Washington, DC: U.S. Government Printing Office.

U.S. Department of Commerce, Bureau of the Census. (1987) *Who's minding the kids?*. Current Population Reports, Series P-70, No. 9. Washington, DC: U.S. Government Printing Office.

U.S. offers new rules covering child support. (1986, December 3). *New York Times*, p. B-15.

U.S. General Accounting Office. (1975). *The Equal Employment Opportunity Program for federal nonconstruction contractors can be improved*. Washington, DC: U.S. Government Printing Office.

When the stork brings the sack. (1986, October 11). *The Economist*.

Wiseman, M. (1986). Workfare and welfare policy. *Focus, 9*(3), 1–8.

Index

357